The UK
Air Fryer
Cookbook

Tasty, Affordable & Easy Air Fryer Recipes to Help You
Make the Best Tasting Food for Family & Friends

Caitlin Naylor

Contents

Introduction

Nearly all kitchens are tight on counter space. Even when you have a lot of it, it's simple to fill with the newest kitchen gadgets and get cluttered. You should, however, create place for an air fryer.

An air fryer is similar to an oven in that it bakes and roasts food, but it differs from an oven in that it uses less oil than a conventional oven and has heating elements that are only on the top. This makes food incredibly crispy in a matter of minutes. Due of the focused heat source and the positioning and size of the fan, air fryers typically heat up very quickly and cook food quickly and evenly.

The clean-up is just another fantastic benefit of air frying. Most baskets and racks for air fryers can go in the dishwasher. We advise using a decent dish brush, such as this one from Casabella, for any dishes that cannot be put in the dishwasher. Without making you crazy, it will reach every nook and cranny that helps with air circulation.

A countertop gadget called an air fryer essentially functions as a small convection oven. It uses heat and airflow from an internal fan instead of a lot of oil or fat to crisp up the chips and cook your chicken wings evenly.

Fundamentals of Air Fryer

What is Air Fryer?

The air fryer is an ubiquitous kitchen appliance for frying foods like meat, pastries, and potato chips.

Heated air is blown around the dish to produce a crunchy, crispy surface.

This also leads to the Maillard reaction, a chemical process. When heat is present, the reaction between an amino acid and a reducing sugar alters the colour and flavour of food

Air-fried foods are marketed as a healthier alternative to deep-fried ones due to their lower fat and calorie content.

Food can be air-fried with just a tablespoon (15 mL) of oil and still come out tasting and feeling like it was deep-fried.

Benefits of Using It

Healthy

An air fryer uses significantly less oil than a deep fryer, which is its principal health advantage. A large portion of the utilized oil also drains away without being absorbed by the food. As a result, you consume fewer calories and fat.

These fryers' convection method encourages the Maillard reaction, a chemical process that results in browning. This has the added benefit of making the food look better while also enhancing its flavour while having less fat.

Crispier Cuisine

Being able to generate crispy food without using oil is one of the best features of air fryers. They accomplish this by enclosing food in a perforated basket or on a rack with extremely hot air from all sides utilizing convection-style heating.

As a result, air fryers are ideal for producing crispy chips, onion rings, fish fingers, and other conventional fried food kinds.

Because it can cover the entire surface of the meal and because the frying basket allows any excess fat to drop away, an air fryer yields crispier results than a conventional convection oven.

Quicker

Air fryers cook food far more quickly than the majority of traditional alternative ways because of how they operate. The rapid frying procedure is made possible by maintaining and constantly circulating the tremendous heat generated inside the fryer.

Many versions either don't need to be heated up before use or only take a little time to do so. Depending on the particular meals, cooking times can be cut by more than 30 to 50 percent as compared to using a standard oven.

Fewer Messes

Compared to deep fryers, air fryers are much less dirty. That's because the cooking procedure only requires a small amount of oil, and it's this that makes the bulk of the mess. An air fryer may be cleaned most easily with a soft-bristle brush, dish soap, and water.

Secure

Air fryers are generally safer because they are self-contained appliances and because little hot fat is used in the cooking process. Splashes and burns are less of a problem. In order to prevent the food from burning, machines are also made to turn off when the timer expires.

More Adaptable

An air fryer can be used to prepare most dishes that

are typically cooked in a deep fryer just as well or even better. There are numerous recipes to experiment with. Surprisingly, baked items, vegetables, and steaks all perform nicely.

Avoid Distributing Heat and Odor
Air fryers retain heat, so unlike conventional ovens, they don't raise the temperature of your kitchen. If you reside in a smaller home or apartment, this quality is especially helpful. Due to the small amount of oil needed, there aren't any of the intense aromas that can come from deep frying.

Smaller in Size
Kitchen equipment like air fryers are comparatively small; they are a little larger than toasters. They work well in spaces where size can be an issue, like a small kitchen.
They may be utilized in an RV or camper while traveling, as well as on a campsite, thanks to their ease of portability.

Reasonable
Air fryers are surprisingly affordable to purchase, especially given how practical and adaptable they are. They normally cost between $50 and $150 and are offered by online sellers.
However, I would advise avoiding the less expensive models and choosing quality even if it costs a bit more.

Simple to Use
Most of the time, air fryers are quite simple to use and require little supervision during cooking. Simply place the food into the basket, set the timer and temperature, and let the fryer handle the rest.
If you need any inspiration, there are several simple recipes available. I find frying veggies to be really simple and gratifying; the roasting effect makes the vegetables appetizing.

Great for Vegetable
Are you and the people you love finicky eaters of vegetables? Vegetables can be crisped up and made tastier by air frying. Many individuals find that air-frying vegetables like cauliflower, broccoli, or Brussels sprouts improves their texture. There are also a tonne of recipes available

online that offer choices for breading veggies to cook in an air fryer (like the buffalo cauliflower below). Some even include healthier alternatives like crumbs made from grains or chickpeas. This is especially useful if you're aiming to increase the number of plant-based meals in your weekly menu or follow a plant-based diet.

Step-By-Step Air Frying

Setup before First Use
You should take off all of the stickers and the air fryer's packing before using it for the first time. After that, place on a solid, heat-resistant surface.
Make sure the air fryer is set up far from surfaces and items. This will stop steam from doing any harm.
You should remove the basket from the air fryer using the handle in order to get rid of all the plastic packaging. Utilize the basket release button to separate the inner and outer baskets.
Use a non-abrasive sponge or a dishwasher to thoroughly clean both baskets. With a slightly moist towel, clean the basket's interior and outside.
The basket can be dried with a dry towel. Put the basket back inside the air fryer after that.

The Air Fryer Is Running a Test
Before utilising the air fryer for cooking, you should test it at least once.
This will assist you in becoming familiar with the various features of your air fryer and ensuring that it is operating properly.
The air fryer can be examined as follows: Connect the air fryer's power plug. A full air fryer basket should be used. Next, give the air fryer some time to warm up.
You will see a preheat button on your air fryer if it has multiple functions. Small, pricey air fryers typically use analogue control systems.
These will need to be manually warmed up. In order to manually preheat, heat for 5 minutes at 400°F. When the

preheating process is finished, the air fryer will beep. After that, remove the air fryer's basket and give it five minutes to cool. After that, re-place the empty basket inside the air fryer.

Decide on the time and temperature you want. Now check to see if the air fryer is operating correctly. The air fryer will automatically switch off and keep making the "beep beep" sound when the cooking time is up.

Then, using the handle, remove the air fryer basket, allowing it to cool for 10 to 30 minutes. If everything goes as planned, your air fryer will be prepared for use.

A Few Pointers for the Air Fryer Basket Only remove the air fryer's basket when cooking and cleaning food. Avoid repeatedly removing the basket. The handle's button guard stops the user from unintentionally hitting the release button. To release the basket, slide the button guard forward. When taking out the basket, never hit the basket release button. This is because the basket may fall and create mishaps if the release button is pressed while the basket is being carried. When you're ready, merely press the basket release button. Make sure the surface you plan to set it on is secure and heat-resistant. The air fryer's handle is affixed to the inside basket rather than the outside basket. As a result, your outer basket will drop when you press the release button on the basket.

A Few Pointers for the Air Fryer Basket Only remove the air fryer's basket when cooking and cleaning food.

Avoid repeatedly removing the basket. The handle's button guard stops the user from unintentionally hitting the release button.

To release the basket, slide the button guard forward. When taking out the basket, never hit the basket release button.

This is because the basket may fall and create mishaps if the release button is pressed while the basket is being carried.

When you're ready, merely press the basket release button. Make sure the surface you plan to set it on is secure and heat-resistant.

The air fryer's handle is affixed to the inside basket rather than the outside basket. As a result, your outer basket will drop when you press the release button on the basket.

An Instruction Guide

It is necessary to heat up the air fryer before using it to cook. This is done so that once the air fryer is preheated, the food would cook more quickly and have a crispy exterior.

A multi-purpose device can be instantly pre-heated by pressing the preheat button. However, manual preheating is required for little, low-cost air fryers.

The air fryer needs to be manually preheated for five minutes at 400°F. After the air fryer has finished preheating, remove the air fryer basket and add the food.

However, keep in mind that the basket shouldn't include too much food. because if the basket is overfilled, the food may not be cooked properly. After filling the air fryer basket with food, place it inside the appliance.

Next, decide when and at what temperature meals should be served. While cooking, you can also change the temperature and time.

Start the air fryer by pressing the start button.. But after you start cooking, you have to keep an eye on it to make sure it doesn't get too done or burnt.

You can combine the ingredients midway through cooking or flip the meal over to ensure that it is thoroughly cooked.

When the cooking time is up, the air fryer will beep. Next, take out the air fryer basket. But mind the heat of the steam.

After separating the inner and outer baskets, serve the food. Separate the inner from the outer basket while keeping the basket on a flat surface.

The basket must completely cool before cleaning.

What Is an Air Fryer's Mechanism?

Let's first talk about an air fryer's operation before moving on to its uses and advantages.

In order to provide the same level of crispiness as traditional fried dishes, air fryers work by moving hot air around a food product. By eliminating high-fat and high-calorie oils from the cooking process, these have the desired impact. Compared to other deep-frying methods, the air fryer uses a very small amount of oil. Instead of using many cups of oil, you may cook your favourite foods using just one scoop.

Around the food, heated air that can reach 400 degrees Fahrenheit is pushed by a fan. Similar to deep-fried dishes, the foods are cooked on the outside first by the circulating air, leaving the interiors mushy. The bottom of the dish has a basket where any grease, if any, is collected from the food.

According to research, air fryers employ heated air with tiny oil droplets to remove moisture from the meal. As a result, it yields fried meals of the same type but with substantially less fat.

The Millard effect, which air fryers cause to happen, enhances the colour and flavour of the food they fry. So, the main question here is, "What does an air fryer do?"

Important Things to Keep in Mind

- Constantly keep the grate in the basket. This allows hot air to circulate around the food and keeps it from resting in additional oil.
- Air fryers emit a sound. You can hear the fans rotating when it's running.
- It is useful. To ensure equal browning, remove the basket every few minutes and turn the food around. You are welcome to remove the basket and examine it. Any time during the cooking process is OK for doing this. There is no need to turn off the machine because it shuts off when the basket is removed.
- Check if the drawer is fully inserted as a result to avoid a fault. The air fryer will alert you by suddenly going silent.
- You're not used to how rapidly food cooks! It's one of the nicest aspects about the air fryer. In the manual for your air fryer, there is probably a helpful table with frying times and temperatures for common foods.
- If there is less food in the basket, the cook time will be cut; if there is more food, the cook time will be extended. You might need a slightly lower temperature. Many air fryer recipes call for lower temperature settings than traditional recipes. Even if this might seem dubious, believe it.
- A slightly lower temperature will help prevent food from being excessively black or crispy on the exterior while still ensuring that the inside is cooked through because air fryers heat up rapidly and circulate the hot air.

Straight from Store

Size and Volume

Size is an important factor, particularly if your kitchen is small. A medium-sized air fryer can hold between 3.7 and 4.1 litres of food. They are so little that they should easily fit in most kitchens. However, there is a clear correlation between size and capacity. Choosing a small or medium-sized fryer may compel you to cook meals in batches, which you don't want to do if you have a large family or frequently host parties. Make your pick carefully because larger air fryers tend to be bulkier and can cook food more quickly for more people.

Controls

Most air fryers have dials for managing the temperature and timer. If you want more accuracy, look for higher-

end models with digital controls. Even the ability to establish custom temperatures and LED displays that display information are included. Additionally, these air fryers include settings that make frying simpler. Additionally, keep an eye out for the rapidly expanding category of intelligent air fryers. They have Wi-Fi connectivity, allowing you to control cooking settings from your phone.

Cleaning

Regularly cleaning your air fryer completely is essential. Thankfully, cleaning an air fryer doesn't require a lot of work. Simply take out its drawer and wash it while turning on the water. The inside basket, which is frequently removable, can be fully washed with dishwashing detergent. These baskets' non-stick coating often prevents food from sticking. Some variants also feature a dishwasher-safe construction.

Air fryers allow for the rapid and simple preparation of healthy cuisine without sacrificing flavour. The majority of chefs suggest reducing cooking or baking times by 20% because this expedites food preparation. For instance, air frying for 24 minutes should be sufficient if the original recipe asks for conventional cooking for 30 minutes. Users must also experiment with temperature settings to avoid overcooking. You can use free tools like the Oven to Air Fryer converter to calculate the correct temperature and cooking time for oven recipes. Chefs frequently advise spraying or brushing some oil on the food halfway through cooking to increase browning and crispiness.

Cleaning and Caring for Your Air Fryer

There are several different types of air fryers available. None, of course, are as stylish or well-made as Ree's! For comprehensive instructions, it is therefore advisable to periodically review the owner's manual for your particular model. But by giving an air fryer a fast once-over at the very least after every other usage, cleaning one is made simple. Chelsea suggests cleaning anything you make that is particularly messy, such as something with sauce or marinade, the same day to prevent a stuck-on mess. Mae Plummer is the author of Mae's Menu's recipes. "It gets tougher to remove anything from the air fryer the longer something sticks."

Cleaning your air fryer on a regular basis will not only make the task simpler, but it will also stop the accumulation of food particles that could otherwise result in issues, unpleasant odours, or even—worst case scenario—a fire. The quickest and simplest method to quickly clean your air fryer is as follows:

Before unplugging your fryer after usage, allow it to cool completely.

The basket, tray, or other item should be removed and washed in the sink with warm water and dish soap. Drying is more effective at night.

Use a moist, soapy cloth, sponge, or paper towel to clean the inside of the fryer, being especially careful to protect the heating element. Use a damp cloth to reclean the area, then dry it off.

Use a gentle towel to clean the fryer's outside.

Place the removable frying parts inside the fryer once they have dried.

How should I thoroughly clean my air fryer?

The process is largely the same as the quick cleanup you do after cooking, with a few more stages. According to chef Sylvia Fountaine, air fryers are really just little convection ovens with a nonstick drawer. Feasting at Home is her recipe blog. You can therefore treat caked-on food similarly to how you would treat a non-stick pan. "The air fryer basket needs to have a cup of water filled. After a brief period of intense heat, the air fryer should be turned off. Debris and cooked-on fat are easily removed using heat and water. Opening the drawer reveals that a significant amount of dirt was rapidly eliminated without the use of soap or washing."

Are your fryer's removable parts still filthy? Use a toothbrush with soft bristles to gently scrub them after 30 minutes in hot, soapy water. A toothpick can be used to (gently) reach places that are challenging to clean, including the perforations in the grate. Never, however, should the entire air fryer be filled with water.

How Can Sticky Residue Be Removed from an Air Fryer?

Try Fountaine's procedure, but if the inside of your air fryer feels unusually oily, add a little dish soap to the water. Use a grease-fighting product like Dawn Ultra if at all possible. To make cleaning the air fryer after use simpler, you might also be able to use disposable aluminium foil or parchment paper liners. Please make sure they are compatible with your toaster oven air fryer by reading your owner's handbook.

Clean Up the Sham Right Away

Get into the habit of wiping out grease and food residue as soon as you can because doing so will make it more difficult to remove them later. This is especially true if you leave them in the air fryer overnight or for several days at a time. After every usage, give your air fryer a good cleaning even if you don't immediately get around to a deeper clean. This will stop the oils from drying out. Additionally, clean up any crumbs left over after using the air fryer. Another straightforward option is to immediately wash the air fryer basket after use with warm, soapy water, then clean it later when it's more convenient.

Prepare Your Basket

By lining your frying basket, you can significantly reduce the amount of cleanup required after cooking. Find a dishwasher-safe, easily removable basket insert if you can. You won't have to deep clean your air fryer as regularly as a result. If you can't find one, you may just use parchment paper or tin foil sparingly. To inhibit ventilation and prevent the food from overcooking, do not, however, block the openings in the basket. Additionally, never put tin foil or parchment paper in the bottom of the drawer when using an air fryer.

Be Wary of Non-stick

Customers have complained about the non-stick coating on some air fryer parts wearing off over time on our website and in other places. In spite of the fact that we haven't observed this (our testing evaluates performance immediately out of the box), our advise for other nonstick cookware is still applicable here: If the non-stick coating is peeled, avoid using the air fryer and avoid using steel wool, metal utensils, or any other abrasives as they may scratch or chip the non-stick coating. Instead, attempt phoning the manufacturer's customer care and requesting a new basket, or consider returning the air fryer to the retailer.

Frequently Asked Questions & Notes

Describe the Air Fryer

Large countertop equipment called "air fryers" make a bold claim: wonderfully fried meals using very little oil (often less than a tablespoon). However, an air fryer is not at all a fryer, despite the catchy name. It is a little convection oven that uses a fan to move hot air around food as it cooks. By using convection cooking in this manner, food can be prepared with a similar level of crispiness to fried food but using significantly less oil. However, the extremely hot air is also perfect for roasting and even makes it possible to prepare foods that you would typically grill.

Is Deep Frying Unhealthy?

Yes, the air fryer works as intended: Instead of using quarts of oil, a cook may use a little bit to get perfectly crisp results for chips, poultry, fish, and more. However, we discovered that the outcomes resemble those of an oven-fried dish more so than a deep-fried one. Foods that are air-fried or baked instead of deep-fried taste much thinner because fat is necessary for the "fried" flavour. However, we discovered that food cooked in the greatest air fryers was even better than food cooked in ovens.

Does the Air Fryer Need to Be Preheated?

An oven heats up slower than an air fryer. When creating the recipes for our air fryer cookbook, Air Fryer Perfection, we discovered that the total cooking time for food added to a cold air fryer was the same as when we waited a few minutes for the air fryer to heat up before adding our food. Additionally, skipping the preheating was practical. One benefit of utilising an air fryer rather than an oven is that you can cook food much more quickly because you don't need to pre-heat the appliance.

What Is the Capacity of an Air Fryer?

Depending on the cuisine, most conventional air fryers can fit enough food for 2 to 4 servings. It's crucial to avoid stuffing the basket too full. If you decide to prepare an air frying recipe in multiple batches, begin monitoring the second batch for doneness a few minutes earlier because the air fryer will already The second batch might cook more rapidly if it's hot.

How to Avoid Adhering?

We advise lightly misting the basket with vegetable oil spray before adding dishes that are prone to sticking, like breaded chicken or delicate fish. Additionally, cleanup and the removal of some meals, particularly fish, can be simplified by using a foil sling.

How Can My Air Fryer Be Cleaned?

The majority of the air fryer's removable elements, such the drawer and basket on many versions, are dishwasher-safe, but you should always check the handbook before doing so. Additionally, you should occasionally clean the main body of your air fryer because food splatters and grease can amass around the heating element and result in smoking. Some types' heating elements can be more easily accessed by flipping the air fryer over. Before cleaning the interior of your air fryer, make sure it is fully cool. Use a light detergent. Run the air fryer briefly after cleaning it to help the interior air out.

What should I Do If I Smell Smoke during Air Frying or If the Smell Coming from My Air Fryer Changes?

Keep your air fryer clean! We discovered that a dirty air fryer was the main cause of smoking and odour issues. Make careful to clean the area around the air fryer's heating element to get rid of any accumulated residue if you notice a lot of smoke or smell burning even though your food hasn't really burned. Check periodically for food splatter with a mild detergent while it's cool.

4-Week Diet Plan

Week 1

Day 1:
Breakfast: Garlic Potatoes
Lunch: Waldorf Salad with Pecans
Snack: Air-fryer Egg Rolls
Dinner: Avocado Prawns-Beans Bowl
Dessert: Honey Pears with Ricotta

Day 2:
Breakfast: Potato Boats with Bacon and Cheese
Lunch: Air Fried Asparagus with Parmesan
Snack: Italian Crispy Stuffed Olives
Dinner: Salsa Verde Chicken
Dessert: Grilled Fruit Skewers

Day 3:
Breakfast: Spinach Frittata with Feta
Lunch: Mouth-Watering Baby Potatoes
Snack: Parmesan Cheese Aubergine Sticks
Dinner: Mini Beef Meatloaves
Dessert: Greek Peaches with Blueberries

Day 4:
Breakfast: Basil Egg Cups
Lunch: Roasted Corn
Snack: Fried Pita Chips
Dinner: Quick Pork Chops
Dessert: Walnut-Stuffed Apples

Day 5:
Breakfast: Pepper Rings with Salsa
Lunch: Cauliflower Quesadillas
Snack: Classic Scotch Eggs
Dinner: Lasagna Casserole
Dessert: Honey Apple-Peach Crisp

Day 6:
Breakfast: Ham and Cheese Muffins
Lunch: Roasted Broccoli
Snack: Savoury Green Bean Fries
Dinner: BBQ Meatballs
Dessert: Strawberry Crumble

Day 7:
Breakfast: Veggie Mini Quiche
Lunch: Mediterranean Roasted Veggies
Snack: Garlic Prawns
Dinner: Caramelized Salmon
Dessert: Berries Crumble

Week 2

Day 1:
Breakfast: Refreshing Blueberry Porridge
Lunch: Spicy Corn Fritters
Snack: Simple Low-Carb Honey Mustard
Dinner: Fried Chicken
Dessert: Apple-Blueberry Pies

Day 2:
Breakfast: Toast Sticks
Lunch: Asian Stir-Fried Veggies
Snack: Stuffed Mushrooms
Dinner: Smoky Calamari Rings
Dessert: Oatmeal-Carrot Cups

Day 3:
Breakfast: Toaster Pastries
Lunch: Breaded Avocado Fries
Snack: Sesame Mushroom Toast
Dinner: Classic Polish Sausage
Dessert: Dark Chocolate Cookies

Day 4:
Breakfast: Raisin Granola Bars
Lunch: Crisp Carrot Chips
Snack: Wrapped Sausages
Dinner: Tasty Coconut Prawn
Dessert: Frosted Chocolate Cake

Day 5:
Breakfast: Cinnamon Bagels
Lunch: Bacon with Brussels Sprouts
Snack: Thai-style Cauliflower Bites
Dinner: Spicy Chicken and Potatoes
Dessert: Maple Chocolate Chip Cookies

Day 6:
Breakfast: Banana-Nut Muffins
Lunch: Roasted Tomatoes
Snack: Waffle Fry Nachos with Bacon
Dinner: Sriracha Pork Ribs
Dessert: Cinnamon Crisps

Day 7:
Breakfast: Scrambled Eggs
Lunch: Breaded Pepper Strips
Snack: Breaded Prawn Toast
Dinner: Mustard Ham
Dessert: Crusted Lemon Bars

Week 3

Day 1:
Breakfast: Sausage and Onion Patties
Lunch: Delicious Broccoli Cheese Tots
Snack: Pesto Bruschetta
Dinner: Beef-Fried Buttermilk Steak
Dessert: Raspberry Streusel Cake

Day 2:
Breakfast: Hard Eggs
Lunch: Roasted Peppers with Parsley
Snack: Kale Chips with Yogurt Sauce
Dinner: Crispy Mayo Chicken Tenders
Dessert: Peach Oat Crumble

Day 3:
Breakfast: Vegetable Bacon Hash
Lunch: Spicy Corn and Beans
Snack: Curried Sweet Potato Fries
Dinner: Mayo Fish Taco Bowl
Dessert: Chocolate Cheesecake

Day 4:
Breakfast: Sausage-Cheese Balls
Lunch: Homemade Roasted Carrots
Snack: Special Beef-Mango Skewers
Dinner: Mayo Prawns Burgers
Dessert: Cheese Pound Cake

Day 5:
Breakfast: Classic Dijon Scotch Eggs
Lunch: Maple Sweet Potatoes
Snack: Tasty Pot Stickers
Dinner: Fajita Flank Steak Rolls
Dessert: Cinnamon Apple Fritters

Day 6:
Breakfast: Vanilla Strawberry Muffins
Lunch: Balsamic Brussels Sprouts with Bacon
Snack: Awesome Cheese Wontons
Dinner: Herbed Crouton-Crusted Pork Chops
Dessert: Mayonnaise Chocolate Cake

Day 7:
Breakfast: Savoury Puffed Egg Tarts
Lunch: Flaxseed Cheese Rolls
Snack: Mayo Artichoke Hearts
Dinner: Homemade Chicken Satay
Dessert: Cinnamon Apple-Pecan Jars

Week 4

Day 1:
Breakfast: Hearty Steak and Eggs
Lunch: Tasty Onion Rings
Snack: Crusted Mozzarella Balls
Dinner: Stuffed Chicken Breast
Dessert: Tasty Banana Nut Cake

Day 2:
Breakfast: Cinnamon Toast Sticks
Lunch: Fried Green Beans
Snack: Stuffed Jalapeño Poppers
Dinner: Lemony Fried Prawns
Dessert: Vanilla Pancake Cake

Day 3:
Breakfast: Scotch Eggs with Breadcrumbs
Lunch: Spicy Roasted Salsa
Snack: Garlic Croutons with Parmesan
Dinner: Pork Cabbage Burgers
Dessert: Classic Shortbread Sticks

Day 4:
Breakfast: An Egg in a Hole
Lunch: Thyme Butternut Squash
Snack: Spicy Cumin Chickpeas
Dinner: Teriyaki Chicken Wings
Dessert: Fancy Chocolate Lava Cakes

Day 5:
Breakfast: Quick Bacon Strips
Lunch: Citrus-Honey Broccoli Florets
Snack: Crispy Potato Chips
Dinner: Mustard Pork Tenderloin
Dessert: Tasty Banana Bread Muffins

Day 6:
Breakfast: Cheese, Sausage, and Egg Burrito
Lunch: Delicious Roasted Carrots
Snack: Ranch Oyster Crackers
Dinner: Blue Cheese Beef Burgers
Dessert: Chocolate Pavlova

Day 7:
Breakfast: Shakshuka Cups
Lunch: Lemon Butter Asparagus
Snack: Apple Chips with Cinnamon
Dinner: Italian Garlic Scallops
Dessert: Sweet Blueberries Jubilee

Chapter 1 Breakfast Recipes

Garlic Potatoes

Prep time: 10 minutes | Cook time: 20 minutes | Serves: 6

1½ teaspoons olive oil, divided, plus more for misting	2 teaspoons seasoned salt, divided
4 large potatoes, skins on, cut into cubes	1 teaspoon minced garlic, divided
	2 large peppers, red or green
	½ onion, diced

1. Cut the peppers into 2.5cm chunks. 2. Lightly mist the air fryer basket with olive oil. 3. In a medium bowl, toss the potatoes with ½ teaspoon of olive oil. Sprinkle with 1 teaspoon of seasoned salt and ½ teaspoon of minced garlic. Stir to coat. 4. Place the seasoned potatoes in the air fryer basket in a single layer. 5. Then cook at 205°C for 5 minutes. Shake the basket and cook for another 5 minutes. 6. Meanwhile, in a medium bowl, toss the peppers and onion with the remaining ½ teaspoon of olive oil. 7. Sprinkle the peppers and onions with the remaining 1 teaspoon of seasoned salt and ½ teaspoon of minced garlic. Stir to coat. 8. Add the seasoned onions and pepper to the air fryer basket with the potatoes. Then cook for 5 minutes. Shake the basket halfway and cook for an additional 5 minutes.
Per Serving: Calories 210; Fat 1.4g; Sodium 791mg; Carbs 45.4g; Fibre 5.8g; Sugar 3g; Protein 5.4g

Potato Boats with Bacon and Cheese

Prep time: 10 minutes | Cook time: 20 minutes | Serves: 4

Olive oil	4 eggs
Salt	2 tablespoons chopped, cooked bacon
2 large russet potatoes, scrubbed	100g shredded cheddar cheese
Freshly ground black pepper	

1. Poke holes in the potatoes. Let it microwave on full power for 5 minutes. 2. Then turn over the potatoes and cook until the potatoes are fork tender, for about 3 to 5 minutes. 3. Lengthwise cut the potatoes in halves and then scoop out the inside of the potatoes with a spoon. To make a sturdy "boat", leave a layer of potato. 4. Lightly spray the air fryer basket with olive oil. Spray the skin side of the potatoes with oil and sprinkle with salt and pepper to taste. 5. Place the potato skins in the air fryer basket skin side down. Crack one egg into each potato skin. 6. Sprinkle ½ tablespoon of bacon pieces and 25g of shredded cheese on top of each egg. Sprinkle with salt and pepper to taste. 7. Air fry at 175°C until the yolk is slightly runny, 5 to 6 minutes, or until the yolk is fully cooked, 7 to 10 minutes.
Per Serving: Calories 392; Fat 19.4g; Sodium 294mg; Carbs 35g; Fibre 2.5g; Sugar 2g; Protein 19.8g

Spinach Frittata with Feta

Prep time: 10 minutes | Cook time: 20 minutes | Serves: 4

Olive oil	30g baby spinach leaves, shredded
5 eggs	75g halved grape tomatoes
¼ teaspoon salt	110g crumbled feta cheese
⅛ teaspoon freshly ground black pepper	

1. Spray a small round air fryer-friendly pan with olive oil. 2. In a medium bowl, whisk together salt, eggs, and pepper and whisk to combine. 3. Add the spinach and stir to combine. 4. Pour ½ cup of the egg mixture into the pan. 5. Sprinkle 35g of the tomatoes and 30g of the feta on top of the egg mixture. 6. Cover the pan with aluminum foil. Then secure it around the edges. 7. Place the pan carefully into the air fryer basket. 8. Air fry at 175°C for 12 minutes. Transfer the foil from the pan and cook until the eggs are set, 5 to 7 minutes. 9. Transfer the frittata onto a serving platter. Repeat with the remaining ingredients.
Per Serving: Calories 226; Fat 16g; Sodium 451mg; Carbs 5.8g; Fibre 0.4g; Sugar 4.5g; Protein 14g

Prawns and Cheese Frittata

Prep time: 15 minutes | Cook time: 20 minutes | Serves: 4

1 teaspoon olive oil, plus more for spraying	Salt
½ small red pepper, finely diced	Freshly ground black pepper
1 teaspoon minced garlic	4 eggs, beaten
1 (100g) can tiny prawns, drained	4 teaspoons ricotta cheese

1. Spray four ramekins with olive oil. 2. Set a medium frying pan over medium-low heat, and heat 1 teaspoon of olive oil. Add the pepper and garlic and sauté until the pepper is soft, about 5 minutes. 3. Add the prawns, salt, and pepper, and mix to season the prawns. Then cook until warm, for 1 to 2 minutes. Remove from the heat. 4. Add the eggs and stir to combine. Pour one quarter of the mixture into each ramekin. 5. Place 2 ramekins in the air fryer basket and cook for 6 minutes. 6. Remove the air fryer basket from your air fryer and stir the mixture in each ramekin. Top each frittata with 1 teaspoon of ricotta cheese. Then transfer the air fryer basket back to the air fryer and cook at 175°C until the eggs are firm and the top is lightly browned, for 4 to 5 minutes. 7. Repeat with the remaining two ramekins.
Per Serving: Calories 101; Fat 6.2g; Sodium 207mg; Carbs 1.2g; Fibre 0g; Sugar 0.5g; Protein 9.5g

Veggie Mini Quiche

Prep time: 10 minutes | Cook time: 15 minutes | Serves: 4

1 teaspoon olive oil, plus more for spraying	4 eggs, beaten
100g coarsely chopped mushrooms	50g shredded Cheddar cheese
30g fresh baby spinach, shredded	60g shredded mozzarella cheese
	¼ teaspoon salt
	¼ teaspoon black pepper

1. Spray 4 silicone baking cups with olive oil and set aside. 2. Set a medium sauté pan over medium heat, warm 1 teaspoon of olive oil. Add the mushrooms and sauté until soft, for 3 to 4 minutes. Then add the spinach to cook until wilted, for 1 to 2 minutes. Set aside. 3. In a medium bowl, whisk together the eggs, Cheddar cheese, mozzarella cheese, salt, and pepper. Gently fold the mushrooms and spinach into the egg mixture. 4. Pour ¼ of the mixture into each silicone baking cup. 5. Place the baking cups into the air fryer basket and air fry at 175°C for 5 minutes. Stir the mixture in each ramekin slightly and air fry until the egg has set, an additional 3 to 5 minutes.
Per Serving: Calories 158; Fat 10g; Sodium 411mg; Carbs 2g; Fibre 0.7g; Sugar 0.9g; Protein 14g

Basil Egg Cups

Prep time: 5 minutes | Cook time: 10 minutes | Serves: 4

Olive oil	4 teaspoons grated Parmesan cheese
240ml marinara sauce	Salt
4 eggs	Freshly ground black pepper
4 tablespoons shredded mozzarella cheese	Chopped fresh basil, for garnish

1. Lightly spritz olive oil over the 4 ramekins. 2. Divide the marinara sauce evenly into each ramekin. 3. In each ramekin, crack one egg just on top of the marinara sauce. 4. Sprinkle 1 tablespoon of Parmesan and 1 tablespoon of mozzarella on top of each egg. Season with salt and pepper. 5. Cover each ramekin with aluminum foil. Then arrange two of the ramekins in the air fryer basket. 6. Air fry at 175°C for 5 minutes and remove the aluminum foil. Then air fry until the top is lightly browned and the egg white is cooked, for another 2 to 4 minutes. For a firmer yolk, cook for 3 to 5 more minutes. 7. Repeat with the remaining two ramekins. Garnish with basil and serve.
Per Serving: Calories 135; Fat 8g; Sodium 806mg; Carbs 6g; Fibre 1.2g; Sugar 3.8g; Protein 9.6g

Pepper Rings with Salsa

Prep time: 5 minutes | Cook time: 10 minutes | Serves: 4

Olive oil	Salt
1 large red, yellow, or orange pepper, cut into four 1.5cm rings	Freshly ground black pepper
4 eggs	2 teaspoons salsa

1. Lightly spray a small round air fryer–friendly pan with olive oil. 2. Place 2 pepper rings on the pan. Then crack one egg into each pepper ring. Season with salt and black pepper. 3. Top each egg with ½ teaspoon of salsa. 4. Place the pan in the air fryer basket. Air fry at 175°C until the yolk is slightly runny, 5 to 6 minutes or until the yolk is fully cooked, 8 to 10 minutes. 5. Repeat with the remaining 2 pepper rings. Serve hot.
Per Serving: Calories 76; Fat 4.3g; Sodium 83mg; Carbs 3g; Fibre 1g; Sugar 2g; Protein 6g

Ham and Cheese Muffins

Prep time: 10 minutes | Cook time: 10 minutes | Serves: 6

Olive oil	135g diced ham
4 eggs, beaten	50g shredded Cheddar cheese
340g frozen hash browns, thawed	½ teaspoon Cajun seasoning

1. Lightly spray 12 silicone muffin cups with olive oil. 2. Mix together the hash browns, eggs, ham, Cheddar cheese, and Cajun seasoning in a medium bowl. 3. Spoon a heaping 1½ tablespoons of hash brown mixture into each muffin cup. 4. Place the muffin cups in the air fryer basket. 5. Then air fry at 175°C until the muffins are golden brown on top and the center has set up, for 8 to 10 minutes.
Per Serving: Calories 263; Fat 17g; Sodium 406mg; Carbs 17g; Fibre 1.8g; Sugar 0.3g; Protein 11g

Refreshing Blueberry Porridge

Prep time: 10 minutes | Cook time: 25 minutes | Serves: 6

120g quick oats	85g honey
1¼ teaspoons ground cinnamon, divided	1 teaspoon vanilla extract
½ teaspoon baking powder	1 egg, beaten
Pinch salt	295g blueberries
240ml unsweetened vanilla almond milk	Olive oil
	1½ teaspoons sugar, divided

1. In a large bowl, mix the baking powder, 1 teaspoon of cinnamon, oats, and salt. 2. In a medium bowl, whisk together the almond milk, honey, vanilla and egg. 3. Pour the liquid ingredients into the oats mixture and stir to combine. Fold in the blueberries. 4. Lightly spray a round air fryer–friendly pan with oil. 5. Add half the blueberry mixture to the pan. 6. Sprinkle ⅛ teaspoon of cinnamon and ½ teaspoon sugar over the top. 7. Use the aluminum foil to cover the pan and place gently in the air fryer basket. 8. Air fry for 20 minutes. Remove the foil and air fry at 180°C for an additional 5 minutes. Transfer the mixture to a shallow bowl. Repeat with the remaining blueberry mixture, ½ teaspoon of sugar, and ⅛ teaspoon of cinnamon. 9. Transfer to serving bowls.
Per Serving: Calories 264; Fat 4g; Sodium 55mg; Carbs 53g; Fibre 3.7g; Sugar 37.8g; Protein 5.8g

Peanut Butter Banana Bread Pudding

Prep time: 10 minutes | Cook time: 20 minutes | Serves: 4

Olive oil	1 teaspoon ground cinnamon
2 medium ripe bananas, mashed	1 teaspoon vanilla extract
120ml low-fat milk	2 slices whole-grain bread, torn
2 tablespoons peanut butter	into bite-sized pieces
2 tablespoons maple syrup	20g quick oats

1. Tear the bread slices into bite-sized pieces. 2. Lightly spray four individual ramekins or one air fryer–safe baking dish with olive oil. 3. Combine the peanut butter, milk, bananas, maple syrup, cinnamon, and vanilla in a large mixing bowl. Mix with an electric mixer until they are fully combined. 4. Add the bread pieces and stir to coat in the liquid mixture. 5. Stir in oats until they are well combined. 6. Transfer the mixture to the baking dish or divide between the ramekins. Cover with aluminum foil. Place 2 ramekins in the air fryer basket and air fry at 175°C until heated through, 10 to 12 minutes. 7. Remove the foil and cook for 6 to 8 more minutes. Repeat with the remaining 2 ramekins.
Per Serving: Calories 231; Fat 6.4g; Sodium 330mg; Carbs 35.3g; Fibre 4g; Sugar 16.4g; Protein 9g

Toast Sticks

Prep Time: 10 minutes | Cook Time: 9 minutes | Serves: 4

Oil, for spraying	1 teaspoon ground cinnamon
6 large eggs	8 slices bread, cut into thirds
320ml milk	Syrup of choice, for serving
2 teaspoons vanilla extract	

1. Preheat the air fryer to 185°C. Line the air fryer basket with parchment paper and spray with oil. 2. Whisk the eggs, milk, vanilla, and cinnamon in a small bowl. 3. Dunk one piece of bread in the egg mixture, making sure to coat both sides. Work quickly so the bread doesn't get soggy, and then immediately transfer the bread to the air fryer basket. 4. Do the same with the remaining bread, and make sure the pieces don't touch each other. You can work in batches. 5. Cook the bread pieces in the preheated air fryer for 9 minutes, flipping halfway through. 6. When cooked, enjoy the bread slices with your favourite syrup.
Per Serving: Calories 271; Fat 11.13g; Sodium 338mg; Carbs 24.98g; Fibre 1.4g; Sugar 6.92g; Protein 15.54g

Toaster Pastries

Prep Time: 10 minutes | Cook Time: 11 minutes | Serves: 6

Oil, for spraying	250g icing sugar
1 (375g) ready-made pie case	3 tablespoons milk
6 tablespoons jam or preserves of choice	1 to 2 tablespoons sprinkle of choice

1. Preheat the air fryer to 175°C. Line the air fryer basket with parchment and spray lightly with oil. 2. Cut the piecrust into 12 rectangles, about 8 by 10cm each. You need reroll the dough scraps to get 12 rectangles. 3. Spread 1 tablespoon of jam in the centre of 6 rectangles, leaving ½cm around the edges. 4. Pour some water into a small bowl and use the water to moisten the edge of each rectangle. 5. Top each rectangle with another and use your fingers to press around the edges. Using the tines of a fork, seal the edges of the dough and poke a few holes in the top of each one. Place the pastries in the prepared basket. 6. Cook the pastries for 11 minutes. Let cool completely after cooking. 7. Mix the icing sugar and milk in a medium bowl. Spread the icing over the tops of the pastries and add sprinkles. 8. Serve immediately.
Per Serving: Calories 513; Fat 20.1g; Sodium 212mg; Carbs 84.14g; Fibre 7.2g; Sugar 68.73g; Protein 2.53g

Granola Cereal

Prep Time: 10 minutes | Cook Time: 30 minutes | Serves: 7

Oil, for spraying	1 tablespoon toasted sesame oil
120g gluten-free rolled oats	or vegetable oil
60g chopped walnuts	1 teaspoon ground cinnamon
45g chopped almonds	½ teaspoon salt
60g pumpkin seeds	55g dried cranberries
85g maple syrup or honey	

1. Preheat the air fryer to 120°C. Line the air fryer basket with parchment and spray lightly with oil. 2. Combine the oats, walnuts, almonds, pumpkin seeds, maple syrup, sesame oil, cinnamon, and salt in a large bowl. 3. Arrange the mixture in an even layer in the prepared basket. 4. Cook the mixture in the preheated air fryer for 30 minutes, stirring every 10 minutes. 5. Put the granola in a bowl, add the dried cranberries and toss to combine. 6. Let the dish cool to room temperature before storing in an airtight container.
Per Serving: Calories 182; Fat 9.9g; Sodium 191mg; Carbs 25.97g; Fibre 4.4g; Sugar 9.52g; Protein 7.1g

Raisin Granola Bars

Prep Time: 5 minutes | Cook Time: 15 minutes | Serves: 6

Oil, for spraying	melted
120g gluten-free rolled oats, divided	3 tablespoons honey
50g packed light brown sugar	1 tablespoon vegetable oil
1 teaspoon ground cinnamon	1 teaspoon vanilla extract
8 tablespoons unsalted butter,	2 tablespoons raisins

1. Line the baking pan with parchment paper and spray lightly with oil. 2. In a blender, Pulse about half of the oats until smooth in the blender, and then transfer to a medium bowl. 3. Add the remaining oats, brown sugar, and cinnamon and stir to combine; add the butter, honey, vegetable oil, and vanilla and stir to combine. Fold in the raisins. 4. Transfer the mixture to the baking pan, and press into an even layer. 5. Cook the mixture at 160°C for 10 minutes; when the time is up, increase the heat to 180°C and cook for 5 minutes more. 6. When cooked, let the dish cool to room temperature, and then freeze before cutting into bars and serving.
Per Serving: Calories 202; Fat 14.15g; Sodium 11mg; Carbs 22.8g; Fibre 3.3g; Sugar 9.29g; Protein 4.17g

Cinnamon Bagels

Prep Time: 30 minutes | Cook Time: 10 minutes | Serves: 4

Oil, for spraying
35g raisins
125g self-rising flour, plus more for dusting
240g plain Greek yogurt
1 teaspoon ground cinnamon
1 large egg

1. Line the air fryer basket with parchment and spray lightly with oil. 2. Place the raisins in a bowl of hot water, and let sit for 10 to 15 minutes, until they have plumped. This will make them extra juicy. 3. In a large bowl, Mix the flour, yogurt, and cinnamon in a large bowl until a ball is formed. 4. Drain the raisins and gently work them into the ball of dough. 5. Flour the work surface and place the dough on it. Roll each piece into a 20 or 23-cm-long rope, and shape it into a circle, pinching the ends together to seal. 6. Beat the egg in a bowl, and brush the egg onto the tops of the dough. 7. Place the dough in the prepared basket. 8. Cook the dough at 175°C for 10 minutes. 9. Serve warm.
Per Serving: Calories 163; Fat 3.43g; Sodium 403mg; Carbs 26.74g; Fibre 1.2g; Sugar 2.98g; Protein 5.92g

Banana-Nut Muffins

Prep Time: 5 minutes | Cook Time: 15 minutes | Serves: 10

Oil, for spraying
2 very ripe bananas
100g packed light brown sugar
80ml vegetable oil
1 large egg
1 teaspoon vanilla extract
90g plain flour
1 teaspoon baking powder
1 teaspoon ground cinnamon
60g chopped walnuts

1. Preheat the air fryer to 160°C. Spray 10 silicone muffin cups lightly with oil. 2. In a medium bowl, mash the bananas. 3. Add the brown sugar, oil, egg, and vanilla to the banana bowl, and stir to combine; fold in the flour, baking powder, and cinnamon; add the walnuts and fold a few times to distribute throughout the batter. 4. Divide the batter equally among the prepared muffin cups and place them in the basket. You can work in batches. 5. Cook the muffins in the preheated air fryer for 15 minutes, or until golden brown and a toothpick inserted into the centre of a muffin comes out clean. 6. Let the muffins cool on a wire rack before serving.
Per Serving: Calories 164; Fat 11.77g; Sodium 5mg; Carbs 13.36g; Fibre 1.2g; Sugar 2.76g; Protein 2.2g

Scrambled Eggs

Prep Time: 5 minutes | Cook Time: 10 minutes | Serves: 2

1 teaspoon unsalted butter
2 large eggs
2 tablespoons milk
2 tablespoons shredded cheddar
cheese
Salt
Freshly ground black pepper

1. Place the butter in the baking pan and cook in the air fryer at 150°C for 1 to 2 minutes until melted. 2. In a small bowl, Beat the eggs with milk, and cheese in a bowl, and season with salt and black pepper. Transfer the mixture to the baking pan. 3. Cook them for 3 minutes. Stir the eggs and push them toward the centre of the pan. 4. Cook for another 2 minutes, then stir again. 5. Cook for another 2 minutes, until the eggs are just cooked. 6. Serve warm.
Per Serving: Calories 88; Fat 6.93g; Sodium 171mg; Carbs 2.12g; Fibre 0g; Sugar 1.35g; Protein 4.2g

Hard Eggs

Prep Time: 5 minutes | Cook Time: 15 minutes | Serves: 6

Oil, for spraying
6 large eggs

1. Preheat the air fryer to 130°C. 2. Line the air fryer basket with parchment and spray lightly with oil. 2. Place the eggs in the air fryer basket. 3. Cook the eggs for 15 minutes. 4. Fill a bowl with water and ice, and then transfer the cooked eggs to the bowl; let the eggs sit for 1 minute or until cool enough to handle. 5. Use the paper towel to pat the eggs dry, and serve immediately. 6. You can refrigerate the cooked eggs for up to 7 days.
Per Serving: Calories 72; Fat 4.76g; Sodium 71mg; Carbs 0.36g; Fibre 0g; Sugar 0.19g; Protein 6.28g

Grilled Grapefruit with Cinnamon

Prep time: 5 minutes | Cook time: 4 minutes | Serves: 2

1 large grapefruit, cut in half
1 tablespoon granular erythritol
2 teaspoons ground cinnamon
⅛ teaspoon ground ginger
2 teaspoons butter, divided into 2 pats

1. Preheat air fryer at 205°C for 3 minutes. 2. Using a paring knife, cut each grapefruit section away from the inner membrane, keeping the sections remaining in the fruit. 3. In a small bowl, combine erythritol, cinnamon, and ginger. Sprinkle over tops of grapefruit halves. Place 1 pat butter on top of each half. 4. Place grapefruit halves in ungreased air fryer basket and cook 4 minutes. 5. Transfer to a medium serving plate and serve warm.
Per Serving: Calories 118; Fat 4g; Sodium 31mg; Carbs 21.8g; Fibre 3.2g; Sugar 17.9g; Protein 1.2g

Sausage and Onion Patties

Prep time: 10 minutes | Cook time: 20 minutes | Serves: 4

300g pork sausage
1 tablespoon peeled and grated yellow onion
1 teaspoon dried thyme
⅛ teaspoon ground cumin
⅛ teaspoon red pepper flakes
¼ teaspoon salt
¼ teaspoon freshly ground black pepper
1 tablespoon water

1. Preheat air fryer at 175°C for 3 minutes. 2. Combine sausage, onion, thyme, cumin, red pepper flakes, salt, and black pepper in a large bowl. Form into eight patties. 3. Pour water into bottom of air fryer to ensure minimum smoke from fat drippings. Place 4 patties in air fryer basket lightly greased with olive oil and cook 5 minutes. 4. Flip patties and cook an additional 5 minutes. 5. Transfer patties to a large serving plate and repeat cooking with remaining sausage patties. Serve warm.
Per Serving: Calories 181; Fat 9g; Sodium 193mg; Carbs 0.7g; Fibre 0.2g; Sugar 0.2g; Protein 21.9g

Sausage-Cheese Balls

Prep time: 10 minutes | Cook time: 12 minutes | Serves: 4

115g loose chorizo
340g pork sausage meat
2 tablespoons canned green chilies, including juice
25g cream cheese, room temperature
25g shredded sharp Cheddar cheese

1. Before cooking, heat your air fryer to 205°C, for about 3 minutes. 2. In a large bowl, combine all ingredients. Form mixture into sixteen 2.5cm balls. Place sausage balls in ungreased air fryer basket. 3. Cook for 6 minutes, then shake basket and cook an additional 6 minutes until a meat thermometer ensures an internal temperature of at least 60°C. 4. Transfer to a large serving plate and serve warm.
Per Serving: Calories 456; Fat 38.5g; Sodium 1136mg; Carbs 2.3g; Fibre 0.1g; Sugar 1.2g; Protein 24.8g

Air-Fried Eggs

Prep time: 5 minutes | Cook time: 15 minutes | Serves: 8

8 large eggs
240g ice cubes
480g water

1. Preheat air fryer at 120°C for 3 minutes. 2. Add eggs to ungreased air fryer basket. Cook for 15 minutes. 3. Add the ice cubes and water to a large bowl. Transfer cooked eggs to this water bath immediately to stop cooking process. After 5 minutes, peel eggs and serve.
Per Serving: Calories 72; Fat 4.7g; Sodium 72mg; Carbs 0.4g; Fibre 0g; Sugar 0.2g; Protein 6.3g

Air Fried Bacon Strips

Prep time: 5 minutes | Cook time: 12 minutes | Serves: 4

2 tablespoons water
8 slices bacon, halved

1. Before cooking, heat your air fryer to 205°C, for about 3 minutes. 2. Pour water into bottom of air fryer to ensure minimum smoke from fat drippings. Place half of bacon in ungreased air fryer basket and cook for 3 minutes. Flip, then cook an additional 3 minutes. 3. Transfer cooked bacon to a medium paper towel–lined serving plate and repeat cooking with remaining bacon. Serve warm.
Per Serving: Calories 212; Fat 20.4g; Sodium 245mg; Carbs 0.4g; Fibre 0g; Sugar 0.4g; Protein 6.5g

Classic Dijon Scotch Eggs

Prep time: 10 minutes | Cook time: 14 minutes | Serves: 4

455g pork sausage
2 teaspoons Dijon mustard
2 teaspoons peeled and grated yellow onion
1 tablespoon chopped fresh chives
1 tablespoon chopped fresh parsley
⅛ teaspoon ground nutmeg
½ teaspoon salt
¼ teaspoon freshly ground black pepper
4 large hard-boiled eggs, peeled
1 large egg, beaten
100g parmesan, grated
2 teaspoons olive oil

1. Before cooking, heat your air fryer to 175°C, for about 3 minutes. 2. Combine sausage, mustard, onion, chives, parsley, nutmeg, salt, and pepper in a large bowl. Separate mixture into four even balls. 3. Form sausage balls evenly around hard-boiled eggs, then dip in beaten egg and dredge in parmesan. 4. Place sausage balls in air fryer basket lightly greased with olive oil. Cook 7 minutes, then gently turn and brush lightly with olive oil. Cook an additional 7 minutes. 5. Transfer to a suitable serving plate and serve warm.
Per Serving: Calories 481; Fat 32.8g; Sodium 1406mg; Carbs 16.7g; Fibre 1.7g; Sugar 9g; Protein 29g

Shakshuka Cups

Prep time: 10 minutes | Cook time: 22 minutes | Serves: 4

1 tablespoon olive oil
½ medium yellow onion, peeled and diced
2 cloves garlic, peeled and minced
1 (1-cm) knob turmeric, peeled and minced
1 (360g) can diced tomatoes, including juice
1 tablespoon no-sugar-added tomato paste
½ teaspoon smoked paprika
½ teaspoon salt
½ teaspoon granular erythritol
¼ teaspoon ground cumin
¼ teaspoon ground coriander
⅛ teaspoon cayenne pepper
4 small peppers, any colour, tops removed and seeded
4 large eggs
2 tablespoons feta cheese crumbles
2 tablespoons chopped fresh parsley

1. Set a suitable saucepan over medium heat and then add olive oil to heat for 30 seconds. Add onion and stir-fry for 10 minutes until softened. 2. Add garlic and turmeric to pan and heat another minute. Add diced tomatoes, tomato paste, paprika, salt, erythritol, cumin, coriander, and cayenne pepper. Remove from heat and stir. 3. Before cooking, heat your air fryer to 175°C, for about 3 minutes. 4. Place peppers in ungreased air fryer basket. Divide tomato mixture among peppers. Crack one egg onto tomato mixture in each pepper. 5. Cook for 9 minutes, then remove from air fryer and sprinkle feta cheese on top of eggs. Then return in air fryer and cook for 1 minute. 6. Remove from air fryer and let rest 5 minutes on a large serving plate. Garnish with parsley and serve warm.
Per Serving: Calories 341; Fat 24g; Sodium 1172mg; Carbs 14.8g; Fibre 3.4g; Sugar 9.6g; Protein 18.4g

Cheese, Sausage, and Egg Burrito

Prep time: 5 minutes | Cook time: 30 minutes | Serves: 6

6 eggs
Salt
Pepper
Cooking oil
75g red pepper, chopped
75g green pepper, chopped
200g chicken sausage meat
140g salsa
50g shredded Cheddar cheese
6 medium (20cm) flour tortillas

1. In a medium bowl, whisk the eggs. Season the whisked eggs with salt and pepper. 2. Set a frying pan over medium-high heat. Spray with cooking oil. Add the whisked eggs. Scramble for 2 to 3 minutes, until fluffy. 3. Remove the fluffy eggs from the frying pan and set aside. 4. Spray the frying pan with more oil if needed. Add the chopped pepper. Cook until the peppers are soft, for 2 to 3 minutes. 5. Add the chicken sausage to the frying pan. Break the sausage into smaller pieces with a spatula or spoon. Cook until the sausage is brown, for about 3 to 4 minutes. 6. Stir in the salsa and scrambled eggs until well combined. Remove the frying pan from heat. 7. Divide the mixture evenly onto the tortillas. 8. Fold the sides of tortilla in toward the middle and then roll up from the bottom to form the burrito with a toothpick or moisten the outside edge of the tortilla with a small amount of water with a cooking brush or just your fingers. 9. Spray the burritos with cooking oil and then place them evenly in the air fryer to avoid

stack. Cook in batches if needed. Then let them cook at 205°C for 8 minutes. 10. Open the air fryer and flip the burritos. Cook until crisp, for an additional 2 minutes. If necessary, repeat the cooking steps for the remaining burritos. 11. Sprinkle the cheddar cheese over the burritos. Cool before serving.
Per Serving: Calories 376; Fat 18.7g; Sodium 673mg; Carbs 29g; Fibre 2g; Sugar 4g; Protein 22g

Vanilla Strawberry Muffins

Prep time: 10 minutes| Cook time: 7 minutes| Serves: 6

50g almond flour
15g granular erythritol
½ teaspoon baking powder
⅛ teaspoon salt
75g hulled and finely chopped
fresh strawberries
¼ teaspoon vanilla extract
3 tablespoons butter, melted
2 large eggs
1 tablespoon chopped fresh basil

1. Before cooking, heat your air fryer to 190°C, for about 3 minutes. 2. In a large bowl, combine almond flour, erythritol, baking powder, and salt. Set aside. 3. In a medium bowl, combine strawberries, vanilla, butter, and eggs. Pour wet ingredients into large bowl with dry ingredients. Gently combine. 4. Add basil to batter. Do not overmix. Spoon batter into six silicone cupcake liners lightly greased with olive oil. 5. Place liners in air fryer basket and cook for 7 minutes. 6. Transfer muffins in silicone liners to a cooling rack to cool for 5 minutes, then serve.
Per Serving: Calories 145; Fat 8.2g; Sodium 122mg; Carbs 14.6g; Fibre 1.2g; Sugar 1g; Protein 4g

Paprika Hash Browns

Prep time: 15 minutes| Cook time: 20 minutes| Serves: 4

4 russet potatoes, peeled
1 teaspoon paprika
Salt
Freshly ground black pepper
Cooking oil spray

1. Shred the peeled russet potatoes with a box grater or food processor. If your grater has different hole sizes, use the largest holes. 2. Place the potatoes in a suitable bowl of cold water. Let sit for 5 minutes. (Cold water helps remove excess starch from the potatoes.) Stir them to help dissolve the starch. 3. Insert the crisper plate into the basket of your air fryer. To preheat, set your air fryer on Air Fry mode and set the temperature to 180°C and time to 3 minutes. 4. Drain and pat them with paper towels until the potatoes are completely dry. Season the potatoes with the paprika, salt, and pepper. 5. Once it is preheated, spray the crisper plate with cooking oil. Spray the potatoes with the cooking oil and place them into the basket. 6. Select AIR FRY, set the temperature to 180°C, and set the time to 20 minutes. Remove the basket and shake the potatoes halfway after cooking for 5 minutes. Reinsert the basket to resume cooking. Continue shaking the basket every 5 minutes (a total of 4 times) until the hash browns are done. 7. When the cooking is complete, remove the hash browns from the basket and serve warm.
Per Serving: Calories 293; Fat 0.4g; Sodium 19mg; Carbs 67g; Fibre 5g; Sugar 2.4g; Protein 8g

Pumpkin and Walnut Muffins

Prep time: 10 minutes| Cook time: 7 minutes| Serves: 6

50g almond flour
15g granular erythritol
½ teaspoon baking powder
¼ teaspoon pumpkin pie spice
⅛ teaspoon ground nutmeg
⅛ teaspoon salt
60g pumpkin purée
¼ teaspoon vanilla extract
3 tablespoons butter, melted
2 large eggs
30g crushed walnuts

1. Before cooking, heat your air fryer to 190°C, for about 3 minutes. 2. In a large bowl, combine flour, erythritol, baking powder, pumpkin pie spice, nutmeg, and salt. Set aside. 3. In a medium bowl, combine pumpkin purée, vanilla, butter, and eggs. Pour wet ingredients into bowl with dry ingredients and gently combine. 4. Add walnuts to batter. Do not overmix. Spoon batter into six silicone cupcake liners lightly greased with olive oil. 5. Place cupcake liners in the air fryer basket and cook for 7 minutes. 6. Transfer muffins in silicone liners to a cooling rack to cool for 5 minutes, then serve.
Per Serving: Calories 193; Fat 12g; Sodium 134mg; Carbs 17g; Fibre 1.6g; Sugar 8.4g; Protein 5.5g

Maple Chicken and Waffles

Prep time: 10 minutes| Cook time: 30 minutes| Serves: 4

8 whole chicken wings	65g plain flour
1 teaspoon garlic powder	Cooking oil spray
Chicken seasoning, for preparing the chicken	8 frozen waffles
Freshly ground black pepper	Pure maple syrup, for serving (optional)

1. In a medium bowl, combine the chicken and garlic powder and season with chicken seasoning and pepper. Toss to coat. 2. Place the seasoned chicken to a resealable plastic bag and add the flour. Seal the bag and shake it to coat the chicken thoroughly. 3. Insert the crisper plate into the air fryer basket and then put the basket into the unit. 4. To preheat, set your air fryer on Air Fry mode and set the temperature to 205°C and time to 3 minutes. 5. Once the unit is preheated, spray the cooking oil over the crisper plate. Transfer the marinated chicken from the bag to the basket with tongs. It is okay to stack the chicken wings on top of each other. Spray them with cooking oil. 6. Set the air fryer on Air Fry mode at 205°C, and set the time to 20 minutes. 7. Remove the basket and shake the wings halfway after cooking for 5 minutes. Return the basket to resume cooking. Shake the basket every 5 minutes until the chicken is fully cooked. 8. When the cooking is complete, remove the cooked chicken from the basket; cover to keep warm. 9. Rinse the basket and crisper plate with warm water. Insert them back into the unit. 10. Set the air fryer on Air Fry mode, adjust the temperature setting to 180°C, and set the time to 3 minutes. Once the unit is preheated, spray the cooking oil over the crisper plate. Working in batches, place the frozen waffles into the basket. Do not stack them. Spray the waffles with cooking oil. 11. Set the air fryer on Air Fry mode, adjust the temperature setting to 180°C, and set the time to 6 minutes. When the cooking is complete, repeat the cooking steps with the remaining waffles. 12. Serve the waffles with the chicken and a touch of maple syrup, if desired.
Per Serving: Calories 338; Fat 9g; Sodium 638mg; Carbs 43.7g; Fibre 2.3g; Sugar 3.7g; Protein 19g

Savoury Puffed Egg Tarts

Prep time: 10 minutes| Cook time: 17 to 20 minutes| Serves: 2

⅓ sheet frozen puff pastry, thawed	2 eggs
Cooking oil spray	¼ teaspoon salt, divided
50g shredded Cheddar cheese	1 teaspoon minced fresh parsley (optional)

1. Insert the crisper plate into the basket of your air fryer. 2. To preheat, set your air fryer on Bake mode and set the temperature to 200°C and time to 3 minutes. 3. Lay the puff pastry sheet on a piece of parchment paper and cut it in half. 4. Once the unit is preheated, spray the crisper plate with cooking oil. Transfer the 2 squares of pastry to the basket, keeping them on the parchment paper. 5. Select BAKE, set the temperature to 200°C, and set the time to 20 minutes. 6. After 10 minutes, use a metal spoon to press down the centre of each pastry square to make a well. Divide the cheese equally between the baked pastries. On top of the cheese, carefully crack an egg, and sprinkle each with the salt. Resume cooking for 7 to 10 minutes. 7. When the cooking is complete, the eggs will be cooked through. Sprinkle each with parsley (if using) and serve.
Per Serving: Calories 404; Fat 29.4g; Sodium 638mg; Carbs 19g; Fibre 0.6g; Sugar 0.6g; Protein 15g

Hearty Steak and Eggs

Prep time: 8 minutes| Cook time: 14 minutes| Serves: 4

Cooking oil spray	1 teaspoon freshly ground black pepper, divided
4 (100g) New York strip steaks	
1 teaspoon granulated garlic, divided	4 eggs
1 teaspoon salt, divided	½ teaspoon paprika

1. Insert the crisper plate into the basket of your air fryer. 2. To preheat, set your air fryer on Air Fry mode and adjust the temperature to 180°C and time to 3 minutes. 3. Once the unit is preheated, spray the crisper plate with cooking oil. Place 2 steaks into the basket; do not oil or season them at this time. 4. Select AIR FRY, set the temperature to 180°C, and set the time to 9 minutes. After 5 minutes, open the unit and flip the steaks. Sprinkle each with ¼ teaspoon of granulated garlic, ¼ teaspoon of salt, and ¼ teaspoon of pepper.

Resume cooking until the steaks register at least 60°C on a food thermometer. 5. When the cooking is complete, transfer the steaks to a plate and tent with aluminum foil to keep warm. Repeat the cooking steps with the remaining steaks. 6. Spray 4 ramekins with olive oil. Crack 1 egg into each ramekin. Sprinkle the eggs with the paprika and remaining ½ teaspoon each of salt and pepper. Working in batches, place 2 ramekins into the basket. 7. Select BAKE, set the temperature to 165°C, and set the time to 5 minutes. 8. When the cooking is complete and the eggs are cooked to 70°C, remove the ramekins and repeat with the remaining 2 ramekins. Serve the eggs with the steaks.
Per Serving: Calories 317; Fat 10g; Sodium 762mg; Carbs 1g; Fibre 0.3g; Sugar 0.2g; Protein 55g

Maple Sage Links

Prep time: 10 minutes | Cook time: 9 minutes | Serves: 8

300g mild pork sausage meat, loosen or removed from casings	¼ teaspoon salt
1 teaspoon rubbed sage	¼ teaspoon freshly ground black pepper
2 tablespoons pure maple syrup	1 tablespoon water
⅛ teaspoon cayenne pepper	

1. Before cooking, heat your air fryer to 205°C, for about 3 minutes. 2. Combine pork, sage, maple syrup, cayenne pepper, salt, and black pepper. Form into eight links. 3. Pour water into bottom of air fryer. Place links in air fryer basket. Cook for 9 minutes. 4. Transfer to a plate and serve warm.
Per Serving: Calories 265; Fat 26g; Sodium 339mg; Carbs 3.5g; Fibre 0.1g; Sugar 3g; Protein 3.3g

Bacon, Egg, and Cheddar Cheese Roll Ups

Prep Time: 15 minutes | Cook Time: 15 minutes | Serves: 4

2 tablespoons unsalted butter	12 slices bacon
40g chopped onion	100g shredded sharp Cheddar cheese
½ medium green pepper, seeded and chopped	
6 large eggs	145g mild salsa, for dipping

1. Melt butter in a medium frying pan over medium heat. Then add the chopped onion and pepper to the frying pan and sauté until fragrant and onions are translucent, about 3 minutes. 2. Whisk the eggs in a small bowl and pour the mixture into frying pan. Scramble the eggs with onions and peppers until fluffy and fully cooked, about 5 minutes. Remove from heat and set aside. 3. Place three slices of bacon side by side on work surface, overlapping about ½cm. Place 35g scrambled eggs in a heap on the side closest to you and sprinkle 25g cup cheese on top of the eggs. 4. Tightly roll the bacon around the eggs and secure them with a toothpick as needed. Evenly put each roll into the air fryer basket. 5. Adjust the temperature to 175°C and set the timer for 15 minutes. Rotate the rolls halfway through the cooking time. 6. Bacon will be brown and crispy when completely cooked. Serve immediately with salsa for dipping.
Per Serving: Calories 165; Fat 13.6g; Sodium 264mg; Carbs 5.07g; Fibre 0.3g; Sugar 1.06g; Protein 5.34g

Scrambled Eggs with Cheese

Prep time: 5 minutes | Cook time: 7 minutes | Serves: 2

4 large eggs	1 tablespoon goat cheese crumbles
¼ teaspoon salt	
⅛ teaspoon freshly ground black pepper	1 tablespoon chopped fresh parsley, divided
2 teaspoons sour cream	

1. Before cooking, heat your air fryer to 205°C, for about 3 minutes. 2. In a small bowl, whisk together eggs, salt, and pepper. 3. Add egg mixture to a cake tin lightly greased with olive oil. Add barrel to air fryer basket and cook for 5 minutes. 4. Remove cake tin from air fryer and use a silicone spatula to stir eggs. Add sour cream, goat cheese, and half of parsley. Place barrel back in the air fryer and cook an additional 2 minutes. 5. Transfer eggs to a medium serving dish and garnish with remaining parsley. Serve warm.
Per Serving: Calories 370; Fat 29.8g; Sodium 614mg; Carbs 2.3g; Fibre 0.1g; Sugar 1g; Protein 22g

Cinnamon Toast Sticks

Prep time: 5 minutes | Cook time: 15 minutes | Serves: 12

4 thick bread,each cut into 3 sticks
1 tablespoon butter
1 egg
1 teaspoon stevia

1 teaspoon ground cinnamon
60ml milk
1 teaspoon vanilla extract
Cooking oil

1. In a suitable microwave-safe bowl, add the butter. Then microwave it for 15 seconds, or until the butter has melted. 2. Remove the bowl from the microwave. Add the egg, stevia, cinnamon, milk, and vanilla extract. Whisk until fully combined. 3. Spray the air fryer basket with cooking oil. 4. Dredge each of the bread sticks in the egg mixture. Add the French toast sticks in the air fryer. It is okay to stack them. Spray the French toast sticks with cooking oil. Cook at 190°C for 8 minutes. 5. Open the air fryer and flip each of the French toast sticks. Cook until the French toast sticks are crisp, for an additional 4 minutes. Cool before serving.
Per Serving: Calories 44; Fat 2g; Sodium 64mg; Carbs 5.5g; Fibre 0.5g; Sugar 0.9g; Protein 1.7g

Scotch Eggs with Breadcrumbs

Prep time: 10 minutes | Cook time: 15 minutes | Serves: 6

455g pork breakfast sausage meat
6 large hard-boiled eggs, peeled
125g all-purpose flour

2 large eggs, beaten
200g plain bread crumbs

1. Preheat the air fryer to 190°C. 2. Separate sausage into six equal amounts and flatten into patties. 3. Form sausage patties around hard-boiled eggs, completely enclosing them. 4. In three separate small bowls, place flour, eggs, and bread crumbs. 5. Roll each sausage-covered egg first in flour, then egg, and finally bread crumbs. Place rolled eggs in the air fryer basket and spritz them with cooking spray. 6. Cook at 190°C for 15 minutes, turning halfway through cooking time and spraying any dry spots with additional cooking spray. Serve warm.
Per Serving: Calories 555; Fat 35g; Sodium 1730mg; Carbs 23g; Fibre 1g; Sugar 1.3g; Protein 33.5g

An Egg in a Hole

Prep time: 5 minutes | Cook time: 40 minutes | Serves: 4

4 slices white sandwich bread
4 large eggs

½ teaspoon salt
¼ teaspoon ground black pepper

1. Preheat the air fryer to 175°C. Spritz cooking spray over a 15cm round cake pan. 2. Place pieces of bread in one layer in the prepared pan until just fit, working in batches as necessary. 3. Cut out a circle with a small cup or cookie cutter in the centre of each bread slice. Crack an egg directly into each cutout and sprinkle eggs with salt and pepper. 4. Cook for 5 minutes, then carefully turn and cook for an additional 5 minutes or less, depending on your preference. Serve warm.
Per Serving: Calories 126; Fat 5.4g; Sodium 460mg; Carbs 10.5g; Fibre 0.6g; Sugar 1.5g; Protein 8g

Simple Morning Quiche

Prep time: 10 minutes | Cook time: 18 minutes | Serves: 4

1 (23cm) refrigerated piecrust
2 large eggs
60g heavy cream
½ teaspoon salt

¼ teaspoon ground black pepper
50g shredded Cheddar cheese
2 slices bacon, cooked and crumbled

1. Preheat the air fryer to 160°C. Spray a 15cm pie pan with cooking spray. Trim piecrust to fit the pan. 2. In a medium bowl, whisk together eggs, heavy cream, salt, and pepper. Stir in Cheddar and bacon. 3. Pour egg mixture into crust and cook for 18 minutes until firm, brown, and a knife inserted into the centre comes out clean. Serve warm.
Per Serving: Calories 428; Fat 29.6g; Sodium 715mg; Carbs 30.2g; Fibre 1.1g; Sugar 0.6g; Protein 10g

Egg and Cream Cheese

Prep time: 5 minutes | Cook time: 10 minutes | Serves: 4

1 sheet frozen puff pastry dough, thawed

1 large egg, beaten
100g full-fat cream cheese, softened
30g icing sugar

1 teaspoon vanilla extract
½ teaspoon lemon juice

1. Preheat the air fryer to 160°C. 2. Unfold puff pastry and cut into four equal squares. For each pastry, fold all four corners partway to the centre, leaving a 2.5cm square in the centre. 3. Brush egg evenly over folded puff pastry. 4. In a medium bowl, mix icing sugar, cream cheese, vanilla, and lemon juice. Scoop 2 tablespoons of mixture into the centre of each pastry square. 5. Place danishes directly in the air fryer basket and cook for 10 minutes until puffy and golden brown. Cool for 5 minutes before serving.
Per Serving: Calories 167; Fat 10g; Sodium 149mg; Carbs 14g; Fibre 0.2g; Sugar 8g; Protein 4.7g

Almond Chocolate-Hazelnut Bear Claws

Prep time: 5 minutes | Cook time: 10 minutes | Serves: 4

1 sheet frozen puff pastry dough, thawed
1 large egg, beaten

150g chocolate-hazelnut spread
1 tablespoon icing sugar
1 tablespoon sliced almonds

1. Preheat the air fryer to 160°C. 2. Unfold puff pastry and cut into four equal squares. 3. Brush egg evenly over puff pastry. 4. To make each bear claw, spread 2 tablespoons chocolate-hazelnut spread over a pastry square. Fold square horizontally to form a triangle and cut four evenly spaced slits about halfway through the top of folded square. Repeat with remaining spread and pastry squares. 5. Sprinkle icing sugar and almonds over bear claws and place directly in the air fryer basket. Cook for 10 minutes until puffy and golden brown. Serve warm.
Per Serving: Calories 119; Fat 7.5g; Sodium 49mg; Carbs 10g; Fibre 0.6g; Sugar 4g; Protein 3g

Quick Bacon Strips

Prep Time: 5 minutes | Cook Time: 12 minutes | Serves: 4

8 slices bacon

1. Place bacon strips into the air fryer basket. 2. Adjust the temperature to 205°C and set the timer for 12 minutes. 3. After 6 minutes, flip bacon and continue cooking time. 4. Serve warm.
Per Serving: Calories 88; Fat 6.2g; Sodium 355mg; Carbs 0.2g; Fibre 0g; Sugar 0g; Protein 5.8g

Vegetable Bacon Hash

Prep time: 10 minutes | Cook time: 12 minutes | Serves: 4

25 small Brussels sprouts, halved
2 mini sweet peppers, seeded and diced
1 small yellow onion, peeled and diced

3 slices bacon, diced
2 tablespoons fresh orange juice
¼ teaspoon salt
1 teaspoon orange zest

1. Before cooking, heat your air fryer to 175°C, for about 3 minutes. 2. In a medium bowl, combine all ingredients except orange zest. 3. Add mixture to ungreased air fryer basket. Cook for 6 minutes, then toss and cook an additional 6 minutes. Serve warm.
Per Serving: Calories 154; Fat 8g; Sodium 268mg; Carbs 16.4g; Fibre 5.3g; Sugar 4g; Protein 7.2g

Cheddar Cheesy Cauliflower Hash Browns

Prep Time: 20 minutes | Cook Time: 12 minutes | Serves: 4

1 (300g) steamer bag cauliflower
1 large egg

100g shredded sharp Cheddar cheese

1. Place the bag of cauliflower in your microwave and cook according to package instructions. Allow to cool completely and put cauliflower into a cheesecloth or kitchen towel and squeeze to remove excess moisture. 2. Mash cauliflower with a fork and add egg and cheese. 3. Cut a piece of parchment to fit your air fryer basket. Take ¼ of the mixture and form it into a hash brown patty shape. Place it onto the parchment and into the air fryer basket, working in batches if necessary. 4. Adjust the temperature setting to 205°C and set the timer for 12 minutes. 5. Flip the hash browns halfway through the cooking time. When completely cooked, they will be golden brown. 6. Serve immediately.
Per Serving: Calories 154; Fat 11g; Sodium 225mg; Carbs 4.7g; Fibre 1.7g; Sugar 1.8g; Protein 10g

Breakfast Sausage Stuffed with Poblanos

Prep Time: 15 minutes | Cook Time: 15 minutes | Serves: 4

225g spicy pork breakfast sausage meat
4 large eggs
100g full-fat cream cheese, softened
55g canned diced tomatoes and

green chiles, drained
4 large poblano peppers
8 tablespoons shredded pepper jack cheese
115g full-fat sour cream

1. Crumble and brown the sausage meat in a medium frying pan over medium heat until no pink remains. Remove the pork sausage and then drain the fat from the pan. Crack the large eggs into the pan, scramble, and cook until no longer runny. 2. Place cooked sausage in a large bowl and fold in cream cheese. Mix in diced tomatoes and chiles. Gently fold in eggs. 3. Cut a 10cm - 13cm slit in the top of each poblano and remove the seeds and white membrane with a small knife. Separate the filling into four servings and then spoon carefully into each pepper. Top each pepper with 2 tablespoons of pepper jack cheese. 4. Place each pepper into the air fryer basket. 5. Adjust the temperature to 175°C and set the timer for 15 minutes. 6. Peppers will be soft and cheese will be browned when ready. 7. Serve immediately with sour cream on top.
Per Serving: Calories 1282; Fat 100.28g; Sodium 2706mg; Carbs 16.49g; Fibre 0.8g; Sugar 5.75g; Protein 77.77g

Scrambled Eggs with Cheddar Cheese

Prep Time: 5 minutes | Cook Time: 15 minutes | Serves: 2

4 large eggs
2 tablespoons unsalted butter, melted

50g shredded sharp Cheddar cheese

1. Crack eggs into 10cm round baking dish and whisk. Place dish into the air fryer basket. 2. Adjust the temperature to 205°C and set the timer for 10 minutes. 3. After 5 minutes, stir the eggs and add the butter and cheese. Let cook for 3 more minutes and stir again. 4. Allow eggs to finish cooking for an additional 2 minutes or remove if they are to your desired liking. 5. Use a fork to fluff. Serve warm.
Per Serving: Calories 179; Fat 16.74g; Sodium 21mg; Carbs 1.22g; Fibre 0g; Sugar 0.19g; Protein 5.85g

Breakfast Bake with Loaded Cauliflower

Prep Time: 15 minutes | Cook Time: 20 minutes | Serves: 4

6 large eggs
60g heavy whipping cream
160g chopped cauliflower
100g shredded medium Cheddar cheese
1 medium avocado, peeled and

pitted
8 tablespoons full-fat sour cream
2 spring onions, sliced on the bias
12 slices bacon, cooked and crumbled

1. Whisk eggs and cream together in a medium bowl. Pour into a 15-cm round baking dish. 2. Add cauliflower and mix, then top with Cheddar. Place dish into the air fryer basket. 3. Adjust the temperature to 160°C and set the timer for 20 minutes. 4. When completely cooked, eggs will be firm and cheese will be browned. Slice into four pieces. 5. Slice avocado and divide evenly among pieces. Top each piece with 2 tablespoons sour cream, sliced spring onions, and crumbled bacon.
Per Serving: Calories 349; Fat 27.54g; Sodium 597mg; Carbs 11.48g; Fibre 4.2g; Sugar 1.54g; Protein 15.4g

Vanilla and Cinnamon Roll sticks

Prep Time: 10 minutes | Cook Time: 7 minutes | Serves: 4

110g shredded mozzarella cheese
25g full-fat cream cheese
30g blanched finely ground almond flour
½ teaspoon baking soda
10g granular sweetener, divided
1 teaspoon vanilla extract
1 large egg

2 tablespoons unsalted butter, melted
½ teaspoon ground cinnamon
3 tablespoons powdered sweetener
2 teaspoons unsweetened vanilla almond milk

1. Place mozzarella in a large microwave-safe bowl and break cream cheese into small pieces and place into bowl. Microwave for 45 seconds. 2. Stir in almond flour, baking soda, 5g granular sweetener,

and vanilla. A soft dough should form. Microwave the mix for additional 15 seconds if it becomes too stiff. 3. Mix egg into the dough, using your hands if necessary. 4. Cut a piece of parchment to fit your air fryer basket. Press the dough into an 20cm × 13cm rectangle on the parchment and cut into eight (2.5cm) sticks. 5. Mix butter, cinnamon, and remaining granular sweetener in a small bowl. Brush half the butter mixture over the top of the sticks and place them into the air fryer basket. 6. Adjust the temperature to 205°C and set the timer for 7 minutes. 7. Halfway through the cooking time, flip the sticks and brush with remaining butter mixture. When done, sticks should be crispy. 8. To make glaze, whisk powdered sweetener and almond milk in a small bowl. Drizzle over cinnamon sticks. Serve warm.
Per Serving (2 sticks): Calories 97; Fat 4.04g; Sodium 296mg; Carbs 33.42g; Fibre 4.1g; Sugar 1.98g; Protein 8.57g

Crumbled Sausage and Scrambled Egg

Prep Time: 15 minutes | Cook Time: 15 minutes | Serves: 4

170g shredded mozzarella cheese
50g blanched finely ground almond flour
25g full-fat cream cheese
1 large whole egg

4 large eggs, scrambled
225g cooked breakfast sausage, crumbled
8 tablespoons shredded mild Cheddar cheese

1. Add mozzarella, almond flour, and cream cheese in a large microwave-safe bowl. Microwave for 1 minute. Stir until the mixture is smooth and forms a ball. Add the large egg and stir until dough forms. 2. Place dough between two sheets of parchment and roll out to ½cm thickness. Cut the dough into four rectangles. 3. Mix scrambled eggs and cooked sausage together in a large bowl. Divide the mixture evenly among each piece of dough, placing it on the lower half of the rectangle. Sprinkle each with 2 tablespoons Cheddar. 4. Fold over the rectangle to cover the egg and meat mixture. Pinch, roll, or use a wet fork to close the edges completely. 5. Cut a piece of parchment to fit your air fryer basket and place the calzones onto the parchment. Place parchment into the air fryer basket. 6. Adjust the temperature to 195°C and set the timer for 15 minutes. 7. Flip the calzones halfway through the cooking time. When done, calzones should be golden in colour. Serve immediately.
Per Serving: Calories 387; Fat 26.56g; Sodium 732mg; Carbs 7.03g; Fibre 2.6g; Sugar 2.02g; Protein 30.88g

Black Pepper and Cauliflower Avocado Toast

Prep Time: 15 minutes | Cook Time: 8 minutes | Serves: 2

1 (300g) steamer bag cauliflower
55g shredded mozzarella cheese
1 ripe medium avocado

1 large egg
¼ teaspoon ground black pepper
½ teaspoon garlic powder

1. Cook cauliflower as the package instructed. Remove the cauliflower from the bag and place them into a cheesecloth or clean towel to remove any excess moisture. 2. Place the cauliflower into a large bowl and then mix together with egg and mozzarella. Cut a piece of parchment paper to fit your air fryer basket. Separate the cauliflower mixture into two servings, and place it on the parchment in two mounds. Press out the cauliflower mounds into a ½cm-thick rectangle. Place the parchment into your air fryer basket. 3. Adjust the temperature to 205°C and set the timer for 8 minutes. 4. Flip the cauliflower halfway through the cooking time. 5. When the timer beeps, remove the parchment and allow the cauliflower to cool for 5 minutes. 6. Cut the avocado open and then remove the pit. Scoop out the inside, place it in a medium bowl, and mash it with garlic powder and pepper. Spread onto the cauliflower. Serve immediately.
Per Serving: Calories 233; Fat 17.01g; Sodium 222mg; Carbs 10.98g; Fibre 7.4g; Sugar 1.44g; Protein 12.56g

Simple Air Fryer "Hard-Boiled" Eggs

Prep Time: 2 minutes | Cook Time: 18 minutes | Serves: 4

4 large eggs
240ml water

1. Place eggs into a 15 x 5cm round baking-safe dish and pour water over eggs. Place dish into the air fryer basket. 2. Adjust the temperature to 150°C and set the timer for 18 minutes. 3. Store cooked eggs in the refrigerator until ready to use or peel and eat warm.
Per Serving: Calories 55; Fat 4.51g; Sodium 9mg; Carbs 0.61g; Fibre 0g; Sugar 0.1g; Protein 2.7g

Breakfast Sausage and Cheese Balls

Prep Time: 10 minutes | Cook Time: 12 minutes | Serves: 4

455g pork breakfast sausage
55g shredded Cheddar cheese
25g full-fat cream cheese,
softened
1 large egg

1. Mix the pork breakfast sausage, shredded cheddar cheese, cream cheese, and 1 egg in a large bowl. Form the mixture into sixteen (2.5cm) balls. Place the balls evenly into your air fryer basket. 2. Adjust the temperature setting to 205°C and set the timer for 12 minutes. 3. Shake the basket two or three times during cooking. Sausage balls will be browned on the outside and have an internal temperature of at least 60°C when completely cooked. 4. Serve warm.
Per Serving: Calories 548; Fat 43.83g; Sodium 2408mg; Carbs 1.92g; Fibre 0g; Sugar 0.44g; Protein 34.06g

Cheddar Cheesy Pepper Eggs

Prep Time: 10 minutes | Cook Time: 15 minutes | Serves: 4

4 medium green peppers
75g cooked ham, chopped
¼ medium onion, peeled and
chopped
8 large eggs
115g mild Cheddar cheese

1. Cut the tops off each pepper. Remove the seeds and the white membranes with a small knife. Place ham and onion into each pepper. 2. Crack 2 eggs into each pepper. Top with 30g cheese per pepper. Place into the air fryer basket. 3. Adjust the temperature to 200°C and set the timer for 15 minutes. 4. When fully cooked, peppers will be tender and eggs will be firm. Serve immediately.
Per Serving: Calories 152; Fat 9.84g; Sodium 292mg; Carbs 6.33g; Fibre 0.8g; Sugar 2.78g; Protein 9.96g

Poached Eggs with Whole Grain Avocado

Prep Time: 5 minutes | Cook Time: 7 minutes | Serves: 4

Olive oil cooking spray
4 large eggs
Salt
Black pepper
4 pieces whole grain bread
1 avocado
Red pepper flakes (optional)

1. Preheat the air fryer to 160°C. Lightly coat the inside of four small oven-safe ramekins with olive oil cooking spray. 2. Crack one egg into each ramekin, and season with salt and black pepper. 3. Place the ramekins into the air fryer basket. Close and set the timer to 7 minutes. 4. While the eggs are cooking, toast the bread in a toaster. 5. Slice the avocado in half lengthwise, remove the pit, and scoop the flesh into a small bowl. Season with salt, black pepper, and red pepper flakes, if desired. Using a fork, smash the avocado lightly. 6. Spread a quarter of the smashed avocado evenly over each slice of toast. 7. Remove the eggs from the air fryer, and gently spoon one onto each slice of avocado toast before serving.
Per Serving: Calories 140; Fat 11.99g; Sodium 13mg; Carbs 5.9g; Fibre 3.5g; Sugar 1.02g; Protein 3.91g

Baked Egg and Mushroom Cups with Baby Spinach

Prep Time: 5 minutes | Cook Time: 15 minutes | Serves: 6

Olive oil cooking spray
6 large eggs
1 garlic clove, minced
½ teaspoon salt
½ teaspoon black pepper
Pinch red pepper flakes
200g mushrooms, sliced
30g fresh baby spinach
2 spring onions, white parts and green parts, diced

1. Preheat the air fryer to 160°C. Lightly coat the inside of six silicone muffin cups or a six-cup muffin tin with olive oil cooking spray. 2. Beat the eggs, garlic, salt, pepper, and red pepper flakes in a large bowl for 1 to 2 minutes, or until well combined. 3. Fold in the mushrooms, spinach, and spring onions. 4. Divide the mixture evenly among the muffin cups. 5. Place into the air fryer and bake for 12 to 15 minutes, or until the eggs are set. 6. Remove and allow to cool for 5 minutes before serving.
Per Serving: Calories 173; Fat 4.97g; Sodium 212mg; Carbs 30.33g; Fibre 4.6g; Sugar 1.34g; Protein 6.67g

Spinach and Swiss Frittata with Black Pepper Mushrooms

Prep Time: 10 minutes | Cook Time: 20 minutes | Serves: 4

Olive oil cooking spray
8 large eggs
½ teaspoon salt
½ teaspoon black pepper
1 garlic clove, minced
60g fresh baby spinach
100g mushrooms, sliced
1 shallot, diced
110g shredded Swiss cheese, divided
Hot sauce, for serving (optional)

1. To prepare, heat your air fryer to 180°C in advance. Lightly spritz the inside of a 15cm round cake pan with olive oil cooking spray. 2. Beat the eggs, salt, pepper, and garlic in a large bowl for 1 to 2 minutes, or until well combined. 3. Fold in the spinach, mushrooms, shallot, and 55g of the Swiss cheese. 4. Pour the seasoned egg mixture into the prepared cake pan, and sprinkle the remaining 55g of Swiss over the top. 5. Place into the air fryer and bake for 18 to 20 minutes, or until the eggs are set in the centre. 6. Remove from the air fryer and allow to cool for 5 minutes. Drizzle with hot sauce (if using) before serving.
Per Serving: Calories 262; Fat 14.02g; Sodium 334mg; Carbs 24.52g; Fibre 3.7g; Sugar 1.11g; Protein 13.07g

Mushroom-and-Tomato Stuffed Hash

Prep Time: 10 minutes | Cook Time: 20 minutes | Serves: 4

Olive oil cooking spray
1 tablespoon plus 2 teaspoons olive oil, divided
100g mushrooms, diced
1 spring onions, white parts and green parts, diced
1 garlic clove, minced
300g shredded potatoes
½ teaspoon salt
¼ teaspoon black pepper
1 Roma tomato, diced
55g shredded mozzarella

1. To prepare, heat your air fryer to 195°C. Lightly spritz the inside of a 15-cm cake pan with olive oil cooking spray. 2. Heat 2 teaspoons olive oil over medium heat in a small frying pan. Add the mushrooms, spring onion, and garlic, and cook for 4 to 5 minutes, or until they have softened and are beginning to show some colour. Remove from heat. 3. Meanwhile, combine the potatoes, salt, pepper, and the remaining tablespoon olive oil in a large bowl. Toss until all potatoes are well coated. 4. Pour half of the potatoes into the bottom of the cake pan. Top with the mushroom mixture, tomato, and mozzarella. Spread the remaining potatoes over the top. 5. Bake in the air fryer for 12 to 15 minutes, or until the top is golden brown. 6. Remove from the air fryer and allow to cool for 5 minutes before slicing and serving.
Per Serving: Calories 179; Fat 1.6g; Sodium 406mg; Carbs 36.54g; Fibre 5.6g; Sugar 2.24g; Protein 9.05g

Simple Whole Wheat Banana-Walnut Bread

Prep Time: 10 minutes | Cook Time: 23 minutes | Serves: 6

Olive oil cooking spray
2 ripe medium bananas
1 large egg
60g nonfat plain Greek yogurt
60ml olive oil
½ teaspoon vanilla extract
2 tablespoons raw honey
120g whole wheat flour
¼ teaspoon salt
¼ teaspoon baking soda
½ teaspoon ground cinnamon
30g chopped walnuts

1. To prepare, heat your air fryer to 180°C. Lightly coat the inside of an 20-by-10-cm loaf tin with olive oil cooking spray. (Or use two smaller loaf tins) 2. Mash the bananas with a fork in a large bowl. Add the egg, yogurt, olive oil, vanilla, and honey. Mix until well combined and mostly smooth. 3. Sift the whole wheat flour, salt, baking soda, and cinnamon into the wet mixture, then stir until just combined. Do not overmix. 4. Gently fold in the walnuts. 5. Pour into the prepared loaf tin and spread to distribute evenly. 6. Place the loaf tin in the air fryer basket and bake for 20 to 23 minutes, or until golden brown on top and a toothpick inserted into the centre comes out clean. 7. Allow the bread to cool for 5 minutes before serving.
Per Serving: Calories 237; Fat 12.6g; Sodium 296mg; Carbs 29.93g; Fibre 3.5g; Sugar 10.79g; Protein 4.06g

Low-Calorie Honey-Apricot Granola with Greek Yogurt

Prep Time: 10 minutes | Cook Time: 30 minutes | Serves: 6

85g rolled oats
65g dried apricots, diced
30g almond slivers
30g walnuts, chopped
30g pumpkin seeds
40g hemp hearts
85g to 110g raw honey, plus more for drizzling
1 tablespoon olive oil
1 teaspoon ground cinnamon
¼ teaspoon ground nutmeg
¼ teaspoon salt
2 tablespoons sugar-free dark chocolate chips (optional)
735g nonfat plain Greek yogurt

1. To prepare, heat your air fryer to 125°C. Line parchment paper over the air fryer basket. 2. Combine the oats, apricots, almonds, walnuts, pumpkin seeds, hemp hearts, honey, olive oil, cinnamon, nutmeg, and salt in a large bowl, mixing so that the honey, oil, and spices are well distributed. 3. Pour the mixture onto the parchment paper and spread it into an even layer. 4. Bake for 10 minutes, then shake or stir and spread back out into an even layer. Continue baking for 10 minutes more, then repeat the process of shaking or stirring the mixture. Bake for an additional 10 minutes before removing from the air fryer. 5. Allow the granola to cool completely before stirring in the chocolate chips (if using) and pouring into an airtight container for storage. 6. For each serving, top 120g Greek yogurt with 60g granola and a drizzle of honey, if needed.
Per Serving: Calories 171; Fat 8.19g; Sodium 157mg; Carbs 28.11g; Fibre 4g; Sugar 14.91g; Protein 5.27g

Low-Calorie Blueberry Muffins

Prep Time: 10 minutes | Cook Time: 15 minutes | Serves: 6

Olive oil cooking spray
120g unsweetened applesauce
85g raw honey
120g nonfat plain Greek yogurt
1 teaspoon vanilla extract
1 large egg
190g plus 1 tablespoon whole wheat flour, divided
½ teaspoon baking soda
½ teaspoon baking powder
½ teaspoon salt
75g blueberries, fresh or frozen

1. To prepare, heat your air fryer to 180°C. Lightly coat the inside of six silicone muffin cups or a six-cup muffin tin with olive oil cooking spray. 2. Combine the applesauce, honey, yogurt, vanilla, and egg in a large bowl, and mix until smooth. 3. Sift in the flour, the baking soda, baking powder, and salt into the wet mixture, then stir until just combined. 4. Toss the blueberries with the remaining 1 tablespoon flour in a small bowl, then fold the mixture into the muffin batter. 5. Divide the mixture evenly among the prepared muffin cups and place into the basket of the air fryer. Bake for 12 to 15 minutes, or until golden brown on top and a toothpick inserted into the middle of one of the muffins comes out clean. 6. Then allow the muffins to cool for 5 minutes before serving.
Per Serving: Calories 184; Fat 1.63g; Sodium 303mg; Carbs 40.63g; Fibre 3.8g; Sugar 18.11g; Protein 4.63g

Whole-Wheat Blueberry Breakfast Cobbler

Prep Time: 5 minutes | Cook Time: 15 minutes | Serves: 4

40g whole-wheat pastry flour
¾ teaspoon baking powder
Dash sea salt
120ml low fat milk
2 tablespoons pure maple syrup
½ teaspoon vanilla extract
Cooking oil spray
75g fresh blueberries
30g plain store-bought granola

1. Whisk the flour, baking powder, and salt in a medium bowl. Add the maple syrup, milk, and vanilla extract, and gently whisk, just until thoroughly combined. 2. Preheat the unit by selecting BAKE, setting the temperature to 175°C, and setting the time to 3 minutes. Select START/STOP to begin. 3. Spray a 15-by-5-cm round baking pan with cooking oil and pour the batter into the pan. Top evenly with the blueberries and granola. 4. Once the unit is preheated, place the pan into the basket. 5. Select BAKE, set the temperature to 175°C, and set the time to 15 minutes. Select START/STOP to begin. 6. When the cooking is complete, the cobbler should be nicely browned and a knife inserted into the middle should come out clean. Enjoy plain or topped with a little vanilla yogurt.
Per Serving: Calories 109; Fat 1.36g; Sodium 55mg; Carbs 22.86g; Fibre 1.6g; Sugar 14.24g; Protein 2.48g

Simple Granola

Prep Time: 5 minutes | Cook Time: 40 minutes | Serves: 4

85g rolled oats
3 tablespoons pure maple syrup
1 tablespoon sugar
1 tablespoon neutral-flavoured oil, such as refined coconut,
sunflower, or safflower
¼ teaspoon sea salt
¼ teaspoon ground cinnamon
¼ teaspoon vanilla extract

1. Insert the crisper plate into the basket and the basket into the unit. To preheat the unit, select BAKE, setting the temperature to 120°C, and setting the time to 3 minutes. Select START/STOP to begin. 2. Stir together the oats, maple syrup, sugar, oil, salt, cinnamon, and vanilla in a medium bowl until thoroughly combined. Transfer the granola to a 15-by-5-cm round baking pan. 3. Once the unit is preheated, place the pan into the basket. 4. Select BAKE, set the temperature to 120°C and set the time to 40 minutes. Select START/STOP to begin. 5. After 10 minutes, stir the granola well. Resume cooking, stirring the granola every 10 minutes, for a total of 40 minutes, or until the granola is lightly browned and mostly dry. 6. When the cooking is complete, place the granola on a plate to cool. Store the completely cooled granola in an airtight container in a cool, dry place for 1 to 2 weeks.
Per Serving: Calories 230; Fat 6.1g; Sodium 148mg; Carbs 38g; Fibre 4.2g; Sugar 11g; Protein 6.6g

Fresh Mixed Berry Muffins

Prep Time: 15 minutes | Cook Time: 12 to 17 minutes | Serves: 8

165g plus 1 tablespoon plain flour, divided
50g granulated sugar
2 tablespoons light brown sugar
2 teaspoons baking powder
2 eggs
180ml whole milk
80ml safflower oil
145g mixed fresh berries

1. Stir together 165g of flour, the granulated sugar, brown sugar, and baking powder in a medium bowl until mixed well. 2. Whisk the eggs, milk, and oil in a small bowl until combined. Stir the egg mixture together with the dry ingredients just until combined. 3. Toss the mixed berries with the remaining 1 tablespoon of flour in another small bowl until coated. Gently stir the berries into the batter. 4. Double up 16 foil muffin cups to make 8 cups. 5. Insert the crisper plate into the basket and the basket into the unit. Preheat the unit by selecting BAKE, setting the temperature to 155°C, and setting the time to 3 minutes. Select START/STOP to begin. 6. Once the unit is preheated, place 4 cups into the basket and fill each three-quarters full with the batter. 7. Select BAKE, set the temperature to 155°C, and set the time for 17 minutes. Select START/STOP to begin. 8. After about 12 minutes, check the muffins. If they spring back when lightly touched with your finger, they are done. If not, resume cooking. 9. When the cooking is done, transfer the muffins to a wire rack to cool. 10. Repeat the steps with the remaining muffin cups and batter. 11. Let the muffins cool for 10 minutes before serving.
Per Serving: Calories 280; Fat 13.8g; Sodium 90mg; Carbs 33.54g; Fibre 1g; Sugar 12.32g; Protein 5.75g

Low-Calorie Baked Peach Oatmeal

Prep Time: 5 minutes | Cook Time: 30 minutes | Serves: 6

Olive oil cooking spray
165g certified gluten-free rolled oats
480ml unsweetened almond milk
85g raw honey, plus more for drizzling (optional)
120g nonfat plain Greek yogurt
1 teaspoon vanilla extract
½ teaspoon ground cinnamon
¼ teaspoon salt
230g diced peaches, divided, plus more for serving (optional)

1. To prepare, heat your air fryer to 195°C. Lightly spritz the inside of a 15cm cake pan with olive oil cooking spray. 2. Mix together the oats, almond milk, honey, yogurt, vanilla, cinnamon, and salt in a large bowl until well combined. 3. Fold in 115g of the peaches and then pour the mixture into the prepared cake pan. 4. Sprinkle the remaining peaches across the top of the oatmeal mixture. Bake in the air fryer for 30 minutes. 5. Allow to set and cool for 5 minutes before serving with additional fresh fruit and honey for drizzling, if desired.
Per Serving: Calories 221; Fat 4.97g; Sodium 138mg; Carbs 49.62g; Fibre 5.8g; Sugar 28.47g; Protein 8.33g

Simple Strawberry Breakfast Tarts

Prep Time: 15 minutes | Cook Time: 10 minutes | Serves: 6

2 refrigerated piecrusts
160g strawberry preserves
1 teaspoon cornflour
Cooking oil spray
120g low-fat vanilla yogurt

25g cream cheese, at room
temperature
3 tablespoons icing sugar
Rainbow sprinkles, for decorating

1. Place the piecrusts on a flat surface. Cut each piecrust into 3 rectangles with a knife or a pizza cutter, for 6 total. Discard any unused dough from the piecrust edges. 2. Stir together the preserves and cornflour in a small bowl. Mix well, ensuring there are no lumps of cornflour remaining. 3. Scoop 1 tablespoon of the strawberry mixture onto the top half of each piece of piecrust. 4. Fold the bottom of each piece up to enclose the filling. Using the back of a fork, press along the edges of each tart to seal. 5. Insert the crisper plate into the basket and the basket into the unit. Preheat the unit by selecting BAKE, setting the temperature to 190°C, and setting the time to 3 minutes. Select START/STOP to begin. 6. Once the unit is preheated, spray the crisper plate with cooking oil. Working in batches, spray the breakfast tarts with cooking oil and place them into the basket in a single layer. Do not stack the tarts. 7. Select BAKE, set the temperature to 190°C, and set the time to 10 minutes. Select START/STOP to begin. 8. When the cooking is complete, the tarts should be light golden brown. Let the breakfast tarts cool fully before removing them from the basket. 9. Repeat the steps for the remaining breakfast tarts. 10. Stir together the yogurt, cream cheese, and icing sugar in a small bowl. Spread the breakfast tarts with the frosting and top with sprinkles.
Per Serving: Calories 48; Fat 1.71g; Sodium 35mg; Carbs 6.93g; Fibre 0.2g; Sugar 6.1g; Protein 1.49g

Bagels with Everything

Prep Time: 10 minutes | Cook Time: 10 minutes | Serves: 2

60g self-rising flour, plus more
for dusting
120g plain Greek yogurt
1 egg
1 tablespoon water

4 teaspoons everything bagel
spice mix
Cooking oil spray
1 tablespoon butter, melted

1. Using a wooden spoon, stir together the flour and yogurt in a large bowl until a tacky dough forms. Lightly spread a thin layer of flour over a clean work surface and then transfer the dough onto the surface. Roll the dough into a ball. 2. Cut the dough into 2 pieces and roll each piece into a log. Form each log into a bagel shape, pinching the ends together. 3. Whisk the egg and water in a small bowl. Brush the egg wash on the bagels. 4. Sprinkle 2 teaspoons of the spice mix on each bagel and gently press it into the dough. 5. Insert the crisper plate into the basket and the basket into the unit. Preheat the unit by selecting BAKE, setting the temperature to 165°C, and setting the time to 3 minutes. Select START/STOP to begin. 6. Once the unit is preheated, spray the crisper plate with cooking spray. Drizzle the bagels with the butter and place them into the basket. 7. Select BAKE, set the temperature to 165°C, and set the time to 10 minutes. Select START/STOP to begin. 8. When the cooking is complete, the bagels should be lightly golden on the outside. Serve warm.
Per Serving: Calories 716; Fat 13.88g; Sodium 442mg; Carbs 119.53g; Fibre 8.9g; Sugar 12.39g; Protein 27.63g

Simple Red Pepper and Feta Frittata

Prep Time: 10 minutes | Cook Time: 20 minutes | Serves: 4

Olive oil cooking spray
8 large eggs
1 medium red pepper, diced
½ teaspoon salt

½ teaspoon black pepper
1 garlic clove, minced
120g feta, divided

1. Preheat the air fryer to 180°C. Lightly coat the inside of a 15-cm round cake pan with olive oil cooking spray. 2. Beat the eggs for 1 to 2 minutes, or until well combined in a large bowl. 3. Add the pepper, salt, black pepper, and garlic to the eggs, and mix together until the pepper is distributed throughout. 4. Fold in 60g of the feta cheese. 5. Pour the egg-pepper mixture into the prepared cake pan, and sprinkle the remaining 60g of feta over the top. 6. Place the pan into the preheated air fryer and bake for 18 to 20 minutes, or until the eggs are set in the centre. 7. Remove from the air fryer and allow to cool for 5

minutes before serving.
Per Serving: Calories 171; Fat 13.18g; Sodium 480mg; Carbs 4.28g; Fibre 0.7g; Sugar 2.22g; Protein 8.44g

Whole Wheat Breakfast Pita

Prep Time: 5 minutes | Cook Time: 6 minutes | Serves: 2

1 whole wheat pita
2 teaspoons olive oil
½ shallot, diced
¼ teaspoon garlic, minced
1 large egg

¼ teaspoon dried oregano
¼ teaspoon dried thyme
⅛ teaspoon salt
2 tablespoons shredded Parmesan
cheese

1. Preheat the air fryer to 195°C. 2. Brush the top of the pita with olive oil, then spread the diced shallot and minced garlic over the pita. 3. Crack the egg into a suitable bowl or ramekin, and season it with oregano, thyme, and salt. 4. Place the pita into the air fryer basket, and gently pour the egg onto the top of the pita. Sprinkle with cheese over the top. 5. Bake for 6 minutes. 6. Allow the pita to cool for 5 minutes before cutting into pieces for serving.
Per Serving: Calories 126; Fat 8.52g; Sodium 312mg; Carbs 8.94g; Fibre 1.1g; Sugar 0.18g; Protein 4.18g

Savory Potato Hash

Prep Time: 15 minutes | Cook Time: 18 minutes | Serves: 6

2 medium sweet potatoes, peeled
and cut into 2.5cm cubes
½ green pepper, diced
½ red onion, diced
100g mushrooms, diced
tablespoons olive oil

1 garlic clove, minced
½ teaspoon salt
½ teaspoon black pepper
½ tablespoon chopped fresh
rosemary

1. To prepare, heat your air fryer to 195°C. 2. Toss the sweet potato cubes, pepper, onion, mushrooms, olive oil, garlic clove, salt, black pepper, and the chopped fresh rosemary together in a large bowl until the vegetables are well coated and seasonings distributed. 3. Pour the vegetables into the air fryer basket, making sure they are in a single even layer. (If using a smaller air fryer, you may need to do this in two batches.) 4. Cook for 9 minutes, then toss or flip the vegetables. Cook for 9 minutes more. 5. Transfer to a serving bowl or individual plates and enjoy.
Per Serving: Calories 141; Fat 4.79g; Sodium 211mg; Carbs 24.73g; Fibre 3.7g; Sugar 3.89g; Protein 2.74g

Caprese Breakfast Pizza with Mozzarella Pearls and Basil Leaves

Prep Time: 5 minutes | Cook Time: 6 minutes | Serves: 2

1 whole wheat pita
2 teaspoons olive oil
¼ garlic clove, minced
1 large egg
⅛ teaspoon salt

55g diced tomato
30g mozzarella pearls
6 fresh basil leaves
½ teaspoon balsamic vinegar

1. Preheat the air fryer to 195°C. 2. Brush the top of the pita with olive oil, then spread the minced garlic over the pita. 3. Crack the egg into a small bowl or ramekin and season it with salt. 4. Place the pita into the air fryer basket, and gently pour the egg onto the top of the pita. Top with the tomato, mozzarella pearls, and basil. 5. Bake for 6 minutes. 6. Remove the pita pizza from the air fryer and drizzle balsamic vinegar over the top. 7. Allow to cool for 5 minutes before cutting into pieces for serving.
Per Serving: Calories 198; Fat 7.46g; Sodium 225mg; Carbs 28.56g; Fibre 5.2g; Sugar 1.06g; Protein 5.44g

Chapter 2 Vegetable and Side Recipes

Waldorf Salad with Pecans

Prep time: 15 minutes | Cook time: 14 minutes | Serves: 4

2 Granny Smith apples, cored and cut into chunks
2 teaspoons olive oil, divided
225g red grapes
120g mayonnaise
2 tablespoons freshly squeezed lemon juice
1 tablespoon honey
3 celery stalks, sliced
55g coarsely chopped pecans

1. Put the chopped apples in the air fryer basket and drizzle with 1 teaspoon olive oil; toss to coat. 2. Set or preheat the air fryer for 205°C. Place the basket in the air fryer and roast for 4 minutes. Remove the basket. 3. Add the grapes to the basket and drizzle with the remaining 1 teaspoon of olive oil; toss again. Then roast for 8 to 10 minutes longer, shaking the basket halfway through cooking time, until tender. 4. Meanwhile, whisk together the mayonnaise, lemon juice, and honey in a medium bowl. 5. Add the celery and pecans to the dressing and stir to combine. 6. Place the roasted apples and grapes in the bowl and stir gently to coat the fruit with the dressing. Serve or refrigerate for 2 hours before serving.
Per Serving: Calories 309; Fat 21g; Sodium 244mg; Carbs 29.5g; Fibre 4.6g; Sugar 22g; Protein 3.8g

Air Fried Asparagus with Parmesan

Prep time: 5 minutes | Cook time: 8 minutes | Serves: 4

455g fresh asparagus
1 tablespoon olive oil
1 teaspoon freshly squeezed lemon juice
½ teaspoon sea salt
⅛ teaspoon freshly ground black pepper
3 tablespoons grated Parmesan cheese

1. Rinse the asparagus and trim down the woody ends where they break naturally. 2. Add the asparagus in the air fryer basket and drizzle with the lemon juice and olive oil, then sprinkle with the pepper and salt; toss to coat. Sprinkle with the Parmesan cheese and toss again. 3. Set the air fryer to 205°C before cooking. Place the basket in the air fryer and roast for 7 to 8 minutes, shaking once during cooking time, until the asparagus are tender and the cheese is light golden brown in places. 4. Serve.
Per Serving: Calories 123; Fat 4.6g; Sodium 361mg; Carbs 5g; Fibre 2.4g; Sugar 2g; Protein 3.6g

Mouth-Watering Baby Potatoes

Prep time: 15 minutes | Cook time: 27 minutes | Serves: 4

10 to 12 baby potatoes
1 tablespoon olive oil
1 tablespoon butter, melted
½ teaspoon sea salt
⅛ teaspoon freshly ground black pepper
½ teaspoon dried thyme
80ml vegetable stock

1. Scrub the potatoes. Cut them in half. 2. Add the olive oil and butter in a 18cm round pan and swirl to coat the bottom. Add the potatoes, cut side down, in a single layer. You may have to use more or fewer potatoes, depending on how many will fit in the pan. The cut side has to sit flat on the pan bottom. 3. Put the pan in the air fryer basket and place the basket in the air fryer. Set or preheat to 205°C and roast the potatoes for 12 minutes. Remove the pan from the basket and shake to loosen the potatoes. 4. Sprinkle the potatoes with the salt, pepper, and thyme and pour the vegetable stock into the pan around the potatoes. 5. Return to the air fryer and roast for another 10 to 15 minutes or until the liquid is fully absorbed and the potatoes are tender when pierced with a fork. Serve.
Per Serving: Calories 417; Fat 6.7g; Sodium 387mg; Carbs 82g; Fibre 10.4g; Sugar 3.8g; Protein 9.5g

Roasted Corn

Prep time: 5 minutes | Cook time: 15 minutes | Serves: 4

300g frozen corn kernels, thawed and drained
1 small onion, diced
2 garlic cloves, sliced
2 tablespoons butter, melted
1 teaspoon chili powder
½ teaspoon cayenne pepper
½ teaspoon sea salt
⅛ teaspoon freshly ground black pepper
60g whipping cream

1. Combine the corn, onion, garlic, butter, chili powder, cayenne pepper, salt, and black pepper in a 15cm metal bowl that fits into your air fryer basket. 2. Set or preheat the air fryer to 205°C. Place the bowl in the basket and roast for 10 minutes, shaking the basket once during cooking time, until some of the kernels start to turn gold around the edges. 3. Remove the basket and pour the cream over the corn; stir to mix. Then return the basket to the air fryer and roast for another 5 minutes or until the cream has thickened slightly. 4. Serve.
Per Serving: Calories 181; Fat 9.7g; Sodium 362mg; Carbs 21g; Fibre 2.5g; Sugar 3.4g; Protein 3.2g

Cauliflower Quesadillas

Prep time: 15 minutes | Cook time: 24 minutes | Serves: 4

110g frozen cauliflower rice or fresh riced cauliflower
3 tablespoons vegetable stock
3 spring onions, sliced
4 (25g) flour tortillas
100g shredded cheddar cheese
1 teaspoon dried oregano
50g shredded Parmesan cheese
1 tablespoon olive oil

1. Combine the cauliflower rice, vegetable stock, and spring onions in a 15cm metal bowl. Put the bowl in the air fryer basket of your air fryer. 2. Set or preheat the air fryer to 190°C and cook the cauliflower mixture until tender, 7 to 8 minutes. Drain if necessary. 3. Put the tortillas on the work surface. Put 25 g of cheddar cheese on one side of each tortilla, then sprinkle with the oregano. 4. Divide the cauliflower rice mixture over the Havarti and oregano, then sprinkle with the Parmesan cheese. Then fold the tortillas in half, enclosing the filling, folding in the edges about 4.5cm. 5. Brush the olive oil over the tortillas. Place the quesadillas, two at a time, in the air fryer basket. Fry at 190°C for 6 to 8 minutes, turning the quesadillas over once during cooking time, until crisp, and the cheese is melted. 6. Repeat with remaining quesadillas. Cut each quesadilla into halves to serve.
Per Serving: Calories 358; Fat 19.8g; Sodium 794mg; Carbs 29g; Fibre 2.2g; Sugar 2.7g; Protein 16.3g

Sweet and Spicy Hashed Brown Potatoes

Prep time: 15 minutes | Cook time: 22 minutes | Serves: 4

2 medium sweet potatoes, peeled
2 tablespoons olive oil
2 teaspoons chili powder
½ teaspoon ground cumin
½ teaspoon sea salt
⅛ teaspoon cayenne pepper

1. Shred the sweet potatoes on the large side of a grater. Place the shredded potatoes in a bowl of cool water for 10 minutes, then drain well. Pat dry using paper towels. 2. Combine the sweet potatoes, olive oil, chili powder, cumin, salt, and cayenne pepper in a large bowl and toss to coat. 3. Put the seasoned potatoes in the air fryer basket of your air fryer. 4. Set or preheat the air fryer to 205°C. Fry for 10 minutes, then remove the basket and shake the potatoes. Return the basket and continue cooking for another 10 to 12 minutes or until the potatoes are crunchy and tender. Serve.
Per Serving: Calories 122; Fat 7g; Sodium 350mg; Carbs 14.2g; Fibre 2.4g; Sugar 4.4g; Protein 1.3g

Roasted Broccoli

Prep time: 10 minutes | Cook time: 15 minutes | Serves: 4

1 bunch fresh broccoli, cut into florets
2 tablespoons olive oil
1 teaspoon five-spice powder
¼ teaspoon onion powder
¼ teaspoon sea salt
⅛ teaspoon freshly ground black pepper

1. Place the broccoli into a large bowl and drizzle with the olive oil. Toss to coat. 2. Sprinkle with the five-spice powder, onion powder, salt, and pepper and toss again. 3. Arrange the broccoli into the air fryer basket of your air fryer. 4. Set or preheat the air fryer to 205°C. Roast the broccoli for 8 minutes. 5. Remove the basket and then shake it to redistribute the broccoli. Return the basket and roast for another 5 to 7 minutes until the broccoli is tender with slightly browned edges. Serve immediately.
Per Serving: Calories 98; Fat 7.3g; Sodium 207mg; Carbs 4g; Fibre 3.2g; Sugar 0.7g; Protein 4.3g

Mediterranean Roasted Veggies

Prep time: 15 minutes | Cook time: 20 minutes | Serves: 4

225g cherry tomatoes
1 yellow pepper, sliced
1 small courgette, sliced
150g button mushrooms, halved lengthwise
2 tablespoons olive oil
1 teaspoon dried basil

½ teaspoon dried oregano
½ teaspoon dried thyme
½ teaspoon garlic powder
½ teaspoon sea salt
⅛ teaspoon freshly ground black pepper

1. Put the tomatoes, pepper, courgette, and mushrooms in the air fryer basket. Add olive oil and toss to coat. Then sprinkle with the basil, oregano, thyme, garlic powder, salt, and pepper and toss again. Put the basket in the air fryer. 2. Heat the air fryer to 190°C before cooking and roast for 15 to 20 minutes, tossing twice during cooking time, until the vegetables are tender. 3. Serve.
Per Serving: Calories 93; Fat 7.1g; Sodium 297mg; Carbs 6.9g; Fibre 1.7g; Sugar 2.2g; Protein 2.3g

Asian Stir-Fried Veggies

Prep time: 15 minutes | Cook time: 13 minutes | Serves: 4

80ml vegetable stock
2 tablespoons low-sodium soy sauce
1 tablespoon hoisin sauce
1 tablespoon corn flour
1 teaspoon grated fresh ginger

2 teaspoons sesame oil
90g broccoli florets
70g chopped Bok choy
50g sliced shiitake mushrooms
1 red pepper, sliced
2 garlic cloves, sliced

1. Whisk the vegetable stock, soy sauce, hoisin sauce, corn flour, and ginger in a small bowl; set aside. 2. Coat the inside of a 15cm metal bowl with the sesame oil. Add the broccoli, Bok choy, shiitake mushrooms, red pepper, and garlic and toss. Put the bowl in the air fryer basket of your air fryer. 3. Set or preheat the air fryer to 205°C. Fry for 8 to 10 minutes, stirring halfway through cooking time, until the vegetables are crisp-tender. 4. Stir the stock mixture again and add it to the vegetables; stir gently. 5. Continue cooking for another 1 to 3 minutes or until the sauce has thickened. Stir again and serve.
Per Serving: Calories 77; Fat 3g; Sodium 417mg; Carbs 11g; Fibre 2.8g; Sugar 2.9g; Protein 3.6g

Breaded Avocado Fries

Prep Time: 20 minutes | Cook Time: 8 minutes | Serves: 6

Olive oil
4 slightly under-ripe avocados, cut in half, pits removed
155g whole-wheat panko bread crumbs

¾ teaspoon freshly ground black pepper
1½ teaspoons paprika
¾ teaspoon salt
3 eggs

1. Spray the air fryer basket lightly with olive oil. 2. Carefully remove the skin from the avocado leaving the flesh intact. Cut each avocado half lengthwise into 5 to 6 slices. 3.In a small bowl, mix together the panko bread crumbs, black pepper, paprika, and salt. 4. In a separate small bowl, beat the eggs. 5.Coat each avocado slice in the egg and then in the panko mixture, pressing the panko mixture gently into the avocado so it sticks. 6. Place the avocado slices in the fryer basket in a single layer. Lightly spray with olive oil. 7.Air fry them for 6 to 8 minutes at 175°C, turning the slices over and spraying lightly with olive oil halfway through. 8. Serve warm.
Per Serving: Calories 379; Fat 23.14g; Sodium 332mg; Carbs 36.98g; Fibre 10.1g; Sugar 1.13g; Protein 9.67g

Spicy Pickle Fries

Prep Time: 15 minutes | Cook Time: 15 minutes | Serves: 4

Olive oil
125g whole-wheat flour
1 teaspoon paprika
1 egg

135g whole-wheat panko bread crumbs
1 (600g) jar spicy dill pickle spears

1. Lightly spray the air fryer basket lightly with olive oil. 2. Mix the whole-wheat flour and paprika in a small bowl. 3. Beat the egg in another small bowl. 4. Put the panko bread crumbs in the third small. 5. Pat the pickle spears dry with paper towels. 6. Dip each pickle spear in the flour mixture, then coat in the egg, and finally dredge in the panko bread crumbs. 7. Place each pickle spear in the fryer basket in a

single layer, leaving a little space between each one. Spray the pickles lightly with olive oil. 8. Air fry them at 205°C for 15 minutes, turning the pickles over halfway through. 9. Serve directly after cooking.
Per Serving: Calories 295; Fat 3.78g; Sodium 88mg; Carbs 55.23g; Fibre 4.6g; Sugar 0.46g; Protein 10.93g

Crisp Carrot Chips

Prep Time: 15 minutes | Cook Time: 10 minutes | Serves: 4

1 tablespoon olive oil plus more for spraying

4 to 5 medium carrots, trimmed
1 teaspoon seasoned salt

1. Lightly spray the air fryer basket lightly with olive oil. 2. Cut the carrots into very thin slices. 3. In a medium bowl, toss the carrot slices with 1 tablespoon of olive oil and the seasoned salt. 4. Add half of the carrots to the air fryer basket. 5. Air fry the carrots at 200°C for 10 minutes until crispy, shaking the basket halfway through. The longer you cook the carrot slices, the crispier they will become. Watch closely because smaller slices could burn. 6. Do the same with the remaining carrots. 7. Serve and enjoy.
Per Serving: Calories 55; Fat 3.55g; Sodium 623mg; Carbs 5.84g; Fibre 1.7g; Sugar 2.89g; Protein 0.57g

Spicy Corn on Cob

Prep Time: 10 minutes | Cook Time: 16 minutes | Serves: 4

Olive oil
2 tablespoons grated Parmesan cheese
1 teaspoon chili powder
1 teaspoon garlic powder
1 teaspoon ground cumin

1 teaspoon paprika
1 teaspoon salt
¼ teaspoon cayenne pepper, optional
4 ears fresh corn, shucked

1. Lightly spray the air fryer basket with olive oil. 2. Mix the Parmesan cheese, chili powder, garlic powder, cumin, paprika, salt, and cayenne pepper in a bowl. 3. Lightly spray the ears of corn with olive oil, and sprinkle them with the seasoning mixture. 4. Place the ears of corn in the air fryer basket in a single layer. 5. Air fry the ears of corn at 205°C for 7 minutes. 6. Turn the corn over and air fry for 7 to 9 minutes more until lightly browned. 7. Serve warm.
Per Serving: Calories 142; Fat 2.7g; Sodium 669mg; Carbs 29.06g; Fibre 4.5g; Sugar 4.76g; Protein 5.72g

Bacon with Brussels Sprouts

Prep Time: 10 minutes | Cook Time: 10 minutes | Serves: 4

Olive oil
400g fresh Brussels sprouts, trimmed and halved
1 tablespoon crumbled cooked bacon

2 teaspoons balsamic vinegar
1 teaspoon olive oil
1 teaspoon salt
1 teaspoon pepper

1. Lightly spray the air fryer basket with olive oil. 2. Toss the Brussels sprouts with the crumbled bacon, balsamic vinegar, olive oil, salt, and pepper in a bowl. 3. Place the Brussels sprouts in the air fryer basket. 4. Air fry them at 175°C for 10 minutes until they are fork-tender and lightly browned, shaking the basket and lightly spraying with the olive oil halfway through. 5. Serve.
Per Serving: Calories 73; Fat 2.15g; Sodium 644mg; Carbs 11.81g; Fibre 4.5g; Sugar 3.46g; Protein 4.31g

Roasted Tomatoes

Prep Time: 10 minutes | Cook Time: 6 minutes | Serves: 4

Olive oil
4 Roma tomatoes, cut into 1cm slices
Salt

60g shredded mozzarella cheese
25g shredded Parmesan cheese
Freshly ground black pepper
Parsley flakes

1. Lightly spray the air fryer basket with olive oil. 2. Lightly season the tomato slices with salt. 3. Place the tomato slices in the air fryer basket in a single layer. 4. Sprinkle each tomato slice with 1 teaspoon of mozzarella cheese, and top each with ½ teaspoon of shredded Parmesan cheese, then season them with black pepper and sprinkle parsley flakes. 5. Air fry them at 190°C for 5 to 6 minutes until the cheese is melted, bubbly, and lightly browned. 6. Serve warm.
Per Serving: Calories 74; Fat 3.07g; Sodium 261mg; Carbs 5.29g; Fibre 1.5g; Sugar 2.61g; Protein 7.12g

Breaded Pepper Strips

Prep Time: 15 minutes | Cook Time: 7 minutes | Serves: 4

Olive oil
65g whole-wheat panko bread crumbs
½ teaspoon paprika
½ teaspoon garlic powder
½ teaspoon salt
1 egg, beaten
2 red, orange, or yellow peppers, cut into 1cm-thick slices

1. Lightly spray the air fryer basket with olive oil. 2. In a medium shallow bowl, mix together the panko bread crumbs, paprika, garlic powder, and salt. 3. In another small shallow bowl, whisk the egg with 1½ teaspoons of water to make an egg wash. 4. Dip the pepper slices in the egg wash to coat, then dredge them in the panko bread crumbs until evenly coated. 5. Place the pepper slices in the fryer basket in a single layer. Lightly spray the pepper strips with oil. 6. Air fry them at 205°C for 4 to 7 minutes until lightly browned. 7. Carefully remove from fryer basket to ensure that the coating does not come off. Serve immediately.
Per Serving: Calories 143; Fat 3.03g; Sodium 319mg; Carbs 22.23g; Fibre 1.5g; Sugar 0.27g; Protein 6.03g

Flavourful Broccoli

Prep Time: 10 minutes | Cook Time: 20 minutes | Serves: 4

½ teaspoon olive oil, plus more for spraying
455g fresh broccoli, cut into florets
½ tablespoon minced garlic
Salt
1½ tablespoons soy sauce
1 teaspoon white vinegar
2 teaspoons hot sauce or sriracha
1½ teaspoons honey
Freshly ground black pepper

1. Lightly spray the air fryer basket with olive oil. 2. In a large bowl, Toss the broccoli florets with ½ teaspoon of olive oil and the minced garlic, and then season them with salt. 3. Place the broccoli in the fryer basket in a single layer. 4. Air fry them at 205°C for 15 to 20 minutes until lightly browned and crispy, shaking the basket every 5 minutes. Do the same with the remaining broccoli. 5. In a small bowl, whisk together the soy sauce, white vinegar, hot sauce, honey, and black pepper. If the honey doesn't incorporate well, microwave the mixture for 10 to 20 seconds until the honey melts. 6. In a large bowl, toss the cooked broccoli with the sauce mixture, and season with additional salt and pepper, if desired. 7. Serve immediately.
Per Serving: Calories 58; Fat 2.23g; Sodium 229mg; Carbs 7.33g; Fibre 3.2g; Sugar 3.8g; Protein 4.11g

Delicious Broccoli Cheese Tots

Prep Time: 20 minutes | Cook Time: 15 minutes | Serves: 4

Olive oil
300g frozen broccoli, thawed and drained
1 large egg
1½ teaspoons minced garlic
25g grated Parmesan cheese
25g shredded reduced-fat sharp Cheddar cheese
50g seasoned whole-wheat bread crumbs
Salt
Freshly ground black pepper

1. Lightly spray the air fryer basket with olive oil. 2. Gently squeeze the thawed broccoli to remove any excess liquid. 3. Add the broccoli, egg, garlic, Parmesan cheese, Cheddar cheese, bread crumbs, salt, and pepper to the food processor, and pulse until it resembles a coarse meal. 4. Scoop up the broccoli mixture and shape into 24 ovals "tater tot" shapes. 5. Place the tots in the air fryer basket in a single layer, being careful to space them a little bit apart. Lightly spray the tots with oil. 6. Air fry them at 190°C for 6 to 7 minutes, turning the tots over and cook for an additional 6 to 8 minutes or until lightly browned and crispy. 7. Serve and enjoy.
Per Serving: Calories 107; Fat 5.71g; Sodium 235mg; Carbs 8.25g; Fibre 2.7g; Sugar 1.56g; Protein 7.23g

Roasted Peppers with Parsley

Prep time: 10 minutes | Cook time: 11 minutes | Serves: 4

1 red pepper, sliced
1 yellow pepper, sliced
1 orange pepper, sliced
1 tablespoon olive oil
1 teaspoon freshly squeezed lemon juice
1 teaspoon dried Italian seasoning
½ teaspoon sea salt
⅛ teaspoon freshly ground black pepper
10g chopped fresh flat-leaf parsley

1. Combine the peppers in the air fryer basket. Drizzle with the olive oil and lemon juice, and sprinkle with the Italian seasoning, salt, and pepper. Toss to coat. Place the basket in the air fryer. 2. Set or preheat the air fryer to 175°C. Roast for 8 to 11 minutes, shaking once during cooking time, until the peppers are tender and starting to brown around the edges. 3. Sprinkle with the parsley and serve.
Per Serving: Calories 57; Fat 3.6g; Sodium 353mg; Carbs 6g; Fibre 1.2g; Sugar 1.3g; Protein 1.3g

Homemade Roasted Carrots

Prep time: 5 minutes | Cook time: 22 minutes | Serves: 4

240g baby carrots
1 large carrot, peeled and sliced 1cm thick
1 tablespoon freshly squeezed orange juice
2 teaspoons olive oil
1 teaspoon butter, melted
1 teaspoon dried dill weed
½ teaspoon sea salt
⅛ teaspoon freshly ground black pepper

1. Use paper towel to dry the carrots and place them in the air fryer basket. 2. Combine the orange juice, butter, olive oil, dill weed, salt, and pepper in a small bowl and mix well. Then drizzle the mixture over the carrots and toss to coat. Place the basket in the air fryer. 3. Heat the air fryer to 205°C before cooking. Roast for 10 minutes, then shake the basket and roast for another 8 to 12 minutes or until the carrots are soft and glazed. Serve.
Per Serving: Calories 61; Fat 3.4g; Sodium 349mg; Carbs 7.6g; Fibre 2.1g; Sugar 3.8g; Protein 0.8g

Spicy Corn Fritters

Prep time: 15 minutes | Cook time: 15 minutes per batch | Serves: 4

65g plain flour
1 teaspoon chili powder
½ teaspoon baking powder
½ teaspoon sea salt
⅛ teaspoon freshly ground black
pepper
195g frozen corn kernels, thawed
1 large egg, beaten
1 tablespoon honey
1 garlic clove, minced

1. Combine the flour, chili powder, baking powder, salt, and pepper in a medium bowl and mix well. 2. In a small bowl, combine the corn, egg, honey, and garlic and mix well. 3. Add the corn mixture to the flour mixture and stir just until combined. Add more flour to get a thick batter that holds its shape when dropped from a spoon as needed. 4. Prepare the air fryer basket by lining it with parchment paper. Drop two to four measures of the fritter batter onto the paper, 4.5cm apart. Place the basket in the air fryer. 5. Heat the air fryer to 190°C before cooking and fry for 10 to 15 minutes, until they are golden brown and hot. Repeat with the remaining batter, if needed. Serve.
Per Serving: Calories 148; Fat 2g; Sodium 315mg; Carbs 28.7g; Fibre 2g; Sugar 6g; Protein 4g

Dijon Veggie Kabobs

Prep time: 15 minutes | Cook time: 11 minutes | Serves: 4

1 (200g) package button mushrooms, rinsed
1 green pepper, sliced
1 yellow pepper, sliced
150g cherry tomatoes
1 tablespoon freshly squeezed lemon juice
1 tablespoon olive oil
2 teaspoons Dijon mustard
½ teaspoon dried marjoram
½ teaspoon sea salt
⅛ teaspoon freshly ground black pepper

1. Build the skewers with the mushrooms, peppers, and cherry tomatoes, alternating vegetables for a nice appearance. 2. Whisk the mustard, marjoram, lemon juice, olive oil, salt, and pepper in a small bowl. Brush this mixture onto the vegetables. 3. Heat the air fryer to 205°C before cooking. Roast the skewers for 8 to 11 minutes, turning once halfway through cooking time, until the vegetables are tender and starting to brown. Serve.
Per Serving: Calories 224; Fat 4.2g; Sodium 329mg; Carbs 48.7g; Fibre 7.7g; Sugar 3g; Protein 6.6g

Maple Sweet Potatoes

Prep time: 15 minutes | Cook time: 22 minutes | Serves: 4

2 sweet potatoes	1 tablespoon brown sugar
2 tablespoons maple syrup	½ teaspoon sea salt
1 tablespoon butter, melted	Pinch nutmeg

1. Rinse the sweet potatoes and peel them, then cut into 1cm cubes. Put the sweet potatoes in the air fryer basket. 2. Combine the maple syrup, butter, brown sugar, salt, and nutmeg in a small bowl and mix well. Drizzle half of this mixture over the sweet potatoes, tossing to coat. Put the basket in the air fryer. 3. Heat the air fryer to 205°C before cooking. Roast the potatoes for 10 minutes, then remove the basket from the air fryer, toss, and drizzle with the rest of the butter mixture; toss again. 4. Return the basket to the air fryer and continue cooking for another 8 to 12 minutes or until the potatoes are tender and glazed. Serve.
Per Serving: Calories 123; Fat 3g; Sodium 329mg; Carbs 23g; Fibre 2g; Sugar 11.7g; Protein 1.1g

Jalapeño and Cheese Cauliflower Mash Bake

Prep time: 10 minutes | Cook time: 15 minutes | Serves: 6

1 (300g) steamer bag cauliflower florets, cooked according to package instructions	50g shredded sharp Cheddar cheese
2 tablespoons salted butter, softened	20g pickled jalapeños
50g cream cheese, softened	½ teaspoon salt
	¼ teaspoon ground black pepper

1. Combine all the listed ingredients above in a food processor. Pulse twenty times until cauliflower is smooth and all ingredients are combined. 2. Spoon mash into an ungreased 15cm round nonstick baking dish. Place dish into air fryer basket. Adjust the temperature setting to 195°C and set the timer for 15 minutes. The top will be golden brown when done. 3. Serve warm.
Per Serving: Calories 108; Fat 8.6g; Sodium 402mg; Carbs 4.3g; Fibre 2g; Sugar 0.5g; Protein 4.7g

Delicious Burger Bun

Prep time: 2 minutes | Cook time: 5 minutes | Serves: 1

2 tablespoons salted butter, melted	¼ teaspoon baking powder
25g blanched finely ground almond flour	⅛ teaspoon apple cider vinegar
	1 large egg, whisked

1. Pour butter into an ungreased 10cm ramekin. Add baking powder, flour, and vinegar to ramekin and stir until combined. Add egg and stir until batter is mostly smooth. 2. Place ramekin into air fryer basket. Adjust the temperature to 175°C and set the timer for 5 minutes. 3. When done, the centre will be firm and the top slightly browned. Let cool, about 5 minutes, then remove from ramekin and slice in half. Serve.
Per Serving: Calories 422; Fat 39g; Sodium 203mg; Carbs 7.8g; Fibre 3.6g; Sugar 2g; Protein 14.2g

Balsamic Brussels Sprouts with Bacon

Prep time: 5 minutes | Cook time: 12 minutes | Serves: 4

175g trimmed and halved fresh Brussels sprouts	¼ teaspoon ground black pepper
2 tablespoons olive oil	2 tablespoons balsamic vinegar
¼ teaspoon salt	2 slices cooked bacon, crumbled

1. Toss Brussels sprouts in olive oil in a large bowl, then sprinkle with salt and pepper. 2. Place into ungreased air fryer basket. Adjust the temperature setting to 190°C and set the timer for 12 minutes, shaking the basket halfway through cooking. Brussels sprouts will be tender and browned when done. 3. Place sprouts in a large serving dish and drizzle with balsamic vinegar. Sprinkle bacon over top. Serve warm.
Per Serving: Calories 113; Fat 9g; Sodium 255mg; Carbs 5.5g; Fibre 1.7g; Sugar 2.2g; Protein 3.5g

Simple Roasted Asparagus

Prep time: 5 minutes | Cook time: 12 minutes | Serves: 4

1 tablespoon olive oil	¼ teaspoon salt
455g asparagus spears, ends trimmed	¼ teaspoon ground black pepper
	1 tablespoon salted butter, melted

1. Drizzle olive oil over asparagus spears in a large bowl and sprinkle with salt and pepper. 2. Place spears into ungreased air fryer basket. Adjust the temperature setting to 190°C and set the timer for 12 minutes, shaking the basket halfway through cooking. Asparagus will be lightly browned and tender when done. 3. Transfer to a large dish and drizzle with butter. Serve warm.
Per Serving: Calories 70; Fat 5.4g; Sodium 163mg; Carbs 4.5g; Fibre 2.4g; Sugar 2.1g; Protein 2.5g

Tasty Onion Rings

Prep time: 10 minutes| Cook time: 5 minutes| Serves: 8

1 large egg	1 large white onion, peeled and sliced into 8 (½cm) rings
30g plain flour	
50g, parmesan, grated	

1. Peel the large white onion and slice into 8 (½cm) rings. 2. Whisk egg in a medium bowl. Place flour and parmesan in two separate medium bowls. Dip each onion ring into egg, then coat in flour. Dip coated onion ring in egg once more, then press gently into parmesan to cover all sides. 3. Place rings into ungreased air fryer basket. Adjust the temperature setting to 205°C and set the timer for 5 minutes, turning the onion rings halfway through cooking. Onion rings will be golden and crispy when done. Serve warm.
Per Serving: Calories 43; Fat 1.6g; Sodium 14mg; Carbs 4.6g; Fibre 0.6g; Sugar 0.8g; Protein 2.5g

Fried Green Beans

Prep time: 5 minutes| Cook time: 8 minutes| Serves: 4

2 teaspoons olive oil	¼ teaspoon salt
225g fresh green beans, ends trimmed	¼ teaspoon ground black pepper

1. Drizzle olive oil over green beans in a large bowl and sprinkle with salt and pepper. 2. Place green beans into ungreased air fryer basket. Adjust the temperature setting to 175°C and set the timer for 8 minutes, shaking the basket two times during cooking. 3. Green beans will be dark golden and crispy at the edges when done. Serve warm.
Per Serving: Calories 33; Fat 2.5g; Sodium 147mg; Carbs 2.6g; Fibre 1.1g; Sugar 0.5g; Protein 0.7g

Cheese Flatbread Dippers

Prep time: 5 minutes| Cook time: 8 minutes| Serves: 4

120g shredded mozzarella cheese	50g blanched finely ground almond flour
25g cream cheese, broken into small pieces	

1. Place mozzarella into a large microwave-safe bowl. Add cream cheese pieces. Microwave on high 60 seconds, then stir to combine. Add flour and stir until a soft ball of dough forms. 2. Cut dough ball into two equal pieces. Cut a suitable piece of parchment paper to fit into air fryer basket. Press each dough piece into a 12cm round on ungreased parchment. 3. Place parchment with dough into air fryer basket. Adjust the temperature setting to 175°C and set the timer for 8 minutes. Carefully flip the flatbread over halfway through cooking. Flatbread will be golden brown when done. 4. Let flatbread cool 5 minutes, then slice each round into six triangles. Serve warm.
Per Serving: Calories 168; Fat 11.6g; Sodium 244mg; Carbs 4.6g; Fibre 2.3g; Sugar 1.5g; Protein 13.3g

Tender-Crisp Mini Poppers

Prep time: 10 minutes| Cook time: 8 minutes| Serves: 4

100g cream cheese, softened	8 mini sweet peppers, tops removed, seeded, and halved lengthwise
30g chopped fresh spinach leaves	
½ teaspoon garlic powder	

1. Mix cream cheese, spinach, and garlic powder in a medium bowl. Place 1 tablespoon mixture into each sweet pepper half and press down to smooth. 2. Place poppers into ungreased air fryer basket. Adjust the temperature setting to 205°C and set the timer for 8 minutes. 3. Poppers will be done when cheese is browned on top and peppers are tender-crisp. Serve warm.
Per Serving: Calories 137; Fat 8.5g; Sodium 133mg; Carbs 13.3g; Fibre 2g; Sugar 1g; Protein 4.2g

Spicy Corn and Beans

Prep time: 10 minutes | Cook time: 10 minutes | Serves: 4

1 (375g) can black beans, drained and rinsed
155g frozen corn kernels
1 red pepper, seeded and chopped
1 jalapeño pepper, sliced
2 garlic cloves, sliced

1 tablespoon olive oil
1 tablespoon freshly squeezed lime juice
2 teaspoons chili powder
½ teaspoon sea salt
⅛ teaspoon cayenne pepper

1. Combine the black beans, corn, pepper, jalapeño pepper, and garlic in the air fryer basket. 2. Drip the lime juice and olive oil and toss to coat. Sprinkle with the chili powder, salt, and cayenne pepper and toss again. Place the basket in the air fryer. 3. Set or preheat the air fryer to 175°C. Roast the vegetables for 10 minutes, shaking the basket halfway through cooking time, until hot and tender. Serve.
Per Serving: Calories 104; Fat 4.5g; Sodium 334mg; Carbs 15g; Fibre 3g; Sugar 2.7g; Protein 2.6g

Flaxseed Cheese Rolls

Prep time: 10 minutes| Cook time: 12 minutes| Serves: 6

120g shredded mozzarella cheese
25g cream cheese, broken into small pieces
100g blanched finely ground

almond flour
40g ground flaxseed
½ teaspoon baking powder
1 large egg, whisked

1. Place mozzarella, cream cheese, and flour in a large microwave-safe bowl. Microwave on high 1 minute. Mix until smooth. 2. Add flaxseed, baking powder, and egg to mixture until fully combined and smooth. Microwave an additional 15 seconds if dough becomes too firm. 3. Separate dough into six equal pieces and roll each into a ball. Place rolls into ungreased air fryer basket. Adjust the temperature setting to 160°C and set the timer for 12 minutes, turning rolls halfway through cooking. Allow rolls to cool completely before serving, for about 5 minutes.
Per Serving: Calories 233; Fat 17.8g; Sodium 179mg; Carbs 7.6g; Fibre 4.7g; Sugar 1.7g; Protein 13.8g

Savoury Roasted Brussels Sprouts

Prep time: 5 minutes| Cook time: 10 minutes| Serves: 6

455g fresh Brussels sprouts, trimmed and halved
2 tablespoons coconut oil
½ teaspoon salt

¼ teaspoon ground black pepper
½ teaspoon garlic powder
1 tablespoon salted butter, melted

1. Place Brussels sprouts into a large bowl. Then drizzle with coconut oil and sprinkle with salt, pepper, and garlic powder. 2. Place Brussels sprouts into ungreased air fryer basket. Adjust the temperature setting to 175°C and set the timer for 10 minutes, shaking the basket three times during cooking. Brussels sprouts will be dark golden and tender when done. 3. Place cooked sprouts in a large serving dish and drizzle with butter. Serve warm.
Per Serving: Calories 84; Fat 6g; Sodium 223mg; Carbs 7g; Fibre 3g; Sugar 1.7g; Protein 2.6g

Spicy Roasted Salsa

Prep time: 5 minutes| Cook time: 30 minutes| Serves: 8

2 large tomatoes, cored and cut into large chunks
½ medium white onion, peeled and large-diced
½ medium jalapeño, seeded and

large-diced
2 cloves garlic, peeled and diced
½ teaspoon salt
1 tablespoon coconut oil
60ml fresh lime juice

1. Place tomatoes, onion, and jalapeño into an ungreased 15cm round nonstick baking dish. Add garlic, then sprinkle with salt and drizzle with coconut oil. 2. Place dish into air fryer basket. Adjust the temperature setting to 150°C and set the timer for 30 minutes. Vegetables will be dark brown around the edges and tender when done. 3. Pour the vegetables into a food processor or blender. Add lime juice. Process on low speed 30 seconds until only a few chunks remain. 4. Transfer salsa to a sealable container and refrigerate at least 1 hour. Serve chilled.
Per Serving: Calories 29; Fat 1.8g; Sodium 148mg; Carbs 3.4g; Fibre 0.7g; Sugar 1.7g; Protein 0.6g

Homemade Roasted Radishes

Prep time: 5 minutes | Cook time: 18 minutes | Serves: 4

455g radishes, ends trimmed if needed

2 tablespoons olive oil
½ teaspoon sea salt

1. Preheat the air fryer to 180°C. 2. In a large bowl, drizzle the radishes with olive oil and sea salt. 3. Pour the radishes into the air fryer and cook for 10 minutes. Stir or turn the radishes over and cook for 8 minutes more, then serve.
Per Serving: Calories 80; Fat 6.9g; Sodium 315mg; Carbs 4.7g; Fibre 1.8g; Sugar 2.8g; Protein 0.7g

Simple Stuffed Red Peppers

Prep time: 10 minutes | Cook time: 20 minutes | Serves: 4

2 red peppers, with seeds and stems removed
200g cooked brown rice
2 Roma tomatoes, diced
1 garlic clove, minced
¼ teaspoon salt
¼ teaspoon black pepper

100g ricotta
3 tablespoons fresh basil, chopped
3 tablespoons fresh oregano, chopped
25g shredded Parmesan, for topping

1. Preheat the air fryer to 180°C. 2. Half the peppers. Combine salt, pepper, garlic, tomatoes, and brown rice in a medium bowl. 3. Divide the rice filling evenly among the four pepper halves. 4. In a small bowl, combine the ricotta, basil, and oregano. Put the herbed cheese over the top of the rice mixture in each pepper. 5. Place the peppers into the air fryer and roast for 20 minutes. 6. Remove and serve with shredded Parmesan on top.
Per Serving: Calories 149; Fat 5.7g; Sodium 260mg; Carbs 17.8g; Fibre 2.4g; Sugar 3.2g; Protein 7.4g

Homemade Ratatouille

Prep time: 15 minutes | Cook time: 40 minutes | Serves: 6

2 russet potatoes, cubed
75g Roma tomatoes, cubed
1 aubergine, cubed
1 courgette, cubed
1 red onion, chopped
1 red pepper, chopped
2 garlic cloves, minced
1 teaspoon dried mint
1 teaspoon dried parsley

1 teaspoon dried oregano
½ teaspoon salt
½ teaspoon black pepper
¼ teaspoon red pepper flakes
80ml olive oil
1 (200g) can tomato paste
60ml vegetable stock
60ml water

1. Preheat the air fryer to 160°C. 2. In a large bowl, combine the potatoes, tomatoes, aubergine, courgette, onion, garlic, mint, parsley, oregano, pepper, black pepper, red pepper flakes, and salt. 3. In a small bowl, mix together the olive oil, tomato paste, stock, and water. 4. Pour the oil-and-tomato-paste mixture over the vegetables and toss until everything is coated. 5. Pour the coated vegetables into the air fryer basket in an even layer and roast for 20 minutes. After 20 minutes, stir well and spread out again. Roast for an additional 10 minutes, then repeat the process and cook for another 10 minutes.
Per Serving: Calories 238; Fat 12.4g; Sodium 251mg; Carbs 30.5g; Fibre 6.3g; Sugar 10.8g; Protein 5g

Thyme Butternut Squash

Prep time: 15 minutes | Cook time: 20 minutes | Serves: 4

1 medium butternut squash, cubed into 2.5cm pieces
2 tablespoons olive oil
¼ teaspoon salt

¼ teaspoon garlic powder
¼ teaspoon black pepper
1 tablespoon fresh thyme
25g grated Parmesan cheese

1. Preheat the air fryer to 180°C. 2. Combine the cubed squash with the olive oil, salt, garlic powder, pepper, and thyme in a large bowl until the squash is well coated. 3. Pour this mixture into the air fryer basket, and roast for 10 minutes. Stir and roast another 8 to 10 minutes more. 4. Remove the squash from the air fryer and toss with freshly grated Parmesan cheese before serving.
Per Serving: Calories 127; Fat 8.6g; Sodium 262mg; Carbs 11.5g; Fibre 2g; Sugar 2g; Protein 2.7g

Parmesan Radishes

Prep time: 10 minutes | Cook time: 10 minutes | Serves: 6

455g radishes, ends removed, quartered
2 tablespoons salted butter, melted
½ teaspoon garlic powder

½ teaspoon dried parsley
¼ teaspoon dried oregano
¼ teaspoon ground black pepper
25g grated Parmesan cheese

1. Place radishes into a medium bowl and drizzle with butter. Sprinkle with garlic powder, parsley, oregano, and pepper, then place into ungreased air fryer basket. Adjust the temperature setting to 175°C and set the timer for 10 minutes, shaking the basket three times during cooking. Radishes will be done when tender and golden. 2. Place radishes into a large serving dish and sprinkle with Parmesan cheese. Serve warm.
Per Serving: Calories 55; Fat 3.8g; Sodium 112mg; Carbs 4g; Fibre 1.3g; Sugar 2g; Protein 1.7g

Garlic Crusted Aubergine Slice

Prep time: 5 minutes | Cook time: 25 minutes | Serves: 4

1 egg
1 tablespoon water
50g whole wheat bread crumbs
1 teaspoon garlic powder
½ teaspoon dried oregano

½ teaspoon salt
½ teaspoon paprika
1 medium aubergine, sliced into ½cm-thick rounds
1 tablespoon olive oil

1. Preheat the air fryer to 180°C. 2. Beat the egg and water in a medium shallow bowl until frothy. 3. In a separate medium shallow bowl, mix together bread crumbs, garlic powder, oregano, salt, and paprika. 4. Immerse each aubergine slice into the egg mixture, then into the bread crumb mixture, coating the outside with crumbs. Then arrange the slices in the bottom of the air fryer basket in a single layer. 5. Drizzle the tops of the aubergine slices with the olive oil, then fry for 15 minutes. Turn each slice and cook for an additional 10 minutes.
Per Serving: Calories 154; Fat 6.8g; Sodium 419mg; Carbs 18.8g; Fibre 5g; Sugar 5.9g; Protein 5.6g

Spicy Garlic Beetroot

Prep time: 10 minutes | Cook time: 30 minutes | Serves: 4

4 beetroot, cleaned, peeled, and sliced
1 garlic clove, minced
2 tablespoons chopped fresh dill

¼ teaspoon salt
¼ teaspoon black pepper
3 tablespoons olive oil

1. Preheat the air fryer to 195°C. 2. In a large bowl, mix the beetroot, garlic, chopped dill, salt, black pepper, and olive oil until the beetroot are well coated with the oil. 3. Pour the beet mixture into the air fryer basket, and roast for 15 minutes before stirring, then continue roasting for 15 minutes more.
Per Serving: Calories 136; Fat 10.8g; Sodium 210mg; Carbs 10g; Fibre 3.1g; Sugar 5.6g; Protein 1.9g

Citrus-Honey Broccoli Florets

Prep time: 5 minutes | Cook time: 12 minutes | Serves: 6

360g broccoli florets (approximately 1 large head)
2 tablespoons olive oil
½ teaspoon salt

120ml orange juice
1 tablespoon raw honey
Orange wedges, for serving (optional)

1. Preheat the air fryer to 180°C. 2. In a large bowl, combine the broccoli, olive oil, salt, orange juice, and honey. Toss the broccoli in the liquid until well coated. 3. Pour the broccoli mixture into the air fryer basket and cook for 6 minutes. Stir and cook for 6 minutes more. 4. Serve alone or with orange wedges for additional citrus flavor, if desired.
Per Serving: Calories 73; Fat 4.7g; Sodium 203mg; Carbs 7.7g; Fibre 1.1g; Sugar 5.8g; Protein 1g

Perfect Polenta Muffins

Prep time: 5 minutes | Cook Time: 10 minutes | Serves: 12

60g plain flour
85g Polenta

50g granulated sugar
½ teaspoon baking powder

55g salted butter, melted
120ml buttermilk

1 large egg

1. Preheat the air fryer to 175°C. 2. In a container, whisk together flour, polenta, sugar, and baking powder. 3. Add butter, buttermilk, and egg to dry mixture. Stir until well combined. 4. Divide batter evenly among twelve silicone or aluminum muffin cups, filling cups about halfway. Working in batches as needed, put in the air fryer and cook them for 10 minutes until golden brown. 5. Let cool 5 minutes before serving.
Per Serving: Calories 83; Fat 3.19g; Sodium 853mg; Carbs 11.89g; Fibre 0.4g; Sugar 2.66g; Protein 1.59g

Popular Macaroni and Cheese

Prep Time: 5 minutes | Cook Time: 25 minutes | Serves: 4

240g dry elbow macaroni
240ml chicken stock
120ml whole milk
2 tablespoons salted butter,

melted
200g sharp cheddar cheese, shredded, divided
½ teaspoon ground black pepper

1. Preheat the air fryer to 175°C. 2. In a 15cm baking dish, combine macaroni, stock, milk, butter, half the cheddar, and pepper. Stir to combine. 3. Put in the air fryer basket and cook them for 12 minutes. 4. Stir in remaining cheddar, then return the air fryer basket to the air fryer and cook them for 13 minutes more. 5. Stir macaroni and cheese until creamy. Let cool 10 minutes before serving.
Per Serving: Calories 355; Fat 14.34g; Sodium 918mg; Carbs 49.52g; Fibre 0.9g; Sugar 8.91g; Protein 25.05g

Roasted Red Potatoes with Rosemary

Prep time: 5 minutes | Cook Time: 20 minutes | Serves: 6

455g red potatoes, quartered
60ml olive oil
½ teaspoon salt

¼ teaspoon black pepper
1 garlic clove, minced
4 rosemary sprigs

1. Preheat the air fryer to 180°C. 2. Toss the potatoes with the salt, olive oil, pepper, and garlic in a large bowl until well-coated. 3. Transfer the seasoned potatoes into the air fryer basket and top with the sprigs of rosemary. 4. Roast for 10 minutes. Then stir or toss the potatoes and roast for 10 minutes more. 5. Remove the rosemary sprigs and serve the potatoes. Season with additional salt and pepper, if needed.
Per Serving: Calories 135; Fat 9g; Sodium 208mg; Carbs 12.5g; Fibre 1.5g; Sugar 1g; Protein 1.5g

Perfect Roasted Broccoli

Prep Time: 5 minutes | Cook Time: 8 minutes | Serves: 4

300g Broccoli florets
2 tablespoons olive oil

½ teaspoon salt
¼ teaspoon ground black pepper

1. Preheat the air fryer to 180°C. 2. In a medium bowl, put broccoli and drizzle with oil. Sprinkle with salt and pepper. 3. Put in the air fryer basket and cook them for 8 minutes, shaking the air fryer basket twice during cooking, until the edges are brown and the centre is tender. 4. Serve warm.
Per Serving: Calories 80; Fat 7.17g; Sodium 319mg; Carbs 2.69g; Fibre 2.3g; Sugar0.47g; Protein 2.75g

Easy Sweet Butternut Squash

Prep Time: 10 minutes | Cook Time: 15 minutes | Serves: 8

1 medium Butternut Squash, peeled and cubed
2 tablespoons salted butter, melted

½ teaspoon salt
1½ tablespoons brown sugar
½ teaspoon ground cinnamon

1. Preheat the air fryer to 205°C. 2. In a container, put squash and add butter. Toss to coat. Sprinkle salt, brown sugar, and cinnamon over Squash and toss to fully coat. 3. Put squash in the air fryer basket and cook them for 15 minutes, shaking the air fryer basket three times during cooking, until the edges are golden and the centre is fork-tender.
Per Serving: Calories 23; Fat 1.95 g; Sodium 853mg; Carbs 1.5 g; Fibre 0.4 g; Sugar 1.09g; Protein 0.32g

Flavourful Sweet Roasted Carrots

Prep Time: 5 minutes | Cook Time: 12 minutes | Serves: 4

455g baby carrots
55g brown sugar
2 tablespoons salted butter, melted
¼ teaspoon garlic powder
½ teaspoon salt
¼ teaspoon ground black pepper

1. Preheat the air fryer to 180°C. 2. Put carrots into a 15cm round baking dish. 3. Mix brown sugar, butter, and garlic powder. Pour mixture over carrots and carefully stir to coat. Sprinkle with salt and pepper. 4. Put in the air fryer basket and cook them for 12 minutes, stirring three times during cooking, until carrots are tender.
Per Serving: Calories 127; Fat 4.02g; Sodium 853mg; Carbs 23.22g; Fibre 3.5g; Sugar 17.4g; Protein 1.01g

Sweet Brussels Sprouts

Prep Time: 5 minutes | Cook Time: 15 minutes | Serves: 4

455g Brussels Sprouts, trimmed and halved
2 tablespoons olive oil
½ teaspoon salt
¼ teaspoon ground black pepper

1. Preheat the air fryer to 175°C. 2. In a container, put Brussels sprouts and drizzle with oil. Sprinkle with salt and pepper. 3. Put in the air fryer basket and cook 15 minutes, shaking the air fryer basket three times during cooking. 4. Serve warm.
Per Serving: Calories 110; Fat 7.1g; Sodium 853mg; Carbs 10.42g; Fibre 4.4g; Sugar 2.64g; Protein 3.89g

Golden and Crispy Potato Balls

Prep Time: 15 minutes | Cook Time: 10 minutes | Serves: 4

460g mashed potatoes (about 4 medium russet potatoes)
170g sour cream, divided
1 teaspoon salt
½ teaspoon ground black pepper
100g shredded sharp Cheddar cheese
4 slices bacon, cooked and crumbled
110g panko bread crumbs

1. Preheat the air fryer to 205°C. Cut parchment paper to fit the air fryer basket. 2. In a container, mix mashed potatoes, 115g sour cream, salt, pepper, Cheddar, and bacon. Form twelve balls using 2 tablespoons of the potato mixture per ball. 3. Divide remaining 55g sour cream evenly among mashed potato balls, coating each before rolling in bread crumbs. 4. Put balls on parchment in the air fryer basket and spritz with cooking spray. Cook them for 10 minutes until brown. 5. Serve warm.
Per Serving: Calories 252; Fat 15.37g; Sodium 815mg; Carbs 21.5g; Fibre 2g; Sugar 13.12g; Protein 7.5g

Lemon Butter Asparagus

Prep Time: 5 minutes | Cook Time: 15 minutes | Serves: 4

455g asparagus, ends trimmed
55g salted butter, cubed
Zest and juice of ½ medium lemon
½ teaspoon salt
¼ teaspoon ground black pepper

1. Preheat the air fryer to 190°C. Cut a 15cm × 15cm square of foil. 2. Put asparagus on foil square. 3. Dot asparagus with butter. Sprinkle lemon zest, salt, and pepper on top of asparagus. Drizzle lemon juice over asparagus. 4. Fold foil over asparagus and seal the edges closed to form a packet. 5. Put in the air fryer basket and cook them for 15 minutes until tender. 6. Serve them warm.
Per Serving: Calories 93; Fat 7.82g; Sodium 853mg; Carbs 5.09g; Fibre 2.4g; Sugar 2.43g; Protein 2.65g

Classic Green Bean Casserole

Prep Time: 10 minutes | Cook Time: 20 minutes | Serves: 4

1 (250g) can condensed cream of mushroom soup
60g heavy cream
2 (360g) cans cut green beans, drained
1 teaspoon minced garlic
½ teaspoon salt
¼ teaspoon ground black pepper
55g packaged French fried onions

1. Preheat the air fryer to 160°C. 2. In a 4-litre baking dish, pour soup and cream over green beans and mix to combine. 3. Stir in garlic, salt, and pepper until combined. Top with French fried onions. 4. Put in the air fryer basket and cook for 20 minutes until top is lightly brown and dish is heated through. 5. Serve warm.
Per Serving: Calories 110; Fat 6.27g; Sodium 853mg; Carbs 12.84g; Fibre 3.3g; Sugar 3.97g; Protein 2.89g

Quick Yeast Rolls

Prep Time: 10 minutes | Cook Time: 75 minutes | Serves: 16

4 tablespoons salted butter
50g granulated sugar
240ml hot water
1 tablespoon quick-rise yeast
1 large egg
1 teaspoon salt
315g flour, divided

1. In a microwave-safe bowl, microwave butter for 30 seconds until melted. Pour 2 tablespoons of butter into a container. Add sugar, hot water, and yeast. Mix until yeast is dissolved. 2. Using a rubber spatula, mix in egg, salt, and 280g flour. Dough will be very sticky. 3. Cover bowl with plastic wrap and let rise in a warm put for 1 hour. 4. Sprinkle the remaining 30g flour on dough and turn onto a lightly floured surface. Knead 2 minutes, then cut into sixteen even pieces. 5. Preheat the air fryer to 175°C. Spray a 15cm round cake pan with cooking spray. 6. Sprinkle each roll with flour and arrange in pan. Brush with remaining melted butter. Put pan in the air fryer basket and cook them for 10 minutes until fluffy and golden on top. 7. Serve warm.
Per Serving: Calories 85; Fat 2.35g; Sodium 195mg; Carbs 13.75g; Fibre 0.5g; Sugar 13.12g; Protein 2.07g

Delicious Roasted Carrots

Prep Time: 5 minutes | Cook Time: 12 minutes | Serves: 4

455g baby carrots
2 tablespoons dry ranch seasoning
3 tablespoons salted butter, melted

1. Preheat the air fryer to 180°C. 2. Put carrots into a 15cm round baking dish. Sprinkle carrots with ranch seasoning and drizzle with butter. Gently toss to coat. 3. Put in the air fryer basket and cook them for 12 minutes, stirring twice during cooking, until carrots are tender.
Per Serving: Calories 104; Fat 5.92g; Sodium 420mg; Carbs 11.81g; Fibre 4g; Sugar 4.38g; Protein 1.11g

Delicious Garlic Bread

Prep Time: 10 minutes | Cook Time: 12 minutes | Serves: 6

130g self-rising flour
245g plain full-fat Greek yogurt
55g salted butter, softened
1 tablespoon minced garlic
115g shredded mozzarella cheese

1. Preheat the air fryer to 160°C. Cut parchment paper to fit the air fryer basket. 2. In a container, mix flour and yogurt until a sticky, soft dough forms. Let sit 5 minutes. 3. Turn dough onto a lightly floured surface. Knead dough 1 minute, then replace to prepared parchment. Press out into an 20cm round. 4. Mix Butter and garlic. Brush over dough. Sprinkle with mozzarella. 5. Put in the air fryer and cook them for 12 minutes until edges are golden and cheese is brown.
Per Serving: Calories 173; Fat 5.95g; Sodium 459mg; Carbs 19.47g; Fibre 0.9g; Sugar 3.22g; Protein 10.32g

Cheddar-Garlic Biscuits

Prep Time: 5 minutes | Cook Time: 10 minutes per batch | Serves: 10

250g plain flour
1 tablespoon baking powder
1 teaspoon salt
½ teaspoon garlic powder
170g sour cream
170g salted butter, melted, divided
100g shredded cheddar cheese

1. Preheat the air fryer to 205°C. 2. In a container, mix flour, baking powder, salt, garlic powder, sour cream, and 115g butter until well combined. Gently stir in cheddar. 3. Using your hands, form dough into ten even-sized balls. 4. Put balls in the air fryer basket, working in batches as necessary. Cook them for 10 minutes until golden and crispy on the edges. 5. Remove biscuits from the air fryer and brush with the remaining melted butter to serve.
Per Serving: Calories 199; Fat 11.36g; Sodium 334mg; Carbs 21.24g; Fibre 0.7g; Sugar 0.19g; Protein 3.44g

Crispy Tater Tots

Prep Time: 15 minutes | Cook Time: 25 minutes | Serves: 4

960g water
455g russet potatoes, peeled
½ teaspoon salt
½ teaspoon ground black pepper

1. In a large saucepan over medium-high heat, bring the water to a boil. Add potatoes and boil about 10 minutes until a fork can be easily inserted into them. Drain potatoes and let cool. 2. Preheat the air fryer to 175°C. 3. Grate potatoes into a container. Add salt and pepper and mix gently by hand. 4. Form potatoes into sixteen 1-tablespoon tater tot–shaped balls. Put tater tots in the air fryer basket and spray lightly with cooking spray. 5. Cook them for 15 minutes, shaking the air fryer basket halfway through cooking time, until crispy and brown. 6. Serve warm.
Per Serving: Calories 92; Fat 0.1g; Sodium 301mg; Carbs 21.02g; Fibre 1.6g; Sugar 0.99g; Protein 2.54g

Versatile Cauliflower Tots

Prep Time: 15 minutes | Cook Time: 12 minutes per batch | Serves: 4

1 (250g) steamer bag riced cauliflower
35g Italian bread crumbs
30g plain flour
1 large egg
75g shredded sharp Cheddar cheese
½ teaspoon salt
¼ teaspoon ground black pepper

1. Cook cauliflower according to the package directions. Let cool, then squeeze in a cheesecloth or kitchen towel to drain excess water. 2. Turn on the air fryer and preheat it to 205°C. Cut parchment paper to fit the air fryer basket. 3. In a container, mix drained cauliflower, bread crumbs, flour, egg, and cheddar. Sprinkle in salt and pepper, then mix until well combined. 4. Roll 2 tablespoons of mixture into a tot shape. Repeat to use all of the mixture. 5. Put tots on parchment in the air fryer basket, working in batches as necessary. Spritz with cooking spray. Cook them for 12 minutes, turning tots halfway through cooking time, until golden brown. 6. Serve warm.
Per Serving: Calories 345; Fat 8.14g; Sodium 1346mg; Carbs 58.81g; Fibre 2.26g; Sugar 17.25g; Protein 8.02g

Flavourful Courgette Fries

Prep Time: 5 minutes | Cook Time: 20 minutes | Serves: 4

3 large courgette, trimmed
2 teaspoons salt
2 large eggs, whisked
100g grated Parmesan cheese
110g panko bread crumbs
2 teaspoons Italian seasoning

1. Cut a courgette in half crosswise. Slice down the length of each half, then cut each new piece in half lengthwise, to make eight sticks. Repeat with the remaining courgette for a total of twenty-four sticks. 2. Spread courgette fries in a single layer on top of a paper towel and sprinkle with salt. The salt will help draw out excess moisture. Put more paper towels on top of courgette fries to absorb moisture. Let sit for 30 minutes, changing paper towels out halfway through time. 3. Preheat the air fryer to 205°C. 4. Put eggs in a medium bowl. Put Parmesan, bread crumbs, and Italian seasoning in a zippered storage bag. Dip six fries into egg, then put into storage bag and shake to coat. Remove and repeat with remaining courgette. 5. Spritz fries with cooking spray and put in the air fryer basket, working in batches as necessary. 6. Cook them for 12 minutes until crisp and brown, turning halfway through cooking time. 7. Serve and enjoy.
Per Serving: Calories 163; Fat 9.56g; Sodium 1764 mg; Carbs 9.31g; Fibre 0.6g; Sugar 0.72g; Protein 9.62g

Easy Courgette Chips

Prep Time: 10 minutes | Cook Time: 12 minutes | Serves: 2

Oil, for spraying
1 medium courgette, cut into ½cm-thick slices
50g grated Parmesan cheese
Pinch salt (optional)

1. Line the air fryer basket with parchment and spray some oil on it. 2. Put the courgette in a single layer in the air fryer basket. 3. Sprinkle the courgette with the Parmesan cheese, covering the tops of each chip. 4. Cook them at 185°C for 10 to 12 minutes, or until the cheese is dark golden brown. The courgette will crisp as it cools. 5. Sprinkle with the salt as you like.
Per Serving: Calories 166; Fat 13.78g; Sodium 645mg; Carbs 3.65g; Fibre 0.1g; Sugar 0.02g; Protein 7.25g

Crave-worthy Chicken Courgette Boats

Prep Time: 5 minutes | Cook Time: 9 minutes | Serves: 4

Oil, for spraying
2 medium courgette, cut in half lengthwise
280g shredded rotisserie or leftover chicken
75g cream cheese, softened
60ml Ranch dressing
55g shredded Cheddar cheese
2 tablespoons buffalo sauce
55g shredded mozzarella cheese

1. Preheat the air fryer to 200°C. Line the air fryer basket with parchment and spray some oil on it. 2. Scrape out the inner flesh of the courgette, leaving about ½cm all the way around, to create a boat. 3. Put the boats in the air fryer basket prepared before. 4. Cook them for 3 to 5 minutes, or until just starting to blister. 5. Mix together the chicken, cream cheese, ranch dressing, fheddar cheese, and buffalo sauce. 6. Spoon the chicken mixture into the boats, dividing evenly. Top each with mozzarella cheese. 7. Cook them for 4 minutes until the cheese is melted.
Per Serving: Calories 286; Fat 21.27g; Sodium 869mg; Carbs 6.7g; Fibre 0.5g; Sugar 4.54g; Protein17.82g

Great Southwest-Style Corn Cobs

Prep Time: 5 minutes | Cook Time: 15 minutes | Serves: 6

115g sour cream
1½ teaspoons chili powder
Juice and zest of 1 medium lime
¼ teaspoon salt
6 mini corn cobs
120g crumbled feta cheese

1. Preheat the air fryer to 175°C. 2. Mix sour cream, chili powder, lime zest and juice, and salt. 3. Brush mixture all over corn cobs and put them in the air fryer basket. Cook them for 15 minutes until corn is tender. 4. Sprinkle with cotija.
Per Serving: Calories 221; Fat 5.81g; Sodium 853mg; Carbs 41.28g; Fibre 4.8g; Sugar 0.43g; Protein 8.01g

Green Veggie Trio

Prep Time: 6 minutes | Cook Time: 9 minutes | Serves: 4

180g Broccoli florets
200g green beans
1 tablespoon olive oil
1 tablespoon lemon juice
225g frozen baby peas
2 tablespoons Honey mustard
Pinch salt
Freshly ground black pepper

1. Put the Broccoli and green beans in the air fryer basket of the air fryer. Put 2 tablespoons water in the air fryer pan. Sprinkle the vegetables with the olive oil and lemon juice, and toss. 2. Steam them at 165°C for 6 minutes, then remove the air fryer basket from the air fryer and add the peas. 3. Steam for 3 minutes or until the vegetables are hot and tender. 4. Transfer the vegetables to a serving dish and drizzle with the honey mustard and sprinkle with salt and pepper.
Per Serving: Calories 79; Fat 4.32g; Sodium 310mg; Carbs 7.91g; Fibre 3.7g; Sugar 1.85g; Protein 3.39g

Sesame Carrots

Prep Time: 5 minutes | Cook Time: 6 minutes | Serves: 4-6

455g baby carrots
1 tablespoon sesame oil
½ teaspoon dried dill
Pinch salt
Freshly ground black pepper
6 cloves garlic, peeled
3 tablespoons sesame seeds

1. Put the baby carrots in a medium bowl. Drizzle with sesame oil, add the dill, salt, and pepper, and toss to coat well. 2. Put the carrots in the air fryer basket of the air fryer. Roast them at 195°C for 8 minutes, shaking the air fryer basket once during cooking time. 3. Add the garlic to the air fryer basket. Roast them for 8 minutes, shaking the air fryer basket once during cooking time, or until the garlic and carrots are lightly browned. 4. Transfer to a serving bowl and sprinkle with the sesame seeds before serving.
Per Serving: Calories 77; Fat 4.93g; Sodium 111mg; Carbs 7.78g; Fibre 2.8g; Sugar 2.66g; Protein 1.66g

Peppers with Garlic

Prep Time: 8 minutes | Cook Time: 22 minutes | Serves: 4

1 red pepper
1 yellow pepper
1 orange pepper
1 green pepper
2 tablespoons olive oil, divided
½ teaspoon dried marjoram
Pinch salt
Freshly ground black pepper
1 head garlic

1. Slice the peppers into 2.5cm strips. 2. Toss the peppers with 1 tablespoon of the oil. Sprinkle on the marjoram, salt, and pepper, and toss again. 3. Cut off the top of the garlic head and put the cloves on an oiled square of aluminum foil. Drizzle with the remaining olive oil. Wrap the garlic in the foil. 4. Put the wrapped garlic in the air fryer and roast them at 165°C for 15 minutes, then add the peppers. Roast for 7 minutes or until the peppers are tender and the garlic is soft. Transfer the peppers to a serving dish. 5. Remove the garlic from the air fryer and unwrap the foil. When cool enough to handle, squeeze the garlic cloves out of the papery skin and mix with the peppers.
Per Serving: Calories 88; Fat 7g; Sodium 123 mg; Carbs 6.35g; Fibre 1g; Sugar 1.75g; Protein 1.25g

Wonderful Parmesan French Fries

Prep Time: 5 minutes | Cook Time: 10 minutes | Serves: 4.

230g frozen thin French fries
2 teaspoons olive oil
35g grated Parmesan cheese
½ teaspoon dried thyme
½ teaspoon dried basil
½ teaspoon salt

1. If there is any ice on the French fries, remove it. Put the French fries in the air fryer basket and drizzle with the olive oil. Toss them gently. 2. Air-fry them at 200°C for about 10 minutes, or until the fries are golden brown and hot, shaking the air fryer basket once during cooking time. 3. Immediately put the fries into a serving bowl and sprinkle with the Parmesan, thyme, basil, and salt. 4. Shake to coat and serve hot.
Per Serving: Calories 718; Fat 42.68g; Sodium 853mg; Carbs 78.1g; Fibre 11.5g; Sugar 0.01g; Protein 9.59g

Scalloped Potato Slices

Prep Time: 5 minutes | Cook Time: 20 minutes | Serves: 4

300g pre-sliced refrigerated potatoes
3 cloves garlic, minced
Pinch salt
Freshly ground black pepper
180g heavy cream

1. Layer the potatoes, garlic, salt, and pepper in a 20cm x 20cm x 4cm baking pan. Slowly pour the cream over all. 2. Bake them at 195°C for 15 minutes, until the potatoes are golden brown on top and tender. Check their state and, if needed, bake for 5 minutes until browned.
Per Serving: Calories 139; Fat 8.46g; Sodium 492 mg; Carbs 14.47g; Fibre 1.7g; Sugar 1.24g; Protein 2.18g

Golden Garlic Knots

Prep Time: 10 minutes | Cook Time: 15 minutes | Serves: 5

125g self-rising flour
245g plain full-fat Greek yogurt
80g salted butter, melted
1 teaspoon garlic powder
25g grated Parmesan cheese

1. Preheat the air fryer to 160°C. 2. In a container, mix flour and yogurt and let sit for 5 minutes. 3. Turn dough onto a lightly floured surface and gently knead about 3 minutes until it's no longer sticky. 4. Form dough into a rectangle and roll out until it measures 25cm × 15cm. Cut dough into ten 2.5cm × 15cm strips. 5. Tie each dough strip into a knot. Brush each knot with butter and sprinkle with garlic powder. 6. Put in the air fryer basket and cook for 8 minutes, turning after 6 minutes. 7. Let the dish cool for 2 minutes after cooking, sprinkle with Parmesan, and serve.
Per Serving: Calories 214; Fat 10.48g; Sodium 489mg; Carbs 23.16g; Fibre 0.7g; Sugar 3.53g; Protein 6.65g

Versatile Potato Salad

Prep Time: 5 minutes | Cook Time: 25 minutes | Serves: 4-6

900g tiny red or creamer potatoes, cut in half
1 tablespoon plus 80ml olive oil
Pinch salt

Freshly ground black pepper
1 red pepper, chopped
2 green onions, chopped
80ml lemon juice
3 tablespoons Dijon or yellow mustard

1. Put the potatoes in the air fryer basket and drizzle with 1 tablespoon of the olive oil. Sprinkle with salt and pepper. 2. Roast them at 175°C for 25 minutes, shaking twice during cooking time, until the potatoes are tender and light golden brown. 3. Put the pepper and green onions in a container. 4. Combine the remaining 80ml of olive oil, the lemon juice, and mustard, and mix well with a whisk in a small bowl. 5. When the potatoes are cooked, add them to the bowl with the peppers and top with the dressing. Toss gently to coat. 6. Let cool for 20 minutes. Stir gently again and serve or refrigerate and serve later.
Per Serving: Calories 263; Fat 16.15g; Sodium 492mg; Carbs 27.44g; Fibre 3.5g; Sugar 13.12g; Protein 3.75g

Quick Corn Casserole

Prep Time: 5 minutes | Cook Time: 15 minutes | Serves: 4

Nonstick baking spray with flour
500g frozen yellow corn
3 tablespoons flour
1 egg, beaten
60ml milk
120ml light cream
110g grated Swiss or Havarti cheese
Pinch salt
Freshly ground black pepper
2 tablespoons butter, cut in cubes

1. Spray a 15 x 5cm baking pan with nonstick spray. 2. Combine the corn, flour, egg, milk, and light cream in a medium bowl, and mix until combined. Stir in the cheese, salt, and pepper. 3. Pour this mixture into the prepared baking pan. Dot with the butter. 4. Bake them at 160°C for 15 minutes. 5. Serve warm.
Per Serving: Calories 321; Fat 19.26g; Sodium 853mg; Carbs 26.53g; Fibre 2g; Sugar 4.43g; Protein 10.62g

Tasty Roasted Sweet Potatoes

Prep Time: 5 minutes | Cook Time: 25 minutes | Serves: 4

2 sweet potatoes, peeled and cut into 2.5cm cubes
1 tablespoon olive oil
Pinch salt
Freshly ground black pepper
½ teaspoon dried thyme
½ teaspoon dried marjoram
25cm grated Parmesan cheese

1. Put the sweet potato cubes in the air fryer basket and drizzle with the olive oil, gently toss them. Sprinkle with the salt, pepper, thyme, and marjoram, and toss again. 2. Roast them at 165°C for 20 minutes, shaking the air fryer basket once during cooking time. 3. Remove the air fryer basket from the air fryer and shake the potatoes again. Sprinkle evenly with the Parmesan cheese and return to the air fryer. 4. Roast them for 5 minutes or until the potatoes are tender. 5. Serve warm.
Per Serving: Calories 57 ; Fat 5.17g; Sodium 210mg; Carbs 0.94g; Fibre 0g; Sugar 0.01g; Protein 1.86g

Classic Parmesan French Fries

Prep Time: 5 minutes | Cook Time: 45 minutes | Serves: 4

3 large russet potatoes, peeled, trimmed, and sliced into 1 × 10cm sticks
2½ tablespoons olive oil, divided
2 teaspoons minced garlic
½ teaspoon salt
¼ teaspoon ground black pepper
1 teaspoon dried parsley
25g grated Parmesan cheese

1. Put potato sticks in a container of cold water and let soak for 30 minutes. 2. Preheat the air fryer to 175°C. 3. Drain potatoes and gently pat dry. Put in a large, dry bowl. 4. Pour 2 tablespoons oil over potatoes; add garlic, salt, and pepper, then toss to fully coat. 5. Put fries in the air fryer basket and cook for 15 minutes, shaking the air fryer basket twice during cooking, until fries are golden and crispy on the edges. 6. Put fries into a clean medium bowl and drizzle with remaining ½ tablespoon oil. Sprinkle parsley and Parmesan over fries and toss to coat.
Per Serving: Calories 308; Fat 8.73g; Sodium 853mg; Carbs 51.63g; Fibre 3.7g; Sugar 1.88g; Protein 7.85g

Crisp Brussels Sprouts

Prep Time: 8 minutes | Cook Time: 20 minutes | Serves: 4

455g fresh Brussels Sprouts
1 tablespoon olive oil
½ teaspoon salt
⅛ teaspoon pepper
25g grated Parmesan cheese

1. Trim the bottoms from the brussels sprouts and pull off any discoloured leaves. Toss with the olive oil, salt, and pepper, and put in the air fryer basket. 2. Roast them at 165°C for 20 minutes, shaking the air fryer basket twice during cooking time. 3. Transfer the brussels sprouts to a serving dish and toss with the Parmesan cheese.
Per Serving: Calories 105; Fat 5.46g; Sodium 432mg; Carbs 11.16g; Fibre4.3g; Sugar 2.57g; Protein 5.64g

Butter Flaky Biscuits

Prep Time: 10 minutes | Cook Time: 15 minutes | Serves: 8

55g salted butter
250g self-rising flour
¼ teaspoon salt
65ml whole milk

1. Preheat the air fryer to 160°C. Cut parchment paper to fit the air fryer basket. 2. Put butter in the freezer 10 minutes. In a container, mix flour and salt. 3. Grate butter into bowl and use a wooden spoon to evenly distribute. Add milk and stir until a soft dough forms. 4. Turn dough onto a lightly floured surface. Gently press and flatten dough until mostly smooth and uniform. Gently roll into an 20cm × 25cm rectangle. Use a sharp knife dusted in flour to cut dough into eight squares. 5. Put biscuits on parchment paper in the air fryer basket, working in batches as necessary, and cook them for 15 minutes until golden brown on the top and edges and feel firm to the touch. 6. Let the dish cool 5 minutes before serving.
Per Serving: Calories 163; Fat 4.76g; Sodium 853mg; Carbs 25.83g; Fibre 0.8g; Sugar 2.7g; Protein 3.74g

Crispy Sweet Potato Fries

Prep Time: 35 minutes | Cook Time: 10 minutes | Serves: 4

2 large sweet potatoes, trimmed and sliced into ½cm × 10cm sticks
1 tablespoon olive oil
½ teaspoon salt

1. Put sweet potato sticks in a container of cold water and let soak for 30 minutes. 2. Preheat the air fryer to 195°C. 3. Drain potatoes and gently pat dry. Put in a large, dry bowl. Drizzle with oil and sprinkle with salt, then toss to fully coat. 4. Put fries in the air fryer basket and cook for 10 minutes, shaking the air fryer basket three times during cooking, until fries are tender and golden brown. 5. Serve warm.
Per Serving: Calories 111; Fat 3.51g; Sodium 323mg; Carbs 18.64g; Fibre 3g; Sugar 5.83g; Protein 1.81g

Perfect Potato Wedges

Prep Time: 10 minutes | Cook Time: 20 minutes | Serves: 4

1.4L water
4 large russet potatoes, sliced into wedges
2 teaspoons seasoned salt
120ml whole milk
60g all-purpose flour

1. In a large saucepan over medium-high heat, bring water to a boil. 2. Carefully put potato wedges into boiling water and cook 5 minutes. 3. Preheat the air fryer to 205°C. 4. Drain potatoes into a colander, then rinse under cold running water 1 minute until they feel cool to the touch. 5. Put potatoes in a container and sprinkle with seasoned salt. Pour milk into bowl, then toss wedges to coat. 6. Put flour on a large plate. Gently dredge each potato wedge in flour on both sides to lightly coat. 7. Put wedges in the air fryer basket and spritz both sides with cooking spray. Cook them for 15 minutes, turning after 10 minutes, until wedges are golden brown.
Per Serving: Calories 376; Fat 1.39g; Sodium 1202mg; Carbs 82.54g; Fibre 5.2g; Sugar 6.25g; Protein 10.42g

Chapter 3 Snack and Starter Recipes

Apple Chips with Cinnamon

Prep time: 10 minutes | Cook time: 32 minutes | Serves: 4

Oil, for spraying
2 Red Delicious or Honeycrisp apples
¼ teaspoon ground cinnamon, divided

1. Prepare the air fryer basket by lining it with parchment and spray lightly with oil. 2. Trim the uneven ends off the apples. Cut the apples into very thin slices with a mandoline on the thinnest setting. Discard the cores. 3. Place half of the apple slices in a single layer in the prepared basket and sprinkle with half of the cinnamon. 4. Place a metal air fryer trivet on top of the apples to keep them from flying around while they are cooking. 5. Cook at 150°C for 16 minutes, flipping every 5 minutes to ensure even cooking. Repeat with the remaining apple slices and cinnamon. 6. Let cool to room temperature before serving. The chips will firm up as they cool.
Per Serving: Calories 63; Fat 0.2g; Sodium 1mg; Carbs 15g; Fibre 2.5g; Sugar 11g; Protein 0.3g

Ranch Oyster Crackers

Prep time: 3 minutes | Cook time: 12 minutes | Serves: 6

Oil, for spraying
60ml olive oil
2 teaspoons dry ranch seasoning
1 teaspoon chili powder
½ teaspoon dried dill
½ teaspoon granulated garlic
½ teaspoon salt
1 (225g) bag oyster crackers

1. Preheat the air fryer to 160°C. Prepare the air fryer basket by lining it with parchment and spray lightly with oil. 2. Mix the olive oil, ranch seasoning, chili powder, dill, garlic, and salt in a large bowl. Add the crackers and toss until evenly coated. 3. Place the mixture in the prepared basket. 4. Cook for 10 to 12 minutes, shaking or stirring every 3 to 4 minutes, or until crisp and golden brown.
Per Serving: Calories 263; Fat 12.8g; Sodium 676mg; Carbs 32.5g; Fibre 1.5g; Sugar 0.7g; Protein 4.2g

Crispy Potato Chips

Prep time: 35 minutes | Cook time: 27 minutes | Serves: 4

Oil, for spraying
4 medium yellow potatoes
1 tablespoon oil
⅛ to ¼ teaspoon fine sea salt

1. Prepare the air fryer basket by lining it with parchment and spray lightly with oil. 2. Then cut the potatoes into very thin slices with a mandoline. 3. Place the slices in a bowl of cold water and let soak for about 20 minutes. 4. Drain the potatoes, transfer them to a plate lined with paper towels, and pat dry. 5. Drizzle the oil over the potatoes, sprinkle with the salt, and toss to combine. Transfer to the prepared basket. 6. Cook at 95°C for 20 minutes. Toss the chips, increase the heat to 205°C, and cook for another 5 to 7 minutes, until crispy.
Per Serving: Calories 314; Fat 3.7g; Sodium 100mg; Carbs 64.5g; Fibre 8.1g; Sugar 2.9g; Protein 7.5g

Crusted Pickle Chips

Prep time: 1 hour 20 minutes | Cook time: 12 minutes | Serves: 4

Oil, for spraying
310g sliced dill or sweet pickles, drained
240ml buttermilk
250g plain flour
2 large eggs, beaten
210g panko bread crumbs
¼ teaspoon salt

1. Prepare the air fryer basket by lining it with parchment and spray lightly with oil. 2. In a shallow bowl, combine the pickles and buttermilk and let soak for at least 1 hour, then drain. 3. Place the bread crumbs, flour, and beaten eggs in separate bowls. 4. Coat each pickle chip lightly in the flour, dip in the eggs, and dredge in the bread crumbs. Be sure each one is evenly coated. 5. Place the pickle chips in the prepared basket, sprinkle with the salt, and spray lightly with oil. Work in batches as needed. 6. Cook at 200°C for 5 minutes, flip, and cook for another 5 to 7 minutes, or until crispy. Serve hot.
Per Serving: Calories 335; Fat 4.2g; Sodium 980mg; Carbs 61.5g; Fibre 3g; Sugar 5g; Protein 11.8g

Spicy Cumin Chickpeas

Prep time: 5 minutes | Cook time: 17 minutes | Serves: 3

Oil, for spraying
1 (390g) can chickpeas, drained
1 teaspoon chili powder
½ teaspoon ground cumin
½ teaspoon salt
½ teaspoon granulated garlic
2 teaspoons lime juice

1. Prepare the air fryer basket by lining it with parchment and spray lightly with oil. Place the chickpeas in the prepared basket. 2. Cook at 200°C for 17 minutes, shaking or stirring the chickpeas and spraying lightly with oil every 5 to 7 minutes. 3. Mix the chili powder, garlic, cumin, and salt in a small bowl. 4. When there is 2 to 3 minutes remained, sprinkle half of the seasoning mix over the chickpeas. Finish cooking. 5. Place the chickpeas to a medium bowl and toss with the remaining seasoning mix and the lime juice. Serve immediately.
Per Serving: Calories 209; Fat 4.3g; Sodium 774mg; Carbs 34g; Fibre 9.7g; Sugar 6g; Protein 10.6g

Garlic Croutons with Parmesan

Prep time: 3 minutes | Cook time: 12 minutes | Serves: 4

Oil, for spraying
160g cubed French bread
1 tablespoon grated Parmesan cheese
3 tablespoons olive oil
1 tablespoon granulated garlic
½ teaspoon unsalted salt

1. Prepare the air fryer basket by lining it with parchment and spray lightly with oil. 2. Mix the bread, Parmesan cheese, olive oil, garlic, and salt in a large bowl, tossing with your hands to evenly distribute the seasonings. Transfer the coated bread cubes to the prepared basket. 3. Cook at 175°C for 10 to 12 minutes, stirring once after 5 minutes, or until crisp and golden brown.
Per Serving: Calories 195; Fat 12g; Sodium 195mg; Carbs 18.2g; Fibre 1g; Sugar 2g; Protein 3.6g

Stuffed Jalapeño Poppers

Prep time: 10 minutes | Cook time: 20 minutes | Serves: 4

Oil, for spraying
200g cream cheese
75g gluten-free bread crumbs, divided
2 tablespoons chopped fresh
parsley
½ teaspoon granulated garlic
½ teaspoon salt
10 jalapeño peppers, halved and seeded

1. Prepare the air fryer basket by lining it with parchment and spray lightly with oil. 2. Mix the cream cheese, half of the bread crumbs, the parsley, garlic, and salt in a medium bowl. 3. Fill the jalapeño halves with the mixture. Gently press the stuffed jalapeños in the remaining bread crumbs. 4. Place the stuffed jalapeños in the prepared basket. 5. Cook at 185°C for 20 minutes, or until the cheese is melted and the bread crumbs are crisp and golden brown.
Per Serving: Calories 259; Fat 17.5g; Sodium 688mg; Carbs 19g; Fibre 2g; Sugar 4.7g; Protein 7g

Crusted Mozzarella Balls

Prep time: 1 hour 50 minutes | Cook time: 5 minutes | Serves: 3 to 4

1 (200g) package mini mozzarella balls or 4 to 5 mozzarella cheese sticks cut into bite-size pieces
1 large egg
25g bread crumbs
30g panko bread crumbs
½ teaspoon onion powder
½ teaspoon garlic powder
½ teaspoon salt
30g plain flour
Oil, for spraying

1. Line a baking sheet with parchment paper. 2. Put the mozzarella balls in a zip-top plastic bag, seal, and place in the freezer for at least 30 minutes. 3. Whisk the egg in a suitable bowl and set aside. 4. In another shallow bowl, mix together the bread crumbs, panko bread crumbs, onion powder, garlic powder, and salt. 5. Place the frozen mozzarella balls and the flour in another zip-top plastic bag, seal, and shake well to coat the balls with flour. 6. Dip each mozzarella ball in the egg, then dredge in the bread crumb mixture. Transfer to the prepared baking sheet. 7. Place the baking sheet in the freezer for at least 1 hour. 8. Heat the air fryer to 185°C before cooking. Prepare the air fryer basket by lining it with parchment and spray lightly with oil. 9. Transfer the mozzarella balls to the prepared basket. Work in batches as needed. Spray lightly with oil. 10. Cook until golden brown and crispy, for about 5 minutes.
Per Serving: Calories 265; Fat 11.8g; Sodium 941mg; Carbs 28g; Fibre 1.6g; Sugar 2.2g; Protein 11.3g

Mayo Artichoke Hearts

Prep time: 10 minutes | Cook time: 12 minutes | Serves: 10

Oil, for spraying
3 (100g) cans quartered artichokes, drained and patted dry
120g mayonnaise

110g panko bread crumbs
35g grated Parmesan cheese
Salt
Freshly ground black pepper

1. Prepare the air fryer basket by lining it with parchment and spray lightly with oil. 2. Place the artichokes on a plate. Put the mayonnaise and bread crumbs in separate bowls. 3. Working one at a time, dredge each artichoke piece in the mayonnaise, then in the bread crumbs to cover. 4. Place the artichokes in the prepared basket. Work in batches as needed. 5. Cook at 185°C for 10 to 12 minutes, or until crispy and golden brown. 6. Sprinkle with the Parmesan cheese and season with salt and black pepper. Serve immediately.
Per Serving: Calories 158; Fat 5.7g; Sodium 303mg; Carbs 22.8g; Fibre 11g; Sugar 2g; Protein 6.5g

Awesome Cheese Wontons

Prep time: 15 minutes | Cook time: 6 minutes | Serves: 5

Oil, for spraying
20 wonton wrappers

100g cream cheese

1. Prepare the air fryer basket by lining it with parchment and spray lightly with oil. 2. Pour some water in a small bowl. 3. Arrange a wonton wrapper and place 1 teaspoon of cream cheese in the center. 4. Dip your finger in the water and moisten the edge of the wonton wrapper. Fold over the opposite corners to make a triangle and press the edges together. 5. Pinch the corners of the triangle together to form a classic wonton shape. Place the wonton in the prepared basket. Repeat with the remaining wrappers and cream cheese. You may need to work in batches, depending on the size of your air fryer. 6. Cook at 205°C for 6 minutes, or until golden brown around the edges.
Per Serving: Calories 439; Fat 8.4g; Sodium 831mg; Carbs 75g; Fibre 2.3g; Sugar 0.8g; Protein 14g

Tasty Pot Stickers

Prep Time: 20 minutes | Cook Time: 10 minutes | Serves: 10

45g finely chopped cabbage
35g finely chopped red pepper
2 green onions, finely chopped
1 egg, beaten
2 tablespoons cocktail sauce

2 teaspoons low-sodium soy sauce
30 wonton wrappers
3 tablespoons water, plus more for brushing the wrappers

1. Mix the cabbage, pepper, green onions, egg, cocktail sauce, and soy sauce in a bowl. 2. Place 1 teaspoon of the mixture in the centre of one wonton wrapper, fold the wrapper in half to cover the filling, and then dampen the edges with water and seal well. 3. You can also crimp the edges with your fingers and brush them with water. 4. Add 3 tablespoons of water to the suitable pan under the air fryer basket, transfer the wontons to the basket, and Steam the wontons in 2 batches at 180°C for 9 to 10 minutes. 5. Serve warm.
Per Serving: Calories 293; Fat 1.94g; Sodium 617mg; Carbs 57.16g; Fibre 2.2g; Sugar 0.95g; Protein 10.32g

Special Beef-Mango Skewers

Prep Time: 10 minutes | Cook Time: 7 minutes | Serves: 4

340g beef sirloin tip, cut into 2.5cm cubes
2 tablespoons balsamic vinegar
1 tablespoon olive oil
1 tablespoon honey

½ teaspoon dried marjoram
Pinch salt
Freshly ground black pepper
1 mango

1. Mix the beef cubes with balsamic vinegar, olive oil, honey, marjoram, salt, and pepper in a medium bowl, and then let them marinate. 2. Cut the mango skin off, carefully cut around the oval pit to remove the flesh, then cut the mango flesh into 2.5cm cubes. 3. Alternatively thread metal skewers, three beef cubes and two mango cubes. 4. Place the skewers in the air fryer basket, and grill them at 200°C for 4 to 7 minutes until the beef cubes are browned and reach an internal temperature of 60°C. 5. Serve hot.
Per Serving: Calories 213; Fat 7.28g; Sodium 88mg; Carbs 18.33g; Fibre 1.4g; Sugar 16.98g; Protein 18.91g

Curried Sweet Potato Fries

Prep Time: 5 minutes | Cook Time: 12 minutes | Serves: 4

120g sour cream
135g mango chutney
3 teaspoons curry powder, divided

230g frozen sweet potato fries
1 tablespoon olive oil
Pinch salt
Freshly ground black pepper

1. Mix the sour cream, chutney, and 1½ teaspoons of curry powder in a small bowl. Set aside for later. 2. Place the sweet potatoes in a medium bowl, drizzle them with the olive oil, and sprinkle them with the remaining 1½ teaspoons curry powder, salt, and pepper, then transfer them to the air fryer basket. 3. Bake the potatoes at 200°C for 8 to 12 minutes until they are crisp and golden brown, tossing them halfway through. 4. Enjoy the sweet potatoes with the chutney dip.
Per Serving: Calories 255; Fat 7.03g; Sodium 74mg; Carbs 45.09g; Fibre 4.1g; Sugar 2.92g; Protein 4.4g

Kale Chips with Yogurt Sauce

Prep Time: 10 minutes | Cook Time: 5 minutes | Serves: 4

240g Greek yogurt
3 tablespoons lemon juice
2 tablespoons honey mustard
½ teaspoon dried oregano

1 bunch curly kale
2 tablespoons olive oil
½ teaspoon salt
⅛ teaspoon pepper

1. Combine the yogurt, lemon juice, honey mustard, and oregano in a small bowl. 2. Remove the stems and ribs from the kale, and cut the leaves into 5 – 8cm pieces. 3. Coat the kale with olive oil, salt, and pepper. 4. Place the coated kale in the air fryer basket, and air fry them at 200°C for 5 minutes until they are crisp, tossing them halfway through. 5. Serve the kale with the yogurt sauce.
Per Serving: Calories 113; Fat 9.18g; Sodium 411mg; Carbs 5.72g; Fibre 1g; Sugar 3.66g; Protein 3.18g

Artichoke Triangles

Prep Time: 15 minutes | Cook Time: 9 minutes | Serves: 6

1 egg white
55g minced drained artichoke hearts
3 tablespoons grated mozzarella cheese

½ teaspoon dried thyme
6 sheets frozen puff pastry, thawed
2 tablespoons melted butter

1. Combine the ricotta cheese, egg white, artichoke hearts, mozzarella cheese, and thyme in a small bowl. 2. Cover the pastry with a damp kitchen towel before using to avoid they dry out. 3. Place one sheet on the work surface at a time, and cut one into thirds lengthwise. 4. Put about 1½ teaspoons of the filling on each strip at the base, fold the bottom right-hand tip of puff pastry over the filling to meet the other side in a triangle, then continue folding in a triangle. 5. Brush each triangle with butter to seal the edges. Do the same with the remaining pastry and filling. 6. Bake the triangles at 205°C for 3 to 4 minutes until they are golden brown, you can bake them in 3 batches. 7. Serve warm.
Per Serving: Calories 121; Fat 6.64g; Sodium 231mg; Carbs 11.82g; Fibre 1.2g; Sugar 0.73g; Protein 3.51g

Homemade Arancini

Prep Time: 15 minutes | Cook Time: 22 minutes | Serves: 6

400g cooked and cooled rice or leftover risotto
2 eggs, beaten
150g panko bread crumbs, divided

50g grated Parmesan cheese
2 tablespoons minced fresh basil
16 1.5-cm cubes mozzarella cheese
2 tablespoons olive oil

1. Combine the rice, eggs, 50g of the bread crumbs, Parmesan cheese, and basil in a medium bowl, and then make them into sixteen 3.5-cm balls. 2. Make a hole in each balls, and insert a mozzarella cube. Form the rice mixture firmly around the cheese. 3. Mix the remaining bread crumbs with olive oil in another bowl, and then coat the rice balls with them. 4. Air Fry the rice balls at 205°C for 8 to 11 minutes until golden brown, you can cook them in batches. 5. Serve warm.
Per Serving: Calories 331; Fat 17.85g; Sodium 391mg; Carbs 40.36g; Fibre 9.5g; Sugar 2.13g; Protein 13.94g

Pesto Bruschetta

Prep Time: 10 minutes | Cook Time: 8 minutes | Serves: 4

8 slices French bread, 1cm thick	115g basil pesto
2 tablespoons softened butter	155g chopped grape tomatoes
120g shredded mozzarella cheese	2 green onions, thinly sliced

1. Spread the butter on the bread slices, place the bread slices in the air fryer basket with butter-side up, and then bake them at 175°C for 3 to 5 minutes until they are light golden brown. 2. When the time is up, top each bread slice with some cheese, and then resume baking them for 1 to 3 minutes until the cheese melts. 3. Mix the tomatoes, green onions, and pesto in a small bowl. 4. After baking, transfer the bread slices to the serving plate, and top them with the pesto mixture. Enjoy.
Per Serving: Calories 304; Fat 7.11g; Sodium 675mg; Carbs 44.17g; Fibre 2.8g; Sugar 8.59g; Protein 16.98g

Ranch Chicken French Bread Pizza

Prep time: 10 minutes | Cook time: 12 minutes | Serves: 8

Oil, for spraying	100g cream cheese
1 loaf French bread, cut in half and split lengthwise	3 tablespoons buffalo sauce, and more for serving
4 tablespoons unsalted butter, melted	2 tablespoons dry ranch seasoning
280g shredded or diced rotisserie chicken	240g shredded mozzarella cheese
	80g crumbled blue cheese

1. Prepare the air fryer basket by lining it with parchment and spray lightly with oil. 2. Brush the cut sides of the bread with the melted butter. Place the bread in the prepared basket. You may need to work in batches, depending on the size of your air fryer. 3. Cook at 205°C for 5 to 7 minutes, or until the bread is toasted. 4. Mix the chicken, cream cheese, buffalo sauce, and ranch seasoning in a medium bowl. 5. Divide the mixture equally among the toasted bread and spread in an even layer. 6. Top with the mozzarella cheese and blue cheese and cook for another 3 to 5 minutes, or until the cheese is melted. 7. Set aside and cool for 2 to 3 minutes before cutting into 5cm slices. Serve with additional buffalo sauce for drizzling.
Per Serving: Calories 1093; Fat 57g; Sodium 1509mg; Carbs 74.8g; Fibre 3.5g; Sugar 7.5g; Protein 67g

Savory Tater Tot Kebabs

Prep time: 15 minutes | Cook time: 20 minutes | Serves: 6

Oil, for spraying	½ teaspoon granulated garlic
1 (500g) bag frozen tater tots	2 tablespoons chopped fresh chives, for garnish
50g shredded cheddar cheese	
55g bacon bits	

1. Preheat the air fryer to 205°C. Prepare the air fryer basket lining it with parchment and spray lightly with oil. 2. Place the tater tots in the prepared basket. They should cover the bottom with a few extra on top. Work in batches as needed. 3. Cook for 15 minutes, shaking after 7 or 8 minutes. 4. Let cool to room temperature. Thread 5 or 6 tots on each skewer. 5. Place the skewers in the air fryer, sprinkle with the cheese, bacon bits, and garlic, and cook until just golden brown and crispy, for another 5 minutes. 6. Sprinkle with the chives and serve.
Per Serving: Calories 175; Fat 8.2g; Sodium 272mg; Carbs 18.6g; Fibre 1g; Sugar 14.5g; Protein 7.5g

Worcestershire Cheese Bread Bowl

Prep time: 10 minutes | Cook time: 28 minutes | Serves: 6

1 (15cm) round loaf bread, unsliced	60ml whole milk
2 tablespoons olive oil	100g shredded cheese
150g cream cheese, at room temperature	100g shredded provolone cheese
120g mayonnaise	25g grated Parmesan cheese
	2 spring onions, sliced
	1 teaspoon Worcestershire sauce

1. Cut off the top 2.5cm of the bread. Use a serrated bread knife to cut around the inside of the loaf, leaving about a 2.5cm shell. Do not cut through the bottom. Cut the pieces of bread and the top of the loaf into 2.5cm cubes and drizzle with the olive oil. 2. Heat the air fryer to 190°C before cooking. Put the bread cubes in the air fryer basket and bake for 5 to 8 minutes, shaking halfway through cooking time, until toasted. Place in a serving bowl. Keep the air fryer set to 190°C.

3. Meanwhile, beat the cream cheese with the mayonnaise and milk until smooth. Stir in the shredded cheese, provolone, and Parmesan cheeses, spring onions, and Worcestershire sauce. 4. Divide the cheese mixture into the centre of the bread shell. Put the filled bread in the air fryer basket and place the basket in the air fryer. 5. Bake the cheese bread at 190°C for 15 to 20 minutes until the cheese is melted and starts to brown on top, stirring the mixture halfway through cooking time. Serve with the toasted bread and bread sticks, if desired.
Per Serving: Calories 364; Fat 32g; Sodium 674mg; Carbs 4.6g; Fibre 0.4g; Sugar 3g; Protein 15g

Fried Tortellini with Mayonnaise

Prep Time: 10 minutes | Cook Time: 20 minutes | Serves: 4

180g mayonnaise	½ teaspoon dried oregano
2 tablespoons mustard	150g bread crumbs
1 egg	2 tablespoons olive oil
65g flour	300g frozen cheese tortellini

1. Combine the mayonnaise and mustard in a small bowl. Set aside. 2. Beat the egg in another bowl, and mix the flour and oregano in the third bowl, and then combine the bread crumbs with olive oil in the fourth bowl. 3. Dip the tortellini into the egg, then into the flour and into the egg again, and coat them with the bread crumbs. 4. Air Fry them at 195°C for 10 minutes until they are crisp and golden brown on the outside, shaking the basket halfway through. 5. Serve the tortellini with the mayonnaise.
Per Serving: Calories 500; Fat 28.22g; Sodium 743mg; Carbs 45.96g; Fibre 2.7g; Sugar 1.92g; Protein 15.29g

Breaded Prawn Toast

Prep Time: 15 minutes | Cook Time: 12 minutes | Serves: 6

3 slices firm white bread	2 tablespoons corn flour
95g finely chopped peeled and deveined raw prawn	¼ teaspoon ground ginger
1 egg white	Pinch salt
2 cloves garlic, minced	Freshly ground black pepper
	2 tablespoons olive oil

1. Cut the crusts from the bread, and crumble the crusts to make bread crumbs. Set aside. 2. Mix the prawn with the egg white, garlic, corn flour, ginger, salt, and pepper in a bowl. 3. Spread the prawn mixture on the bread to the edges, and then cut each slice into 4 strips. 4. Mix the bread crumbs with olive oil, and coat the prawn with them. 5. Place the prawn mixture in the air fryer basket in a single layer, and Air Fry them at 175°C for 3 to 6 minutes until crisp and golden brown. 6. Serve hot.
Per Serving: Calories 102; Fat 5.02g; Sodium 227mg; Carbs 9.02g; Fibre 1.3g; Sugar 0.75g; Protein 5.09g

Simple Falafel with Garlic-Yogurt Sauce

Prep time: 5 minutes| Cook time: 15 minutes| Serves: 4

For the Falafel

1 (375g) can chickpeas, drained and rinsed	½ tablespoon ground cumin
10g fresh parsley	1 tablespoon whole-wheat flour
2 garlic cloves, minced	Salt

For the Garlic-Yogurt Sauce

240g nonfat plain Greek yogurt	1 tablespoon chopped fresh dill
1 garlic clove, minced	2 tablespoons lemon juice

To make the falafel: 1. Preheat the air fryer to 180°C. 2. Put the chickpeas into a food processor. Pulse until mostly chopped, then add the parsley, garlic, and cumin and pulse for another 1 to 2 minutes, or until the ingredients are combined and turning into a dough. 3. Add the flour. Pulse a few more times until combined. The dough will have texture, but the chickpeas should be pulsed into small bits. 4. Using clean hands, roll the dough into 8 balls of equal size, then pat the balls down a bit so they are about 1cm thick disks. 5. Spray the basket of the air fryer with olive oil cooking spray, then place the falafel patties in the basket in a single layer, making sure they don't touch each other. 6. Fry in the air fryer at 180°C for 15 minutes.
To make the garlic-yogurt sauce: 1. In a small bowl, combine the yogurt, garlic, dill, and lemon juice. 2. Once the falafel is done cooking and nicely browned on all sides, remove them from the air fryer and season with salt.
Serve hot with a side of dipping sauce.
Per Serving: Calories 132; Fat 2.3g; Sodium 154mg; Carbs 20.2g; Fibre 5g; Sugar 4g; Protein 9.3g

Wrapped Sausages

Prep time: 15 minutes | Cook time: 12 minutes | Serves: 7

Oil, for spraying
1 (300g) package thick-cut bacon
1 (300g) package cocktail sausages
2 teaspoons chili powder
2 tablespoons maple syrup
2 tablespoons packed light brown sugar

1. Prepare the air fryer basket by lining it with parchment and spray lightly with oil. (The parchment will catch drippings. If your air fryer has an outer tray, you can also line it with foil.) 2. Cut each bacon strip lengthwise into thirds and wrap a piece around each sausage, securing with a toothpick. 3. Place the wrapped sausages in the prepared basket in a single layer and sprinkle with the chili powder. Work in batches as needed. Brush the sausages with the maple syrup and sprinkle with the brown sugar. 4. Cook at 170°C for 6 minutes, flip, and cook for another 6 minutes, or until the bacon is crisp. 5. Remove the toothpicks and serve immediately.
Per Serving: Calories 476; Fat 18g; Sodium 924mg; Carbs 72.6g; Fibre 2.4g; Sugar 64.5g; Protein 12.5g

Thai-style Cauliflower Bites

Prep time: 15 minutes | Cook time: 15 minutes | Serves: 6

Oil, for spraying
1 medium head cauliflower, cut into florets
2 tablespoons olive oil
2 teaspoons granulated garlic
¼ teaspoon smoked paprika
120ml–180ml sweet chili sauce
¼ teaspoon sesame seeds

1. Preheat the air fryer to 205°C. Prepare the air fryer basket by lining it with parchment and spraying lightly with oil. 2. Add the cauliflower in a large bowl and drizzle with olive oil, tossing until fully coated. Sprinkle with the garlic and paprika and toss again until coated. 3. Place the cauliflower in the prepared basket, taking care not to overlap the pieces. Work in batches as needed. 4. Cook for 15 minutes, or until the cauliflowers are browned and crispy, flipping every 5 minutes. 5. Transfer the cauliflowers to a large serving bowl and toss with the sweet chili sauce and sesame seeds before serving.
Per Serving: Calories 77; Fat 4.8g; Sodium 318mg; Carbs 7g; Fibre 2.3g; Sugar 3.3g; Protein 1.5g

Fried Crusted Cheese Ravioli

Prep time: 10 minutes | Cook time: 5 minutes | Serves: 8

Oil, for spraying
2 large eggs
105g panko bread crumbs
25g grated Parmesan cheese
1 teaspoon onion powder
1 teaspoon granulated garlic
½ teaspoon dry Italian dressing mix
½ teaspoon salt
1 (500g) package refrigerated cheese ravioli

1. Preheat the air fryer to 205°C. Prepare the air fryer basket by lining it with parchment and spray lightly with oil. 2. Whisk the eggs in a suitable bowl and set aside. 3. In another medium bowl, mix together the bread crumbs, Parmesan cheese, onion powder, garlic, Italian dressing mix, and salt. 4. Add the ravioli to the eggs and toss gently to coat. 5. Transfer the ravioli to the bread crumb mixture and toss until evenly coated. 6. Arrange the coated ravioli in a single layer in the prepared basket. You may need to work in batches, depending on the size of your air fryer. Spray lightly with oil. 7. Cook the ravioli in your air fryer for 3 to 5 minutes, or until hot and crispy.
Per Serving: Calories 103; Fat 3.4g; Sodium 476mg; Carbs 13.4g; Fibre 1.2g; Sugar 3.2g; Protein 4.8g

Apricots and Cheese in Blankets

Prep time: 20 minutes | Cook time: 24 minutes | Serves: 6

6 dried apricots, halved lengthwise
4 tablespoons (50g) cream cheese
½ sheet frozen puff pastry,
thawed
4 tablespoons honey mustard
2 tablespoons butter, melted

1. Stuff each apricot half with a teaspoon of cream cheese and set aside. 2. Roll out the puff pastry until it is 15 by 30cm. Cut in half lengthwise for two 8-by-30-cm rectangles. Cut each rectangle into six 8cm strips for a total of 12 puff pastry strips. 3. Spread 1 teaspoon of honey mustard onto each strip. Place a filled apricot on each strip and roll up the pastry, pinching the seam closed but leaving the ends open.

4. Place 6 filled pastries in the air fryer basket. Then brush the top of each with some of the melted butter. 5. Set or preheat the air fryer to 190°C. Put the basket in the air fryer. Bake the pastries for 8 to 12 minutes or until the pastry is golden brown. 6. Repeat with the other six pastries, then serve.
Per Serving: Calories 190; Fat 16.5g; Sodium 320mg; Carbs 8g; Fibre 1g; Sugar 5.2g; Protein 3.6g

Sesame Mushroom Toast

Prep time: 20 minutes| Cook time: 8 minutes per batch| Serves: 6

2 teaspoons olive oil
2 (100g) cans sliced mushrooms, drained
3 spring onions, sliced
1 tablespoon grated fresh ginger
1 tablespoon soy sauce
3 slices whole-wheat bread
2 tablespoons sesame seeds

1. Heat the olive oil in a medium saucepan over medium heat. Add the mushrooms and cook, stirring often, for 3 to 4 minutes or until the mushrooms are dry. 2. Add the spring onions, ginger, and soy sauce and cook for another 3 minutes or until the mushrooms have absorbed the soy sauce. 3. Transfer the mixture to a blender or food processor and process until it forms a paste. 4. Cut the bread slices into fourths, making triangles. Spread the mushroom mixture onto the bread triangles, dividing evenly, then sprinkle with the sesame seeds. 5. Heat the air fryer to 190°C before cooking. Working in batches, place the triangles in the air fryer basket in a single layer. Fry for 7 to 8 minutes or until the toast is crisp. Repeat with the remaining triangles. Serve.
Per Serving: Calories 90; Fat 4.3g; Sodium 117mg; Carbs 9.8g; Fibre 2g; Sugar 2.2g; Protein 4g

Focaccia Bites with Grapes

Prep time: 15 minutes| Cook time: 28 minutes| Serves: 4

125g plain flour
½ teaspoon sea salt
1½ teaspoons baking powder
80ml whole milk
4 tablespoons olive oil, divided
100g halved red grapes
2 teaspoons fresh thyme

1. In a medium bowl, combine the flour, salt, and baking powder and mix well. 2. Add the milk and 3 tablespoons of the olive oil and stir just until a dough forms. Divide the dough into two balls. 3. Cut two pieces of parchment paper to fit in your air fryer basket. Press the dough onto each piece of paper, spreading the dough so it almost fills the paper. 4. Dimple the dough with your fingers. Drizzle both with the remaining 1 tablespoon olive oil. 5. Put the grapes on the dough, cut-side down, and press down gently. Sprinkle with the thyme. Place one of the parchment pieces with dough in the air fryer basket. 6. Set or preheat the air fryer to 175°C. Put the basket in the air fryer and bake for 11 to 14 minutes or until the bread is golden brown. Remove the focaccia and repeat with the remaining dough. 7. Cut into squares and serve.
Per Serving: Calories 271; Fat 14.5g; Sodium 303mg; Carbs 32g; Fibre 1.2g; Sugar 6.6g; Protein 4g

Stuffed Mushrooms

Prep time: 5 minutes| Cook time: 8 minutes| Serves: 6

2 tablespoons finely diced red pepper
1 garlic clove, minced
45g cooked quinoa
⅛ teaspoon salt
¼ teaspoon dried oregano
24 button mushrooms, stemmed
50g crumbled feta
3 tablespoons whole wheat bread crumbs
Olive oil cooking spray

1. Preheat the air fryer to 180°C. 2. In a suitable bowl, combine the pepper, garlic, quinoa, salt, and oregano. 3. Fill the mushroom caps with the quinoa stuffing. 4. Add a small piece of feta to the top of each mushroom. 5. Sprinkle a pinch bread crumbs over the feta on each mushroom. 6. Spray the basket of the air fryer with olive oil cooking spray, then gently place the mushrooms into the basket, making sure that they don't touch each other. Work in batches as needed. 7. Place the air fryer basket into the air fryer and bake for 8 minutes. Remove from the air fryer and serve.
Per Serving: Calories 66; Fat 2.6g; Sodium 167mg; Carbs 7.2g; Fibre 1.2g; Sugar 2.2g; Protein 4.4g

Garlic Prawns

Prep time: 5 minutes| Cook time: 6 minutes| Serves: 4

455g medium prawns, cleaned and deveined
60ml plus 2 tablespoons olive oil, divided
Juice of ½ lemon
3 garlic cloves, minced and divided
½ teaspoon salt
¼ teaspoon red pepper flakes
Lemon wedges, for serving (optional)
Marinara sauce, for dipping (optional)

1. Preheat the air fryer to 195°C. 2. In a large bowl, combine the prawns with 2 tablespoons of the olive oil, as well as the lemon juice, ⅓ of the minced garlic, salt, and red pepper flakes. Toss to coat the prawns well. 3. In a small ramekin, combine the remaining 60ml of olive oil and the remaining minced garlic. 4. Tear off a 30-by-30-cm sheet of aluminum foil. Pour the prawns into the centre of the foil, then fold the sides up and crimp the edges so that it forms an aluminum foil bowl that is open on top. Place this packet into the air fryer basket. 5. Roast the prawns for 4 minutes, then open the air fryer and place the ramekin with oil and garlic in the basket beside the prawns packet. Cook for 2 more minutes. 6. Transfer the prawns on a serving plate or platter with the ramekin of garlic olive oil on the side for dipping. You may also serve with lemon wedges and marinara sauce, if desired.
Per Serving: Calories 201; Fat 13.8g; Sodium 1049mg; Carbs 3.3g; Fibre 0.1g; Sugar 0.6g; Protein 15.8g

Baked Feta Potato Skins with Olives

Prep time: 5 minutes | Cook time: 45 minutes | Serves: 4

2 russet potatoes
3 tablespoons olive oil, divided, plus more for drizzling (optional)
1 teaspoon salt, divided
¼ teaspoon black pepper
2 tablespoons fresh coriander,
chopped, plus more for serving
35g Kalamata olives, diced
60g crumbled feta
Chopped fresh parsley, for garnish (optional)

1. Preheat the air fryer to 195°C. 2. Poke 2 to 3 holes in the potatoes with a fork, and then coat each with about ½ tablespoon olive oil and ½ teaspoon salt. 3. Place the potatoes into the air fryer basket and bake for 30 minutes. 4. Remove the potatoes from the air fryer, and slice them in half. Using a spoon, scoop out the flesh of the potatoes, leaving a 1cm layer of potato inside the skins, and set the skins aside. 5. In a medium bowl, combine the scooped potato middles with the remaining 2 tablespoons of olive oil, ½ teaspoon of salt, black pepper, and coriander. Mix until well combined. 6. Divide the potato filling into the now-empty potato skins, spreading it evenly over them. Top each potato with a tablespoon each of the olives and feta. 7. Place the loaded potato skins back into the air fryer and bake for 15 minutes. 8. Serve with additional chopped coriander or parsley and a drizzle of olive oil, if desired.
Per Serving: Calories 270; Fat 13g; Sodium 739mg; Carbs 34.4g; Fibre 2.7g; Sugar 1.5g; Protein 5.4g

Parmesan Artichoke and Olive Pita Flatbread

Prep time: 5 minutes | Cook time: 10 minutes | Serves: 4

2 whole wheat pitas
2 tablespoons olive oil, divided
2 garlic cloves, minced
¼ teaspoon salt
85g canned artichoke hearts, sliced
35g Kalamata olives
25g shredded Parmesan cheese
60g crumbled feta cheese
Chopped fresh parsley, for garnish (optional)

1. Preheat the air fryer to 195°C. 2. Brush each pita with 1 tablespoon olive oil, then sprinkle the minced garlic and salt over the top. 3. Distribute the artichoke hearts, olives, and cheeses evenly between the two pitas, and place both into the air fryer to bake for 10 minutes. 4. Remove the pitas and cut them into 4 pieces each before serving. Sprinkle parsley over the top, if desired.
Per Serving: Calories 165; Fat 11.5g; Sodium 453mg; Carbs 11.8g; Fibre 3g; Sugar 0.8g; Protein 5.4g

Waffle Fry Nachos with Bacon

Prep time: 5 minutes | Cook time: 11 minutes | Serves: 4

Oil, for spraying
1 (500g) package frozen waffle fries
100g shredded cheddar cheese
2 tablespoons bacon bits
1 tablespoon canned diced green
chilies
1 tablespoon sliced olives
70g salsa of choice
1 tablespoon sour cream

1. Prepare the air fryer basket by lining it with parchment and spray lightly with oil. Place the waffle fries in the prepared basket and spray lightly with oil. 2. Cook at 190°C for 8 minutes. Transfer to an air fryer–safe baking pan. 3. Top with the cheese, bacon bits, green chilies, and olives. Raise the heat to 220°C and cook for 2 to 3 minutes, or until the cheese is melted. 4. Top with the salsa and sour cream before serving.
Per Serving: Calories 511; Fat 32g; Sodium 1072mg; Carbs 45.6g; Fibre 7.1g; Sugar 0.7g; Protein 12.3g

Mini Crab Cakes

Prep time: 10 minutes | Cook time: 10 minutes | Serves: 6

200g lump crab meat
2 tablespoons diced red pepper
1 spring onion, white parts and green parts, diced
1 garlic clove, minced
1 tablespoon capers, minced
1 tablespoon nonfat plain Greek
yogurt
1 egg, beaten
25g whole-wheat bread crumbs
¼ teaspoon salt
1 tablespoon olive oil
1 lemon, cut into wedges

1. Preheat the air fryer to 180°C. 2. In a medium bowl, mix the crab, pepper, spring onion, garlic, and capers until combined. 3. Add the yogurt and egg. Stir until incorporated. Mix in the bread crumbs and salt. 4. Divide this mixture into 6 equal portions and pat out into patties. Place the crab cakes into the air fryer basket in a single layer, making sure that they don't touch each other. Brush a bit of the olive oil over the tops of each patty. 5. Bake for 10 minutes. Remove the crab cakes from the air fryer and serve with lemon wedges on the side.
Per Serving: Calories 87; Fat 3.7g; Sodium 286mg; Carbs 4.5g; Fibre 0.4g; Sugar 0.8g; Protein 8.7g

Air Fried Onion Rings

Prep time: 15 minutes | Cook time: 14 minutes | Serves: 4

1 large white onion, peeled and cut into 1 – 1.5cm-thick slices
120ml milk
125g plain flour
2 tablespoons corn flour
¾ teaspoon sea salt, divided
½ teaspoon freshly ground black pepper, divided
¾ teaspoon granulated garlic, divided
150g whole-grain bread crumbs, or gluten-free bread crumbs
Cooking oil spray (coconut, sunflower, or safflower)
Ketchup, for serving (optional)

1. Carefully separate the onion slices into rings—a gentle touch is important here. 2. Place the milk in a shallow bowl and set aside. 3. Make the first breading: In a medium bowl, stir together the flour, corn flour, ¼ teaspoon of salt, ¼ teaspoon of pepper, and ¼ teaspoon of granulated garlic. Set aside. 4. Make the second breading: In a separate medium bowl, stir together the bread crumbs with the remaining ½ teaspoon of salt, the remaining ½ teaspoon of garlic, and the remaining ½ teaspoon of pepper. Set aside. 5. Insert the crisper plate into the basket and the basket into the unit. To preheat, set your air fryer on Air Fry mode and set the temperature to 200°C and time to 3 minutes. 6. Once the unit is preheated, spray the crisper plate and the basket with cooking oil. 7. To make the onion rings, dip one ring into the milk and into the first breading mixture. Dip the ring into the milk again and back into the first breading mixture, coating thoroughly. Dip the ring into the milk one last time and then into the second breading mixture, coating thoroughly. Gently lay the onion ring in the basket. Repeat with additional rings and, as you place them into the basket, do not overlap them too much. Once all the onion rings are in the basket, generously spray the tops with cooking oil. 8. Let it cook in your air fryer on Air Fry mode at 200°C for 14 minutes. 9. After 4 minutes, open the unit and spray the rings generously with cooking oil. Close the unit to resume cooking. After 3 minutes, remove the basket and spray the onion rings again. Remove the rings, turn them over, and place them back into the basket. Generously spray them again with oil. Reinsert the basket to resume cooking. After 4 minutes, generously spray the rings with oil one last time. Resume cooking for the remaining 3 minutes, or until the onion rings are very crunchy and brown. 10. When the cooking is complete, serve the hot rings with ketchup, or other sauce of choice.
Per Serving: Calories 312; Fat 4g; Sodium 748mg; Carbs 60g; Fibre 5.8g; Sugar 5.8g; Protein 11g

Pork-Cabbage Egg Rolls

Prep time: 15 minutes | Cook time: 12 minutes | Serves: 12

Cooking oil spray
2 garlic cloves, minced
300 g pork mince
1 teaspoon sesame oil
60ml soy sauce
2 teaspoons grated peeled fresh

ginger
140g shredded green cabbage
4 spring onions, green parts
(white parts optional), chopped
24 egg roll wrappers

1. Spray cooking oil over a frying pan and place it over medium-high heat. 2. Add the garlic and cook it until fragrant, for about 1 minute. 3. Add the pork mince to the frying pan. Using a spoon, break the pork into smaller chunks. 4. In a small bowl, whisk the sesame oil, soy sauce, and ginger until combined. Stir in the sauce to the frying pan. Combine well and then continue cooking for about 5 minutes until the pork is browned and thoroughly cooked. 5. Stir in the cabbage and spring onions. Transfer the pork mixture to a large bowl. 6. Lay the egg roll wrappers on a clean flat countertop. Dip a basting brush in water and glaze each egg roll wrapper along the edges with the wet brush to soften the dough and make it easier to roll. 7. Stack 2 egg roll wrappers (it works best if you double-wrap the egg rolls). Scoop 1 to 2 tablespoons of the pork mixture into the centre of each wrapper stack. 8. Roll one long side of the wrappers up over the filling. Press firmly on the area with the filling, tucking it in lightly to secure it in place. Fold in the left and right sides. Continue rolling to close. Use the basting brush to wet the seam and seal the egg roll. Repeat with the remaining ingredients. 9. Insert the crisper plate into the basket of your air fryer. 10. To preheat, set your air fryer on Air Fry mode and set the temperature to 205°C and time to 3 minutes. 11. Once the unit is preheated, spray the crisper plate with cooking oil. Place the egg rolls into the basket. It is okay to stack them. Spray them with cooking oil. 12. Let it cook in your air fryer on Air Fry mode at 205°C for 12 minutes. 13. After 8 minutes, use tongs to flip the egg rolls. Reinsert the basket to resume cooking. When the cooking is complete, serve the egg rolls hot.
Per Serving: Calories 295; Fat 8.2g; Sodium 471mg; Carbs 40g; Fibre 1.8g; Sugar 1.6g; Protein 14.3g

Savoury Green Bean Fries

Prep time: 5 minutes| Cook time: 5 minutes| Serves: 4

For the Green Beans
1 egg
2 tablespoons water
1 tablespoon whole-wheat flour
¼ teaspoon paprika
For the Lemon-Yogurt Sauce
120g nonfat plain Greek yogurt
1 tablespoon lemon juice

½ teaspoon garlic powder
½ teaspoon salt
25g whole-wheat bread crumbs
225g whole green beans

¼ teaspoon salt
⅛ teaspoon cayenne pepper

To make the green beans: 1. Preheat the air fryer to 195°C. 2. In a suitable shallow bowl, beat together the egg and water until frothy. 3. In a separate medium shallow bowl, whisk together the flour, paprika, garlic powder, and salt, then mix in the bread crumbs. 4. Spray the cooking spray over the bottom of the air fryer. 5. Dip each green bean into the egg mixture, then into the bread crumb mixture, coating the outside with the crumbs. Add the green beans in a single layer in the bottom of the air fryer basket. 6. Fry in the air fryer for 5 minutes, or until the breading is golden brown.
To make the lemon-yogurt sauce: 1. In a small bowl, combine the yogurt, lemon juice, salt, and cayenne.
Serve the green bean fries alongside the lemon-yogurt sauce as a snack or appetizer.
Per Serving: Calories 79; Fat 1.7g; Sodium 529mg; Carbs 10.9g; Fibre 1.4g; Sugar 1.8g; Protein 5.3g

Gruyère Mushroom Tarts

Prep time: 15 minutes | Cook time: 38 minutes | Serves: 15

2 tablespoons extra-virgin olive
oil, divided
1 small white onion, sliced
200g shiitake mushrooms, sliced
¼ teaspoon sea salt
¼ teaspoon freshly ground black
pepper

60ml dry white wine
1 sheet frozen puff pastry, thawed
100g shredded Gruyère cheese
Cooking oil spray
1 tablespoon thinly sliced fresh
chives

1. Insert the crisper plate into the basket of your air fryer. To preheat, set your air fryer on Bake mode and set the temperature to 150°C and time to 3 minutes. 2. In a heatproof bowl that fits into the basket, stir together 1 tablespoon of olive oil, the onion, and the mushrooms. 3. Once the unit is preheated, place the bowl into the basket. 4. Let it cook in your air fryer on Bake mode at 150°C for 7 minutes. 5. After about 2½ minutes, stir the vegetables. Resume cooking. After another 2½ minutes, the vegetables should be browned and tender. Season with the salt and pepper and add the wine. Resume cooking until the liquid evaporates, about 2 minutes. 6. When the cooking is complete, place the bowl on a heatproof surface. 7. Increase the air fryer temperature to 200°C and set the time to 3 minutes. 8. Flat the puff pastry and cut it into 15 (7.5 x 7. 5cm) squares. Using a fork, pierce the dough and brush both sides with the remaining 1 tablespoon of olive oil. 9. Evenly distribute half the cheese among the puff pastry squares, leaving a 1cm border around the edges. Divide the mushroom-onion mixture among the pastry squares and top with the remaining cheese. 10. Once the unit is preheated, spray the crisper plate with cooking oil. Working in batches, place 5 tarts into the basket; do not stack or overlap. 11. Let it cook in your air fryer on Bake mode at 200°C for 8 minutes. After 6 minutes, check the tarts; if not yet golden brown, resume cooking for about 2 minutes more. When the cooking is complete, remove the tarts and transfer to a wire rack to cool. Repeat the cooking steps with the remaining tarts. 12. Serve garnished with the chives.
Per Serving: Calories 77; Fat 5.7g; Sodium 100mg; Carbs 4.2g; Fibre 0.5g; Sugar 0.9g; Protein 2.7g

Parmesan Mozzarella Sticks

Prep time: 8 minutes | Cook time: 5 minutes | Serves: 4

65g plain flour
1 egg, beaten
55g panko bread crumbs
50g grated Parmesan cheese
1 teaspoon Italian seasoning

½ teaspoon garlic salt
6 mozzarella sticks, halved
crosswise
Olive oil spray

1. Put the flour in a small bowl. 2. In another small bowl, add the beaten egg. 3. In a suitable bowl, stir together the panko, Parmesan cheese, Italian seasoning, and garlic salt. 4. Roll a mozzarella stick half in the flour, dip it into the egg, and then coat the stick with the panko mixture. 5. Press lightly to make sure the bread crumbs stick to the cheese. 6. Repeat the steps with the remaining 11 mozzarella sticks. 7. To preheat, set your air fryer on Air Fry mode and set the temperature to 205°C and time to 3 minutes with the crisper plate inserted in the air fryer basket inside your air fryer. 8. Then spray the olive oil over the crisper plate and line the basket with a sheet of parchment paper. Arrange evenly the mozzarella sticks into the basket and lightly spray them with olive oil. 9. Let it cook in your air fryer on Air Fry mode and set the temperature to 205°C and time to 5 minutes. 10. When the mozzarella sticks are cooked, they should be golden brown and crispy. 11. Let the sticks stand for 1 minute and then transfer them to a serving plate. Serve warm.
Per Serving: Calories 214; Fat 5.5g; Sodium 560mg; Carbs 24.8g; Fibre 1.5g; Sugar 1.4g; Protein 15.5g

Parmesan Cheese Aubergine Sticks

Prep Time: 10 minutes | Cook Time: 24 minutes | Serves: 4

2 large eggs
2 tablespoons heavy cream
50g grated Parmesan cheese
½ teaspoon salt
1 medium aubergine, cut into

1cm rounds, then sliced into
sticks
130g no-sugar-added marinara
sauce, warmed

1. Preheat air fryer to 205°C for 3 minutes. 2. Whisk together eggs and heavy cream in a medium bowl. 3. Combine Parmesan cheese, and salt in a separate shallow dish. 4. Dip aubergine sticks in egg mixture. 5. Dredge it in parmesan mixture. 6. Place half of the aubergine sticks in air fryer basket lightly greased with olive oil. Cook for 6 minutes, then flip it and cook for another 6 minutes. 7. Repeat with remaining aubergine sticks. 8. Transfer it to a large serving plate and serve it with warmed marinara sauce for dipping.
Per Serving: Calories 140; Fat 8.76g; Sodium 526mg; Carbs 10.31g; Fibre 4.1g; Sugar 0g; Protein 6.4g

Classic Scotch Eggs

Prep time: 15 minutes | Cook time: 11 to 13 minutes | Serves: 6

675g lean chicken or turkey sausage
3 raw eggs, divided
150g dried bread crumbs, divided
65g plain flour
6 hard-boiled eggs, peeled
Cooking oil spray

1. In a large bowl, combine 1 raw egg, chicken sausage, and 50 g of bread crumbs until well mixed. Divide the mixture into 6 pieces and then flatten each into a long oval. 2. Beat the remaining 2 raw eggs in a shallow bowl. 3. Place the flour in a small bowl. 4. Place the remaining 100 g of bread crumbs in a second small bowl. 5. Coat each hard-boiled egg with the flour and then wrap each with one piece of chicken sausage. 6. Then roll the wrapped eggs in the flour. Dip with the beaten eggs. Drop in the bread crumbs to coat well. 7. Insert the crisper plate into the basket of your air fryer. 8. To preheat, set your air fryer on Air Fry mode and set the temperature to 190°C and time to 3 minutes. 9. Spray the cooking oil over the preheated crisper plate and then arrange the eggs into the air fryer basket in a single layer. Spray them with oil. 10. Let it cook in your air fryer on Air Fry mode at 190°C for 13 minutes. 11. Turn the eggs with tongs halfway through cooking and then spray them with more oil. 12. Continue cooking for 5 to 7 minutes more, or until the chicken is thoroughly cooked and the Scotch eggs are browned. When the cooking is complete, serve warm.
Per Serving: Calories 445; Fat 24g; Sodium 931mg; Carbs 13.5g; Fibre 0.5g; Sugar 1.3g; Protein 40.7g

Fried Pita Chips

Prep time: 2 minutes| Cook time: 8 minutes| Serves: 2

2 whole-wheat pitas
1 tablespoon olive oil
½ teaspoon salt

1. Preheat the air fryer to 180°C. 2. Cut each pita into 8 wedges. 3. In a medium bowl, toss the pita wedges, olive oil, and salt until the wedges are coated, and the olive oil and salt are evenly distributed. 4. Place the pita wedges into the air fryer basket in an even layer and fry for 6 to 8 minutes. (Depending upon how thick the pita is and how browned you prefer a chip.) 5. Season with additional salt, if desired. Serve alone or with a favorite dip.
Per Serving: Calories 97; Fat 7.1g; Sodium 644mg; Carbs 7.7g; Fibre 1g; Sugar 0.1g; Protein 1.4g

Roasted Avocado Shishito Peppers

Prep Time: 5 minutes | Cook Time: 10 minutes | Serves: 2

1 (100g) bag shishito peppers, whole, rinsed and dried
1 tablespoon avocado oil, plus
more for the basket
1 tablespoon minced garlic
Salt

1. Preheat the air fryer to 205°C. 2. Toss the shishitos with the avocado oil, garlic, and salt in a medium bowl. 3. Lightly spritz the air fryer basket with oil. Place the shishitos in the basket. 4. Air fry at 205°C for 8 to 10 minutes, shaking the basket every 3 to 4 minutes to ensure even cooking. 5. Make sure the peppers are roasted and blistered, but not burned.
Per Serving: Calories 68; Fat 7.02g; Sodium 1mg; Carbs 1.41g; Fibre 0.1g; Sugar 0.04g; Protein 0.27g

Air-Fryer Vegetable Dumplings with Dipping Sauce

Prep Time: 30 minutes | Cook Time: 20 minutes | Serves: 4

For the Dumplings
1 tablespoon extra-virgin olive oil, plus more for spraying
1 (200g) box cremini mushrooms, finely chopped
2 teaspoons minced garlic
For the Dipping sauce
1 tablespoon soy sauce
2 teaspoons rice vinegar
1 teaspoon grated fresh ginger
1 (350g) bag coleslaw mix, refrigerated
1 (300g) package round dumpling wrappers

1 teaspoon sesame oil
½ tablespoon packed brown sugar

To make the dumplings: 1. Set the heat to medium and then add olive oil in a 25cm frying pan. Add the mushrooms, garlic, and ginger and sauté for 2 to 3 minutes, and add the coleslaw mix and sauté for another 4 to 5 minutes, or until the coleslaw is soft. 2. Stir the vegetables frequently and cook it until all the moisture has evaporated and the mixture is dry. 3. Place 2 teaspoons of vegetable filling in the centre of each dumpling wrapper. 4. Moisten the edges of the dumpling wrapper with water. Fold over the wrapper and seal the edges with your fingers, making pleats and pinching the edges to close them well. 5. Preheat the air fryer to 185°C. Lightly spray the air fryer basket with oil, and place the dumplings in a single layer in the basket. (Air fry in batches, if necessary.) Don't forget to lightly spray with oil. 6. Air fry at 185°C for 6 minutes. 7. Flip the dumplings and lightly spray with oil. 8. Air fry for another 6 minutes, or until it's golden brown and crispy.
To make the dipping sauce: 1. While the dumplings are air frying, combine the soy sauce, rice vinegar, sesame oil, and brown sugar in a small bowl, and stir them until the sugar dissolves. 2. Serve the dumplings with the dipping sauce.
Per Serving: Calories 162; Fat 5.27g; Sodium 68mg; Carbs 29.22g; Fibre 0.2g; Sugar 27.5g; Protein 0.5g

Italian Crispy Stuffed Olives

Prep Time: 15 minutes | Cook Time: 10 minutes | Serves: 6

1 (250g) jar garlic- or pimento-stuffed olives
30g plain flour
1 large egg
110g Italian seasoned panko bread crumbs
Extra-virgin olive oil, for spraying

1. Preheat the air fryer to 205°C. 2. Remove the olives from the jar and dry them completely with paper towels. 3. Add the flour to a small shallow bowl. Beat the egg in a second small shallow bowl. Put the bread crumbs in a third small shallow bowl. 4. Toss the olives in the flour. 5. Coat each olive in the beaten egg, then in the breading. 6. Lightly spray the air fryer basket with oil, place the coated olives in a single layer in the basket, and lightly spray with oil. 7. Air fry at 205°C for 6 to 8 minutes, shaking the basket gently after 2 minutes to ensure even cooking. 8. Serve it hot.
Per Serving: Calories 44; Fat 1.07g; Sodium 37mg; Carbs 6.98g; Fibre 0.3g; Sugar 0.36g; Protein 1.51g

Air-fryer Raspberry Brie

Prep Time: 15 minutes | Cook Time: 15 minutes | Serves: 6

1 tablespoon plain flour
1 puff pastry sheet, at room temperature
1 (200g) Brie wheel, refrigerated
80g raspberry preserves
2 tablespoons fresh raspberries
1 large egg
1 tablespoon water
Extra-virgin olive oil, for the basket

1. Preheat the air fryer to 175°C. 2. Dust your work surface with the flour, then roll out the puff pastry sheet. 3. Cut the rind off the Brie and discard it, and place the Brie in the centre of the puff pastry sheet. 4. Spread the raspberry preserves on top of the Brie, and then sprinkle the fresh raspberries on top. 5. Fold up the sides of the puff pastry around the Brie, and press the seams of the pastry together until they are closed. 6. Whisk together the egg and water in a small bowl, and brush the egg wash all over the top and sides of the puff pastry.7. Generously spritz the air fryer basket with oil, and place the pastry-enrobed Brie in the basket. 8. Air fry at 175°C for 10 to 15 minutes, or until the pastry is golden brown and cooked through.
Per Serving: Calories 598; Fat 48.02g; Sodium 1075mg; Carbs 5.6g; Fibre 0.6g; Sugar 4g; Protein 36.13g

Simple Bacon-Wrapped Jumbo Prawn

Prep Time: 10 minutes | Cook Time: 15 minutes | Serves: 6

455g sliced bacon
400g jumbo prawns, peeled and deveined, tails on
Extra-virgin olive oil, for the basket

1. Preheat the fryer to 190°C. 2. Cut the bacon strips in half. Wrap half a strip tightly around each prawn. 3. Spritz the air fryer basket lightly with oil. 4. Place each bacon-wrapped prawn seam-side down in the basket. Air fry at 190°C for 12 to 15 minutes, or until the bacon is crispy and cooked to your preference. 5. Check the progress after about 6 minutes and move the prawns around a little so they don't stick to the basket.
Per Serving: Calories 383; Fat 30.72g; Sodium 1013mg; Carbs 0.63g; Fibre 0g; Sugar 0.63; Protein 24.91g

Simple Low-Carb Honey Mustard

Prep Time: 10 minutes | Cook Time: 0 minutes | Serves: 36

60g mayonnaise
2 tablespoons yellow mustard
1 teaspoon Dijon mustard

¼ teaspoon apple cider vinegar
1 tablespoon granular sweetener

1. Combine all ingredients in a small bowl. 2. Refrigerate it for five days until ready to use.
Per Serving (1 teaspoon): Calories 7; Fat 0.64g; Sodium 31mg; Carbs 0.13g; Fibre 0.1g; Sugar 0.03g; Protein 0.25g

Italian Toasted Ravioli

Prep Time: 15 minutes | Cook Time: 10 minutes | Serves: 6

2 large eggs
2 tablespoons milk
30g plain flour
80g Italian bread crumbs
35g grated Parmesan cheese
1 teaspoon Italian seasoning
¼ teaspoon salt
¼ teaspoon freshly ground black

pepper
1 (200g) package fresh ravioli, refrigerated
Extra-virgin olive oil, for spraying
Marinara sauce, for serving (optional)

1. To prepare, heat your air fryer to 195°C. 2. Pour the milk in a small shallow bowl and whisk together with 2 eggs. Put the flour in a second small shallow bowl. Combine the bread crumbs, Parmesan cheese, Italian seasoning, salt, and pepper in a third small shallow bowl. 3. Coat each ravioli in the flour, in the egg wash, and then in the bread crumb mixture. 4. Lightly spritz the air fryer basket with oil, putting the ravioli in a single layer in the basket and lightly spraying with oil. 5. Air fry at 175°C for 4 minutes. 6. Flip the ravioli and lightly spray with oil. 7. Air fry for another 3 to 4 minutes, or until golden brown and crispy. 8. Serve it with marinara sauce, if using.
Per Serving: Calories 119; Fat 4.88g; Sodium 381mg; Carbs 13.43g; Fibre 1g; Sugar 1.46g; Protein 4.98g

Cheese Pizza Pinwheels

Prep Time: 10 minutes | Cook Time: 20 minutes | Serves: 4

1 tablespoon flour
1 (200g) can crescent dough, refrigerated
125g pizza sauce

55g mozzarella cheese
50g shredded Parmesan cheese
Extra-virgin olive oil, for the basket

1. Preheat the air fryer to 175°C. 2. Lightly coat your work surface with flour, then roll out the sheet of crescent dough. 3. Add the pizza sauce evenly over the crescent dough all the way to the edges. 4. Sprinkle the mozzarella cheese and Parmesan cheese over top of the pizza sauce. 5. Roll up the dough into a long tube. 6. Place the rolled tube in the freezer for about 10 minutes to make cutting easier. 7. Cut the dough roll into 2.5cm slices. 8. Lightly spray the air fryer basket with oil. 9. Place the pinwheel slices in a single layer in the basket. 10. Allow about 1cm between each. 11. Air fry at 175°C for 5 minutes. 12. Shake the basket and air fry for another 2 to 5 minutes, or until golden brown and cooked through.
Per Serving: Calories 111; Fat 4.15g; Sodium 463mg; Carbs 8.95g; Fibre 1g; Sugar 1.42g; Protein 9.26g

Air-fryer Egg Rolls

Prep Time: 15 minutes | Cook Time: 10 minutes | Serves: 5

1 (375g) can black beans, drained and rinsed
165g corn kernels, frozen or canned, drained
1 (100g) can diced green chiles
195g shredded Colby-Jack cheese
1 teaspoon paprika
1 teaspoon chili powder

1 teaspoon salt
½ teaspoon ground cumin
½ teaspoon freshly ground black pepper
1 (300g) package egg roll wrappers
Extra-virgin olive oil, for spraying

1. To prepare, heat the air fryer to 190°C. 2. Combine the black beans, corn, green chiles, cheese, paprika, chili powder, salt, cumin, and pepper in a large bowl. 3. Place an egg roll wrapper on your work surface diagonally. 4. Put some filling onto the centre of the wrapper. 5. Fold the bottom corner over the filling and roll up snugly halfway to cover the filling. 6. Fold in both sides of the wrapper. 7. Moisten the edges of the top corner with water, roll up the rest of the way, and seal the top corner. 8. Repeat steps 2 and 3 with the remaining ingredients. 9. Lightly spray the air fryer basket with oil. 10. Place the egg rolls seam-side down in the basket, leaving at least ½cm between each to ensure even cooking. 11. Lightly spray with oil. 12. Air fry at 190°C for 4 minutes. 13. Flip the egg rolls and lightly spray with oil. 14. Air fry the egg rolls for another 4 to 6 minutes, or until golden brown and crispy.
Per Serving: Calories 269; Fat 18.02g; Sodium 963mg; Carbs 13.66g; Fibre 2.7g; Sugar 1.61g; Protein 15.07g

Baked Jalapeño Poppers

Prep Time: 15 minutes | Cook Time: 10 minutes | Serves: 8

8 large jalapeños
200g cream cheese, at room temperature
55g panko bread crumbs
50g shredded cheese, any variety

2 teaspoons dried parsley
½ teaspoon garlic powder
Extra-virgin olive oil, for the basket

1. Preheat the air fryer to 185°C. 2. Remove the stems of the jalapeños, and then cut them in half lengthwise. 3. Carefully remove the seeds and insides to create boats. 4. Combine the cream cheese, bread crumbs, shredded cheese, parsley, and garlic powder in a medium bowl. 5. Stuff each jalapeño half with the cream cheese mixture. 6. Lightly spritz the air fryer basket with the extra-virgin olive oil, placing the poppers in a single layer in the basket. 7. Air fry at 185°C for 7 to 10 minutes, or until the cheese is bubbly and golden brown and the jalapeños have softened.
Per Serving: Calories 126; Fat 11.15g; Sodium 216mg; Carbs 2.57g; Fibre 0.2g; Sugar 1.17g; Protein 4.31g

Garlic Buffalo Chicken Meatballs

Prep Time: 10 minutes | Cook Time: 15 minutes | Serves: 4

455g chicken mince
55g panko bread crumbs
1 large egg
3 tablespoons buffalo sauce, divided
2 teaspoons minced garlic
1 teaspoon dry ranch dressing

mix
½ teaspoon salt
½ teaspoon freshly ground black pepper
Extra-virgin olive oil, for the basket

1. To prepare. heat the air fryer to 175°C. 2. Combine the chicken, bread crumbs, egg, 1 tablespoon buffalo sauce, garlic, ranch dressing mix, salt, and pepper in a large bowl. 3. Form the mixture into 2.5cm meatballs, and make sure it has about 20 meatballs. 4. Lightly spray the air fryer basket with oil, and place the meatballs in a single layer in the basket. (Air fry in batches, if necessary.) 5. Air fry at 175°C for 6 minutes. 6. Then shake the basket and air fry again for another 6 to 9 minutes, or until browned and cooked through. 7. Toss with the remaining 2 tablespoons buffalo sauce before serving.
Per Serving: Calories 280; Fat 18.94g; Sodium 500mg; Carbs 3.76g; Fibre 0.4g; Sugar 0.88g; Protein 22.47g

Italian Stuffed Mushroom Caps

Prep Time: 15 minutes | Cook Time: 10 minutes | Serves: 5

24 large cremini mushrooms
100g cream cheese, at room temperature
55g shredded mozzarella cheese
50g grated Parmesan cheese
30g Italian seasoned bread crumbs
1 large egg

¼ teaspoon salt
¼ teaspoon freshly ground black pepper
¼ teaspoon onion powder
Dash hot sauce
Extra-virgin olive oil, for spraying

1. Clean the mushrooms gently with a damp paper towel and remove the stems. 2. Use an electric mixer to combine the cream cheese, mozzarella cheese, Parmesan cheese, bread crumbs, egg, salt, pepper, onion powder, and hot sauce in a medium bowl. 3. Preheat the air fryer to 185°C. 4. Spoon the cheese mixture into each mushroom, pressing the mixture into the mushrooms and leaving a little bit mounded over the top. 5. Lightly spray the air fryer basket with oil. 6. Place the stuffed mushrooms in a single layer in the basket. (Air fry in batches, if necessary.), and lightly spray with oil. Air fry at 185°C for 7 to 10 minutes, or until both the mushrooms and the cheese have started to brown lightly on top.
Per Serving: Calories 144; Fat 9.22g; Sodium 405mg; Carbs 6.57g; Fibre 1.4g; Sugar 3.28; Protein 10.73g

Spicy Onion Rings

Prep Time: 15 minutes | Cook Time: 10 minutes | Serves: 6

2 large sweet onions
125g plain flour
1 teaspoon baking powder
2 teaspoons salt, divided
2 large eggs
2 tablespoons milk
215g panko bread crumbs
1 teaspoon smoked paprika

½ teaspoon onion powder
½ teaspoon garlic powder
½ teaspoon freshly ground black pepper
Pinch cayenne pepper
Extra-virgin olive oil, for spraying

1. Cut the ends of the onions off, peel off the skins, slice into ½cm-thick rings, and separate the rings. 2. Combine the flour, baking powder, and 1 teaspoon salt in a small shallow bowl. 3. Whisk together the eggs and milk in a second small shallow bowl. 4. Combine the bread crumbs, paprika, onion powder, garlic powder, black pepper, and cayenne pepper in a third small shallow bowl. 5. Preheat the air fryer to 195°C. 6. Coat the onions in the flour mixture, then in the egg mixture, and then in the bread crumbs. 7. Press on the bread crumbs to ensure they adhere. 8. Lightly spray the air fryer basket with oil, placing the onion rings in a single layer in the basket and lightly spraying with oil. 9. Air fry at 175°C for 5 minutes. 10. Gently flip the onion rings and lightly spray with oil. 11. Air fry the onion rings for another 5 minutes, or until golden brown and crispy.
Per Serving: Calories 166; Fat 2.4g; Sodium 847mg; Carbs 31g; Fibre 2.1g; Sugar 6.6g; Protein 5.24g

Spicy and Sweet Chicken Wings

Prep Time: 10 minutes | Cook Time: 15 minutes | Serves: 6

For the Wings
900g fresh bone-in chicken wings
1 tablespoon baking powder
2 teaspoons salt
For the Sauce
8 tablespoons butter, melted
1 tablespoon lemon-pepper

Extra-virgin olive oil, for spraying

seasoning
2 teaspoons honey

To make the wings: 1. To prepare, heat your air fryer to 205°C. 2. Pat the chicken wings dry with paper towels. 3. Mix together the baking powder and salt in a large zip-top bag. 4. Add the chicken wings, seal the bag, and shake to coat evenly. 5. Lightly spray the air fryer basket with oil. 6. Arrange evenly the chicken wings in a single layer in the basket (Air fry in batches, if necessary.), and lightly spray with oil again. 7. Air fry at 175°C for 7 minutes, and then flip the wings and lightly spray with oil. 8. Air fry for another 6 to 8 minutes, or until the wings are crispy and lightly browned and have reached an internal temperature of 75°C.
To make the sauce: While the wings are air frying, whisk together the melted butter, lemon-pepper seasoning, and honey in a small bowl.
As soon as the wings are done, toss them in the lemon-pepper sauce to coat.
Per Serving: Calories 333; Fat 20.71g; Sodium 1019mg; Carbs 1.95g; Fibre 0g; Sugar 1.94g; Protein 33.39g

Simple Avocado Fries with Dipping Sauce

Prep Time: 20 minutes | Cook Time: 10 minutes | Serves: 6

For the Avocado Fries
4 slightly underripe avocados, halved and pitted
160g panko bread crumbs
¾ teaspoon freshly ground black pepper
For the Dipping Sauce
115g sour cream
115g mayonnaise
2 to 3 teaspoons sriracha

1½ teaspoons paprika
¾ teaspoon salt
3 large eggs
Extra-virgin olive oil, for spraying

½ teaspoon freshly squeezed lemon juice

To make the avocado fries: 1. To prepare, heat your air fryer to 175°C. 2. Carefully remove the skin from the avocados while leaving the flesh intact. 3. Cut each avocado in half lengthwise into 5 to 6 slices, and set it aside. 4. Mix together the bread crumbs, pepper, paprika, and salt in a small shallow bowl. 4. Whisk the eggs in a second small shallow bowl. 5. Coat each avocado slice in the eggs, then in the bread crumbs. Press on the bread crumbs to ensure they adhere. 6. Lightly spray the air fryer basket with oil. 87 Place the avocado fries in a single layer in the basket. 8. Lightly spray with oil.

Air fry the avocado fries at 175°C for 3 to 4 minutes. 9. Gently flip the fries and lightly spray with oil. Air fry for another 3 to 4 minutes, or until golden brown and crispy.
To make the dipping sauce: 1. While they're cooking, combine the sour cream, mayonnaise, sriracha, and lemon juice in a small bowl. 2. Serve it with the fries immediately.
Per Serving: Calories 359; Fat 30.69g; Sodium 519mg; Carbs 18.58g; Fibre 9.6g; Sugar 1.9g; Protein 6.8g

Air-Fryer Parmesan-Asparagus Twists

Prep Time: 15 minutes | Cook Time: 15 minutes | Serves: 6

24 asparagus spears
1 tablespoon extra-virgin olive oil, plus more for the basket
¼ teaspoon salt
¼ teaspoon freshly ground black pepper
Flour, for dusting

1 sheet puff pastry, at room temperature
1 large egg
1 teaspoon water
50g grated Parmesan cheese
¼ teaspoon cayenne pepper

1. Combine the asparagus, olive oil, salt, and black pepper in a large bowl, and toss to coat. 2. Preheat the air fryer to 175°C. 3. Dust your work surface with flour, then unfold the puff pastry sheet. 4. Cut the sheet in half lengthwise, then cut each half into thin strips about 1cm wide, and make it sure it will have 24 strips. 5. Wrap a pastry strip around each asparagus spear, leaving the tip free. 6. Place the wrapped spears on a baking sheet. 7. Whisk together the egg and water in a small shallow bowl. 8. Combine the Parmesan cheese and cayenne pepper in a second small shallow bowl. 9. Brush each wrapped spear with the egg wash, then sprinkle with the cheese mixture. 10. Press on the mixture to ensure it adheres. 11. Lightly spray the air fryer basket with oil, and place the twists in a single layer in the basket, leaving about 1cm of space between each. (Air fry in batches, if necessary.) 12. Air fry at 175°C for 10 minutes, shaking the basket once while cooking, until the pastry is lightly browned.
Per Serving: Calories 67; Fat 5.37g; Sodium 249mg; Carbs 1.85g; Fibre 0.3g; Sugar 0.29g; Protein 3.14g

Loaded Potato Skins with Black Pepper

Prep Time: 10 minutes | Cook Time: 60 minutes | Serves: 6

Extra-virgin olive oil, for greasing the basket
6 medium russet potatoes, scrubbed
Salt
Freshly ground black pepper

6 slices cooked bacon, crumbled
100g shredded cheddar cheese
115g sour cream, for serving
3 spring onions, thinly sliced, for serving

1. To prepare, heat the air fryer to 205°C. 2. Lightly spray the air fryer basket with oil. Lightly spritz the potatoes with oil and season with salt and pepper. Pierce each potato a few times with a fork. 3. Place the potatoes in the basket. Air fry at 205°C for 30 to 40 minutes, until fork-tender. 4. Set aside the potatoes for 5 to 10 minutes, or until cool enough to handle. 5. Cut the potatoes in half lengthwise. Scoop out most of the insides, leaving about ½cm so the potato skins hold their shape and resemble a boat. 6. Season the inside of the potato skins with salt and pepper. 7. Lightly spray with oil. 8. Spread the potato skins evenly in a single layer in the basket, leaving about ½cm of space between each to ensure even cooking. (Air fry in batches, if necessary.) Air fry the potato skins for 8 to 10 minutes, until crispy and golden. 9. Carefully sprinkle the bacon and cheese into each potato skin. 10. Air fry for an additional 2 to 3 minutes, or until the cheese is melted and bubbly. 11. Top with sour cream and spring onions before serving.
Per Serving: Calories 423; Fat 5.37g; Sodium 157mg; Carbs 68.25g; Fibre 4.8g; Sugar 2.55; Protein 11.83g

Fluffy Cheese Bread

Prep Time: 10 minutes | Cook Time: 10 minutes | Serves: 2

110g shredded mozzarella cheese
25g grated Parmesan cheese

1 large egg
½ teaspoon garlic powder

1. Mix all ingredients in a large bowl. 2. Cut a piece of parchment to fit your air fryer basket. 3. Press the mixture into a circle on the parchment and put it into the air fryer basket. 4. Adjust the temperature to 175°C and set the timer for 10 minutes. 5. Serve it warm.
Per Serving: Calories 162; Fat 5.74g; Sodium 650mg; Carbs 4.6g; Fibre 1.1g; Sugar 0.91g; Protein 22.94g

Simple Crab Rangoon

Prep Time: 15 minutes | Cook Time: 10 minutes | Serves: 6

200g cream cheese, at room temperature
1 (150g) white crabmeat, picked through and drained
1 teaspoon minced garlic
½ teaspoon soy sauce
½ teaspoon icing sugar
½ teaspoon dried chives
1 (300g–400g) package wonton wrappers
Extra-virgin olive oil, for spraying

1. To prepare, heat the air fryer to 175°C. 2. Mix together the cream cheese, crabmeat, garlic, soy sauce, icing sugar, and chives in a medium bowl. 3. Lay out the wonton wrappers and place a heaping teaspoon of cream cheese in the centre of each. 4. Dab a bit of water on the outer edges of the wrappers and fold the two ends together to form a small pocket. Pinch the edges tightly to seal. 5. Lightly spritz the air fryer basket with oil. 6. Place the crab rangoon in a single layer in the basket. 7. Lightly spray with oil. Air fry at 175°C for 7 minutes, or until golden brown and crispy.
Per Serving: Calories 131; Fat 10.98g; Sodium 202mg; Carbs 4.99g; Fibre 0.1g; Sugar 1.69g; Protein 3.36g

Simple Fried Pickles

Prep Time: 15 minutes | Cook Time: 15 minutes | Serves: 4

125g plain flour
1 teaspoon paprika
1 large egg
140g panko bread crumbs
1 (600g) jar dill pickle spears
Extra-virgin olive oil, for spraying

1. Preheat the air fryer to 205°C. 2. Combine the flour and paprika in a small shallow bowl. Whisk the egg in a second small shallow bowl. Put the bread crumbs in a third small shallow bowl. 3. Pat the pickle spears dry with paper towels. 4. Coat each pickle spear in the flour mixture, then in the egg, and then in the bread crumbs. 5. Lightly spray the air fryer basket with oil. 6. Place the pickle spears in a single layer in the basket, leaving about ½cm of space between each to ensure even cooking. (Air fry in batches, if necessary.) 7. Lightly spray with oil. Air fry at 205°C for 7 minutes. 8. Gently flip the pickles and air fry for an additional 5 to 8 minutes, or until lightly browned and crispy.
Per Serving: Calories 131; Fat 10.98g; Sodium 202mg; Carbs 4.99g; Fibre 0.1g; Sugar 1.69g; Protein 3.36g

Three-Meat Pizza

Prep Time: 5 minutes | Cook Time: 5 minutes | Serves: 1

55g shredded mozzarella cheese
7 slices pepperoni
35g cooked sausage meat
2 slices bacon, cooked and crumbled
1 tablespoon grated Parmesan cheese
2 tablespoons, sugar-free pizza sauce, for dipping

1. Cover the bottom of a 15cm x 5cm cake pan with mozzarella. 2. Place pepperoni, sausage, and bacon on top of cheese and sprinkle it with Parmesan. 3. Place pan into the air fryer basket. 4. Adjust the temperature to 205°C and set the timer for 5 minutes. 5. Remove it when cheese is bubbling and golden. 6. Serve it warm with pizza sauce for dipping.
Per Serving: Calories 335; Fat 16.66g; Sodium 1135mg; Carbs 12.21g; Fibre 1.1g; Sugar 8.07g; Protein 34.29g

Bacon-Wrapped Brie

Prep Time: 5 minutes | Cook Time: 10 minutes | Serves: 8

4 slices bacon
1 (200g) round Brie

1. Place two slices of bacon to form an X. Place the third slice of bacon horizontally across the centre of the X. 2. Put the fourth slice of bacon vertically across the X, and make sure it looks like a plus sign (+) on top of an X. 3. Place the Brie in the centre of the bacon. 4. Wrap the bacon around the Brie, securing with a few toothpicks. 5. Cut a piece of parchment to fit your air fryer basket and place the bacon-wrapped Brie on top. 6. Put it inside the air fryer basket. Adjust the temperature setting to 205°C and set the timer for 10 minutes. 7. Flip Brie carefully when 3 minutes remain. 8. Finally, bacon will be crispy and cheese will be soft and melty. 9. Cut it into eight slices for serving.

Per Serving: Calories 428; Fat 35.43g; Sodium 805mg; Carbs 0.58g; Fibre 0g; Sugar 0.58g; Protein 0.58g

Smoky Roasted Almonds

Prep Time: 5 minutes | Cook Time: 6 minutes | Serves: 4

160g raw almonds
2 teaspoons coconut oil
1 teaspoon chili powder
¼ teaspoon cumin
¼ teaspoon smoked paprika
¼ teaspoon onion powder

1. Toss all ingredients in a large bowl until almonds are evenly coated with oil and spices. 2. Place almonds into the air fryer basket. 3. Adjust the temperature to 160°C and set the timer for 6 minutes. 4. Toss the air fryer basket halfway through the cooking time, and allow it to cool completely.
Per Serving: Calories 230; Fat 20g; Sodium 20mg; Carbs 8g; Fibre 4.8g; Sugar 1.6g; Protein 7.7g

Thinly Sliced Beef Jerky

Prep Time: 5 minutes | Cook Time: 4 hours | Serves: 10

450g flat iron beef, thinly sliced
60ml soy sauce (or liquid aminos)
2 teaspoons Worcestershire sauce
¼ teaspoon crushed red pepper
flakes
¼ teaspoon garlic powder
¼ teaspoon onion powder

1. Place all ingredients into a plastic storage bag or covered container and marinate them for 2 hours in refrigerator. 2. Place each slice of jerky on the air fryer rack in a single layer. 3. Adjust the temperature to 70°C and set the timer for 4 hours. 4. Cool and store it in airtight container up to 1 week.
Per Serving: Calories 80; Fat 3.47g; Sodium 145mg; Carbs 2.02g; Fibre 0.2g; Sugar 1.41g; Protein 10.24g

Mozzarella-Stuffed Buffalo Meatballs

Prep Time: 15 minutes | Cook Time: 15 minutes | Serves: 4

450g lean beef mince
25g blanched finely ground almond flour
1 teaspoon dried parsley
½ teaspoon garlic powder
¼ teaspoon onion powder
1 large egg
75g low-moisture, whole-milk mozzarella, cubed
110g no-sugar-added pasta sauce
25g grated Parmesan cheese

1. Add beef mince, almond flour, parsley, garlic powder, onion powder, and egg in a large bowl. 2. Fold ingredients together until fully combined. 3. Form the mixture into 5cm balls and use your thumb or a spoon to create an indent in the centre of each meatball. 4. Place a cube of cheese in the centre and form the ball around it. 5. Place the meatballs into the air fryer, working in batches if necessary. 6. Adjust the temperature to 175°C and set the timer for 15 minutes. (Meatballs will be slightly crispy on the outside and fully cooked when at least 80°C internally.) 7. Toss the meatballs in the sauce and sprinkle them with grated Parmesan for serving.
Per Serving: Calories 360; Fat 20.25g; Sodium 190mg; Carbs 8.98g; Fibre 1g; Sugar 5g; Protein 34.89g

Air-Fryer Jalapeño Poppers

Prep Time: 10 minutes | Cook Time: 18 minutes | Serves: 6

1 tablespoon olive oil
115g pork mince
2 tablespoons pitted and finely diced Kalamata olives
2 tablespoons feta cheese
25g cream cheese, room temperature
½ teaspoon dried mint leaves
6 large jalapeños, sliced in half lengthwise and seeded

1. Heat olive oil over medium-high heat 30 seconds in a medium frying pan. 2. Add pork and cook it for 6 minutes until it is no longer pink. Drain fat. 3. Preheat air fryer to 175°C for 3 minutes. 4. Combine cooked pork, olives, feta cheese, cream cheese, and mint leaves in a medium bowl. 5. Press pork mixture into peppers. 6. Place half of poppers in ungreased air fryer basket for 6 minutes. 7. Transfer it to a medium serving plate and repeat cooking with remaining poppers. 8. Serve it warm.
Per Serving: Calories 108; Fat 8.91g; Sodium 138mg; Carbs 0.78g; Fibre 0.1g; Sugar 0.54g; Protein 6.05g

Simple Baked Brie with Orange Marmalade and Spiced Walnuts

Prep Time: 10 minutes	Cook Time: 22 minutes	Serves: 6

120g walnuts	¼ teaspoon powdered sweetener
1 large egg white, beaten	1 (200g) round Brie
⅛ teaspoon ground cumin	2 tablespoons sugar-free orange
⅛ teaspoon cayenne pepper	marmalade
1 teaspoon ground cinnamon	

1. Preheat air fryer at 160°C for 3 minutes. 2. Combine walnuts with egg white in a small bowl, and set aside. 3. Combine cumin, cayenne pepper, cinnamon, and sweetener in a separate small bowl, adding walnuts, drained of excess egg white, and toss them. 4. Place walnuts in ungreased air fryer basket cooking for 6 minutes, and then toss nuts cooking for an additional 6 minutes. 5. Transfer them to a small bowl and cool it about 5 minutes until it's easy to handle. After it's cooled, chop it into smaller bits. 6. Adjust air fryer temperature to 205°C, and put Brie in an ungreased pizza pan or on a piece of parchment paper cut to size of air fryer basket cook for 10 minutes. 7. Transfer Brie to a medium serving plate and garnish it with orange marmalade and spiced walnuts.
Per Serving: Calories 661; Fat 55.97g; Sodium 1083mg; Carbs 3.03g; Fibre 1.1g; Sugar 1.17g; Protein 38.07g

Tasty Ranch Roasted Almonds

Prep Time: 5 minutes	Cook Time: 6 minutes	Serves: 8

315g raw almonds	½ (25g) ranch dressing mix
2 tablespoons unsalted butter, melted	packet

1. Toss almonds in butter to evenly coat in a large bowl. 2. Sprinkle ranch mix over almonds and toss them. 3. Place almonds into the air fryer basket. 4. Adjust the temperature to 160°C and set the timer for 6 minutes. 5. Shake the basket two or three times during cooking. 6. Cool it at least 20 minutes. 7. Store it in an airtight container up to 3 days.
Per Serving: Calories 19; Fat 2.08g; Sodium 1mg; Carbs 0.06g; Fibre 0g; Sugar 0.01g; Protein 0.18g

Italian Pepperoni Pizza Bread

Prep Time: 5 minutes	Cook Time: 20 minutes	Serves: 4

2 large eggs, beaten	½ teaspoon baking powder
2 tablespoons coconut flour	⅛ teaspoon salt
2 tablespoons cassava flour	2 tablespoons grated Parmesan
80g whipping cream	cheese
35g chopped pepperoni	110g no-sugar-added marinara
35g grated mozzarella cheese	sauce, warmed
2 teaspoons Italian seasoning	

1. Preheat air fryer at 150°C for 3 minutes. 2. Combine eggs with coconut flour, cassava flour, whipping cream, pepperoni, mozzarella cheese, Italian seasoning, baking powder, and salt in a medium bowl. 3. Pour batter into an ungreased pizza pan. 4. Place the pan in an air fryer basket cooking for 19 minutes. 5. Sprinkle Parmesan cheese on top for an additional 1 minute. 6. Remove pan from basket and let it set for 5 minutes, then slice it and serve it with warmed marinara sauce.
Per Serving: Calories 81; Fat 4.09g; Sodium 308mg; Carbs 5.45g; Fibre 0.6g; Sugar 1.04g; Protein 5.38g

Air-Fryer Avocado Fries

Prep Time: 10 minutes	Cook Time: 10 minutes	Serves: 2

1 large egg, beaten	¼ teaspoon salt
25g almond flour	1 large avocado, peeled, pitted,
2 tablespoons ground flaxseed	and sliced into 8 "fries"
¼ teaspoon chipotle powder	

1. Preheat air fryer to 190°C for 3 minutes. 2. Place egg in a small dish, and combine almond flour, flaxseed, chipotle powder, and salt in a separate shallow dish. 3. Dip avocado slices into egg. 4. Dredge through flour mixture to coat. 5. Place half of slices in air fryer basket lightly greased with olive oil cooking for 5 minutes. 6. Transfer it to a medium serving plate and repeat cooking with remaining avocado

slices. 7. Serve it warm.
Per Serving: Calories 244; Fat 21.41g; Sodium 305mg; Carbs 11.89g; Fibre 9.6g; Sugar 0.88g; Protein 5.27g

Italian Mozzarella Sticklets

Prep Time: 15 minutes	Cook Time: 10 minutes	Serves: 6

2 tablespoons all-purpose flour	¼ teaspoon Italian seasoning
1 large egg	10 mozzarella sticks, each cut
1 tablespoon whole milk	into thirds
55g plain bread crumbs	2 teaspoons olive oil
¼ teaspoon salt	

1. Add flour in a small bowl. Whisk egg and milk together in another small bowl. 2. Combine bread crumbs, salt, and Italian seasoning in a shallow dish. 3. Roll a mozzarella sticklet in flour, dredge it in egg mixture, and then roll in bread crumb mixture. 4. Shake off excess between each step. 5. Set it aside on a plate and repeat with remaining mozzarella. Place it in freezer for 10 minutes. 6. To prepare, heat your air fryer at 205°C for about 3 minutes. 7. Place half of mozzarella sticklets in fryer basket cooking for 2 minutes. 8. Shake it and lightly brush it with olive oil cooking for an additional 2 minutes. Shake again cooking for an additional 1 minute. 9. Transfer it to a serving dish. Repeat with remaining sticklets and serve warm.
Per Serving: Calories 68; Fat 2.75g; Sodium 173mg; Carbs 8.63g; Fibre 0.5g; Sugar 0.59g; Protein 1.92g

Simple Five Spice Crunchy Edamame

Prep Time: 5 minutes	Cook Time: 16 minutes	Serves: 4

95g ready-to-eat edamame, shelled	1 teaspoon five spice powder
1 tablespoon sesame oil	½ teaspoon salt

1. Preheat air fryer at 175°C for 3 minutes. 2. Toss edamame in sesame oil in a small bowl. 3. Place it in your air fryer basket cooking for 5 minutes. 4. Shake. Cook an additional 5 minutes. 5. Shake again. Cook an additional 6 minutes. 6. Transfer it to a small bowl and toss it with five spice powder and salt. 7. Let it cool for serving.
Per Serving: Calories 46; Fat 3.42g; Sodium 291mg; Carbs 3.62g; Fibre 0.2g; Sugar 0.04g; Protein 0.28g

Spicy Air-Fryer Sunflower Seeds

Prep Time: 10 minutes	Cook Time: 10 minutes	Serves: 4

280g unsalted sunflower seeds	¼ teaspoon salt
2 teaspoons olive oil	1 teaspoon granular sweetener
2 teaspoons chili garlic paste	

1. Preheat air fryer at 160°C for 3 minutes. 2. Combine all ingredients in a medium bowl until seeds are well coated. 3. Place seeds in ungreased air fryer basket cooking for 5 minutes, and shake basket cooking for an additional 5 minutes. 4. Transfer it to a medium serving bowl and serve it.
Per Serving: Calories 815; Fat 73.15g; Sodium 169mg; Carbs 30.37g; Fibre 7.3g; Sugar 13.51g; Protein 22.53g

Roasted Jack-O'-Lantern Seeds with black pepper

Prep Time: 10 minutes	Cook Time: 13 minutes	Serves: 4

235g fresh pumpkin seeds	½ teaspoon dried dill
1 tablespoon butter, melted	¼ teaspoon dried chives
1 teaspoon salt, divided	¼ teaspoon dry mustard
½ teaspoon onion powder	¼ teaspoon celery seed
½ teaspoon dried parsley	¼ teaspoon freshly ground black
½ teaspoon garlic powder	pepper

1. Preheat air fryer at 160°C for 3 minutes. 2. Toss seeds with butter and ½ teaspoon salt in a medium bowl. 3. Place seed mixture in ungreased air fryer basket cooking for 7 minutes. 4. Use a spatula turning seeds, and then cook for an additional 6 minutes. 5. Transfer it to a medium serving bowl, and toss it with remaining ingredients. 6. Serve it.
Per Serving: Calories 368; Fat 31.91g; Sodium 760mg; Carbs 9.44g; Fibre 4g; Sugar 0.8g; Protein 17.82g

Delicious Deviled Eggs

Prep Time: 5 minutes | Cook Time: 15 minutes | Serves: 4

4 large eggs
215g ice cubes
240ml water
2 tablespoons plain Greek yogurt
2 tablespoons pitted and finely chopped Kalamata olives
2 tablespoons goat cheese
crumbles
⅛ teaspoon salt
⅛ teaspoon freshly ground black pepper
2 tablespoons finely chopped fresh mint

1. Preheat air fryer at 120°C for 3 minutes. 2. Place eggs in silicone muffin cups to avoid bumping around and cracking during cooking process. 3. Add silicone cups to air fryer basket cooking for 15 minutes. 4. Add ice and water to a medium bowl. 5. Transfer eggs to water bath immediately to stop cooking process. 6. After 5 minutes, carefully peel eggs. Cut eggs in half lengthwise. Spoon yolks into a separate medium bowl. Arrange white halves on a large plate. Using a fork, blend egg yolks with yogurt, olives, goat cheese, salt, and pepper. 7. Spoon mixture into white halves. 8. Garnish it with mint and serve it.
Per Serving: Calories 300; Fat 18.08g; Sodium 180mg; Carbs 8.57g; Fibre 1.7g; Sugar 2.55g; Protein 8.57g

California Deviled Eggs

Prep Time: 5 minutes | Cook Time: 15 minutes | Serves: 4

4 large eggs
215g ice cubes
240ml water
2 tablespoons mayonnaise
½ teaspoon coconut aminos
¼ medium ripe avocado, peeled, pitted, and diced
¼ teaspoon wasabi powder
2 tablespoons diced cucumber
60g lump crabmeat, shells discarded
1 sheet nori, sliced
8 slices jarred pickled ginger
1 teaspoon toasted sesame seeds

1. Preheat air fryer at 120°C for 3 minutes. 2. Place eggs in silicone muffin cups to avoid bumping around and cracking during cooking process. 3. Add silicone cups to air fryer basket cooking for 15 minutes. 4. Add ice and water to a medium bowl. Transfer eggs to water bath immediately to stop cooking process. After 5 minutes, peel eggs carefully. Cut eggs in half lengthwise. 5. Spoon yolks into a medium bowl. Arrange white halves on a large plate. 6. Using a fork, blend egg yolks, mayonnaise, coconut aminos, avocado, and wasabi powder until smooth. Mix in diced cucumber. 7. Spoon into white halves. 8. Garnish eggs with crabmeat, nori, and pickled ginger. 9. Sprinkle it with sesame seeds and serve it.
Per Serving: Calories 204; Fat 13.63g; Sodium 95mg; Carbs 16.2g; Fibre 3.5g; Sugar 4.96g; Protein 5.67g

Air-Fryer Barbecue Turnip Chips

Prep Time: 10 minutes | Cook Time: 24 minutes | Serves: 2

½ teaspoon smoked paprika
¼ teaspoon chili powder
¼ teaspoon garlic powder
⅛ teaspoon onion powder
⅛ teaspoon cayenne pepper
⅛ teaspoon granular sweetener
1 teaspoon salt, divided
1 large turnip, sliced into ¼ cm-thick circles
2 teaspoons olive oil

1. Preheat air fryer to 205°C for 3 minutes. 2. Combine paprika, chili powder, garlic powder, onion powder, cayenne pepper, sweetener, and ½ teaspoon salt in a small bowl, and set aside. 3. Toss turnip slices with olive oil and ½ teaspoon salt in a medium bowl. 4. Place half of turnip slices in air fryer basket lightly greased with olive oil and cook for 6 minutes. 5. Shake basket and cook for an additional 6 minutes. 6. Transfer chips to a medium bowl and repeat cooking with remaining turnip slices. 7. Toss with seasoning mix. 8. Let rest 15 minutes, then serve it.
Per Serving: Calories 46; Fat 4.71g; Sodium 1179mg; Carbs 0.98g; Fibre 0.4g; Sugar 0.12g; Protein 0.31g

Italian Salsa Verde

Prep Time: 10 minutes | Cook Time: 10 minutes | Serves: 6

340g fresh tomatillos, husked
1 large jalapeño, stem removed
1 bunch (approximately 8) spring onions, both ends trimmed
3 cloves garlic, peeled
½ teaspoon salt
1 tablespoon fresh lime juice
5g fresh coriander leaves

1. Preheat air fryer at 205°C for 3 minutes. 2. Place tomatillos and jalapeño in ungreased air fryer basket, and cook for 5 minutes. 3. Add spring onions and garlic to basket, and cook for an additional 5 minutes. 4. Add tomatillos, jalapeño, spring onions, and garlic to a food processor or blender. 5. Add salt, lime juice, and coriander leaves, and pulse or blend until ingredients are finely chopped. 6. Pour it into a small sealable container and refrigerate until ready to use, up to five days.
Per Serving: Calories 22; Fat 0.6g; Sodium 195mg; Carbs 4.23g; Fibre 1.2g; Sugar 2.35g; Protein 0.71g

Jalapeño Popper

Prep Time: 10 minutes | Cook Time: 18 minutes | Serves: 4

80g riced cauliflower
2 medium jalapeños, seeded and minced
1 large egg
30g grated sharp Cheddar cheese
25g cream cheese, room
temperature
1 tablespoon peeled and grated yellow onion
30g almond flour
½ teaspoon salt
¼ teaspoon garlic powder

1. Preheat air fryer at 190°C for 3 minutes. 2. Combine all ingredients in a medium bowl. Form it into twelve rectangular mounds (about 1 tablespoon each). 3. Cut a piece of parchment paper to fit bottom of air fryer basket. 4. Place six pieces on parchment paper in basket, and cook for 9 minutes. 5. Transfer it to a medium serving plate and repeat cooking with remaining pieces. 6. Let it rest for 5 minutes, and then serve it warm.
Per Serving: Calories 42; Fat 3.27g; Sodium 330mg; Carbs 1.8g; Fibre 0.5g; Sugar 0.77g; Protein 1.65g

Tasty Cauliflower Pizza Crusts

Prep Time: 10 minutes | Cook Time: 24 minutes | Serves: 2

110g cauliflower rice
1 large egg
55g grated mozzarella cheese
1 tablespoon grated Parmesan
cheese
1 clove garlic, peeled and minced
1 teaspoon Italian seasoning
⅛ teaspoon salt

1. Preheat air fryer at 205°C for 3 minutes. 2. Combine cauliflower rice, the large egg, mozzarella cheese, Parmesan cheese, garlic, Italian seasoning, and salt in a medium bowl. 3. Divide mixture in half and spread it into two pizza pans greased with cooking spray. 4. Place one pizza pan in air fryer basket and cook it for 12 minutes. 5. Remove pan from basket and repeat cooking with second pan.
Per Serving: Calories 98; Fat 3.11g; Sodium 535mg; Carbs 5.64g; Fibre 1.8g; Sugar 1.66g; Protein 12.2g

Simple Bone Marrow Butter

Prep Time: 10 minutes | Cook Time: 12 minutes | Serves: 4

900g beef bone marrow bones, cut into 5cm sections
2 cloves garlic, peeled and quartered
5 tablespoons butter, softened
1 tablespoon chopped fresh thyme leaves
¼ teaspoon salt

1. Soak bones in water in a large bowl and refrigerate for 1 hour. 2. Preheat air fryer at 205°C for 3 minutes. 3. Place bones in ungreased air fryer basket, and cook for 12 minutes. 4. Remove it from basket and let it cool for 10 minutes. 5. Push marrow out of bones with a small knife or chopstick. 6. Add a food processor with remaining ingredients and pulse it until smooth. 7. Place mixture on a piece of plastic wrap. Fold sides in to create a log. 8. Spin ends until log is tight. 9. Refrigerate for 1 hour until firm.
Per Serving: Calories 611; Fat 37.93g; Sodium 412mg; Carbs 0.65g; Fibre 0.1g; Sugar 0.03g; Protein 63.47g

Chapter 4 Fish and Seafood Recipes

Dijon Crab Cakes

Prep time: 40 minutes | Cook time: 15 minutes | Serves: 6

4 (150g) cans crab meat, drained
110g whole-wheat panko bread crumbs
35g chopped fresh parsley

4 cloves garlic, minced
4 teaspoons Dijon mustard
2 large eggs, beaten
Olive oil

1. Mix the crab meat, panko bread crumbs, parsley, garlic, and Dijon mustard in a large bowl. Add the eggs and stir to combine. Then cover the bowl and refrigerate for 30 minutes. 2. Spray an air fryer basket lightly with olive oil. 3. Form the mixture into 12 crab cakes. 4. Arrange the crab cakes evenly in the air fryer basket in a single layer. Spray the tops lightly with olive oil. Cook them in batches as needed. 5. Air fry the crab cakes in your air fryer at 180°C for 6 to 8 minutes. Turn the crab cakes over, spray lightly with olive oil, and cook until golden brown, 4 to 7 more minutes.
Per Serving: Calories 242; Fat 4g; Sodium 203mg; Carbs 31.6g; Fibre 9.1g; Sugar 1.3g; Protein 21.8g

Italian Garlic Scallops

Prep time: 10 minutes | Cook time: 15 minutes | Serves: 4

2 teaspoons olive oil, plus more for spraying
1 packet dry zesty Italian dressing mix

1 teaspoon minced garlic
400g small scallops, thawed, patted dry

1. Spray an air fryer basket lightly with olive oil. 2. Combine the olive oil, Italian dressing mix, and garlic in a large plastic zip-top bag. 3 Add the scallops, seal the zip-top bag, and coat the scallops in the seasoning mixture. 4. Add the scallops in the air fryer basket and lightly spray with olive oil. 5. Air fry at 205°C for 5 minutes, shake the basket, and cook until the scallops reach an internal temperature of 50°C, for 5 to 10 more minutes. 6. Serve them over a bowl of cooked quinoa and veggies.
Per Serving: Calories 108; Fat 3.6g; Sodium 482mg; Carbs 4.3g; Fibre 0g; Sugar 0.4g; Protein 13.7g

Lemony Fried Prawns

Prep time: 10 minutes | Cook time: 15 minutes | Serves: 4

2 teaspoons olive oil plus more for spraying
2 teaspoons minced garlic
2 teaspoons lemon juice
½ to 1 teaspoon crushed red

pepper
300g medium cooked prawns, thawed, and deveined, with tails on

1. Spray an air fryer basket lightly with olive oil. 2. Mix the garlic, lemon juice, 2 teaspoons of olive oil, and crushed red pepper to make a marinade in a medium bowl. 3. Toss in the prawns and cover the coated prawns with plastic wrap and place the bowl in the refrigerator for 30 minutes. 4. Then transfer the prepared prawns to the air fryer basket. Air fry at 205°C for 5 minutes. Shake the basket and cook until the prawns are cooked through and nicely browned, an additional 5 to 10 minutes.
Per Serving: Calories 90; Fat 3.5g; Sodium 485mg; Carbs 2.3g; Fibre 0.3g; Sugar 0.7g; Protein 11.8g

Avocado Prawns-Beans Bowl

Prep time: 10 minutes | Cook time: 15 minutes | Serves: 4

1 teaspoon olive oil, plus more for spraying
2 teaspoons lime juice
1 teaspoon honey
1 teaspoon minced garlic
1 teaspoon chili powder
Salt

300g medium cooked prawns, thawed, deveined, peeled
400g cooked brown rice
1 (375g) can seasoned black beans, warmed
1 large avocado, chopped
150g sliced cherry tomatoes

1. Spray an air fryer basket lightly with olive oil. 2. Mix the lime juice, 1 teaspoon of olive oil, honey, garlic, chili powder, and salt to make a marinade in a medium bowl. 3. Toss the prawns in the marinade until well coated. 4. Place the prawns in the air fryer basket. Air fry the prepared prawns at 205°C for 5 minutes. Shake the basket and cook until the prawns are cooked through and starting to brown, an additional 5 to 10 minutes. 5. To assemble the bowls, spoon ¼ of the rice, black beans, avocado, and cherry tomatoes into each of the four bowls. Top with the prawns and serve.
Per Serving: Calories 291; Fat 10.7g; Sodium 509mg; Carbs 35g; Fibre 7.2g; Sugar 3.8g; Protein 16.2g

Lemony Prawn

Prep Time: 5 minutes | Cook Time: 6 minutes | Serves: 2

1 medium lemon
200g medium shelled and deveined prawn

2 tablespoons unsalted butter, melted
½ teaspoon minced garlic

1. Zest the lemon and cut it in half. 2. Place prawn in a large bowl, and squeeze juice from ½ lemon over them. 3. Toss the prawn with the lemon zest and the remaining ingredients, then transfer them to a suitable baking dish. 4. Place the dish in the air fryer basket, and cook the prawn at 205°C for 6 minutes until they are bright pink. 5. Serve the prawn with pan sauce.
Per Serving: Calories 157; Fat 8.93g; Sodium 647mg; Carbs 3.03g; Fibre 0.1g; Sugar 0.61g; Protein 16.04g

Cajun Salmon Fillets

Prep Time: 5 minutes | Cook Time: 7 minutes | Serves: 2

2 (100g) salmon fillets, skin removed
2 tablespoons unsalted butter, melted
⅛ teaspoon ground cayenne

pepper
½ teaspoon garlic powder
1 teaspoon paprika
¼ teaspoon ground black pepper

1. Brush each salmon fillet with butter. 2. Mix the remaining ingredients in a small bowl, and rub the fillet with them. 3. Place fillets in the air fryer basket, and cook them at 200°C for 7 minutes until they have an internal temperature of at least 60°C. 4. Serve warm.
Per Serving: Calories 146; Fat 10.02g; Sodium 35mg; Carbs 1.71g; Fibre 0.6g; Sugar 0.29g; Protein 12.27g

Spiced Prawn

Prep Time: 5 minutes | Cook Time: 6 minutes | Serves: 2

200g medium shelled and deveined prawn
2 tablespoons salted butter, melted

1 teaspoon paprika
½ teaspoon garlic powder
¼ teaspoon onion powder

1. Toss the prawn with the other ingredients in a large bowl, then transfer the prawn to the air fryer basket. 2. Cook the prawn in the air fryer at 205°C for 6 minutes, turning them halfway through. 3. Serve hot.
Per Serving: Calories 155; Fat 8.94g; Sodium 705mg; Carbs 2.59g; Fibre 0.6g; Sugar 0.16g; Protein 15.85g

Fried Marinated Salmon Fillets

Prep time: 1 hour 10 minutes | Cook time: 20 minutes | Serves: 4

1 tablespoon olive oil, plus more for spraying
60ml soy sauce
60ml rice wine vinegar
1 tablespoon brown sugar
1 teaspoon mustard powder

1 teaspoon ground ginger
½ teaspoon freshly ground black pepper
½ teaspoon minced garlic
4 (150g) salmon fillets, skin-on

1. Spray an air fryer basket lightly with olive oil. 2. Combine the brown sugar, the soy sauce, rice wine vinegar, brown sugar, 1 tablespoon of olive oil, mustard powder, ginger, black pepper, and garlic in a small bowl to make a marinade. 3. Place the fillets in a shallow baking dish and pour the marinade over them. Cover the baking dish and then refrigerate it for at least 1 hour, turning the fillets occasionally to keep them well coated in the marinade. 4. Shake off as much marinade as possible from the fillets and place them in the air fryer basket in a single layer, skin side down. Cook the fillets in batches as needed. 5. Air fry the fillets at 185°C for 10 to 15 minutes for medium-rare to medium done salmon or 15 to 20 minutes for well done. The minimum internal temperature should be 60°C at the thickest part of the fillet.
Per Serving: Calories 295; Fat 12.7g; Sodium 341mg; Carbs 6.8g; Fibre 0.5g; Sugar 5.1g; Protein 35.5g

Tasty Coconut Prawn

Prep Time: 5 minutes | Cook Time: 6 minutes | Serves: 2

200g medium shelled and deveined prawn
2 tablespoons salted butter, melted
25g unsweetened shredded coconut

1. Toss the prawn with butter in a large bowl. 2. Coat the prawn with the shredded coconut, and then place them in the air fryer basket. 3. Cook the prawn in the air fryer at 205°C for 6 minutes, turning them halfway through. 4. Serve hot.
Per Serving: Calories 190; Fat 8.28g; Sodium 228mg; Carbs 1.23g; Fibre 0.4g; Sugar 0.79g; Protein 23.1g

Foil-Packet Lemon Salmon

Prep Time: 10 minutes | Cook Time: 12 minutes | Serves: 2

2 (100g) salmon fillets, skin removed
2 tablespoons unsalted butter, melted
½ teaspoon garlic powder
1 medium lemon
½ teaspoon dried dill

1. Place each fillet on a 12cm × 12cm square of aluminum foil. Drizzle them with butter and sprinkle with garlic powder. 2. Zest half of the lemon and sprinkle zest over salmon. Slice other half of the lemon and lay two slices on each piece of salmon. 3. Sprinkle dill over salmon. 4. Fold the foil to fully close packets, and place the foil packets in the air fryer basket. 5. Cook the fillets at 205°C for 12 minutes until they can be easily flaked and have an internal temperature of at least 60°C. 6. Serve warm.
Per Serving: Calories 148; Fat 10g; Sodium 34mg; Carbs 2.54g; Fibre 0.3g; Sugar 0.62g; Protein 12.19g

Fish Sticks

Prep Time: 15 minutes | Cook Time: 10 minutes | Serves: 4

25g parmesan., grates
25g blanched finely ground almond flour
1 tablespoon coconut oil
1 large egg
455g cod fillet, cut into 2cm strips

1. Mix the parmesan, almond flour, and coconut oil in a large bowl. 2. Beat the egg in a medium bowl. 3. Dip each fish stick in the egg, and the coat with the flour mixture. 4. Cook the coated fish sticks in the air fryer at 205°C for 10 minutes until golden. 5. Serve warm.
Per Serving: Calories 169; Fat 5.81g; Sodium 366mg; Carbs 6.12g; Fibre 0.2g; Sugar 0.07g; Protein 21.67g

Crispy Salmon Patties

Prep Time: 10 minutes | Cook Time: 8 minutes | Serves: 2

2 (125g) pouches cooked pink salmon
1 large egg
25g parmesan, grated
2 tablespoons full-fat mayonnaise
2 teaspoons sriracha
1 teaspoon chili powder

1. Mix all ingredients in a large bowl, and form the mixture into four patties. 2. Place the patties in the air fryer basket, and cook them at 205°C for 8 minutes until crispy, flipping them halfway through. 3. Serve and enjoy.
Per Serving: Calories 325; Fat 25.11g; Sodium 370mg; Carbs 1.21g; Fibre 0.6g; Sugar 0.4g; Protein 22.25g

Delicious Firecracker Prawn

Prep Time: 10 minutes | Cook Time: 7 minutes | Serves: 4

455g medium shelled and deveined prawn
2 tablespoons salted butter, melted
¼ teaspoon garlic powder
2 tablespoons sriracha
¼ teaspoon powdered erythritol
60g full-fat mayonnaise
⅛ teaspoon ground black pepper

1. Toss the prawn with butter, and garlic powder, and then transfer to the air fryer basket. 2. Cook the prawn at 205°C for 7 minutes until they are bright pink, flipping them halfway through. 3. Mix the sriracha, powdered erythritol, mayonnaise, and pepper in a large bowl, then toss in the cooked prawn. Enjoy.

Per Serving: Calories 157; Fat 5.5g; Sodium 230mg; Carbs 2.8g; Fibre 0.7g; Sugar 0.83g; Protein 24.85g

Crab Legs with Lemon Butter Dip

Prep Time: 5 minutes | Cook Time: 15 minutes | Serves: 4

55g salted butter, melted and divided
1.3kg crab legs
¼ teaspoon garlic powder
Juice of ½ medium lemon

1. Drizzle the crab legs with 2 tablespoons of butter, and then place the crab legs into the air fryer basket. 2. Cook the crab legs at 205°C for 15 minutes, tossing them halfway through. 3. While cooking the crab legs, mix the garlic powder, lemon juice, and the remaining butter in a small bowl. 4. Crack open crab legs, remove the meat, and dip in lemon butter to enjoy.
Per Serving: Calories 393; Fat 9.25g; Sodium 1862mg; Carbs 2.8g; Fibre 51.6g; Sugar 21.42g; Protein 26.06g

Foil-Packet Lobster Tail with Parsley

Prep Time: 15 minutes | Cook Time: 12 minutes | Serves: 2

2 (150g) lobster tails, halved
2 tablespoons salted butter, melted
Juice of ½ medium lemon
1 teaspoon dried parsley

1. Place the two halved tails on a sheet of aluminum foil, and drizzle them with butter, and lemon juice. 2. Seal the foil packets, covering the tails completely, and then place them in the air fryer basket. 3. Cook the tails at 190°C for 12 minutes. 4. After cooking, sprinkle the tails with dried parsley, and serve immediately.
Per Serving: Calories 136; Fat 8.31g; Sodium 422mg; Carbs 0.99g; Fibre 0.1g; Sugar 0.31g; Protein 26.06g

Simple Fish Sticks

Prep time: 15 minutes | Cook time: 15 minutes | Serves: 4

Olive oil
4 fish fillets (cod, tilapia or pollock)
65g whole-wheat flour
1 teaspoon seasoned salt
2 eggs
155g whole-wheat panko bread crumbs
½ tablespoon dried parsley flakes

1. Spray an air fryer basket lightly with olive oil. 2. Cut the fish fillets lengthwise into "sticks." 3. In a shallow bowl, mix together the whole-wheat flour and seasoned salt. 4. In a small bowl whisk the eggs with 1 teaspoon of water. 5. Mix the panko bread crumbs and parsley flakes in another shallow bowl. 6. Coat each fish stick in the seasoned flour, then in the egg mixture, and dredge them in the panko bread crumbs. 7. Lay the fish sticks evenly in the air fryer basket in a single layer and lightly spray the fish sticks with olive oil. Work in batches as needed. 8. Air fry the fish sticks at 205°C for 5 to 8 minutes. Flip the fish sticks over and lightly spray with the olive oil. Cook until golden brown and crispy, for 5 to 7 more minutes.
Per Serving: Calories 490; Fat 13.3g; Sodium 1107mg; Carbs 49g; Fibre 2.9g; Sugar 0.7g; Protein 41g

Seasoned Catfish Strips

Prep time: 1 hour 15 minutes | Cook time: 20 minutes | Serves: 4

240ml buttermilk
5 catfish fillets, cut into 4.5cm strips
Olive oil
160g polenta
1 tablespoon cajun seasoning

1. Add the buttermilk into a shallow baking dish. Place the catfish in the dish and refrigerate for at least 1 hour to help remove any fishy taste. 2. Spray an air fryer basket lightly with olive oil. 3. In a shallow bowl, combine polenta and cajun seasoning. 4. Shake any excess buttermilk off the catfish. Place each strip in the polenta mixture and coat completely. Press the polenta into the catfish gently to help it stick. 5. Lay the strips evenly in the air fryer basket in a single layer. Lightly spray the catfish with olive oil. You may need to cook the catfish in more than one batch. 6. Air fry at 205°C for 8 minutes. Turn the catfish strips over and lightly spray with olive oil. Cook the catfish strips until they are golden brown and crispy, for 8 to 10 more minutes.
Per Serving: Calories 365; Fat 6.8g; Sodium 359mg; Carbs 35.4g; Fibre 1.8g; Sugar 3.8g; Protein 37.5g

Fried Breaded Fish and Potato Chips

Prep time: 25 minutes | Cook time: 35 minutes | Serves: 4

For the Chips

1 tablespoon olive oil, plus more for spraying
2 large russet potatoes, scrubbed

1 teaspoon salt
½ teaspoon freshly ground black pepper

For the Fish

Olive oil
4 (100g) cod fillets
1½ teaspoons salt, divided plus more as needed
1½ teaspoons black pepper, divided, plus more as needed

65g whole-wheat flour
2 eggs
155g whole-wheat panko bread crumbs
¼ teaspoon cayenne pepper

To make the chips: 1. Spray an air fryer basket lightly with olive oil. 2. Cut the potatoes lengthwise into 1cm-thick slices and then into 1cm-thick fries. 3. In a large bowl, mix together the oil, salt, and pepper and toss with the potatoes to coat. 4. Place the potatoes in a single layer in the air fryer basket. You may need to cook them in batches. 5. Air fry at 205°C for 5 minutes. Shake the basket and cook until the potatoes are lightly browned and crisp, for 5 to 10 more minutes. Set aside and keep warm.

To make the fish: 1. Spray the air fryer basket with olive oil. 2. Season the fillets with salt and black pepper. 3. In a shallow bowl, mix together the whole-wheat flour, ½ teaspoon of salt, and ½ teaspoon of black pepper. 4. In a second bowl, whisk together the eggs, 1 teaspoon of water, and a pinch of salt and pepper. 5. In another shallow bowl, combine the panko bread crumbs, cayenne pepper, and remaining 1 teaspoon of salt and 1 teaspoon of black pepper. Coat each fillet in the seasoned flour, then coat with the egg, and dredge in the panko bread crumb mixture. 6. Place the fillets in the air fryer basket in a single layer. Lightly spray the fish with olive oil. You may need to cook them in batches. 7. Air fry at 205°C for 8 to 10 minutes. Turn the fillets over and lightly spray with olive oil. Cook until golden brown and crispy, for 5 to 10 more minutes.

Per Serving: Calories 694; Fat 22.2g; Sodium 1912mg; Carbs 90.2g; Fibre 10.8g; Sugar 2.2g; Protein 34.6g

Parmesan Tuna Patty Sliders

Prep time: 15 minutes | Cook time: 15 minutes | Serves: 4

Olive oil
3 (125g) cans tuna, packed in water
80g whole-wheat panko bread crumbs

35g shredded Parmesan cheese
1 tablespoon sriracha
¾ teaspoon black pepper
10 whole-wheat slider buns

1. Spray an air fryer basket lightly with olive oil. 2. In a medium bowl combine the tuna, bread crumbs, Parmesan cheese, sriracha, and black pepper and stir to combine. 3. Form the mixture into 10 patties. 4. Then transfer the patties to the air fryer basket in a single layer. Spray the patties lightly with olive oil. Work in batches as needed. 5. Air fry at 175°C for 6 to 8 minutes. Turn the patties over and lightly spray with olive oil. Cook until golden brown and crisp, another 4 to 7 more minutes.

Per Serving: Calories 524; Fat 9.4g; Sodium 805mg; Carbs 76.6g; Fibre 7.7g; Sugar 4.7g; Protein 35.7g

Mayo Salmon Burgers

Prep time: 40 minutes | Cook time: 15 minutes | Serves: 4

Olive oil
4 (125g) cans pink salmon in water, any skin and bones removed, drained
2 eggs, beaten

100g whole-wheat bread crumbs
4 tablespoons light mayonnaise
2 teaspoons Cajun seasoning
2 teaspoons dry mustard
4 whole-wheat buns

1. Spray an air fryer basket lightly with olive oil. 2. Mix the salmon, egg, bread crumbs, mayonnaise, Cajun seasoning, and dry mustard in a medium bowl. Cover with plastic wrap and then let it marinate in the refrigerator for 30 minutes. 3. Shape the mixture into four 1cm thick patties about the same size as the buns. 4. Place the salmon patties in the fryer basket in a single layer and lightly spray the tops with olive oil. Cook them in batches as needed. 5. Air fry the patties at 180°C for 6 to 8 minutes. Turn the patties over and lightly spray with olive oil. Cook until crispy on the outside, for 4 to 7 more minutes. 6. Serve on whole-wheat buns.

Per Serving: Calories 824; Fat 42g; Sodium 1355mg; Carbs 53.3g; Fibre 2.4g; Sugar 19.1g; Protein 55.6g

Caramelized Salmon

Prep time: 1 hour 10 minutes | Cook time: 16 minutes | Serves: 4

3 tablespoons soy sauce
1 tablespoon rice wine or dry sherry
1 tablespoon brown sugar
1 tablespoon toasted sesame oil

1 teaspoon minced garlic
¼ teaspoon minced ginger
4 (150g) salmon fillets, skin-on
Olive oil
½ tablespoon sesame seeds

1. Mix the soy sauce, rice wine, brown sugar, toasted sesame oil, garlic, and ginger in a small bowl. 2. Add the salmon fillets in a shallow baking dish and pour the marinade over the fillets. Cover the baking dish and let it refrigerate for at least 1 hour, turning the fillets occasionally to coat in the marinade. 3. Spray an air fryer basket lightly with olive oil. 4. Shake off any marinade and place the fillets, skin side down, in the air fryer basket in a single layer. Reserve the marinade. Work in batches as needed. 5. Air fry the fillets at 185°C for 8 to 10 minutes. Brush the tops of the salmon fillets with the reserved marinade and sprinkle with sesame seeds. 6. Increase the air fryer temperature setting to 205°C and cook for 2 to 5 more minutes for medium, 1 to 3 minutes for medium rare, or 4 to 6 minutes for well done.

Per Serving: Calories 341; Fat 18.4g; Sodium 919mg; Carbs 5.6g; Fibre 0.4g; Sugar 4.5g; Protein 36.2g

Fried Breaded Calamari

Prep time: 15 minutes | Cook time: 15 minutes | Serves: 4

Olive oil
455g fresh calamari tubes, rinsed and patted dry
½ teaspoon salt, plus more as needed
½ teaspoon pepper, plus more as

needed
125g whole-wheat flour
3 eggs
100g whole-wheat bread crumbs
2 teaspoons dried parsley

1. Spray an air fryer basket lightly with olive oil. 2. Cut the calamari into ½cm rings. Season them with salt and black pepper. 3. In a shallow bowl, combine the whole-wheat flour, ½ teaspoon of salt, and ½ teaspoon of black pepper. 4. Add the beaten eggs in a small bowl and whisk together with 1 teaspoon of water. 5. Add the bread crumbs and parsley in another shallow bowl. 6. Coat the calamari in the flour mixture, coat in the egg, and dredge in the bread crumbs to coat. 7. Spread the calamari in the air fryer basket in a single layer. Spray the calamari lightly with olive oil. Work in batches as needed. 8. Air fry at 195°C until crispy and lightly browned for 10 to 15 minutes, shaking the basket several times during cooking to redistribute and evenly cook.

Per Serving: Calories 514; Fat 12.5g; Sodium 1051mg; Carbs 48.8g; Fibre 4.5g; Sugar 2.3g; Protein 49.5g

Mayo Fish Taco Bowl

Prep time: 10 minutes | Cook time: 12 minutes | Serves: 4

140g finely shredded cabbage
120g mayonnaise
Juice of 1 medium lime, divided
4 (150g) boneless, skinless tilapia

fillets
2 teaspoons chili powder
1 teaspoon salt
½ teaspoon ground black pepper

1. In a large bowl, mix cabbage, mayonnaise, and half of lime juice to make a slaw. Cover and refrigerate while the fish are cooking. 2. Preheat the air fryer to 205°C. 3. Sprinkle tilapia with chili powder, salt, and pepper. Spritz each side with cooking spray. 4. Place fillets in the air fryer basket and cook for 12 minutes, turning halfway through cooking time, until fish is opaque, flakes easily, and reaches an internal temperature of 60°C. 5. Allow fish to cool for 5 minutes before chopping into bite-sized pieces. To serve, place 70g slaw into each bowl and top with one-fourth of fish. Squeeze remaining lime juice over fish. Serve warm.

Per Serving: Calories 414; Fat 19.5g; Sodium 1318mg; Carbs 41.5g; Fibre 4.4g; Sugar 11.4g; Protein 18.5g

Butter Bay Scallops

Prep Time: 5 minutes | Cook Time: 5 minutes | Serves: 4

2 tablespoons butter, melted
Juice from 1 medium lime
¼ teaspoon salt
455g bay scallops

1. Preheat air fryer to 175°C. 2. Coat the scallops with butter, lime juice, and salt in a medium bowl. 3. Transfer the scallops to air fryer basket, and cook them for 5 minutes, tossing them halfway through. 4. Serve warm.
Per Serving: Calories 116; Fat 4.42g; Sodium 593mg; Carbs 4.53g; Fibre 0g; Sugar 0.19g; Protein 13.95g

Breaded Salmon Patty Bites

Prep time: 15 minutes | Cook time: 15 minutes | Serves: 4

Olive oil
4 (125g) cans pink salmon, skinless, boneless in water, drained
2 eggs, beaten
105g whole-wheat panko bread crumbs
4 tablespoons finely minced red pepper
2 tablespoons parsley flakes

1. Spray an air fryer basket lightly with olive oil. 2. Mix together the salmon, eggs, panko bread crumbs, red pepper, parsley flakes, and Old Bay seasoning in a medium bowl. 3. Form the mixture into 20 balls with a small cookie scoop. 4. Place the salmon bites in the air fryer basket in a single layer and spray lightly with olive oil. Work in batches as needed. 5. Air fry at 180°C until crispy for 10 to 15 minutes, shaking the basket a couple of times for even cooking.
Per Serving: Calories 375; Fat 13.8g; Sodium 847mg; Carbs 24.2g; Fibre 2g; Sugar 4g; Protein 36.6g

Smoky Calamari Rings

Prep Time: 15 minutes | Cook Time: 8 minutes | Serves: 4

2 tablespoons tomato paste
1 tablespoon gochujang
1 tablespoon fresh lime juice
1 teaspoon smoked paprika
½ teaspoon salt
100g parmesan, grated
6 calamari tubes, cut into ½cm rings

1. Preheat air fryer to 205°C. Lightly grease the air fryer basket with oil. 2. Whisk the tomato paste, gochujang, lime juice, paprika, and salt in a medium bowl. 3. Add parmesan to a separate shallow dish. 4. Dredge a calamari ring in tomato mixture, shaking off excess, and then roll it through the parmesan. Do the same with the remaining rings. 5. Place the calamari rings in air fryer basket, and cook them for 4 minutes, flipping them halfway through. You can cook them in 2 batches. 6. Serve warm.
Per Serving: Calories 282; Fat 25.95g; Sodium 614mg; Carbs 2.75g; Fibre 0.6g; Sugar 1.27g; Protein 9.32g

Breaded Fish Sticks

Prep Time: 10 minutes | Cook Time: 20 minutes | Serves: 4

For Tartar Sauce
120g mayonnaise
1 tablespoon Dijon mustard
30g small-diced dill pickles
⅛ teaspoon salt
¼ teaspoon freshly ground black pepper
For Fish Sticks
1 large egg, beaten
30g cornflour
25g almond flour
½ teaspoon salt
¼ teaspoon freshly ground black pepper
455g cod, cut into 2.5cm sticks

1. To make the tartar sauce, mix all the tartar sauce ingredients in a small bowl, cover the bowl and refrigerate the mixture for serving. 2. To make the fish sticks: Preheat the air fryer to 175°C. Lightly grease the air fryer basket. 3. Place egg in a small bowl; combine the cornflour, almond flour, salt, and pepper in a separate shallow dish. 4. Dip a fish stick in egg, shaking off excess egg, and roll in flour mixture, then place in a large plate. 5. Do the same with the remaining fish sticks. 6. Place the fish sticks in the air fryer basket, and cook them for 10 minutes, flipping halfway through. You can cook them in 2 batches. 7. Serve warm with tartar sauce on the side.
Per Serving: Calories 227; Fat 11.43g; Sodium 1149mg; Carbs 8.96g; Fibre 1g; Sugar 0.53g; Protein 20.98g

Crab Cakes with Rocket Salad

Prep Time: 15 minutes | Cook Time: 10 minutes | Serves: 2

For Crab Cakes
200g crabmeat, shells discarded
2 tablespoons mayonnaise
½ teaspoon Dijon mustard
½ teaspoon lemon juice
2 teaspoons peeled and minced
yellow onion
¼ teaspoon prepared horseradish
25g almond meal
1 large egg white, beaten
For Salad
1 tablespoon olive oil
2 teaspoons lemon juice
⅛ teaspoon salt
⅛ teaspoon freshly ground black pepper
100g fresh rocket
70g fresh blackberries
30g walnut pieces
2 lemon wedges

1. To make crab cakes: Preheat the air fryer at 205°C for 3 minutes. Lightly grease the air fryer basket with oil. 2. Combine all ingredients, and then form the mixture into four patties. 3. Place the patties into air fryer basket, and cook them for 10 minutes, flipping them halfway through. 4. Transfer crab cakes to a large plate. Set aside. 5. To make salad: Toss the rocket with olive oil, lemon juice, salt, and pepper in a large bowl. 6. Distribute the salad into two medium bowls. 7. Add two crab cakes to each bowl, garnish them with blackberries, walnuts, and lemon wedges. Enjoy.
Per Serving: Calories 431; Fat 20.38g; Sodium 690mg; Carbs 36.68g; Fibre 7g; Sugar 21.48g; Protein 29.61g

Bacon Stuffed Prawns

Prep Time: 10 minutes | Cook Time: 18 minutes | Serves: 4

455g large raw prawns, deveined and shelled
3 tablespoons crumbled goat cheese
2 tablespoons panko bread crumbs
¼ teaspoon Worcestershire sauce
½ teaspoon prepared horseradish
¼ teaspoon garlic powder
2 teaspoons mayonnaise
¼ teaspoon freshly ground black pepper
2 tablespoons water
5 slices bacon, quartered
5g chopped fresh parsley

1. Butterfly prawns by cutting down the spine of each prawns without going all the way through. 2. Combine the goat cheese, bread crumbs, Worcestershire sauce, horseradish, garlic powder, mayonnaise, and pepper in a medium bowl. 3. Preheat air fryer at 205°C for 3 minutes. Pour 2 tablespoons of water in the air fryer basket. 4. Evenly press goat cheese mixture into prawns; wrap a piece of bacon around each piece of prawns to hold in cheese mixture. 5. Place half of prawns in the air fryer basket, cook them for 9 minutes, flipping them halfway through. 6. Garnish the prawns with chopped parsley after cooking. Serve warm.
Per Serving: Calories 286; Fat 16.79g; Sodium 526mg; Carbs 4.41g; Fibre 0.4g; Sugar 1.46g; Protein 29.51g

Efficient Cod Piccata with Roasted Potatoes

Prep Time: 15 minutes | Cook Time: 12 minutes | Serves: 4

4 (100g) cod fillets
1 tablespoon unsalted butter
2 teaspoons capers, drained
1 garlic clove, minced
2 tablespoons freshly squeezed lemon juice
225g asparagus, trimmed
2 large potatoes, cubed
1 tablespoon extra-virgin olive oil
¼ teaspoon salt
¼ teaspoon garlic powder
¼ teaspoon freshly ground black pepper

1. Turn on and preheat the air fryer to 195°C. 2. Put the cod fillets on a large piece of aluminum foil. Add the butter, capers, garlic, and lemon juice over the cod and wrap up the foil to enclose the fish in a pouch. 3. Toss in a large bowl together the asparagus, potatoes, olive oil, salt, garlic powder, and pepper. 4. Replace the potatoes and asparagus to the air fryer basket and cook for 4 minutes. Shake or stir the air fryer basket and carefully place the foil packet of fish on top of the vegetables. Continue cooking for 8 minutes. 5. Let the dish stand for 5 minutes before serving.
Per Serving: Calories 436; Fat 19.03g; Sodium 707mg; Carbs 43.31g; Fibre 10.7g; Sugar 3.41g; Protein 24.88g

Classic Ahi Tuna Steaks

Prep time: 5 minutes| Cook time: 14 minutes| Serves: 2

2 (150g) ahi tuna steaks
2 tablespoons olive oil
3 tablespoons bagel seasoning

1. Preheat the air fryer to 205°C. 2. Drizzle both sides of steaks with oil. Place seasoning on a medium plate and press each side of tuna steaks into seasoning to form a thick layer. 3. Add steaks in the air fryer basket and cook for 14 minutes, turning halfway through cooking time, until internal temperature reaches at least 60°C for well-done. Serve warm.
Per Serving: Calories 672; Fat 16.6g; Sodium 722mg; Carbs 72g; Fibre 6g; Sugar 9g; Protein 56.5g

Snow Crab Legs

Prep time: 5 minutes| Cook time: 15 minutes per batch| Serves: 6

200g fresh shell-on snow crab legs
2 tablespoons olive oil
4 tablespoons salted butter, melted
2 teaspoons lemon juice

1. Preheat the air fryer to 205°C. 2. Drizzle crab legs with oil. Place in the air fryer basket, working in batches as necessary. Cook for 15 minutes, turning once while cooking, until crab turns a bright red-orange. 3. In a small bowl, whisk together butter and lemon juice. Serve as a dipping sauce with warm crab legs.
Per Serving: Calories 588; Fat 13g; Sodium 5047mg; Carbs 0.3g; Fibre 0.1g; Sugar 0g; Protein 109.6g

Coconut Breaded Prawns

Prep time: 10 minutes| Cook time: 10 minutes| Serves: 4

125g plain flour
1 teaspoon salt
2 large eggs
55g panko bread crumbs
80g shredded unsweetened coconut flakes
455g large prawns, peeled and deveined

1. Preheat the air fryer to 190°C. 2. Add flour and salt in a medium bowl and mix well. In a separate medium bowl, whisk eggs. In a third medium bowl, mix bread crumbs and coconut flakes. 3. Dredge prawns first in flour mixture, shaking off excess, then in eggs, letting any additional egg drip off, and finally in bread crumb mixture. Spritz with cooking spray. 4. Place prawns in the air fryer basket. Cook for 10 minutes, turning and spritzing opposite side with cooking spray halfway through cooking, until insides are pearly white and opaque and internal temperature reaches at least 60°C. Serve warm.
Per Serving: Calories 479; Fat 22g; Sodium 1625mg; Carbs 39.2g; Fibre 3.2g; Sugar 8.3g; Protein 29.8g

Parmesan Breaded Tilapia

Prep time: 10 minutes| Cook time: 10 minutes| Serves: 4

1 large egg
40g plain flour
25g grated Parmesan cheese
½ tablespoon lemon pepper
seasoning
4 (150g) boneless, skinless tilapia fillets

1. Preheat the air fryer to 190°C. 2. In a medium bowl, whisk egg. On a large plate, mix flour, Parmesan, and lemon pepper seasoning. 3. Pat tilapia dry. Dip each fillet into egg, gently shaking off excess. Press into flour mixture, then spritz both sides with cooking spray. 4. Place the tilapia fillets in the air fryer basket and cook for 10 minutes, turning halfway through cooking, until fillets are golden and crispy and internal temperature reaches at least 60°C. Serve warm.
Per Serving: Calories 243; Fat 5.9g; Sodium 203mg; Carbs 9.5g; Fibre 0.5g; Sugar 0g; Protein 37.8g

Lemon-Butter Lobster Tails

Prep time: 5 minutes| Cook time: 10 minutes| Serves: 4

4 (150g) lobster tails
2 tablespoons salted butter, melted
2 teaspoons lemon juice
1 tablespoon Cajun seasoning

1. Preheat the air fryer to 205°C. 2. Carefully cut open lobster tails with kitchen scissors and pull back the shell a little to expose the meat. Drizzle butter and lemon juice over each tail, then sprinkle with Cajun seasoning. 3. Place tails in the air fryer basket and cook for 10 minutes until lobster shells are bright red and internal temperature reaches at least 60°C. Serve warm.
Per Serving: Calories 157; Fat 5g; Sodium 820mg; Carbs 1.4g; Fibre 0.3g; Sugar 0.3g; Protein 24.9g

Cod Fillet Sandwich

Prep time: 10 minutes| Cook time: 18 minutes| Serves: 4

4 (75g) cod fillets
½ teaspoon salt
¼ teaspoon ground black pepper
80g unsweetened cornflakes,
crushed
100g Italian bread crumbs
2 large eggs
4 sandwich buns

1. Preheat the air fryer to 190°C. 2. Sprinkle cod with salt and pepper on both sides. 3. In a large bowl, combine cornflakes and bread crumbs. 4. In a medium bowl, whisk eggs. Press each piece of cod into eggs to coat, shaking off excess, then into cornflake mixture to coat evenly on both sides. Spritz with cooking spray. 5. Place the cod in the air fryer basket and cook for 18 minutes, turning halfway through cooking time, until fillets are brown and internal temperature reaches at least 60°C. Place on buns to serve.
Per Serving: Calories 451; Fat 21g; Sodium 1050mg; Carbs 45g; Fibre 3.4g; Sugar 22.6g; Protein 21.8g

Sesame Teriyaki Salmon

Prep time: 5 minutes plus 15 minutes for marinating| Cook time: 12 minutes| Serves: 4

120ml teriyaki sauce
¼ teaspoon salt
1 teaspoon ground ginger
½ teaspoon garlic powder
4 (150g) boneless, skinless salmon fillets
2 tablespoons toasted sesame seeds

1. In a large bowl, whisk teriyaki sauce, salt, ginger, and garlic powder. Add salmon to the bowl, being sure to coat each side with marinade. Cover and let marinate in refrigerator for 15 minutes. 2. Preheat the air fryer to 190°C. 3. Spritz fillets with cooking spray and place in the air fryer basket. Cook for 12 minutes, turning halfway through cooking time, until glaze has caramelized to a dark brown color, salmon flakes easily, and internal temperature reaches at least 60°C. Sprinkle sesame seeds on salmon and serve warm.
Per Serving: Calories 299; Fat 11.5g; Sodium 1000mg; Carbs 7.3g; Fibre 0.8g; Sugar 5g; Protein 39.2g

Great Coconut Prawns with Orange Sauce

Prep Time: 15 minutes | Cook Time: 15 minutes | Serves: 4

40g unsweetened grated coconut
30g whole-wheat bread crumbs
30g whole-wheat flour
¼ teaspoon smoked paprika
¼ teaspoon freshly ground black pepper
¼ teaspoon salt
1 egg
1 teaspoon water
455g medium prawns, peeled and
deveined
Extra-virgin olive oil, in a spray bottle, for greasing
2 tablespoons maple syrup
½ teaspoon rice vinegar
⅛ teaspoon red pepper flakes
60ml freshly squeezed orange juice
1 teaspoon cornflour

1. Turn on and preheat the air fryer to 175°C. 2. Mix in a shallow bowl together the coconut, bread crumbs, flour, paprika, black pepper, and salt. 3. In a separate shallow bowl, whisk together the egg and water. 4. Dip a prawns into the egg, shaking off any excess. Dip it into the coconut–bread crumb mixture, making sure to coat it completely. Do the same with the rest of the prawns. 5. Put the prawns in the air fryer basket in a single layer and spray the tops with olive oil. 6. Cook for 5 minutes. Turn over the prawns and continue cooking for another 2 to 3 minutes. 7. In a small saucepan, combine the maple syrup, vinegar, and red pepper flakes and stir until combined. Mix in a small bowl together the orange juice and cornflour. 8. Add it to the saucepan, and bring to a boil over medium heat. Cook, stirring frequently, for 5 minutes. Remove from the heat and let sit for 5 minutes.
Per Serving: Calories 190; Fat 4.05g; Sodium 871mg; Carbs 18.66g; Fibre 1.4g; Sugar 8.57g; Protein 19.32g

Mayo Prawns Burgers

Prep time: 10 minutes| Cook time: 10 minutes| Serves: 4

250g medium prawns, peeled and deveined
60g mayonnaise
55g panko bread crumbs
¼ teaspoon salt
⅛ teaspoon ground black pepper
4 hamburger buns

1. Preheat the air fryer to 205°C. 2. Add prawns in a food processor and pulse four times until broken down. 3. Scoop the prawns into a large bowl and mix with mayonnaise, bread crumbs, salt, and pepper until well combined. 4. Portion the mixture into four servings and form them into patties. They will feel wet but should be able to hold their shape. 5. Arrange the patties evenly in the air fryer basket and cook for 10 minutes, turning halfway through cooking time, until burgers are brown and internal temperature reaches at least 60°C. Serve warm on buns.
Per Serving: Calories 243; Fat 14g; Sodium 891mg; Carbs 16.3g; Fibre 2g; Sugar 0.7g; Protein 12.5g

Avocado-Salmon Patties

Prep time: 5 minutes| Cook time: 8 minutes| Serves: 4

300g pouched pink salmon
3 tablespoons mayonnaise
35g blanched finely ground almond flour
½ teaspoon Cajun seasoning
1 medium avocado, peeled, pitted, and sliced

1. In a medium bowl, mix salmon, mayonnaise, flour, and Cajun seasoning. Form mixture into four patties. 2. Place patties into ungreased air fryer basket. Adjust the temperature setting to 205°C and set the timer for 8 minutes, turning patties halfway through cooking. Patties will be done when firm and golden brown. 3. Transfer patties to four medium plates and serve warm with avocado slices.
Per Serving: Calories 319; Fat 23.3g; Sodium 486mg; Carbs 7g; Fibre 4.7g; Sugar 1g; Protein 21.8g

Fish-Cabbage Taco Bowl

Prep time: 10 minutes | Cook time: 12 minutes | Serves: 4

½ teaspoon salt
¼ teaspoon garlic powder
¼ teaspoon ground cumin
4 (100g) cod fillets
280g finely shredded green
cabbage
80g mayonnaise
¼ teaspoon ground black pepper
25g chopped pickled jalapeños

1. Sprinkle salt, garlic powder, and cumin over cod and place into ungreased air fryer basket. Adjust the temperature to 175°C and set the timer for 12 minutes, turning fillets halfway through cooking. Cod will flake easily and have an internal temperature of at least 60°C when done. 2. In a large bowl, toss cabbage with mayonnaise, pepper, and jalapeños until fully coated. Serve cod warm over cabbage slaw on four medium plates.
Per Serving: Calories 206; Fat 9.8g; Sodium 1324mg; Carbs 9.5g; Fibre 3.2g; Sugar 4.5g; Protein 20.5g

Spicy Garlic Salmon

Prep time: 5 minutes | Cook time: 7 minutes | Serves: 2

2 (100g) boneless, skinless salmon fillets
2 tablespoons salted butter, softened
⅛ teaspoon cayenne pepper
½ teaspoon garlic powder
1 teaspoon paprika
¼ teaspoon ground black pepper

1. Brush butter over both sides of each fille. In a small bowl, mix remaining ingredients and rub into fish on both sides. 2. Place fillets into an ungreased air fryer basket. Then cook the fillet in your air fryer at 200°C for 7 minutes. The internal temperature will be 60°C when done. Serve warm.
Per Serving: Calories 254; Fat 14.5g; Sodium 501mg; Carbs 1.5g; Fibre 0.6g; Sugar 0.2g; Protein 30.3g

Mustard Butter Salmon

Prep time: 5 minutes | Cook time: 12 minutes | Serves: 4

2 tablespoons salted butter, melted
1 teaspoon maple syrup
1 teaspoon yellow mustard

4 (100g) boneless, skinless salmon fillets
½ teaspoon salt

1. In a small bowl, whisk together butter, syrup, and mustard. Brush ½ mixture over each fillet on both sides. Sprinkle fillets with salt on both sides. 2. Place salmon into ungreased air fryer basket. Adjust the temperature setting to 205°C and set the timer for 12 minutes. Halfway through cooking, brush fillets on both sides with remaining syrup mixture. 3. Salmon will easily flake and have an internal temperature of at least 60°C when done. Serve warm.
Per Serving: Calories 236; Fat 10.3g; Sodium 638mg; Carbs 24.9g; Fibre 1.8g; Sugar 7.1g; Protein 10.6g

Fresh Garlic-Dill Salmon with Tomatoes & Green Beans

Prep Time: 5 minutes | Cook Time: 15 minutes | Serves: 4

4 tablespoons unsalted butter
4 garlic cloves, minced
10g chopped fresh dill
½ teaspoon salt
½ teaspoon freshly ground black pepper
4 (100g) wild-caught salmon fillets, skin removed
1 lemon, thinly sliced
455g green beans, trimmed
150g halved cherry tomatoes

1. Turn on and preheat the air fryer to 200°C. Line the air fryer basket with parchment paper. 2. Mix in a small bowl together the butter, garlic, dill, salt, and pepper. 3. Put the salmon fillets on a large plate and spread the butter mixture over them. 4. Put the salmon in the air fryer basket in a single layer. Put about three-quarters of the lemon slices on top of the fillets. Put the green beans and tomatoes around the fillets. 5. Cook for 12 to 15 minutes. 6. Serve with the remaining lemon slices.
Per Serving: Calories 515; Fat 22.86g; Sodium 1257mg; Carbs 12.4g; Fibre 3g; Sugar 5.85g; Protein 67.52g

Healthy Fish Cakes

Prep Time: 10 minutes | Cook Time: 10 minutes | Serves: 4

2 (125g) cans solid white albacore tuna in water, drained
1 large egg, beaten
160g panko bread crumbs, divided
3 tablespoons finely chopped coriander
2 tablespoons sweet chili sauce
2 tablespoons oyster sauce
2 teaspoons minced garlic
¼ teaspoon cayenne pepper
½ teaspoon salt
½ teaspoon freshly ground black pepper
Extra-virgin olive oil, for spraying

1. Combine the tuna, egg, 80g bread crumbs, coriander, chili sauce, oyster sauce, garlic, and cayenne pepper in a medium bowl. Stir the ingredients lightly with a fork until well mixed, but with some intact tuna chunks for texture. 2. Combine the remaining 80g bread crumbs, the salt, and black pepper in small shallow bowl. 3. Turn on and preheat the air fryer to 195°C. 4. Use a 50g to 75g ice cream scoop to form the tuna mixture into equal-size patties. Coat each patty with the breading. 5. Sprinkle the air fryer basket with oil lightly. Put the fish cakes in a single layer in the air fryer basket. Lightly spray with oil. 6. Air fry for 4 minutes; gently flip the fish cakes and lightly spray with oil, and then air fry them for another 4 minutes.
Per Serving: Calories 185; Fat 5.33g; Sodium 1042mg; Carbs 10.06g; Fibre 1g; Sugar 1.7g; Protein 22.63g

Mouth-watering Catfish

Prep Time: 10 minutes | Cook Time: 12 minutes | Serves: 4

4 (175g) catfish fillets
80g heavy whipping cream
1 tablespoon lemon juice
100g blanched finely ground
almond flour
½ teaspoon salt
¼ teaspoon ground black pepper

1. Place catfish fillets into a large bowl with cream and pour in lemon juice. Stir to coat. 2. Mix flour in a large bowl. 3. Remove each fillet and gently shake off excess cream. Sprinkle with salt and pepper. Press each fillet gently into flour mixture on both sides to coat. 4. Place fillets into ungreased air fryer basket. Adjust the temperature setting to 205°C and set the timer for 12 minutes, turning fillets halfway through cooking. 5. Catfish will be golden brown and have an internal temperature of at least 60°C when done. Serve warm.
Per Serving: Calories 439; Fat 28.3g; Sodium 387mg; Carbs 7.6g; Fibre 3.7g; Sugar 2g; Protein 40.5g

Salmon-Courgette Kebabs

Prep time: 10 minutes | Cook time: 8 minutes | Serves: 2

150g boneless, skinless salmon, cut into 2.5cm cubes
¼ medium red onion
½ medium yellow pepper
½ medium courgette, trimmed
and cut into 1cm slices
1 tablespoon olive oil
½ teaspoon salt
¼ teaspoon ground black pepper

1. Peel the onion and cut into 2.5cm pieces. Remove the seeds from the pepper and cut into 2.5cm pieces. 2. Using one 15cm skewer, skewer 1 piece salmon, then 1 piece onion, 1 piece pepper, and finally 1 piece courgette. Repeat this pattern with additional skewers to make four kebabs total. Drizzle the courgette skewers with olive oil and then sprinkle with salt and black pepper. 3. Place kebabs into ungreased air fryer basket. Adjust the temperature setting to 205°C and set the timer for 8 minutes, turning kebabs halfway through cooking. Salmon will easily flake and have an internal temperature of at least 60°C when done; vegetables will be tender. Serve warm.
Per Serving: Calories 219; Fat 11.6g; Sodium 810mg; Carbs 20.4g; Fibre 1.8g; Sugar 5.7g; Protein 8.4g

Crispy Cajun Lobster Tails

Prep time: 5 minutes | Cook time: 7 minutes | Serves: 4

4 (100g) lobster tails
2 tablespoons salted butter, melted
1½ teaspoons Cajun seasoning,
divided
¼ teaspoon salt
¼ teaspoon ground black pepper
50g grated Parmesan cheese

1. Cut lobster tails open carefully with a pair of scissors and gently pull meat away from shells, resting meat on top of shells. 2. Brush butter over lobster meat and sprinkle with 1 teaspoon Cajun seasoning, ¼ teaspoon per tail. 3. In a small bowl, mix the remaining Cajun seasoning, salt, pepper, and Parmesan cheese. Gently press ¼ mixture onto the meat on each lobster tail. 4. Carefully place tails into an ungreased air fryer basket. Adjust the temperature setting to 205°C and set the timer for 7 minutes. 5. Lobster tails will be crispy and golden on top and have an internal temperature of at least 60°C when done. Serve warm.
Per Serving: Calories 159; Fat 7g; Sodium 848mg; Carbs 1.6g; Fibre 0.2g; Sugar 0g; Protein 21.2g

Enticing Crab Cakes

Prep time: 10 minutes | Cook time: 10 minutes | Serves: 4

200g fresh lump crabmeat
2 tablespoons mayonnaise
15g parmesan, grated
35g seeded and chopped red pepper

1. In a large bowl, mix lump crabmeat, mayonnaise, parmesan, and red pepper together. Separate into four equal sections and form into patties. 2. Cut a piece of parchment to fit air fryer basket. Place patties onto an ungreased parchment and into air fryer basket. Adjust the temperature setting to 195°C and set the timer for 10 minutes, turning patties halfway through cooking. 3. Crab cakes will be golden when done. Serve warm.
Per Serving: Calories 84; Fat 3.6g; Sodium 326mg; Carbs 0g; Fibre 0g; Sugar 0.4g; Protein 11.3g

Lemony Crab Legs

Prep time: 5 minutes | Cook time: 15 minutes | Serves: 4

200g fresh shell-on snow crab legs
2 tablespoons coconut oil
4 tablespoons salted butter, melted
2 teaspoons lemon juice

For the crab legs: 1. Place crab legs into ungreased air fryer basket, working in batches if needed. Drizzle legs with coconut oil. 2. Adjust the temperature to 205°C and set the timer for 15 minutes, shaking the basket three times during cooking. Legs will turn a bright red-orange when done. Serve warm.
For the dipping sauce: In a separate small bowl, whisk butter and lemon juice for dipping. Serve on the side.
Per Serving: Calories 908; Fat 23.3g; Sodium 2738mg; Carbs 7.1g; Fibre 0g; Sugar 0g; Protein 158g

Lemon Butter Fish Fillet

Prep time: 5 minutes | Cook time: 12 minutes | Serves: 4

4 (100g) cod fillets
2 tablespoons salted butter, melted
½ medium lemon, cut into 4 slices

1. Place cod fillets into an ungreased 15cm round nonstick baking dish. Brush tops of fillets with butter. Lay 1 lemon slice on each fillet. 2. Use aluminum foil to cover the baking dish and place into air fryer basket. Adjust the temperature to 175°C and set the timer for 12 minutes, turning fillets halfway through cooking. 3. Fish will be opaque and have an internal temperature of at least 60°C when done. Serve warm.
Per Serving: Calories 115; Fat 4.3g; Sodium 375mg; Carbs 0.8g; Fibre 0g; Sugar 0g; Protein 17.5g

Tuna in Tomatoes

Prep time: 5 minutes | Cook time: 5 minutes | Serves: 2

2 medium beefsteak tomatoes, tops removed, seeded, membranes removed
2 (70g) pouches tuna packed in water, drained
1 medium stalk celery, trimmed and chopped
2 tablespoons mayonnaise
¼ teaspoon salt
¼ teaspoon ground black pepper
2 teaspoons coconut oil
25g shredded mild Cheddar cheese

1. Scoop pulp out of each tomato, leaving 1cm shell. 2. In a medium bowl, mix tuna, celery, mayonnaise, salt, and pepper. Drizzle with coconut oil. Spoon ½ mixture into each tomato and top each with 2 tablespoons Cheddar. 3. Place tomatoes into ungreased air fryer basket. Adjust the temperature setting to 160°C and set the timer for 5 minutes. Cheese will be melted when done. Serve warm.
Per Serving: Calories 234; Fat 15g; Sodium 702mg; Carbs 6.2g; Fibre 2g; Sugar 3.7g; Protein 19.9g

Irresistible Chili-Lime Tilapia

Prep Time: 5 minutes | Cook Time: 8 minutes | Serves: 4

½ teaspoon salt
½ teaspoon freshly ground black pepper
¼ teaspoon garlic powder
¼ teaspoon chili powder
¼ teaspoon smoked paprika
4 (100g) tilapia fillets
2 tablespoons freshly squeezed lime juice

1. Turn on and preheat the air fryer to 205°C. Line the air fryer basket with parchment paper. 2. Mix in a small bowl together the salt, pepper, garlic powder, chili powder, and paprika. 3. Put the fish fillets in a shallow bowl. Pour the lime juice over the fillets and then sprinkle it with the spice blend, making sure to coat all sides well. 4. Put the fish in the air fryer basket in a single layer, leaving space between each fillet. Cook the fish for 4 minutes; turn the fish over and cook for an another 4 to 5 minutes until crispy. 5. Serve immediately.
Per Serving: Calories 116; Fat 2.03g; Sodium 356mg; Carbs 1.14g; Fibre 0.2g; Sugar 0.16g; Protein 23.43g

Easy and Delicious Coriander Butter Baked Mahi Mahi

Prep Time: 5 minutes | Cook Time: 15 minutes | Serves: 4

2 tablespoons butter, melted
2 tablespoons chopped fresh coriander
2 garlic cloves, minced
½ teaspoon salt
¼ teaspoon freshly ground black pepper
¼ teaspoon chili powder
4 (100g) boneless, skinless mahi-mahi fillets

1. Turn on and preheat the air fryer to 190°C. 2. Mix the butter, coriander, garlic, salt, pepper, and chili powder in a small bowl. 3. Put the mahi-mahi fillets on a large plate. Spread the butter mixture over the top of the fillets. 4. Put a piece of parchment paper in the air fryer basket. Put the fish in a single layer in the air fryer basket. Cook them for 6 minutes; turn them over and cook for an another 6 to 7 minutes until flaky.
Per Serving: Calories 103; Fat 7.41g; Sodium 418mg; Carbs 6.62g; Fibre 0.6g; Sugar 1.56g; Protein 2.83g

Lemon-Herb Tuna Steaks

Prep Time: 20 minutes | Cook Time: 7 minutes | Serves: 4

½ tablespoon extra-virgin olive oil	freshly squeezed lemon juice
1 garlic clove, minced	1 tablespoon chopped fresh coriander
¼ teaspoon salt	4 (100g) tuna steaks, about 2.5cm thick
¼ teaspoon chili powder	
1 tablespoon plus 1 teaspoon	1 lemon, thinly sliced

1. In a wide, shallow bowl, mix together the olive oil, garlic, salt, chili powder, lemon juice, and coriander. Put the tuna steaks in the mixture, turning the steaks to coat them on all sides. Cover loosely and set aside to marinate for 20 minutes. 2. Turn on and preheat the air fryer to 195°C. 3. Put a piece of parchment paper in the air fryer basket. Remove the tuna steaks from the marinade and place them in the air fryer basket in one layer. Discard any remaining marinade. Cook for 7 minutes. Remove the air fryer basket from the air fryer and let stand for 5 minutes. 4. Put the tuna steaks on plates, and top them the lemon slices, then enjoy.
Per Serving: Calories 135; Fat 1.37g; Sodium 217mg; Carbs 1.26g; Fibre 0.36g; Sugar 13.12g; Protein 27.8g

Zesty Lemon-Caper Salmon Burgers

Prep Time: 15 minutes | Cook Time: 12 minutes | Serves: 4

455g boneless, skinless salmon fillet	½ teaspoon freshly ground black pepper
1 spring onion, both white and green parts, diced	¼ teaspoon paprika
2 tablespoons clean mayonnaise, plus more for serving	Zest of 1 lemon
	30g whole-wheat bread crumbs
1 egg	4 whole-wheat buns, toasted
1 teaspoon capers, drained	4 teaspoons whole-grain mustard
½ teaspoon salt	4 lettuce leaves
	1 small tomato, sliced

1. Turn on and preheat the air fryer to 205°C. 2. Cut the salmon in half. Cut one half into chunks and place them into a food processor. Add the spring onion, mayonnaise, egg, capers, salt, pepper, paprika, and lemon zest and pulse until the salmon is pureed. 3. Dice the remaining half of salmon into ½cm pieces. 4. Combine the salmon pieces, pureed salmon, and bread crumbs in a large bowl. 5. Form the mixture into 4 patties and place them in the air fryer basket. Cook for 5 minutes. Turn over the patties and continue cooking for an another 5 to 7 minutes. 6. Serve the salmon burgers on the whole-wheat buns with a teaspoon of mustard, more mayonnaise, lettuce, and a slice of tomato.
Per Serving: Calories 293; Fat 11.58g; Sodium 742mg; Carbs 32.74g; Fibre 2.9g; Sugar 7g; Protein 14.65g

Satisfying Parmesan Perch

Prep Time: 5 minutes | Cook Time: 10 minutes | Serves: 5

½ teaspoon salt	2 tablespoons whole-wheat bread crumbs
¼ teaspoon paprika	
¼ teaspoon freshly ground black pepper	4 (100g) ocean perch fillets
1 tablespoon chopped fresh dill	Extra-virgin olive oil, in a spray bottle, for greasing
25g grated Parmesan cheese	1 lemon, quartered

1. Turn on and preheat the air fryer to 205°C. Line the air fryer basket with parchment paper. 2. Combine the salt, paprika, pepper, dill, Parmesan cheese, and bread crumbs in a shallow bowl. 3. Dip the fillets in the Parmesan mixture, turning them to coat on all sides. 4. Put the perch fillets in a single layer in the air fryer basket, and spray the fillets with olive oil. Cook them for 7 to 9 minutes until the crust is golden. 5. Serve the perch fillets with the lemon wedges.
Per Serving: Calories 111; Fat 3.25g; Sodium 612mg; Carbs 4.19g; Fibre 0.5g; Sugar 0.43g; Protein 15.95g

Perfect Haddock Fish Fingers

Prep Time: 10 minutes | Cook Time: 10 minutes | Serves: 4

30g whole-wheat flour	¼ teaspoon dried oregano
¼ teaspoon salt	1 egg
¼ teaspoon freshly ground black pepper	1 teaspoon water
	4 (100g) haddock fillets
¼ teaspoon smoked paprika	1 lemon, thinly sliced (optional)

Malt vinegar, for serving (optional)	Tartar sauce, for serving (optional)
Ketchup, for serving (optional)	

1. Turn on and preheat the air fryer to 205°C. Line the air fryer with parchment paper. 2. In a wide, shallow bowl, mix together the flour, salt, pepper, paprika, and oregano. 3. In a separate wide shallow bowl, whisk together the egg and water. 4. Pat dry the haddock and cut each fillet into 4 strips. Dip each strip into the egg first, letting any excess drip off, and then in the flour mixture until coated on all sides. 5. Put the fish in the air fryer basket in a single layer and cook for 4 minutes. Turn over the fish and continue cooking for an another 4 to 5 minutes until crisp. 6. If desired, serve with sliced lemon, vinegar, ketchup, or tartar sauce.
Per Serving: Calories 204; Fat 3.52g; Sodium 853mg; Carbs 6.71g; Fibre 1g; Sugar 0.52g; Protein 34.82g

Crisp Flounder au Gratin

Prep Time: 5 minutes | Cook Time: 12 minutes | Serves: 4

4 (150g) flounder fillets	½ teaspoon dried oregano
4 tablespoons unsalted butter, melted, divided	½ teaspoon dried basil
	¼ teaspoon freshly ground black pepper
30g whole-wheat panko bread crumbs	
25g grated Parmesan cheese	1 lemon, quartered
½ teaspoon salt	1 tablespoon chopped fresh parsley

1. Turn on and preheat the air fryer to 190°C. 2. Pat dry the fish fillets and brush them with 2 tablespoons of butter, making sure to coat them on all sides. 3. Mix in a small bowl together the remaining 2 tablespoons of butter, bread crumbs, Parmesan cheese, salt, oregano, basil, and pepper until it becomes a moist but crumbly mixture. 4. Dredge the fish in the bread crumb mixture, making sure to press the crumbs onto the fish, until well coated. Put the fillets in the air fryer basket and cook for 5 minutes. Turn and cook them for an another 5 to 7 minutes. 5. Serve with lemon wedges and a sprinkle of fresh parsley.
Per Serving: Calories 377; Fat 24.94g; Sodium 825mg; Carbs 15.8g; Fibre 5.6g; Sugar 1.02g; Protein 22.91g

Delicious Fish and Chips

Prep Time: 25 minutes | Cook Time: 35 minutes | Serves: 4

For Chips

2 large russet potatoes, scrubbed	1 teaspoon seasoned salt
1 tablespoon extra-virgin olive oil, plus more for greasing the air fryer basket	½ teaspoon freshly ground black pepper

For Fish

4 (100g) white fish fillets, such as pollock, cod, or haddock	2 large eggs
	1 teaspoon water
1½ teaspoons salt, divided, plus more for seasoning	160g panko bread crumbs
1½ teaspoons black pepper, divided, plus more for seasoning	¼ teaspoon cayenne pepper
	Extra-virgin olive oil, for spraying
60g plain flour	

1. Turn on and preheat the air fryer to 205°C. 2. Cut the potatoes lengthwise into 1cm thick slices and then again into 1-cm-thick fries. 3. Mix in a large bowl the olive oil with the seasoned salt and pepper, then add the fries and toss to coat. 4. Sprinkle the air fryer basket with oil lightly. Put the fries in a single layer in the air fryer basket. 5. Air fry them for 5 minutes; shake the air fryer basket and air fry for another 5 to 10 minutes. Set aside and keep warm. 6. Season the fish fillets with salt and black pepper. 7. Mix in a small shallow bowl together the flour, ½ teaspoon salt, and ½ teaspoon black pepper. 8. In a second shallow bowl, whisk together the eggs and a pinch each of salt and black pepper. 9. Combine in another bowl the bread crumbs, cayenne pepper, remaining 1 teaspoon salt, and remaining 1 teaspoon black pepper. 10. Turn on and preheat the air fryer to 205°C. 11. Coat each fillet in the seasoned flour, then in the egg, then in the breading. 12. Sprinkle the air fryer basket with oil lightly. Put the coated fillets in a single layer in the air fryer basket. Lightly spray with oil. 13. Air fry them for 8 to 10 minutes; flip the fillets and lightly spray with oil, and air fry them for an another 5 to 10 minutes.
Per Serving: Calories 455; Fat 11. 27g; Sodium 1595mg; Carbs 53.02g; Fibre 3.6g; Sugar 2g; Protein 34.88g

Delicate Crab Ratatouille

Prep Time: 15 minutes | Cook Time: 11 minutes | Serves: 4

125g peeled, cubed aubergine
1 onion, chopped
1 red pepper, chopped
2 large tomatoes, chopped
1 tablespoon olive oil
½ teaspoon dried thyme

½ teaspoon dried basil
Pinch salt
Freshly ground black pepper
330g cooked crabmeat, picked
over

1. Combine the aubergine, onion, pepper, tomatoes, olive oil, thyme, and basil in a 15cm metal bowl, then sprinkle them with salt and pepper. 2. Roast them for 9 minutes at 205°C, then remove the bowl from the air fryer and stir. 3. Add the crabmeat and roast for 2 to 5 minutes until the ratatouille is bubbling and the vegetables are tender. 4. Serve and enjoy.
Per Serving: Calories 320; Fat 11. 27g; Sodium 853mg; Carbs 49.52g; Fibre 3.4g; Sugar 13.12g; Protein 5.85g

Glorious Tropical Tuna Steaks

Prep Time: 40 minutes | Cook Time: 10 minutes | Serves: 4

125g crushed pineapple
70g hoisin sauce
2 tablespoons freshly squeezed
lime juice
1 tablespoon chopped coriander
2 teaspoons honey

1 teaspoon minced fresh ginger
1 teaspoon minced garlic
1 teaspoon extra-virgin olive oil,
plus more for spraying
½ teaspoon sriracha
4 (150g) ahi tuna steaks

1. Combine the pineapple, hoisin sauce, lime juice, coriander, honey, ginger, olive oil, and sriracha in a small bowl. 2. Put three-quarters of the marinade in a large zip-top bag and reserve the remaining marinade. Add the tuna steaks to the zip-top bag and coat them in the marinade. Seal the bag and refrigerate for 30 minutes. 3. Turn on and preheat the air fryer to 195°C. 4. Remove the tuna steaks from the marinade and shake off any excess. 5. Sprinkle the air fryer basket with oil lightly. Put the tuna steaks in a single layer in the air fryer basket. Lightly spray with oil. 6. Air fry them for 5 minutes. Brush the reserved marinade on the tuna steaks, then let them rest for 5 minutes before slicing and serving.
Per Serving: Calories 263; Fat 2.54g; Sodium 336mg; Carbs 15.81g; Fibre 0.8g; Sugar 11.9g; Protein 42.27g

Easy Fish and Chips

Prep Time: 10 minutes | Cook Time: 20 minutes | Serves: 4

4 (100g) fish fillets
Pinch salt
Freshly ground black pepper
½ teaspoon dried thyme
1 egg white

20g crushed potato crisps
2 tablespoons olive oil, divided
2 russet potatoes, peeled and cut
into strips

1. Pat the fish fillets dry and sprinkle with salt, pepper, and thyme. Set aside. 2. In a shallow bowl, beat the egg white until foamy. In another bowl, combine the potato chips and 1 tablespoon of olive oil and mix until combined. 3. Dip the fish fillets into the egg white, then into the crushed potato chip mixture to coat. 4. Toss the fresh potato strips with the remaining 1 tablespoon olive oil. 5. Use your separator to divide the air fryer basket in half, then fry the chips and fish at 205°C. The chips will take about 20 minutes; the fish will take about 10 to 12 minutes to cook.
Per Serving: Calories 423; Fat 18.78g; Sodium 679mg; Carbs 37.4g; Fibre 2.9g; Sugar 1.22g; Protein 26.25g

Juicy Teriyaki Prawn Skewers

Prep Time: 10 minutes | Cook Time: 10 minutes | Serves: 4

455g jumbo prawn, peeled and
deveined
145g teriyaki sauce
1 pineapple, peeled, cored, and

cut into 2.5cm chunks
Extra-virgin olive oil, for the air
fryer basket

1. Turn on and preheat the air fryer to 205°C. 2. Combine the prawn and teriyaki sauce in a medium bowl. 3. Thread the coated prawns and pineapple chunks in an alternating pattern onto 15cm metal skewers. 4. Sprinkle the air fryer basket with oil lightly. Put the skewers in a single layer in the air fryer basket. 5. Air fry for 5 minutes, flipping the skewers and brush more teriyaki sauce onto the prawn, if desired. Air fry them for an another 5 minutes at 205°C. 6. Serve hot.
Per Serving: Calories 193; Fat 2.72g; Sodium 1627mg; Carbs 15.38g; Fibre 0.5g; Sugar 14.07g; Protein 25.55g

Delicate Steamed Tuna

Prep Time: 10 minutes | Cook Time: 10 minutes | Serves: 4

4 small tuna steaks
2 tablespoons low-sodium soy
sauce
2 teaspoons sesame oil
2 teaspoons rice wine vinegar

1 teaspoon grated fresh ginger
⅛ teaspoon pepper
1 stalk lemongrass, bent in half
3 tablespoons lemon juice

1. Put the tuna steaks on a plate. 2. Combine the soy sauce, sesame oil, rice wine vinegar, and ginger in a small bowl. Pour this mixture over the tuna and marinate for 10 minutes. Rub the soy sauce mixture gently into both sides of the tuna, and sprinkle with the pepper. 3. Put the lemongrass on the air fryer basket and put on the top the steaks. Put the lemon juice and 1 tablespoon water in the pan below the air fryer basket. 4. Steam the fish for 8 to 10 minutes at 200°C. 5. When cooked, discard the lemongrass and serve the tuna.
Per Serving: Calories 307; Fat 15.99g; Sodium 810mg; Carbs2.92g; Fibre 0.1g; Sugar 0.41g; Protein 810g

Quick Scallops and Spring Veggies

Prep Time: 10 minutes | Cook Time: 8 minutes | Serves: 4

225g asparagus, ends trimmed,
cut into 5cm pieces
100g sugar snap peas
445g sea scallops
1 tablespoon lemon juice

2 teaspoons olive oil
½ teaspoon dried thyme
Pinch salt
Freshly ground black pepper

1. Put the asparagus and sugar snap peas in the air fryer basket. Cook them for 2 to 3 minutes. 2. Meanwhile, check the scallops for a small muscle attached to the side, and pull it off and discard. 3. Toss in a medium bowl the scallops with the lemon juice, olive oil, thyme, salt, and pepper. Put into the air fryer basket on top of the vegetables. 4. Steam them for 5 to 7 minutes at 205°C, tossing them once during cooking time, until the scallops are just firm when tested with your finger and are opaque in the centre, and the vegetables are tender.
Per Serving: Calories 204; Fat 8.13g; Sodium 684mg; Carbs 5.45g; Fibre 2.5g; Sugar 1.17g; Protein 28.3g

Simple Snapper Scampi

Prep Time: 5 minutes | Cook Time: 10 minutes | Serves: 4

4 (150g) skinless snapper
1 tablespoon olive oil
3 tablespoons lemon juice,
divided
½ teaspoon dried basil

Pinch salt
Freshly ground black pepper
2 tablespoons butter
2 cloves garlic, minced

1. Rub the fish fillets with olive oil and 1 tablespoon of the lemon juice. Sprinkle with the basil, salt, and pepper, and place in the air fryer basket. 2. Grill the fish for 7 to 8 minutes at 195°C. Remove the fish from the air fryer basket and put on a serving plate. Cover to keep warm. 3. In a 15cm x 5cm pan, combine the butter, remaining 2 tablespoons lemon juice, and garlic. Cook in the air fryer for 1 to 2 minutes. 4. Pour this mixture over the fish and serve.
Per Serving: Calories 305; Fat 12.11g; Sodium 853mg; Carbs 1.71g; Fibre 0.2g; Sugar 0.31g; Protein 44.99g

Great Garlic-Ginger Salmon

Prep Time: 10 minutes | Cook Time: 10 minutes | Serves: 4

60ml soy sauce
2 tablespoons extra-virgin olive
oil, plus more for the parchment
paper
2 tablespoons grated fresh ginger

1 tablespoon minced garlic
1 tablespoon balsamic vinegar
4 (100g) boneless, skinless
salmon fillets

1. In a medium bowl, whisk the soy sauce, olive oil, ginger, garlic, and balsamic vinegar. 2. Put the salmon fillets in the marinade, then cover the bowl, and refrigerate them for at least 30 minutes but no longer than 3 hours. 3. Turn on and preheat the air fryer to 180°C. 4. Put a sheet of air fryer perforated parchment paper in the air fryer basket and lightly spray with oil. Put the marinated salmon fillets in a single layer in the air fryer basket. 5. Air fry the salmon fillets for 6 minutes; flip the fillets and air fry for an another 4 to 6 minutes until they have an internal temperature of 60°C.
Per Serving: Calories 129; Fat 8.46g; Sodium 1083mg; Carbs 8.84g; Fibre 0.7g; Sugar 2.5g; Protein 4.73g

Simple Ranch Haddock Fillets

Prep Time: 10 minutes | Cook Time: 10 minutes | Serves: 4

60g plain flour
½ teaspoon salt
½ teaspoon freshly ground black pepper
2 large eggs
160g panko bread crumbs

2 tablespoons dry ranch dressing mix
4 (100g) haddock fillets
Extra-virgin olive oil, for spraying

1. Combine the flour, salt, and pepper in a small bowl. 2. In a second small shallow bowl, whisk the eggs. 3. Combine the bread crumbs and ranch dressing mix in the third bowl. 4. Turn on and preheat the air fryer to 175°C. 5. Lightly coat the haddock fillets in the flour mixture, then in the egg, allowing the excess to drip off. Coat the haddock pieces in the breading. Press on the breading to ensure it adheres. 6. Sprinkle the air fryer basket with oil lightly. Put the coated fillets in a single layer in the air fryer basket. Lightly spray with oil. 7. Air-fry the fillets for 8 minutes; gently flip the haddock fillets and lightly spray with oil, then air fry them for another 4 minutes.
Per Serving: Calories 304; Fat 8.19g; Sodium 838mg; Carbs 19.34g; Fibre 0.9g; Sugar 1.19g; Protein 35.75g

Indulgent Lobster Tails with Butter and Lemon

Prep Time: 10 minutes | Cook Time: 10 minutes | Serves: 2

2 lobster tails
Extra-virgin olive oil, for greasing the air fryer basket
2 tablespoons butter, melted, plus

more for serving (optional)
Salt
1 lemon, cut into wedges

1. Turn on and preheat the air fryer to 205°C. 2. Use kitchen scissors to cut the lobster tails from open end to the tail fins. Do not cut through the tail fins. Spread open the shell with your fingers and push the meat upward so it separates from the bottom shell. Leave the end attached at the tail fin. Hold the lobster meat up and push the shell together under the meat. Place the meat on the top of the shell. 3. Sprinkle the air fryer basket with oil lightly. Put the lobster tails in a single layer in the air fryer basket. Pour the melted butter over the lobster meat and season with salt. 4. Air fry them for 6 to 8 minutes until the lobster reaches an internal temperature of 60°C. 5. Serve the dish with lemon wedges and extra melted butter (optional).
Per Serving: Calories 242; Fat 14.95g; Sodium 1889mg; Carbs 1.66g; Fibre 0.1g; Sugar 0.61g; Protein 24.98g

Flaky Chile-Lime Tilapia

Prep Time: 10 minutes | Cook Time: 15 minutes | Serves: 4

4 teaspoons chili powder
2 teaspoons ground cumin
2 teaspoons garlic powder
1 teaspoon salt
½ teaspoon freshly ground black

pepper
4 (125g – 150g) tilapia fillets
Extra-virgin olive oil, for the parchment paper
2 limes, cut into wedges

1. Turn on and preheat the air fryer to 195°C. 2. Combine in a small bowl the chili powder, cumin, garlic powder, salt, and pepper. 3. Pat the tilapia fillets dry with a paper towel. 4. Press the spice mixture all over the fish. 5. Line the air fryer basket with a sheet of perforated parchment paper, and lightly spray the parchment with oil. 6. Put the seasoned fillets in a single layer in the air fryer basket, leaving 1cm of space between each to ensure even cooking. 7. Air fry the fillets for 10 to 15 minutes until flake easily. 8. Drizzle lime juice over the top, and enjoy.
Per Serving: Calories 144; Fat 3.75g; Sodium 722mg; Carbs 4.98g; Fibre 1.4g; Sugar 0.63g; Protein24.22g

Classic Cod Nuggets

Prep Time: 15 minutes | Cook Time: 51 minutes | Serves: 4

4 (100g) cod fillets
60g plain flour
1 teaspoon seasoned salt
2 large eggs
1 teaspoon water
160g panko bread crumbs

½ tablespoon dried parsley
1 teaspoon lemon-pepper seasoning
Extra-virgin olive oil, for spraying

1. Cut the cod fillets into 2.5cm chunks. 2. Mix in a small shallow bowl together the flour and seasoned salt. 3. In a second small shallow bowl, whisk together the eggs and water. 4. In a third small shallow bowl, mix together the bread crumbs, parsley, and lemon-pepper seasoning. 5. Turn on and preheat the air fryer to 205°C. 6. Coat each cod chunk in the seasoned flour, then in the egg, then in the breading. 7. Sprinkle the air fryer basket with oil lightly. Put the nuggets in a single layer in the air fryer basket. Lightly spray with oil. 8. Air fry for 7 minutes. Flip the nuggets and lightly spray with oil. Air fry for an another 6 to 8 minutes.
Per Serving: Calories 378; Fat 19.29g; Sodium 1067mg; Carbs 26.81g; Fibre 6.1g; Sugar 1.52g; Protein 23.75g

Quick Lemon-Garlic Jumbo Scallops

Prep Time: 10 minutes | Cook Time: 10 minutes | Serves: 4

4 tablespoons unsalted butter, melted
2 tablespoons freshly squeezed lemon juice
1 tablespoon minced garlic
½ teaspoon salt

⅛ teaspoon freshly ground black pepper
455g jumbo sea scallops
Extra-virgin olive oil, for the air fryer basket

1. Turn on and preheat the air fryer to 205°C. 2. Combine the melted butter, lemon juice, garlic, salt, and pepper in a medium bowl. 3. Add the sea scallops and toss to coat. 4. Sprinkle the air fryer basket with oil lightly. Put the scallops in a single layer in the air fryer basket. 5. Air fry for 8 minutes, flipping after 4 minutes.
Per Serving: Calories 211; Fat 9.82g; Sodium 1053mg; Carbs 7.41g; Fibre 0.1g; Sugar 0.21g; Protein 23.92g

Delicious Fried Prawn

Prep Time: 15 minutes | Cook Time: 15 minutes | Serves: 4

2 teaspoons Old Bay seasoning, divided
½ teaspoon garlic powder
½ teaspoon onion powder
½ teaspoon freshly ground black pepper
455g large prawn, deveined, tails

on
2 large eggs
1 teaspoon water
55g panko bread crumbs
Extra-virgin olive oil, for spraying

1. Turn on and preheat the air fryer to 195°C. 2. Mix in a medium bowl together 1 teaspoon Old Bay, the garlic powder, onion powder, and pepper. Add the prawns and toss to coat lightly. 3. Whisk in a small bowl the eggs with the water. 4. Mix the remaining 1 teaspoon Old Bay and the bread crumbs in a small shallow bowl. 5. Coat each prawn in the egg mixture, then the breading. 6. Sprinkle the air fryer basket with oil lightly. Put the prawns in a single layer in the air fryer basket. Do not overcrowd. Lightly spray with oil. 7. Air fry for 10 to 15 minutes, shaking the air fryer basket every 5 minutes.
Per Serving: Calories 134; Fat 4.71g; Sodium 668mg; Carbs 4.44g; Fibre 0.4g; Sugar 0.33g; Protein 17.32g

Amazing Coconut Prawn

Prep Time: 20 minutes | Cook Time: 10 minutes | Serves: 4

60g plain flour
½ teaspoon salt
¼ teaspoon freshly ground black pepper
2 large eggs
Dash hot sauce

75g sweetened shredded coconut
55g panko bread crumbs
455g large uncooked prawns, peeled and deveined
Extra-virgin olive oil, for spraying

1. Combine the flour, salt, and pepper in a small bowl. 2. In a second small shallow bowl, whisk together the eggs and hot sauce. 3. Combine the coconut and bread crumbs in the third bowl. 4. Turn on and preheat the air fryer to 185°C. 5. Lightly coat the prawn in the flour mixture, then in the egg mixture, allowing the excess to drip off. Coat the prawn in the coconut breading. Press on the breading to ensure it adheres. 6. Sprinkle the air fryer basket with oil lightly. Put the coated prawn in a single layer in the air fryer basket. Lightly spray with oil. 7. Air fry the prawn for 5 minutes. Gently flip the prawn and lightly spray with oil, then air fry for another 4 to 5 minutes.
Per Serving: Calories 198; Fat 4.95g; Sodium 1052mg; Carbs 17.77g; Fibre 1.2g; Sugar 1.92g; Protein 19.24g

Wonderful Fried Catfish

Prep Time: 10 minutes | Cook Time: 20 minutes | Serves: 4

240ml buttermilk	1 tablespoon Creole seasoning
4 catfish fillets	Extra-virgin olive oil, for
170g polenta	spraying

1. Pour the buttermilk into a shallow baking dish. Put the catfish in the dish, cover, and refrigerate for at least 1 hour. 2. Turn on and preheat the air fryer to 205°C. 3. Combine the polenta and Creole seasoning in a small bowl. 4. Take the catfish out of the dish and shake off any excess buttermilk. Put each fillet in the polenta mixture. Press on the polenta to ensure it adheres. 5. Sprinkle the air fryer basket with oil lightly. Put the coated catfish strips in a single layer in the air fryer basket. Lightly spray them with oil. 6. Air fry the catfish strips for 7 to 10 minutes; flip the catfish and lightly spray with oil, and air fry for an another 8 to 10 minutes. 7. When done, they should be golden brown and crispy.
Per Serving: Calories 338; Fat 6.83g; Sodium 342mg; Carbs 35.37g; Fibre 1.8g; Sugar 3.8g; Protein 30.96g

Great Breaded Calamari

Prep Time: 15 minutes | Cook Time: 15 minutes | Serves: 4

455g fresh calamari tubes, rinsed and patted dry	3 large eggs
½ teaspoon salt, plus more for seasoning	1 teaspoon water
½ teaspoon freshly ground black pepper, plus more for seasoning	110g panko bread crumbs
	2 teaspoons dried parsley
125g plain flour	Extra-virgin olive oil, for spraying

1. Cut the calamari into ½cm rings. Season with salt and pepper. 2. Combine the flour, salt, and pepper in a small bowl. 3. Beat the eggs with water in the second bowl. 4. Combine the bread crumbs and parsley in the third bowl. 5. Turn on and preheat the air fryer to 195°C. 6. Coat the calamari rings in the seasoned flour, then in the egg, then in the breading. 7. Sprinkle the air fryer basket with oil lightly. Put the breaded calamari in a single layer in the air fryer basket. Lightly spray with oil. 8. Air fry them for 10 to 15 minutes, shaking the air fryer basket a few times, until lightly browned and crispy.
Per Serving: Calories 465; Fat 5.48g; Sodium 439mg; Carbs 103.58g; Fibre 11g; Sugar 65.51g; Protein 7.13g

Delicious Bacon-Wrapped Scallops

Prep Time: 5 minutes | Cook Time: 10 minutes | Serves: 4

455g jumbo sea scallops	fryer basket
455g sliced bacon	Freshly ground black pepper
Extra-virgin olive oil, for the air	

1. Turn on and preheat the air fryer to 205°C. 2. Pat the scallops dry with paper towels and remove any side muscles. 3. Cut the bacon slices in half so you have half a slice for each scallop. 4. Wrap each scallop in bacon and secure the bacon with a toothpick. 5. Sprinkle the air fryer basket with oil lightly. Put the bacon-wrapped scallops in a single layer in the air fryer basket. 6. Air fry for 8 minutes. Flip the scallops and season with pepper. Air fry for another 4 minutes until the scallops are tender and opaque.
Per Serving: Calories 599; Fat 46.63g; Sodium 1289mg; Carbs 7.44g; Fibre 0.1g; Sugar 0.94g; Protein 37.56g

Tasty Cajun Prawn and Veggies

Prep Time: 10 minutes | Cook Time: 15 minutes | Serves: 6

455g jumbo prawn, peeled and deveined	2 tablespoons Cajun seasoning
2 medium courgette, cut into 1cm slices, then cut in half	2 tablespoons extra-virgin olive oil, plus more for the air fryer basket
2 peppers (red, yellow, or orange), cut into 2.5cm chunks	2 fully cooked smoked turkey sausages, cut into 1cm slices

1. Turn on and preheat the air fryer to 205°C. 2. Toss in a large bowl the prawn, courgette, and peppers with the Cajun seasoning and olive oil. Stir in the smoked sausage slices. 3. Sprinkle the air fryer basket with oil lightly. Put the seasoned prawn, vegetables, and sausages in a single layer in the air fryer basket. 4. Air fry for 15 minutes, shaking the air fryer basket every 5 minutes until the vegetables are tender and seared.

Per Serving: Calories 137; Fat 5.93g; Sodium 904mg; Carbs 3.24g; Fibre 0.7g; Sugar 1.21g; Protein 16.45g

Spanish Quick Paella

Prep Time: 7 minutes | Cook Time: 15 minutes | Serves: 4

1 (250g) package frozen cooked rice, thawed	½ teaspoon dried thyme
1 (150g) jar artichoke hearts, drained and chopped	130g frozen cooked small prawns
	100g frozen baby peas
60ml vegetable stock	1
½ teaspoon turmeric	tomato, diced

1. Gently stir the rice, artichoke hearts, vegetable stock, turmeric, and thyme in a suitable pan. 2. Put the pan in the air fryer, and bake the mixture for 8 to 9 minutes at 170°C until the rice is hot. 3. When cooked, transfer the dish to the serving plate, and gently stir in the prawns, peas, and tomato. Enjoy.
Per Serving: Calories 174; Fat 1.97g; Sodium 96mg; Carbs 34.74g; Fibre 5g; Sugar 9.94g; Protein 5.47g

Perfect Coconut Prawn

Prep Time: 15 minutes | Cook Time: 5 minutes | Serves: 4

1 (8-ounce) can crushed pineapple	55g sweetened coconut
115g sour cream	110g panko bread crumbs
80g pineapple preserves	455g uncooked large prawn, thawed if frozen, deveined and shelled
2 egg whites	
85g cornflour	Olive oil for misting

1. Drain the crushed pineapple well, reserving the juice. 2. Combine the pineapple, sour cream, and preserves in a small bowl. Set aside. 3. In a shallow bowl, beat the egg whites with 2 tablespoons of the reserved pineapple liquid. Put the cornflour on a plate. Combine the coconut and bread crumbs on another plate. 4. Dip the prawn into the cornflour, shake it off, then dip into the egg white mixture and finally into the coconut mixture. 5. Put the prawn in the air fryer basket and mist with oil. Air-fry them for 5 to 7 minutes at 205°C.
Per Serving: Calories 352; Fat 4.67g; Sodium 782mg; Carbs 56.15g; Fibre 1.4g; Sugar 28.7g; Protein 20.16g

Great Herbed Salmon

Prep Time: 5 minutes | Cook Time: 12 minutes | Serves: 4

4 (150g) skinless salmon fillets	30g panko bread crumbs
3 tablespoons honey mustard	10g crushed potato crisps
½ teaspoon dried thyme	2 tablespoons olive oil
½ teaspoon dried basil	

1. Put the salmon on a plate. Combine in a small bowl the mustard, thyme, and basil, and spread evenly over the salmon. 2. In another small bowl, combine the bread crumbs and potato chips and mix well. Drizzle in the olive oil and mix until combined. 3. Put the salmon in the air fryer basket and gently but firmly press the bread crumb mixture onto the top of each fillet. 4. Bake them for 9 to 12 minutes at 160°C. 5. Serve warm.
Per Serving: Calories 231; Fat 11.57g; Sodium 305 mg; Carbs 10.92g; Fibre 1g; Sugar 0.32g; Protein 20.42g

Easy Tuna Veggie Stir-Fry

Prep Time: 15 minutes | Cook Time: 10 minutes | Serves: 4

1 tablespoon olive oil	2 cloves garlic, sliced
1 red pepper, chopped	2 tablespoons low-sodium soy sauce
100g green beans, cut into 5cm pieces	
1 onion, sliced	1 tablespoon honey
	225g fresh tuna, cubed

1. Combine the olive oil, pepper, green beans, onion, and garlic in a suitable metal bowl. 2. Cook the bean mixture in the air fryer for 4 to 6 minutes until crisp and tender, stirring once; stir in the soy sauce, honey, and tuna, and cook them for 4 to 6 minutes at 195°C, stirring once, until crisp and tender. 3. Cook them for another 3 to 6 minutes, stirring once. Tuna can be served rare or medium-rare.
Per Serving: Calories 115; Fat 4.18g; Sodium 398mg; Carbs 8.07g; Fibre 1g; Sugar 5.35g; Protein 12.44g

Chapter 5 Poultry Recipes

Prep Day Chicken Breasts

Prep Time: 5 minutes | Cook Time: 9 minutes | Serves: 4

2 teaspoons olive oil
4 (100g) boneless, skinless chicken breasts
½ teaspoon salt
¼ teaspoon ground black pepper

1. Preheat air fryer to 175°C. 2. Lightly brush the chicken breasts with oil, and season them with salt and pepper. 3. Add the chicken breasts to the air fryer basket, and cook them for 9 minutes until they have an internal temperature of at least 75°C, flipping them halfway through. 4. Transfer chicken to a large serving plate and let rest 5 minutes. Chop and refrigerate covered up to 7 days.
Per Serving: Calories 215; Fat 12.75g; Sodium 362mg; Carbs 0.11g; Fibre 0g; Sugar 0g; Protein 23.66g

Salsa Verde Chicken

Prep Time: 5 minutes | Cook Time: 30 minutes | Serves: 4

4 (100g) boneless, skinless chicken thighs
245g salsa verde

1. Preheat air fryer at 175°C for 3 minutes. 2. Place chicken thighs in a suitable cake barrel, and cover them with salsa verde. 3. Place the pan in air fryer basket, and cook the chicken things for 30 minutes until they have an internal temperature of at least 75°C. 4. Let the chicken thighs rest for 5 minutes before serving.
Per Serving: Calories 269; Fat 18.95g; Sodium550mg; Carbs 4.65g; Fibre 1.2g; Sugar 2.56g; Protein 19.73g

Chicken Bulgogi with Rice

Prep Time: 15 minutes | Cook Time: 11 minutes | Serves: 4

For Quick Pickled Carrots
2 medium carrots, grated
60ml rice vinegar
2 teaspoons granulated sugar
⅛ teaspoon salt
For Chicken and Bulgogi Sauce
2 tablespoons tamari
2 teaspoons sesame oil
1 tablespoon light brown sugar
1 tablespoon rice vinegar
1 tablespoon lime juice
2 cloves garlic, peeled and minced
2 teaspoons minced fresh ginger
3 spring onions, sliced, whites and green separated
6 (100g) boneless, skinless chicken thighs, cut into 2.5cm cubes
800g cooked white rice
2 teaspoons sesame seeds

1. To make Quick Pickled Carrots, combine all the Quick Pickled Carrots ingredients in a medium bowl, cover the bowl and refrigerate the carrots until ready to use. 2. To make Chicken and Bulgogi Sauce, whisk the tamari, sesame oil, brown sugar, rice vinegar, lime juice, garlic, ginger, and whites of spring onions in a large bowl; add chicken thighs and let them marinate for 10 minutes. 3. Preheat air fryer at 175°C for 3 minutes. 4. Place the marinated chicken things in air fryer basket. Reserve the remaining marinade. 5. Cook the chicken things for 11 minutes until they have an internal temperature of 75°C, pouring the remaining marinade over them halfway through. 6. Place the chicken thighs over rice on serving plates, garnish with spring onion greens and sesame seeds, and then serve with Quick Pickled Carrots on the side.
Per Serving: Calories 336; Fat 8.35g; Sodium 630mg; Carbs 52.87g; Fibre 2.1g; Sugar 4.79g; Protein 10.78g

Breaded Drumsticks

Prep Time: 10 minutes | Cook Time: 20 minutes | Serves: 2

455g chicken drumsticks
240ml buttermilk
75g gluten-free bread crumbs
½ teaspoon smoked paprika
½ teaspoon garlic powder
½ teaspoon salt

1. Toss the drumsticks with buttermilk in a bowl, then cover the bowl and refrigerate the drumsticks overnight. 2. Preheat the air fryer at 175°C for 3 minutes. Lightly grease the air fryer basket with cooking oil. 3. Combine bread crumbs, paprika, garlic powder, and salt in a shallow dish. Shake excess buttermilk off drumsticks and dredge in bread crumb mixture. 4. Add chicken to air fryer basket, and cook them for 12 minutes. 5. When the time is up, increase the cooking temperature to 205°C, flip the drumsticks and resume cooking them for 8 minutes until they have an internal temperature of at least 75°C,

turning them over once more halfway through. 6. Let the dish cool for 5 minutes before serving.
Per Serving: Calories 340; Fat 7.72g; Sodium 1631mg; Carbs 13.28g; Fibre 0.6g; Sugar 6.69g; Protein 51.51g

Flavourful Chicken Legs

Prep Time: 10 minutes | Cook Time: 36 minutes | Serves: 4

240g plain Greek yogurt
1 tablespoon Dijon mustard
1 teaspoon smoked paprika
1 teaspoon garlic powder
1 teaspoon dried oregano
1 teaspoon dried thyme
⅛ teaspoon ground nutmeg
1 teaspoon salt
1 teaspoon ground black pepper
6 (100g) chicken legs
3 tablespoons butter, melted

1.Toss the chicken legs with yogurt, Dijon mustard, smoked paprika, garlic powder, dried oregano, dried thyme, nutmeg, salt, and pepper in a bowl, then cover the bowl, and refrigerate them for 60 minutes to overnight. 2. Preheat air fryer at 190°C for 3 minutes. Lightly grease the air fryer basket with cooking oil. 3. Shake excess marinade from chicken. Add the chicken legs to air fryer basket, and cook them for 10 minutes. 4. When the time is up, lightly brush them with melted butter, flip them and brush the other side with butter, and then resume cooking them for 8 minutes more until they have an internal temperature of at least 75°C. 5. You can cook the chicken legs in 2 batches. 6. Let the chicken legs stand for 5 minutes before serving.
Per Serving: Calories 399; Fat 22.25g; Sodium 1503mg; Carbs 4.68g; Fibre 0.8g; Sugar 2.99g; Protein 44.16g

Greek Chicken Salad

Prep Time: 10 minutes | Cook Time: 10 minutes | Serves: 2

For Dressing
240g plain Greek yogurt
½ medium English cucumber, peeled and small-diced
1 teaspoon chopped fresh dill
1 teaspoon chopped fresh mint
For Chicken
455g boneless, skinless chicken cutlets, cut into 1cm-thick strips
For Salad
90g mixed greens
40g diced peeled red onion
10 kalamata olives, pitted and
½ teaspoon salt
1 teaspoon lemon juice
2 cloves garlic, peeled and minced
½ teaspoon salt
¼ teaspoon ground black pepper
halved
1 large Roma tomato, diced
60g feta cheese crumbles

1. Preheat air fryer at 175°C for 3 minutes. Lightly grease the air fryer basket with cooking oil. 2. To make dressing, mix all the dressing ingredients in a small bowl, cover the bowl, and refrigerate the dressing for up to 7 days. 3. To make chicken, place chicken strips in medium bowl, and season them with salt and pepper. 4. Add chicken strips to air fryer basket, and cook them for 10 minutes until they have an internal temperature of at least 75°C, gently tossing them halfway through. 5. To make salad, add mixed greens to two medium salad bowls, garnish with onions, olives, tomatoes, and feta cheese. Top with chicken and drizzle with dressing. Enjoy.
Per Serving: Calories 515; Fat 28.6g; Sodium 1816mg; Carbs 17.35g; Fibre 4.8g; Sugar 10.22g; Protein 49.7g

Mozzarella Chicken Pizza Crust

Prep Time: 10 minutes | Cook Time: 25 minutes | Serves: 4

445g chicken thigh mince
25g grated Parmesan cheese
55g shredded mozzarella

1. Mix the chicken thigh meat, Parmesan cheese, and shredded mozzarella together in a large bowl. Separate into four even parts. 2. Cut out four (15cm) circles of parchment paper and press each portion of the chicken-cheese mixture out onto one of the circles. Then place the circles into the air fryer basket, working in batches as needed. 3. Adjust the temperature setting to 190°C and set the timer for 25 minutes. 4. Flip the crust halfway through the cooking time. 5. Once fully cooked, you may top it with cheese and your favorite toppings and cook for 5 additional minutes. Or, you may place crust into the refrigerator or freezer and top when ready to eat.
Per Serving: Calories 183; Fat 6.41g; Sodium 325 mg; Carbs 1.36g; Fibre 0.3g; Sugar 0.21g; Protein 28.55g

Barbecue Chicken Legs

Prep Time: 10 minutes | Cook Time: 36 minutes | Serves: 4

4 spring onions, sliced, whites and greens separated
60ml tamari
2 tablespoons sesame oil
25g honey
2 tablespoons gochujang

4 cloves garlic, peeled and minced
½ teaspoon ground ginger
1 teaspoon salt
½ teaspoon ground white pepper
6 (100g) chicken legs

1. Mince whites of spring onions. Set the greens aside. 2. Combine tamari, sesame oil, honey, gochujang, garlic, ginger, salt, pepper, and whites of spring onions in a medium bowl. Reserve 60ml of the marinade. 3. Add chicken legs to the tamari mixture bowl, then cover the bowl and refrigerate them for 30 minutes. 4. Preheat air fryer at 175°C for 3 minutes. Lightly grease the air fryer basket with cooking oil. 5. Add the chicken legs to air fryer basket, and cook 10 minutes. 6. Flip the chicken legs, and increase the cooking temperature to 205°C, then resume cooking them for 8 minutes until they have an internal temperature of at least 75°C. 7. You can cook the chicken legs in 2 batches. 8. Let the chicken legs stand for 5 minutes after cooking, then toss them with the remaining sauce, garnish with the sliced spring onion greens, and enjoy.
Per Serving: Calories 354; Fat 14.08g; Sodium 1818mg; Carbs 21.86g; Fibre 0.9g; Sugar 18.74g; Protein 35.28g

Cream Chicken Patties

Prep Time: 10 minutes | Cook Time: 26 minutes | Serves: 4

60g crumbled blue cheese
60g sour cream
⅛ teaspoon salt
3 tablespoons buffalo wing sauce, divided

455g chicken mince
2 tablespoons finely grated carrot
2 tablespoons finely diced celery
1 large egg white

1. Combine blue cheese, sour cream, salt, and 1 tablespoon of buffalo wing sauce in a small bowl, cover the bowl, and refrigerate them until ready to serve patties. 2. Preheat air fryer at 175°C for 3 minutes. Lightly grease the air fryer basket with cooking oil. 3. Mix chicken, carrot, celery, egg white and the remaining buffalo sauce in a large bowl, then make the mixture into 4 patties, making a slight indentation in middle of each. 4. Place the patties in the air fryer basket, and cook them for 13 minutes, flipping them halfway through. 5. You can cook then patties in batches. 6. Serve the patties with blue cheese sauce.
Per Serving: Calories 222; Fat 6.03g; Sodium 430mg; Carbs 11.86g; Fibre 1.7g; Sugar 7.03g; Protein 29.03g

Chicken Satay Kebabs

Prep Time: 10 minutes | Cook Time: 24 minutes | Serves: 4

For Peanut Sauce
65g creamy peanut butter
1 tablespoon pure maple syrup
1 tablespoon tamari
1 tablespoon lime juice
¼ teaspoon sriracha
For Marinade
240ml coconut milk
1 tablespoon Peanut Sauce
1 teaspoon sriracha
1 tablespoon chopped fresh

2 teaspoons finely chopped peeled yellow onion
¼ teaspoon minced fresh ginger
1 clove garlic, peeled and minced
2 tablespoons water

coriander
2 (200g) boneless, skinless chicken breasts, cut into 8 (2.5cm) strips

1. To make peanut sauce, mix all the sauce ingredients in a small bowl, and set aside. Reserve 1 tablespoon. 2. To make marinade, combine reserved Peanut Sauce, coconut milk, sriracha, and coriander in a medium bowl. Toss in the chicken strips, then cover the bowl and refrigerate for 15 minutes. 3. Preheat air fryer at 175°C for 3 minutes. 4. Skewer chicken and place them on kebab rack. 5. Place kebab rack in air fryer basket, and cook them for 12 minutes. You can cook them in batches. 6. Serve warm with Peanut Sauce on the side.
Per Serving: Calories 424; Fat 22.84g; Sodium 484mg; Carbs 23.96g; Fibre 2.8g; Sugar 15.5g; Protein 32.52g

Curry Chicken Salad

Prep Time: 10 minutes | Cook Time: 18 minutes | Serves: 2

2 (200g) boneless, skinless chicken breasts

1 teaspoon salt
¼ teaspoon ground black pepper

180g mayonnaise
1 tablespoon fresh lime juice
1 teaspoon curry powder
70g chopped golden raisins

1 small Granny Smith apple, peeled, cored, and grated
1 medium spring onion, minced
2 tablespoons chopped pecans

1. Preheat air fryer at 175°C for 3 minutes. Lightly grease the air fryer basket with cooking oil. 2. Season the chicken breasts with salt and pepper. 3. Add chicken breasts to air fryer basket, and cook them for 9 minutes until they have an internal temperature of at least 75°C, shaking the basket gently and flipping the chicken breast halfway through. 4. You can cook them in batches. 5. Let the chicken breasts stand for 7 minutes, then chop them and toss them in a large bowl with the remaining ingredients, then cover the bowl and refrigerate them until ready to eat.
Per Serving: Calories 526; Fat 23.64g; Sodium 1347mg; Carbs 54.81g; Fibre 4.9g; Sugar 32.5g; Protein 27.84g

Cheesy Hasselback Chicken

Prep time: 10 minutes | Cook time: 19 minutes | Serves: 2

Oil, for spraying
2 (200g) boneless, skinless chicken breasts
50g cream cheese, softened

30g bacon bits
20g chopped pickled jalapeños
50g shredded cheddar cheese, divided

1. Prepare the air fryer basket by lining it with parchment and lightly spraying it with oil. 2. Make multiple cuts across the top of each chicken breast, cutting only halfway through. 3. In a medium bowl, mix together the cream cheese, bacon bits, jalapeños, and 25g of cheddar cheese. Spoon some of the mixture into each cut. 4. Place the chicken in the prepared basket. Cook at 175°C for 14 minutes. Sprinkle the chicken with the remaining 25g of cheese and continue cooking until the cheese is melted, for about 2 to 5 minutes. The internal temperature reaches 75°C.
Per Serving: Calories 627; Fat 30g; Sodium 1875mg; Carbs 6g; Fibre 1.8g; Sugar 1.4g; Protein 81g

Spicy Garlic Chicken

Prep time: 5 minutes | Cook time: 30 minutes | Serves: 4

Oil, for spraying
4 (150g) boneless, skinless chicken breasts
1 tablespoon olive oil
1 tablespoon paprika

1 tablespoon packed light brown sugar
½ teaspoon cayenne pepper
½ teaspoon onion powder
½ teaspoon granulated garlic

1. Line the air fryer basket with parchment and spray lightly with oil. 2. Brush the chicken with the olive oil. 3. Mix the paprika, brown sugar, cayenne pepper, onion powder, and garlic in a small bowl and sprinkle it over the chicken. 4. Place the chicken in the prepared basket. You may need to work in batches, depending on the size of your air fryer. 5. Cook the prepared chicken in your air fryer at 180°C for 15 minutes, flip, and continue cooking it until the internal temperature reaches 75°C, about 15 minutes. Serve immediately.
Per Serving: Calories 319; Fat 10g; Sodium 831mg; Carbs 4.8g; Fibre 1g; Sugar 3.6g; Protein 51g

Cheddar Chicken with Enchilada Sauce

Prep time: 10 minutes | Cook time: 8 minutes | Serves: 4

Oil, for spraying
420g shredded cooked chicken
1 package taco seasoning
8 flour tortillas, at room temperature

120g canned black beans, rinsed and drained
100g shredded cheddar cheese
1 (250g) can enchilada sauce

1. Prepare the air fryer basket by lining it with parchment and lightly spraying it with oil. (The parchment will keep the sauce and cheese from dripping through the holes.) 2. Mix the chicken and taco seasoning in a small bowl. 3. Divide the mixture among the tortillas. Top with the black beans and green chilies. Carefully roll up each tortilla. 4. Place the enchiladas, seam-side down, in the prepared basket. Work in batches as needed. 5. Spoon the enchilada sauce over the enchiladas. Use just enough sauce to keep them from drying out. You can add more sauce when serving. Sprinkle the cheese on top. 6. Cook at 180°C for 5 to 8 minutes, or until heated through and the cheese is melted. 7. Place 2 enchiladas on each serving plate and top with more enchilada sauce, if desired.
Per Serving: Calories 838; Fat 34.3g; Sodium 1526mg; Carbs 76.8g; Fibre 9g; Sugar 6g; Protein 53.6g

Ranch Chicken Nachos

Prep time: 5 minutes | Cook time: 5 minutes | Serves: 8

Oil, for spraying
420g shredded cooked chicken
1 (25g) package ranch seasoning
60g sour cream
80g corn tortilla chips

35g bacon bits
100g shredded cheddar cheese
1 tablespoon chopped spring onions

1. Prepare the air fryer basket by lining it with parchment and lightly spraying it with oil. 2. Mix the chicken, ranch seasoning, and sour cream in a small bowl. 3. Place the tortilla chips in the prepared basket and top with the chicken mixture. Add the bacon bits, cheddar cheese, and spring onions. 4. Cook at 220°C for 3 to 5 minutes, or until heated through and the cheese is melted.
Per Serving: Calories 254; Fat 15.4g; Sodium 377mg; Carbs 7.6g; Fibre 1g; Sugar 0g; Protein 20g

Chicken Cordon Bleu with Ham and Cheese

Prep time: 15 minutes | Cook time: 20 minutes | Serves: 4

Oil, for spraying
2 (200g) boneless, skinless
chicken breasts
4 slices Swiss cheese
4 slices deli ham
90g plain flour

1 large egg, lightly beaten
100g bread crumbs
½ teaspoon salt
½ teaspoon freshly ground black pepper

1. Preheat the air fryer to 190°C. Prepare the air fryer basket by lining it with parchment and lightly spraying it with oil. 2. Cut each chicken breast in half through its thickness to make 4 thin cutlets. Using a meat tenderizer, pound each cutlet until it is about ¾ inch thick. 3. Top each cutlet with a cheese slice and then a ham slice. Roll up the chicken and secure with a toothpick to hold it closed. 4. Place the beaten egg, flour, and bread crumbs in three separate bowls. 5. Coat each chicken roll in the flour, dip in the egg, and dredge in the bread crumbs until evenly coated. Season with the salt and black pepper. 6. Place the chicken rolls in the prepared basket and spray with oil. You may need to work in batches, depending on the size of your air fryer. 7. Cook for 10 minutes, flip, spray with more oil, and cook until golden brown, about 10 minutes. The internal temperature shall reach 75°C and the juices run clear.
Per Serving: Calories 520; Fat 15.6g; Sodium 1373mg; Carbs 39g; Fibre 2g; Sugar 2.2g; Protein 52.8g

Chili Chicken Fajita

Prep time: 7 minutes | Cook time: 20 minutes | Serves: 4

Oil, for spraying
455g boneless, skinless chicken
breasts, thinly sliced
2 peppers, seeded and thinly
sliced
1 onion, thinly sliced

1 tablespoon olive oil
2 teaspoons chili powder
1 teaspoon salt
1 teaspoon ground cumin
4 corn or flour tortillas, at room
temperature

1. Assorted toppings, such as shredded cheese, guacamole, shredded lettuce, chopped tomato, or sour cream. 2. Line the air fryer basket with parchment and spray lightly with oil. 3. Place the chicken, peppers, onion, olive oil, chili powder, salt, and cumin in a zip-top plastic bag, seal, and shake until evenly coated. Transfer the mixture to the prepared basket. 4. Cook at 180°C for 16 to 20 minutes, stirring after 10 minutes. The internal temperature of the chicken shall reach 75°C and the juices will run clear. 5. To warm the tortillas, stack them on a microwave-safe plate with a damp paper towel between each one and microwave for 30 to 60 seconds. Spoon the chicken mixture on top and serve with toppings on the side.
Per Serving: Calories 380; Fat 17.3g; Sodium 1173mg; Carbs 27.3g; Fibre 3.2g; Sugar 2.8g; Protein 29g

Ginger Chicken Thighs with Pineapple

Prep time: 7 minutes plus 30 minutes to marinate | Cook time: 15 minutes | Serves: 4

Oil, for spraying
4 (150g) boneless, skinless
chicken thighs
1 (200g) can pineapple chunks,

drained, 60 ml juice reserved
60ml soy sauce
50g packed light brown sugar
2 tablespoons ketchup

1 tablespoon minced garlic   2 teaspoons ground ginger

1. Prepare the air fryer basket by lining it with parchment and lightly spraying it with oil. 2. Pierce the chicken thighs several times with a fork and place them in a zip-top plastic bag. 3. Add together the reserved pineapple juice, soy sauce, brown sugar, ketchup, garlic, and ginger in a small bowl and whisk well. 4. Pour half of the sauce into the zip-top bag with the chicken, seal, and refrigerate for at least 30 minutes. 5. Place the chicken in the prepared basket, reserving the marinade. 6. Cook at 180°C for 7 minutes, flip, and cook for another 8 minutes. When cooked, the internal temperature reaches 75°C and the juices run clear. 7. Meanwhile, in a small saucepan over medium heat, bring the marinade to a boil, then simmer to thicken, stirring frequently, for 8 to 10 minutes. 8. Top the chicken thighs with the pineapple chunks and sauce and serve.
Per Serving: Calories 456; Fat 18.4g; Sodium 1052mg; Carbs 30g; Fibre 1.3g; Sugar 26.4g; Protein 42.4g

Garlic Turkey Breast with Parsley

Prep time: 10 minutes | Cook time: 60 minutes | Serves: 4

Oil, for spraying
1 (1.2kg) bone-in turkey breast
2 tablespoons unsalted butter,
melted

½ teaspoon granulated garlic
¼ teaspoon poultry seasoning
⅛ teaspoon salt
⅛ teaspoon dried parsley

1. Preheat the air fryer to 175°C. Prepare the air fryer basket by lining it with parchment and lightly spraying it with oil. 2. Place the turkey breast in the prepared basket, breast-side up, spray with oil, and cook for 20 minutes. Flip and cook, breast-side down, for another 20 minutes. Flip again and resume cooking for 15 minutes, until the internal temperature reaches 75°C. 3. Mix together the melted butter, garlic, poultry seasoning, salt, and parsley in a small bowl. 4. Brush the butter mixture all over the turkey and cook for another 5 minutes, or until the skin is browned and crispy.
Per Serving: Calories 570; Fat 27.8g; Sodium 281mg; Carbs 0g; Fibre 0g; Sugar 0g; Protein 74.7g

Honey-Mustard Chicken Salad

Prep time: 10 minutes | Cook time: 10 to 13 minutes | Serves: 4

3 boneless, skinless chicken
breasts, cut into 2.5cm cubes
1 small red onion, sliced
1 orange pepper, sliced
4 tablespoons honey mustard

salad dressing, divided
½ teaspoon dried thyme
120g mayonnaise
2 tablespoons lemon juice

1. Place the chicken, onion, pepper, and squash in the air fryer basket. Drizzle with 1 tablespoon of the honey mustard salad dressing, add the thyme, and toss. 2. Roast at 205°C for 10 to 13 minutes or until the chicken is 75°C on a food thermometer, tossing the food once during cooking time. 3. Transfer the vegetables and chicken to a bowl and mix in the remaining 3 tablespoons of honey mustard salad dressing, the mayonnaise, and lemon juice. Serve on lettuce leaves, if desired.
Per Serving: Calories 337; Fat 19.3g; Sodium 765mg; Carbs 9.3g; Fibre 1.6g; Sugar 4.8g; Protein 31g

Mayo Pretzel-Crusted Chicken

Prep time: 10 minutes| Cook time: 12 minutes| Serves: 4

80g mini twist pretzels
120g mayonnaise
2 tablespoons honey
2 tablespoons yellow mustard

4 (150g) boneless, skinless
chicken breasts
1 teaspoon salt
½ teaspoon ground black pepper

1. Preheat the air fryer to 190°C. 2. Slice the chicken breasts in half lengthwise. 3. In a food processor, place pretzels and pulse ten times. 4. In a medium bowl, mix mayonnaise, honey, and mustard. 5. Sprinkle chicken with salt and pepper, then brush with sauce mixture until well coated. 6. Pour pretzel crumbs onto a shallow plate and press each piece of chicken into them until well coated. 7. Spritz chicken with cooking spray and place in the air fryer basket. Cook for 12 minutes, turning halfway through cooking time, until edges are golden brown and the internal temperature reaches at least 75°C. Serve warm.
Per Serving: Calories 616; Fat 17.4g; Sodium 1784mg; Carbs 61.8g; Fibre 5.6g; Sugar 9g; Protein 56.5g

Cheese Spaghetti Pie

Prep Time: 15 minutes | Cook Time: 22 minutes | Serves: 4

For Ricotta Cheese Layer

160g ricotta cheese	cheese
1 tablespoon grated Parmesan	½ teaspoon salt

For Spaghetti Crust

2 tablespoons butter, melted	¼ teaspoon salt
1 large egg	150g dry gluten-free spaghetti,
100g grated Parmesan cheese	cooked according to instructions

For Toppings

2 teaspoons olive oil	225g chicken mince
55g diced peeled yellow onion	240ml marinara sauce
50g diced seeded green pepper	60g grated mozzarella cheese

1. To make the ricotta cheese layer, combine all the Ricotta Cheese Layer ingredients in a small bowl. 2. To make the spaghetti crust, mix the butter, egg, Parmesan, and salt in a large bowl; stir in the drained, cooled cooked spaghetti. Set aside. 3. To make the toppings, heat the olive oil in a medium skillet over medium heat for 30 seconds; add onion and pepper, and cook them for 3 minutes until onions are translucent; add the chicken mince, and stir-fry for 5 minutes until no longer pink. 4. Preheat the air fryer at 175°C for 3 minutes. Lightly grease the air fryer basket with cooking oil. 5. Gently press spaghetti mixture into an 18cm spring-form pan, spread ricotta mixture evenly on top. Top with toppings mixture, followed by marinara sauce. 6. Place spring-form pan in air fryer basket, and cook for 10 minutes. 7. Spread mozzarella cheese evenly on top, and cook for an additional 4 minutes. 8. Transfer pan to a cutting board and let rest 20 minutes. Once set, release sides of spring-form pan. Slice and serve pie.

Per Serving: Calories 355; Fat 19.34g; Sodium 1321mg; Carbs 22.5g; Fibre 2.4g; Sugar 3.77g; Protein 23.46g

Garlicky Wings

Prep Time: 5 minutes | Cook Time: 25 minutes | Serves: 4

900g bone-in chicken wings,	½ teaspoon onion powder
separated at joints	½ teaspoon garlic powder
½ teaspoon salt	1 teaspoon dried dill
½ teaspoon ground black pepper	

1. Toss the chicken wings with salt, pepper, onion powder, garlic powder, and dill in a large bowl until evenly coated. 2. Place the chicken wings in the air fryer basket in a single layer. 3. Cook the wings at 205°C for 25 minutes until they have an internal temperature of at least 75°C, shaking the basket every 7 minutes during cooking. 4. Serve warm.

Per Serving: Calories 291; Fat 8.12g; Sodium 475mg; Carbs 1.06g; Fibre 0.3g; Sugar 0.03g; Protein 50.05g

Fajita Chicken Thigh Meatballs

Prep Time: 10 minutes | Cook Time: 20 minutes | Serves: 6

455g chicken thigh mince	and finely chopped
½ medium green pepper, seeded	50g shredded pepper jack cheese
and finely chopped	1 (25g) packet gluten-free fajita
¼ medium yellow onion, peeled	seasoning

1. Combine all ingredients in a large bowl, form the mixture into eighteen 5cm balls. 2. Place the balls in the air fryer basket in a single layer. 3. Cook the meatballs at 175°C for 20 minutes, turning the poppers halfway through cooking. 4. When there are 5 minutes left, increase temperature to 205°C to give the poppers a dark golden-brown color, shaking the basket once more when there are 2 minutes left. 5. Serve warm.

Per Serving: Calories 221; Fat 15.09g; Sodium 333mg; Carbs 2.7g; Fibre 0.5g; Sugar 0.75g; Protein 15.44g

Pesto Chicken Pizzas

Prep Time: 10 minutes | Cook Time: 12 minutes | Serves: 4

455g chicken thigh mince	60g basil pesto
¼ teaspoon salt	120g shredded mozzarella cheese
⅛ teaspoon ground black pepper	4 grape tomatoes, sliced

1. Line the air fryer basket with parchment paper. 2. Mix the chicken mince with mix with salt and pepper in a large bowl. Divide mixture into four equal sections. 3. Wet your hands with water to prevent sticking, then press each section into a 15cm circle onto a piece of ungreased parchment. 4. Place each chicken crust in the air fryer

basket, working in batches if needed. 4. Cook the crusts at 175°C for 10 minutes, turning them halfway through cooking. 5. When the time is up, spread 1 tablespoon pesto across the top of each crust, then sprinkle with 30g mozzarella and top with 1 sliced tomato, then resume cooking them for 2 minutes until the cheese is melted and brown. 6. Serve warm.

Per Serving: Calories 307; Fat 19.03g; Sodium 452mg; Carbs 4.92g; Fibre 1.6g; Sugar 2.82g; Protein 28.55g

Pickle-Brined Chicken

Prep Time: 1 hour 15 minutes | Cook Time: 20 minutes | Serves: 4

4 (100g) boneless, skinless	50g parmesan, grated
chicken thighs	½ teaspoon salt
80ml dill pickle juice	¼ teaspoon ground black pepper
1 large egg	

1. Place chicken thighs in a large sealable bowl or bag and pour pickle juice over them. Place sealed bowl or bag into refrigerator and allow to marinate at least 1 hour up to overnight. 2. Beat the egg in a small bowl; place the parmesan in another medium bowl. 3. Remove chicken thighs from marinade. Shake off excess pickle juice and pat thighs dry with a paper towel. Sprinkle with salt and pepper. 4. Dip each thigh into egg and gently shake off excess. Press into parmesan to coat each side. 5. Place thighs into ungreased air fryer basket, and cook them at 205°C for 20 minutes until they have an internal temperature of at least 75°C. 6. Serve warm.

Per Serving: Calories 159; Fat 10.38g; Sodium 685mg; Carbs 0.56g; Fibre 0.2g; Sugar 0.17g; Protein 15.02g

Thyme Roasted Chicken

Prep Time: 10 minutes | Cook Time: 60 minutes | Serves: 6

1 (1.8kg) chicken	1 teaspoon baking powder
2 teaspoons dried thyme	1 medium lemon
1 teaspoon garlic powder	2 tablespoons salted butter,
½ teaspoon onion powder	melted
2 teaspoons dried parsley	

1. Rub chicken with thyme, garlic powder, onion powder, parsley, and baking powder. 2. Slice lemon and place four slices on top of chicken, breast side up, and secure with toothpicks. Place remaining slices inside of the chicken. 3. Place entire chicken into the air fryer basket, breast side down. 4. Adjust the temperature to 175°C and set the timer for 60 minutes. 5. After 30 minutes, flip chicken so breast side is up. 6. When done, internal temperature should be 75°C and the skin golden and crispy. To serve, pour melted butter over entire chicken.

Per Serving: Calories 363; Fat 10.74g; Sodium 248mg; Carbs 1.18g; Fibre 0.2g; Sugar 0.23g; Protein 61.67g

Chicken Fajitas

Prep Time: 10 minutes | Cook Time: 10 to 14 minutes | Serves: 4

Cooking oil spray	divided
4 boneless, skinless chicken	½ teaspoon dried oregano
breasts, sliced crosswise	8 corn tortillas
1 small red onion, sliced	70g torn butter lettuce leaves
2 red peppers, seeded and sliced	2 avocados, peeled, pitted, and
120ml spicy ranch salad dressing,	chopped

1. Insert the crisper plate into the basket and the basket into the unit. Preheat the unit by selecting BAKE, setting the temperature to 190°C, and setting the time to 3 minutes. Select START/STOP to begin. 2. Once the unit is preheated, spray the crisper plate with cooking oil. Place the chicken, red onion, and red pepper into the basket. Drizzle with 1 tablespoon of the salad dressing and season with the oregano. Toss to combine. 3. Select BAKE, set the temperature to 190°C, and set the time to 14 minutes. Select START/STOP to begin. 4. After 10 minutes, check the chicken. If a food thermometer inserted into the chicken registers at least 75°C, it is done. If not, resume cooking. 5. When the cooking is complete, transfer the chicken and vegetables to a bowl and toss with the remaining salad dressing. 6. Serve the chicken mixture family-style with the tortillas, lettuce, and avocados, and let everyone make their own plates.

Per Serving: Calories 919; Fat 42.05g; Sodium 1070mg; Carbs 62.72g; Fibre 10.1g; Sugar 7.41g; Protein 72.06g

Cheese Broccoli–Stuffed Chicken

Prep Time: 15 minutes | Cook Time: 20 minutes | Serves: 4

50g cream cheese, softened
90g chopped fresh broccoli, steamed
50g shredded sharp Cheddar cheese
4 (150g) boneless, skinless

chicken breasts
2 tablespoons mayonnaise
¼ teaspoon salt
¼ teaspoon garlic powder
⅛ teaspoon ground black pepper

1. Combine cream cheese, broccoli, and Cheddar in a medium bowl. 2. Cut a 10cm pocket into each chicken breast. Evenly divide mixture between chicken breasts; stuff the pocket of each chicken breast with the mixture. 3. Spread ¼ tablespoon mayonnaise per side of each chicken breast, then sprinkle both sides of breasts with salt, garlic powder, and pepper. 4. Place stuffed chicken breasts in air fryer basket, and cook them at 175°C for 20 minutes, turning them halfway through cooking. 5. When done, chicken will be golden and have an internal temperature of at least 75°C. 6. Serve warm.
Per Serving: Calories 200; Fat 15.22g; Sodium 387mg; Carbs 1.52g; Fibre 0.4g; Sugar 0.64g; Protein 14.12g

Spiced Chicken Thighs

Prep Time: 10 minutes | Cook Time: 25 minutes | Serves: 4

4 (100g) bone-in, skin-on chicken thighs
½ teaspoon salt
½ teaspoon garlic powder

2 teaspoons chili powder
1 teaspoon paprika
1 teaspoon ground cumin
1 small lime, halved

1. Pat chicken thighs dry and sprinkle with salt, garlic powder, chili powder, paprika, and cumin. 2. Squeeze juice from ½ lime over thighs, and then place the thighs in air fryer basket. 3. Cook the thighs at 195°C for 25 minutes until they are crispy and browned with an internal temperature of at least 75°C, turning thighs halfway through cooking. 4. Drizzle with remaining lime juice, and serve warm.
Per Serving: Calories 74; Fat 5.1g; Sodium 354mg; Carbs 2.5g; Fibre 0.8g; Sugar 0.36g; Protein 5.15g

Parmesan Fried Chicken

Prep Time: 40 minutes | Cook Time: 20 minutes | Serves: 4

60ml buffalo sauce
4 (100g) boneless, skinless chicken breasts
½ teaspoon paprika

½ teaspoon garlic powder
¼ teaspoon ground black pepper
50g parmesan, finely grated

1. Toss the chicken breasts with buffalo sauce in a large sealable bag, then place the bag in the refrigerator to let them marinate for at least 30 minutes up to overnight. 2. Remove chicken from marinade but do not shake excess sauce off chicken. Sprinkle the thighs with paprika, garlic powder, and pepper on both sides. 3. Place parmesan in a large bowl, and evenly coat each chicken breast with them on both sides. 4. Place chicken in the air fryer basket, and cook them at 205°C for 20 minutes until they are golden and have an internal temperature of at least 75°C, turning chicken halfway through cooking. 5. Serve warm.
Per Serving: Calories 160; Fat 7.22g; Sodium 460mg; Carbs 8.01g; Fibre 0.3g; Sugar 6.13g; Protein 14.91g

Chicken Tenders with Carrots and Potatoes

Prep time: 10 minutes| Cook time: 18 to 20 minutes| Serves: 4

455g chicken tenders
1 tablespoon honey
Pinch salt
Freshly ground black pepper
50g soft fresh bread crumbs

½ teaspoon dried thyme
1 tablespoon olive oil
2 carrots, sliced
12 small red potatoes

1. Toss the chicken tenders with honey, salt, and pepper in a medium bowl. 2. Combine the bread crumbs, thyme, and olive oil in a shallow bowl, and mix. 3. Coat the tenders in the bread crumbs, pressing firmly onto the meat. 4. Place the carrots and potatoes in the air fryer basket and top with the chicken tenders. 5. Roast at 195°C for 18 to 20 minutes or until the chicken is cooked to 75°C and the vegetables are tender, shaking the basket halfway during the cooking time.
Per Serving: Calories 553; Fat 7.4g; Sodium 220mg; Carbs 90.5g; Fibre 10g; Sugar 12.6g; Protein 33.4g

Savoury Wings

Prep Time: 5 minutes | Cook Time: 25 minutes | Serves: 4

900g bone-in chicken wings, separated at joints

1 teaspoon salt
½ teaspoon ground black pepper

1. Sprinkle the chicken wings with salt and pepper, then place in the air fryer basket in a single layer. 2. Cook the chicken wings at 205°C for 25 minutes until they are golden brown and have an internal temperature of at least 75°C, shaking the basket every 7 minutes during cooking. 3. Serve warm.
Per Serving: Calories 287; Fat 8.04g; Sodium 765mg; Carbs 0.24g; Fibre 0.1g; Sugar 0g; Protein 49.87g

Chicken and Cheese Nacho Bake

Prep time: 5 minutes| Cook time: 7 minutes| Serves: 4

50 tortilla chips
280g shredded cooked chicken breast, divided
200g shredded cheese, divided

45g sliced pickled jalapeño peppers, divided
80g diced red onion, divided

1. Preheat your air fryer to 150°C. 2. Use foil to make a bowl shape that fits the shape of the air fryer basket. Then layer half the tortilla chips in the bottom of foil bowl, then top with 140g chicken, 100g cheese, 20g jalapeños, and 40g onion. Repeat with remaining chips and toppings. 3. Place foil bowl in the air fryer basket and cook for 7 minutes until cheese is melted and toppings heated through. Serve warm.
Per Serving: Calories 480; Fat 25.5g; Sodium 339mg; Carbs 24g; Fibre 2g; Sugar 2g; Protein 37g

Garlic Chicken Tenders

Prep time: 10 minutes| Cook time: 12 minutes| Serves: 4

455g boneless, skinless chicken breast tenderloins
120g mayonnaise
100g grated Parmesan cheese

105g panko bread crumbs
½ teaspoon garlic powder
1 teaspoon salt
½ teaspoon ground black pepper

1. Preheat your air fryer to 205°C. 2. In a large bowl, add chicken and mayonnaise and toss to coat. 3. In a medium bowl, mix Parmesan, bread crumbs, garlic powder, salt, and pepper. Press chicken into bread crumb mixture to fully coat. Spritz with cooking spray and place in the air fryer basket. 4. Cook for 12 minutes, flipping once while cooking, until tenders are golden and crisp on the edges and internal temperature reaches at least 75°C. Serve warm.
Per Serving: Calories 424; Fat 23g; Sodium 1610mg; Carbs 32.9g; Fibre 2.4g; Sugar 6.9g; Protein 20.3g

Crispy Buttermilk Fried Chicken

Prep time: 15 minutes plus 30 minutes for marinating| Cook time: 50 minutes| Serves: 4

4 (150g) boneless, skinless chicken thighs
180ml buttermilk
80ml hot sauce

1½ tablespoons Cajun seasoning, divided
125g plain flour
1 large egg

1. Preheat your air fryer to 190°C. 2. Add chicken thighs, buttermilk, hot sauce, and ½ tablespoon of Cajun seasoning in a large bowl, and toss to coat. Cover it and let the chicken thighs marinate in the refrigerator for at least 30 minutes. 3. Whisk together the flour with ½ tablespoon of Cajun seasoning in a large bowl. In a medium bowl, whisk the egg. 4. Remove chicken from marinade and sprinkle with remaining ½ tablespoon Cajun seasoning. 5. Dredge chicken by dipping it into whisked egg, then pressing into flour to fully coat. Spritz with cooking spray and place into the air fryer basket. 6. Cook for 20 minutes, turning halfway through cooking time until the chicken is golden brown. The internal temperature shall reach at least 75°C. Serve warm.
Per Serving: Calories 545; Fat 26g; Sodium 1594mg; Carbs 28g; Fibre 1.3g; Sugar 3g; Protein 46g

Chicken Sandwiches with Buffalo Sauce

Prep time: 15 minutes| Cook time: 20 minutes| Serves: 4

4 (150g) boneless, skinless chicken thighs
1 (25g) packet dry ranch seasoning

60ml buffalo sauce
4 (25g) slices pepper jack cheese
4 sandwich buns

1. Preheat the air fryer to 190°C. 2. Sprinkle each chicken thigh with ranch seasoning and spritz with cooking spray. 3. Then transfer the chicken thighs to the air fryer basket and cook for 20 minutes, turning chicken halfway through, until chicken is brown at the edges and internal temperature reaches at least 75°C. 4. Drizzle buffalo sauce over chicken, top with a slice of cheese, and place on buns to serve.
Per Serving: Calories 752; Fat 41.5g; Sodium 1329mg; Carbs 41.6g; Fibre 1g; Sugar 23g; Protein 51g

Zesty Parmesan Chicken Drumsticks

Prep time: 10 minutes| Cook time: 20 minutes| Serves: 4

8 (100g) chicken drumsticks
1 teaspoon salt
½ teaspoon ground black pepper

30g dry ranch seasoning
55g panko bread crumbs
50g grated Parmesan cheese

1. Preheat the air fryer to 190°C. 2. Sprinkle drumsticks with salt, pepper, and ranch seasoning. 3. In a paper lunch bag, combine bread crumbs and Parmesan. Add drumsticks to the bag and shake to coat. Spritz with cooking spray. 4. Place the chicken drumsticks in your air fryer basket and cook for 20 minutes, turning halfway through cooking time, until the internal temperature reaches at least 75°C. Serve warm.
Per Serving: Calories 499; Fat 25g; Sodium 1762mg; Carbs 16.8g; Fibre 1.8g; Sugar 1.8g; Protein 46.8g

Crispy Mayo Chicken Thighs

Prep time: 10 minutes| Cook time: 25 minutes| Serves: 4

120g mayonnaise
4 bone-in, skin-on chicken thighs
1 teaspoon salt

½ teaspoon ground black pepper
2 teaspoons Italian seasoning
100g Italian bread crumbs

1. Preheat the air fryer to 185°C. 2. Brush mayonnaise over chicken thighs on both sides. Sprinkle thighs with salt, pepper, and Italian seasoning. 3. Place bread crumbs into a resealable plastic bag and add thighs. Shake to coat. 4. Remove thighs from bag and spritz with cooking spray. Place the crumbs-coated chicken thighs in the air fryer basket and cook for 25 minutes, turning thighs after 15 minutes, until skin is golden and crispy and internal temperature reaches at least 75°C. Serve warm.
Per Serving: Calories 333; Fat 16.7g; Sodium 1437mg; Carbs 21g; Fibre 2g; Sugar 2g; Protein 23g

Chicken and Cheese Enchiladas

Prep time: 10 minutes | Cook time: 15 minutes per batch | Serves: 4

360g barbecue sauce, divided
420g shredded cooked chicken
8 (15cm) flour tortillas

150g shredded cheese, divided
55g diced red onion

1. Preheat your air fryer to 175°C. 2. In a large bowl, mix 240g barbecue sauce and shredded chicken. 3. Place 30g chicken onto each tortilla and top with 2 tablespoons cheese. 4. Roll each tortilla and then place seam side down into two 15cm round baking dishes. Brush tortillas with remaining sauce, top with remaining cheese, and sprinkle with onion. 5. Working in batches, place in the air fryer basket and cook for 15 minutes until the sauce is bubbling and cheese is melted. Serve warm.
Per Serving: Calories 865; Fat 32.5g; Sodium 1996mg; Carbs 93.5g; Fibre 3.5g; Sugar 39.7g; Protein 47g

Cheddar Chicken Taquitos

Prep time: 5 minutes | Cook time: 8 minutes | Serves: 4

210g shredded cooked chicken
100g full-fat cream cheese, softened

100g shredded sharp Cheddar cheese
12 (15cm) white corn tortillas

1. Preheat the air fryer to 175°C. 2. Mix chicken, cream cheese, and Cheddar cheese in a large bowl. 3. Place 3 tablespoons chicken mixture onto each tortilla and roll. Spritz each roll with cooking spray. 4. Place the rolls evenly in the air fryer basket, seam side down, and cook for 8 minutes, turning halfway through cooking time, until crispy and brown. Serve warm.
Per Serving: Calories 454; Fat 23g; Sodium 359mg; Carbs 34.8g; Fibre 4.5g; Sugar 2.4g; Protein 27.5g

Teriyaki Chicken-Pineapple Kebabs

Prep time: 10 minutes | Cook time: 15 minutes | Serves: 4

180ml teriyaki sauce, divided
4 (100g) boneless, skinless chicken thighs, cubed
1 teaspoon salt
½ teaspoon ground black pepper

165g pineapple chunks
1 medium red pepper
¼ medium yellow onion, peeled and cut into 2.5cm cubes

1. Remove the seeds from the medium red pepper and cut into 2.5cm cubes. 2. In a large bowl, pour 120ml teriyaki sauce over chicken and sprinkle with salt and black pepper. Cover it and let them marinate in refrigerator for 1 hour. 3. Soak eight 15cm skewers in water at least 10 minutes to prevent burning. Preheat your air fryer to 205°C. 4. Place a cube of chicken on skewer, then a piece of pineapple, pepper, and onion. Repeat with remaining chicken, pineapple, and vegetables. 5. Brush kebabs with remaining 60ml teriyaki sauce and place in the air fryer basket. Cook for 15 minutes, turning twice during cooking, until chicken reaches an internal temperature of at least 75°C and vegetables are tender. Serve warm.
Per Serving: Calories 320; Fat 10.4g; Sodium 2030mg; Carbs 24.6g; Fibre 1.5g; Sugar 22g; Protein 31g

Garlic Popcorn Chicken

Prep time: 10 minutes | Cook time: 12 minutes | Serves: 4

1½ teaspoons salt, divided
1 teaspoon ground black pepper, divided
1½ teaspoons garlic powder, divided

1 tablespoon mayonnaise
455g boneless, skinless chicken breast, cut into 2.5cm cubes
110g panko bread crumbs

1. Preheat your air fryer to 175°C. 2. Cut the chicken breasts into 2.5cm cubes. 3. In a large bowl, combine 1 teaspoon salt, ½ teaspoon pepper, 1 teaspoon garlic powder, and mayonnaise. Add chicken cubes and toss to coat. 4. Place the bread crumbs in a suitable resealable bag and add remaining ½ teaspoon salt, ½ teaspoon pepper, and ½ teaspoon garlic powder. Place the chicken into the bag and toss to evenly coat. 5. Spritz chicken with cooking spray and place in the air fryer basket. Cook them for 12 minutes, turning halfway through cooking time, until chicken is golden brown and internal temperature reaches at least 75°C. Serve warm.
Per Serving: Calories 238; Fat 8g; Sodium 1248mg; Carbs 29.4g; Fibre 2g; Sugar 6.6g; Protein 11.8g

Cheddar Chicken and Broccoli Casserole

Prep time: 10 minutes | Cook time: 30 minutes | Serves: 4

455g boneless, skinless chicken breast, cubed
1 teaspoon salt
½ teaspoon ground black pepper
185g uncooked instant long-grain

white rice
90g chopped broccoli florets
240ml chicken stock
100g shredded sharp Cheddar cheese

1. Preheat the air fryer to 205°C. 2. In a 15cm round baking dish, add chicken and sprinkle with salt and pepper. 3. Then transfer the seasoned chicken to your air fryer basket and cook for 10 minutes, stirring twice during cooking. 4. Add rice, broccoli, stock, and Cheddar. Stir until combined. Cover with foil, being sure to tuck foil under the bottom of the dish to ensure the air fryer fan does not blow it off. 5. Place dish back in the air fryer basket and cook for 20 minutes until rice is tender. Serve warm.
Per Serving: Calories 500; Fat 20.4g; Sodium 1319mg; Carbs 44.6g; Fibre 2.5g; Sugar 6.2g; Protein 32.5g

Mayo Chicken Patties

Prep time: 10 minutes | Cook time: 15 minutes | Serves: 4

455g chicken breast mince
100g shredded sharp Cheddar cheese
50g plain bread crumbs
1 teaspoon salt
½ teaspoon ground black pepper
2 tablespoons mayonnaise
105g panko bread crumbs

1. Preheat your air fryer to 205°C. 2. In a large bowl, mix chicken, Cheddar cheese, plain bread crumbs, salt, and pepper until well combined. Separate into four portions and form into patties 1cm thick. 3. Brush each patty with mayonnaise, then press into panko bread crumbs to fully coat. Spritz with cooking spray. 4. Place the coated patties in the air fryer basket and cook for 15 minutes, flipping once while cooking, until patties are golden brown and internal temperature reaches at least 75°C. Serve warm.
Per Serving: Calories 411; Fat 23.4g; Sodium 1034mg; Carbs 14.8g; Fibre 1g; Sugar 1.5g; Protein 33.5g

Breaded Chicken Nuggets

Prep time: 15 minutes | Cook time: 10 minutes | Serves: 4

455g chicken breast mince
1½ teaspoons salt, divided
¾ teaspoon ground black pepper,
divided
150g plain bread crumbs, divided
2 large eggs

1. Preheat your air fryer to 205°C. 2. In a large bowl, mix chicken, 1 teaspoon salt, ½ teaspoon pepper, and 50g bread crumbs. 3. In a small bowl, whisk eggs. In a separate medium bowl, mix remaining 100g bread crumbs with remaining ½ teaspoon salt and ¼ teaspoon pepper. 4. Scoop 1 tablespoon chicken mixture and flatten it into a nugget shape. 5. Dip into eggs, shaking off excess before rolling in bread crumb mixture. Repeat with remaining chicken mixture to make twenty nuggets. 6. Place the chicken nuggets in the air fryer basket and spritz with cooking spray. Cook for 10 minutes, turning halfway through cooking time, until internal temperature reaches 75°C. Serve warm.
Per Serving: Calories 392; Fat 15g; Sodium 1276mg; Carbs 30g; Fibre 2g; Sugar 2.6g; Protein 32g

Greek Chicken Stir-Fry

Prep Time: 15 minutes | Cook Time: 15 minutes | Serves: 2

1 (150g) chicken breast, cut into 2.5cm cubes
½ medium courgette, chopped
½ medium red pepper, seeded and chopped
¼ medium red onion, peeled and
sliced
1 tablespoon coconut oil
1 teaspoon dried oregano
½ teaspoon garlic powder
¼ teaspoon dried thyme

1. Place the chicken breasts, courgette, pepper, red onion, coconut oil, dried oregano, garlic powder, and the dried thyme into a large mixing bowl and toss until the coconut oil coats the meat and vegetables. Then pour the jichicken mixture from the bowl into the air fryer basket. 2. Adjust the temperature setting to 190°C and set the timer for 15 minutes. 3. Shake the air fryer basket halfway through the cooking time to redistribute the food. Serve immediately.
Per Serving: Calories 215; Fat 14.73g; Sodium 55mg; Carbs 2.21g; Fibre 0.5g; Sugar 0.66g; Protein 18.23g

Chicken, Spinach, and Feta Bites

Prep Time: 10 minutes | Cook Time: 12 minutes | Serves: 4

455g chicken thigh mince
70g frozen spinach, thawed and drained
80g crumbled feta
¼ teaspoon onion powder
½ teaspoon garlic powder
10g grated parmesan

1. Mix the chicken thigh meat, spinach, feta, onion powder, garlic powder, and the parmesan in a large bowl. Roll the chicken-pork mixture into 5cm and place evenly into the air fryer basket, working in batches if needed. 2. Adjust the temperature setting to 175°C and set the timer for 12 minutes. 3. When done, internal temperature will be 75°C. Serve immediately.
Per Serving: Calories 182; Fat 7.64g; Sodium 234mg; Carbs 1.46g; Fibre 0.4g; Sugar 0.61g; Protein 25.69g

Buffalo Chicken Cheese Sticks

Prep Time: 5 minutes | Cook Time: 8 minutes | Serves: 2

135g shredded cooked chicken
60ml buffalo sauce
115g shredded mozzarella cheese
1 large egg
60g crumbled feta

1. In a large bowl, mix the cooked chicken, buffalo sauce, mozzarella cheese, and then whisk the egg. Cut a suitable piece of parchment to fit your air fryer basket and press the mixture into a 1cm thick circle. 2. Sprinkle the mixture with the crumbled feta cheese and place them into the air fryer basket. 3. Adjust the temperature setting to 205°C and set the timer for 8 minutes. 4. Flip over the cheese mixture, when the cooking time passed 5 minutes. 5. Allow them to cool for 5 minutes before cutting into sticks. Serve warm.
Per Serving: Calories 334; Fat 9.44g; Sodium 1030mg; Carbs 17.5g; Fibre 1.3g; Sugar 13.58g; Protein 43g

Italian Chicken Thighs

Prep Time: 5 minutes | Cook Time: 20 minutes | Serves: 2

4 bone-in, skin-on chicken thighs
2 tablespoons unsalted butter, melted
1 teaspoon dried parsley
1 teaspoon dried basil
½ teaspoon garlic powder
¼ teaspoon onion powder
¼ teaspoon dried oregano

1. Brush the unsaltedd butter over chicken thighs and sprinkle the dried parsley, basil, garlic powder, onion powder, and the dried oregano over the thighs. Place thighs into the air fryer basket. 2. Adjust the temperature setting to 195°C and set the timer for 20 minutes. 3. Halfway through the cooking time, flip the thighs. 4. When fully cooked, internal temperature will be at least 75°C and skin will be crispy. Serve warm.
Per Serving: Calories 493; Fat 39.14g; Sodium 159mg; Carbs 1.6g; Fibre 0.3g; Sugar 0.06g; Protein 31.96g

Stuffed Chicken Breast

Prep Time: 15 minutes | Cook Time: 25 minutes | Serves: 4

2 (150g) boneless, skinless chicken breasts
¼ medium white onion, peeled and cut into slices
1 medium green pepper, seeded
and sliced
1 tablespoon coconut oil
2 teaspoons chili powder
1 teaspoon ground cumin
½ teaspoon garlic powder

1. Slice each chicken breast completely in half lengthwise into two even pieces. Using a meat tenderizer, pound out the chicken until it's about ½cm thickness. 2. Lay each slice of chicken out and place three slices of onion and four slices of green pepper on the end closest to you. Begin rolling the peppers and onions tightly into the chicken. Secure the roll with either toothpicks or a couple pieces of butcher's twine. 3. Drizzle coconut oil over chicken. Sprinkle each side with chili powder, cumin, and garlic powder. Place the rolls evenly into the air fryer basket. 4. Adjust the temperature to 175°C and set the timer for 25 minutes. 5. Serve warm.
Per Serving: Calories 117; Fat 7.68g; Sodium 68mg; Carbs 2.9g; Fibre 0.8g; Sugar 0.98g; Protein 9.51g

Chicken Patties

Prep Time: 15 minutes | Cook Time: 12 minutes | Serves: 4

455g chicken thigh mince
55g shredded mozzarella cheese
1 teaspoon dried parsley
½ teaspoon garlic powder
¼ teaspoon onion powder
1 large egg
50g parmesan, grated

1. Mix chicken micne, mozzarella, parsley, garlic powder, and onion powder in a large bowl. Form them into four patties. 2. Place the four patties in the freezer for about 15–20 minutes until they are just about to firm up. 3. Whisk the large egg in a medium bowl. Add the parmesan to a large bowl. 4. Dip each chicken patty with the egg and press into parmesan until fully coated. Place the four patties evenly into the air fryer basket. 5. Adjust the temperature setting to 180°C and set the timer for 12 minutes. 6. Patties will be firm and cooked to an internal temperature of 75°C when done. Serve immediately.
Per Serving: Calories 202; Fat 7.37g; Sodium 223mg; Carbs 1.08g; Fibre 0.3g; Sugar 0.26g; Protein 31.17g

Chicken and Spinach Salad

Prep Time: 10 minutes | Cook Time: 20 minutes | Serves: 4

3 (125g) boneless, skinless chicken breasts, cut into 2.5cm cubes
5 teaspoons extra-virgin olive oil
½ teaspoon dried thyme
1 medium red onion, sliced
1 red pepper, sliced
1 small courgette, cut into strips
3 tablespoons freshly squeezed lemon juice
180g fresh baby spinach leaves

1. Insert the crisper plate into the basket and the basket into the unit. Preheat the unit by selecting AIR ROAST, setting the temperature to 190°C, and setting the time to 3 minutes. Select START/STOP to begin. 2. Combine the chicken, olive oil, and thyme in a large bowl. Toss to coat. Transfer to a medium metal bowl that fits into the basket. 3. Once the unit is preheated, place the bowl into the basket. 4. Select AIR ROAST, set the temperature to 190°C, and set the time to 20 minutes. Select START/STOP to begin. 5. After 8 minutes, add the red onion, red pepper, and courgette to the bowl. Resume cooking. After about 6 minutes more, stir the chicken and vegetables. Resume cooking. 6. When the cooking is complete, a food thermometer inserted into the chicken should register at least 75°C. Remove the bowl from the unit and stir in the lemon juice. 7. Put the spinach in a serving bowl and top with the chicken mixture. Toss to combine and serve immediately.
Per Serving: Calories 102; Fat 5.97g; Sodium 108 mg; Carbs 3.73g; Fibre 1.3g; Sugar 1.17g; Protein 9.06g

Marinara Chicken with Cheeses

Prep Time: 10 minutes | Cook Time: 20 minutes | Serves: 4

2 (100g) boneless, skinless chicken breasts
2 egg whites, beaten
110g Italian bread crumbs
50g grated Parmesan cheese
2 teaspoons Italian seasoning
Salt
Freshly ground black pepper
Cooking oil spray
200g marinara sauce
55g shredded mozzarella cheese

1. Cut the boneless and skinless chicken breasts in half horizontally to create 4 thin cutlets on a cutting board with a knife blade parallel. On a solid surface, pound the cutlets to flatten them with your hands, a rolling pin, a kitchen mallet, or a meat hammer. 2. Pour the egg whites into a bowl large enough to dip the chicken. 3. In another bowl large enough to dip a chicken cutlet in, stir together the bread crumbs, Parmesan cheese, and Italian seasoning, and season with salt and pepper. 4. Dip each cutlet into the egg whites and into the breadcrumb mixture to coat. 5. Insert the crisper plate into the basket and the basket into the unit. Preheat the unit by selecting AIR FRY, setting the temperature to 190°C, and setting the time to 3 minutes. Select START/STOP to begin. 6. Once the unit is preheated, spray the crisper plate with cooking oil. Working in batches, place 2 chicken cutlets in the basket. Spray the chicken with cooking oil. 7. Select AIR FRY, set the temperature to 190°C, and set the time to 7 minutes. Select START/STOP to begin. 8. When the cooking is complete, repeat steps 6 and 7 with the remaining cutlets. 9. Top the chicken cutlets with the marinara sauce and shredded mozzarella cheese. If the chicken will fit into the basket without stacking, you can prepare all 4 at once. Otherwise, do these 2 cutlets at a time. 10. Select AIR FRY, set the temperature to 190°C, and set the time to 3 minutes. Select START/STOP to begin. 11. The cooking is complete when the cheese is melted and the chicken reaches an internal temperature of 75°C. Cool for 5 minutes before serving.
Per Serving: Calories 192; Fat 8.26g; Sodium 574mg; Carbs 11.41g; Fibre 1.6g; Sugar 3.64g; Protein 17.26g

Sweet and Spicy General Tso's Chicken

Prep Time: 10 minutes | Cook Time: 14 minutes | Serves: 4

1 tablespoon sesame oil
1 teaspoon minced garlic
½ teaspoon ground ginger
240ml chicken stock
4 tablespoons soy sauce, divided
½ teaspoon sriracha, plus more for serving
2 tablespoons hoisin sauce
4 tablespoons cornflour, divided
4 boneless, skinless chicken breasts, cut into 2.5cm pieces
Olive oil spray
2 medium spring onions, sliced, green parts only
Sesame seeds, for garnish

1. Set a suitable saucepan over low heat, combine the sesame oil, garlic, and ginger and cook for 1 minute. 2. Add the chicken stock, 2 tablespoons of soy sauce, the sriracha, and hoisin sauce. Whisk to combine. 3. Whisk in 2 tablespoons of cornflour and continue cooking over low heat until the sauce starts to thicken, about 5 minutes. Remove the pan from heat, cover, and then set aside. 4. Insert the crisper plate into the basket and the basket into the unit. Preheat the unit by selecting BAKE, setting the temperature 205°C, and setting the time to 3 minutes. Select START/STOP to begin. 5. Toss together the chicken, remaining 2 tablespoons of soy sauce, and remaining 2 tablespoons of cornflour in a medium bowl. 6. Once the unit is preheated, spray the crisper plate with olive oil. Place the chicken into the basket and spray it with olive oil. 7. Select BAKE, set the temperature to 205°C, and set the time to 9 minutes. Select START/STOP to begin. 8. After 5 minutes, remove the basket, shake, and spray the chicken with more olive oil. Reinsert the basket to resume cooking. 9. When the cooking is up, a food thermometer inserted into the chicken should register at least 75°C. Transfer the chicken breasts to a large bowl and toss it with the sauce. Garnish with the spring onions and sesame seeds and serve.
Per Serving: Calories 308; Fat 11.62g; Sodium 680mg; Carbs 16.06g; Fibre 0.9g; Sugar 5.72g; Protein 32.7g

Ranch Chicken Wings

Prep Time: 10 minutes, plus 30 minutes to marinate | Cook Time: 40 minutes | Serves: 4

2 tablespoons water
2 tablespoons hot pepper sauce
2 tablespoons unsalted butter, melted
2 tablespoons apple cider vinegar
1 (25g) envelope ranch salad
dressing mix
1 teaspoon paprika
1.8kg chicken wings, tips removed
Cooking oil spray

1. In a large bowl, whisk the water, hot pepper sauce, melted butter, vinegar, salad dressing mix, and paprika until combined. 2. Add the wings and toss to coat. Then cover the bowl and marinate the wings in the refrigerator for 4 to 24 hours for best results. However, you can just let the wings stand for 30 minutes in the refrigerator. 3. Insert the crisper plate into the air fryer basket and the air fryer basket into the unit. Preheat the air fryer by selecting AIR FRY, setting the temperature to 205°C, and setting the timer to 3 minutes. 4. Once the unit is preheated, spray the crisper plate with cooking oil. Working in batches, put half the wings into the basket; it is okay to stack them. Refrigerate the remaining wings. 5. Select AIR FRY, set the temperature to 205°C, and set the time to 20 minutes. Select START/STOP to begin. 6. Remove and shake the air fryer basket every 5 minutes, three more times, until the chicken is browned and glazed and a food thermometer inserted into the wings registers 75°C. 7. Repeat the cooking steps with the remaining wings. 8. When the cooking is complete, serve warm.
Per Serving: Calories 660; Fat 24.5g; Sodium 440mg; Carbs 2.94g; Fibre 0.5g; Sugar 1.59g; Protein 100.52g

Crispy Chicken Thighs and Carrots

Prep Time: 10 minutes | Cook Time: 22 minutes | Serves: 4

4 bone-in, skin-on chicken thighs
2 carrots, cut into 5cm pieces
2 tablespoons extra-virgin olive oil
2 teaspoons poultry spice
1 teaspoon sea salt, divided
2 teaspoons chopped fresh rosemary leaves
Cooking oil spray
300g cooked white rice

1. Brush the chicken thighs and carrots with olive oil. Sprinkle both with the poultry spice, salt, and rosemary. 2. Insert the crisper plate into the basket and the basket into the unit. Preheat the unit by selecting AIR FRY, setting the temperature to 205°C, and setting the time to 3 minutes. Select START/STOP to begin. 3. Once the unit is preheated, spray the crisper plate with cooking oil. Place the carrots into the basket. Add the wire rack and arrange the chicken thighs on the rack. 4. Select AIR FRY, set the temperature to 205°C, and set the time to 20 minutes. Select START/STOP to begin. 5. When the cooking is complete, check the chicken temperature. If a food thermometer inserted into the chicken registers 75°C, remove the chicken from the air fryer, place it on a clean plate, and cover with aluminum foil to keep warm. Otherwise, resume cooking for 1 to 2 minutes longer. 6. The carrots can cook for 18 to 22 minutes and will be tender and caramelized; cooking time isn't as crucial for root vegetables. 7. Serve the chicken and carrots with the hot cooked rice.
Per Serving: Calories 595; Fat 36.5g; Sodium 811mg; Carbs 29.53g; Fibre 1.1g; Sugar 0.81g; Protein 34.38g

Buffalo Crumb-Crusted Chicken Strips

Prep Time: 15 minutes | Cook Time: 13 to 17 minutes per batch | Serves: 4

95g flour
2 eggs
2 tablespoons water
110g seasoned panko bread crumbs
2 teaspoons granulated garlic
1 teaspoon salt
1 teaspoon freshly ground black
pepper
16 chicken breast strips, or 3 large boneless, skinless chicken breasts, cut into 2.5cm strips
Olive oil spray
60ml Buffalo sauce, plus more as needed

1. Put the plain flour in a small bowl. 2. In another small bowl, whisk the eggs and the water. 3. In a third bowl, stir the panko, granulated garlic, salt, and pepper together. 4. Then dip each chicken strip in the flour, in the egg, and in the panko mixture to coat. Press the crumbs onto the chicken with your fingers. 5. Insert the crisper plate into the basket and the basket into the unit. Preheat the unit by selecting AIR FRY, setting the temperature to 190°C, and setting the time to 3 minutes. Select START/STOP to begin. 6. Once the unit is preheated, place a parchment paper liner into the basket. Place the chicken strips evenly into the basket, working in batches as needed. Do not stack unless using a wire rack for the second layer. Spray the chicken with olive oil. 7. Select AIR FRY, set the temperature to 190°C, and set the time to 17 minutes. Select START/STOP to begin. 8. After 10 or 12 minutes, remove the basket, flip the chicken, and spray again with olive oil. Reinsert the basket to resume cooking. 9. When the cooking is up, the chicken should be golden brown and crispy and a food thermometer inserted into the chicken should reach 75°C. 10. Repeat steps 6, 7, and 8 with any remaining chicken. 11. Transfer the chicken to a large bowl. Drizzle the Buffalo sauce over the top of the cooked chicken, toss to coat, and serve.
Per Serving: Calories 409; Fat 15.95g; Sodium 922mg; Carbs 30.5g; Fibre 1.2g; Sugar 6.6g; Protein 33.46g

Homemade Chicken Satay

Prep Time: 12 minutes | Cook Time: 12 to 18 minutes | Serves: 4

50g crunchy peanut butter
80ml chicken stock
3 tablespoons low-sodium soy sauce
2 tablespoons freshly squeezed lemon juice
2 garlic cloves, minced
2 tablespoons extra-virgin olive oil
1 teaspoon curry powder
455g chicken tenders
Cooking oil spray

1. Whisk the peanut butter, chicken stock, soy sauce, lemon juice, garlic, olive oil, and curry powder in a medium bowl until smooth. 2. Place 2 tablespoons of this mixture into a small bowl. Transfer the remaining sauce to a serving bowl and set aside. 3. Add the chicken tenders to the bowl with the 2 tablespoons of sauce and stir to coat. Let stand for a few minutes to marinate. 4. Insert the crisper plate into the basket and the basket into the unit. Preheat the unit by selecting AIR FRY, setting the temperature to 200°C, and setting the time to 3 minutes. Select START/STOP to begin. 5. Run a 15cm bamboo skewer lengthwise through each chicken tender. 6. Once the unit is preheated, spray the crisper plate with cooking oil. Working in batches, place half the chicken skewers into the basket in a single layer without overlapping. 7. Select AIR FRY, set the temperature to 200°C, and set the time to 9 minutes. Select START/STOP to begin. 8. After 6 minutes, check the chicken. If a food thermometer inserted into the chicken registers 75°C, it is done. If not, resume cooking. 9. Repeat the 6, 7, and 8 steps with the remaining chicken. 10. When the cooking is complete, serve the chicken with the reserved sauce.
Per Serving: Calories 363; Fat 19.6g; Sodium 799mg; Carbs 14.82g; Fibre 2.3g; Sugar 3.7g; Protein 33.69g

Crispy Mayo Chicken Tenders

Prep Time: 10 minutes | Cook Time: 15 minutes | Serves: 4

110g panko bread crumbs
1 tablespoon paprika
½ teaspoon salt
¼ teaspoon freshly ground black
pepper
16 chicken tenders
110g mayonnaise
Olive oil spray

1. Stir together the panko, paprika, salt, and pepper in a medium bowl. 2. Toss together the chicken tenders and mayonnaise in a large bowl to coat. Transfer the mayo-coated chicken pieces to the bowl of seasoned panko and dredge to coat thoroughly. Press with your fingers until firmly coated. 3. Insert the crisper plate into the basket and the basket into the unit. Preheat the unit by selecting AIR FRY, setting the temperature to 175°C, and setting the time to 3 minutes. Select START/STOP to begin. 4. Once the unit is preheated, place a parchment paper liner into the basket. Place the chicken into the basket and spray it with olive oil. 5. Select AIR FRY, set the temperature to 175°C, and set the time to 15 minutes. Select START/STOP to begin. 6. When the cooking is complete, the tenders will be golden brown and a food thermometer inserted into the chicken should register 75°C. For more even browning, remove the basket halfway through cooking and flip the tenders. Give them an extra spray of olive oil and reinsert the basket to resume cooking. This ensures they are crispy and brown all over. 7. When the cooking is complete, serve.
Per Serving: Calories 407; Fat 16.91g; Sodium 849mg; Carbs 21.37g; Fibre 2.2g; Sugar 2.11g; Protein 40.23g

Chicken Cordon Bleu

Prep Time: 15 minutes | Cook Time: 15 minutes | Serves: 4

4 chicken breast filets
70g chopped ham
70g grated Swiss cheese, or Gruyère cheese
30g plain flour
Pinch salt
Freshly ground black pepper
½ teaspoon dried marjoram
1 egg
110g panko bread crumbs
Olive oil spray

1. Place the chicken breast filets on a work surface and then gently press the chicken to make them thinner with the palm of your hand but to watch out not to tear them. 2. Combine the ham and cheese in a small bowl. Divide the mixture among the chicken filets. Then wrap the chicken rolls, using toothpicks to hold the chicken together. 3. Stir together the flour, salt, pepper, and marjoram in a shallow bowl. 4. In another bowl, beat the egg. 5. Spread the panko on a plate. 6. Dip the chicken in the flour mixture, in the egg, and in the panko to coat thoroughly. Press the panko crumbs into the chicken so they stick well. 7. Insert the crisper plate into the basket and the basket into the unit. Preheat the unit by selecting BAKE, setting the temperature to 190°C, and setting the time to 3 minutes. Select START/STOP to begin. 8. Once the unit is preheated, spray the crisper plate with olive oil. Place the chicken into the basket and spray it with olive oil. 9. Select BAKE, set the temperature to 190°C, and set the time to 15 minutes. Select START/STOP to begin. 10. When the cooking is up, the chicken should be cooked through and a food thermometer inserted into the chicken should register 75°C. Carefully remove the toothpicks and serve.
Per Serving: Calories 464; Fat 20.54g; Sodium 459mg; Carbs 26.22g; Fibre 1.5g; Sugar 1.97g; Protein 40.79g

Spinach and Feta-Stuffed Chicken Breast

Prep Time: 15 minutes | Cook Time: 25 minutes | Serves: 2

1 tablespoon unsalted butter
125g frozen spinach, thawed and drained
½ teaspoon garlic powder, divided
½ teaspoon salt, divided
40g chopped yellow onion
60g crumbled feta
2 (150g) boneless, skinless chicken breasts
1 tablespoon coconut oil

1. Set a suitable frying pan over medium heat, add butter to the pan and sauté spinach for 3 minutes. Sprinkle ¼ teaspoon garlic powder and ¼ teaspoon salt onto spinach and add onion to the pan. 2. Continue sautéing 3 more minutes, then remove from heat and place in medium bowl. Fold feta into spinach mixture. 3. Slice a roughly 10cm slit into the side of each chicken breast, lengthwise. Spoon half of the mixture into each piece and secure closed with a couple toothpicks. Sprinkle outside of chicken with remaining garlic powder and salt. Drizzle with coconut oil. Place chicken breasts into the air fryer basket. 4. Adjust the temperature to 175°C and set the timer for 25 minutes. 5. When completely cooked chicken should be golden brown and have an internal temperature of at least 75°C. Slice and serve warm.
Per Serving: Calories 327; Fat 24.1g; Sodium 864mg; Carbs 5.19g; Fibre 2.3g; Sugar 1.73g; Protein 23.44g

Spicy Chicken and Potatoes

Prep Time: 5 minutes | Cook Time: 25 minutes | Serves: 4

4 bone-in, skin-on chicken thighs	½ teaspoon granulated garlic
½ teaspoon salt or ¼ teaspoon fine salt	¼ teaspoon paprika
2 tablespoons melted unsalted butter	¼ teaspoon hot pepper sauce, such as Tabasco
2 teaspoons Worcestershire sauce	Cooking oil spray
2 teaspoons curry powder	4 medium Yukon gold potatoes, chopped
1 teaspoon dried oregano leaves	1 tablespoon extra-virgin olive oil
½ teaspoon dry mustard	

1. Sprinkle salt over both sides of the chicken thighs. 2. Stir together the melted butter, Worcestershire sauce, curry powder, oregano, dry mustard, granulated garlic, paprika, and your favored hot pepper sauce in a medium bowl. Add the thighs to the sauce and stir to coat. 3. Insert the crisper plate into the basket and the basket into the unit. Preheat the unit by selecting AIR FRY, setting the temperature to 205°C, and setting the time to 3 minutes. Select START/STOP to begin. 4. Once the unit is preheated, spray the crisper plate with cooking oil. In the basket, combine the potatoes and olive oil and toss to coat. 5. Add the wire rack to the air fryer and place the chicken thighs on top. 6. Select AIR FRY, set the temperature setting to 205°C, and set the time to 25 minutes. Select START/STOP to begin. 7. After 19 minutes check the chicken thighs. If a food thermometer inserted into the chicken registers 75°C, transfer them to a clean plate, and then cover it with aluminum foil to keep warm. If they aren't cooked to 75°C, resume cooking for another 1 to 2 minutes until they are done. Remove them from the air fryer along with the rack. 8. Remove the basket and shake it to distribute the potatoes. Reinsert the basket to resume cooking for 3 to 6 minutes, or until the potatoes are crisp and golden brown. 9. When the cooking is complete, serve the chicken with the potatoes.
Per Serving: Calories 656; Fat 38.92g; Sodium 536mg; Carbs 39.22g; Fibre 5.4g; Sugar 2.02g; Protein 36.66g

Buttermilk Fried Chicken

Prep Time: 7 minutes | Cook Time: 20 to 25 minutes | Serves: 4

125g plain flour	2 tablespoons extra-virgin olive oil
2 teaspoons paprika	160g bread crumbs
Pinch salt	6 chicken pieces, drumsticks, breasts, and thigh
Freshly ground black pepper	
80ml buttermilk	Cooking oil spray
2 eggs	

1. In a shallow bowl, stir together the flour, paprika, salt, and pepper. 2. In another bowl, beat the buttermilk and eggs until smooth. 3. In a third bowl, stir together the olive oil and bread crumbs until mixed. 4. Dredge the chicken in the flour, dip in the eggs to coat, and finally press into the bread crumbs, patting the crumbs firmly onto the chicken skin. 5. Insert the crisper plate into the basket and the basket into the unit. Preheat the unit by selecting AIR FRY, setting the temperature to 190°C, and setting the time to 3 minutes. Select START/STOP to begin. 6. Once the unit is preheated, spray the crisper plate with cooking oil. Place the chicken into the basket. 7. Select AIR FRY, set the temperature to 190°C, and set the time to 25 minutes. Select START/STOP to begin. 8. After 10 minutes, flip the chicken. Resume cooking. After 10 minutes more, check the chicken. If a food thermometer inserted into the chicken registers 75°C and the chicken is brown and crisp, it is done. Otherwise, resume cooking for up to 5 minutes longer. 9. When the cooking is complete, let cool for 5 minutes, then serve.
Per Serving: Calories 679; Fat 31.45g; Sodium 399mg; Carbs 32.45g; Fibre 1.7g; Sugar 2g; Protein 62.49g

Korean Chicken Wings

Prep Time: 10 minutes | Cook Time: 25 minutes per batch | Serves: 4

65g gochujang, or red pepper paste	2 teaspoons ground ginger
55g mayonnaise	1.3kg whole chicken wings
2 tablespoons honey	Olive oil spray
1 tablespoon sesame oil	1 teaspoon salt
2 teaspoons minced garlic	½ teaspoon freshly ground black pepper
1 tablespoon sugar	

1. In a large bowl, whisk the gochujang, mayonnaise, honey, sesame

oil, garlic, sugar, and ginger. Set aside. 2. Insert the crisper plate into the basket and the basket into the unit. Preheat the unit by selecting AIR FRY, setting the temperature to 205°C, and setting the time to 3 minutes. Select START/STOP to begin. 3. To prepare the chicken wings, cut the wings in half. The meatier part is the drumette. Cut off and discard the wing tip from the flat part (or save the wing tips in the freezer to make chicken stock). 4. Once the unit is preheated, spray the crisper plate with olive oil. Working in batches, place half the chicken wings into the basket, spray them with olive oil, and sprinkle with the salt and pepper. 5. Select AIR FRY, set the temperature to 205°C, and set the time to 20 minutes. Select START/STOP to begin. 6. After 10 minutes, remove the basket, flip the wings, and spray them with more olive oil. Reinsert the basket to resume cooking. 7. Cook the wings to an internal temperature of 75°C, then transfer them to the bowl with the prepared sauce and toss to coat. 8. Repeat steps 4, 5, 6, and 7 for the remaining chicken wings. 9. Return the coated wings to the basket and air fry for 4 to 6 minutes more until the sauce has glazed the wings and the chicken is crisp. After 3 minutes, check the wings to make sure they aren't burning. Serve hot.
Per Serving: Calories 563; Fat 21.39g; Sodium 974mg; Carbs 12.48g; Fibre 0.4g; Sugar 10.89g; Protein 75.89g

Dijon Roasted Turkey Breast

Prep Time: 20 minutes | Cook Time: 45 minutes | Serves: 6

1 tablespoon olive oil, plus more for spraying	1½ teaspoons thyme
2 garlic cloves, minced	1 teaspoon salt
2 teaspoons Dijon mustard	½ teaspoon freshly ground black pepper
1½ teaspoons rosemary	1.3kg turkey breast, thawed if frozen
1½ teaspoons sage	

1. Spray an air fryer basket lightly with olive oil. 2. Mix together the garlic, olive oil, Dijon mustard, rosemary, sage, thyme, salt, and black pepper in a small bowl for a paste. Smear the paste all over the turkey breast. 3. Place the turkey breast in the fryer basket. 4. Air fry at 185°C for 20 minutes. Flip turkey breast over and baste it with any drippings that have collected in the bottom drawer of the air fryer. Air fry the turkey breast until the internal temperature of the meat reaches at least 75°C, 20 more minutes. 5. If desired, increase the temperature to 205°C, flip the turkey breast over one last time, and air fry for up to 5 minutes to get a crispy exterior. 6. Let the turkey rest for 10 minutes before slicing and serving.
Per Serving: Calories 380; Fat 18.28 g; Sodium 540 mg; Carbs 0.75 g; Fibre 0.3 g; Sugar 0.03 g; Protein 49.83 g

Crispy Chicken Tenders

Prep Time: 15 minutes | Cook Time: 20 minutes | Serves: 4

445g boneless, skinless chicken mini fillets	35g grated parmesan
60ml hot sauce	1 teaspoon chili powder
	1 teaspoon garlic powder

1. In a large bowl, place the boneless chicken mini fillets and pour hot sauce over them. Toss tenders in hot sauce, evenly coating. 2. Mix grated parmesan with chili powder and garlic powder in a second large bowl. 3. Place each tender in the parmesan covering completely. Press down the parmesan into the chicken with wet hands. 4. Place the tenders in a single layer into the air fryer basket. 5. Adjust the temperature to 190°C and set the timer for 20 minutes. 6. Serve warm.
Per Serving: Calories 160; Fat 5.1 g; Sodium 492 mg; Carbs 1.15 g; Fibre 0.3 g; Sugar 0.25 g; Protein 26.01 g

Pepperoni and Chicken Pizza Bake

Prep Time: 10 minutes | Cook Time: 15 minutes | Serves: 4

280g cubed cooked chicken	sauce
20 slices pepperoni	110g shredded mozzarella cheese
225g low-carb, sugar-free pizza	25g grated Parmesan cheese

1. In a 15cm x 5cm round baking dish add chicken, pepperoni, and pizza sauce. Stir so meat is completely covered with sauce. 2. Top with mozzarella and grated Parmesan. Place dish into the air fryer basket. 3. Adjust the temperature setting to 190°C and set the timer for 15 minutes. 4. Dish will be brown and bubbling when cooked. Serve immediately.
Per Serving: Calories 343; Fat 15.67g; Sodium 568mg; Carbs 18.3g; Fibre 0.7g; Sugar 13.18g; Protein 32.76g

Teriyaki Chicken Wings

Prep Time: 1 hour | Cook Time: 25 minutes | Serves: 4

900g chicken wings
120ml sugar-free teriyaki sauce
2 teaspoons minced garlic
¼ teaspoon ground ginger
2 teaspoons baking powder

1. Place all ingredients except baking powder into a large bowl or bag and let marinade for 1 hour in the refrigerator. 2. Place wings into the air fryer basket and sprinkle with baking powder. Gently rub into wings. 3. Adjust the temperature ssetting to 205°C and set the timer for 25 minutes. 4. Toss the basket two or three times during cooking. 5. Wings should be crispy and cooked to at least 75°C internally when done. Serve immediately.
Per Serving: Calories 292; Fat 8.05g; Sodium 199mg; Carbs 1.85g; Fibre 0.1g; Sugar 0.02g; Protein 50.06g

Lime Chicken Thighs

Prep Time: 15 minutes | Cook Time: 22 minutes | Serves: 4

4 bone-in, skin-on chicken thighs
1 teaspoon baking powder
½ teaspoon garlic powder
2 teaspoons chili powder
1 teaspoon cumin
2 medium limes
5g chopped fresh coriander

1. Pat the chicken thighs dry and then sprinkle them with baking powder. 2. Mix garlic powder, chili powder, and cumin in a small bowl and sprinkle the mixture evenly over the chicken thighs, gently rubbing on and under chicken skin. 3. Cut one lime in half and squeeze juice over thighs. Place chicken into the air fryer basket. 4. Adjust the temperature to 195°C and set the timer for 22 minutes. 5. Cut other lime into four wedges for serving and garnish cooked chicken with wedges and coriander.
Per Serving: Calories 441; Fat 32.4g; Sodium 198mg; Carbs 4.15g; Fibre 0.7g; Sugar 0.5g; Protein 32.34g

Cheddar Jalapeño Popper Hasselback Chicken

Prep Time: 20 minutes | Cook Time: 20 minutes | Serves: 2

4 slices bacon, cooked and crumbled
50g full-fat cream cheese, softened
50g shredded sharp Cheddar
cheese, divided
20g sliced pickled jalapeños
2 (150g) boneless, skinless chicken breasts

1. In a medium bowl, place cooked bacon, then fold in cream cheese, half of the Cheddar, and the jalapeño slices. 2. Use a sharp knife to make slits in each of the chicken breasts about ¾ of the way across the chicken, being careful not to cut all the way through. Depending on the size of the chicken breast, you'll likely have 6–8 slits per breast. 3. Transfer the cheese mixture to the slits of the chicken with a spoon. Sprinkle the remaining shredded cheese over chicken breasts and place into the air fryer basket. 4. Adjust the temperature to 175°C and set the timer for 20 minutes. 6. Serve warm.
Per Serving: Calories 426; Fat 30.37g; Sodium 730mg; Carbs 2.98g; Fibre 0g; Sugar 1.75g; Protein 33.68g

Chicken-Avocado Enchiladas

Prep Time: 20 minutes | Cook Time: 10 minutes | Serves: 4

360g shredded cooked chicken
75g enchilada sauce, divided
220g medium-sliced deli chicken
120g shredded medium Cheddar cheese
60g shredded Monterey jack cheese
115g full-fat sour cream
1 medium avocado, peeled, pitted, and sliced

1. In a large bowl, mix shredded chicken and half of the enchilada sauce. Lay slices of deli chicken on a work surface and spoon 2 tablespoons shredded chicken mixture onto each slice. 2. Sprinkle 2 tablespoons of Cheddar onto each roll. Gently roll closed. 3. In a 15cm x 5cm round baking dish, place each roll, seam side down. Pour the remaining sauce over rolls and then top with Monterey jack. Place dish into the air fryer basket. 4. Adjust the temperature setting to 185°C and set the timer for 10 minutes. 5. Enchiladas will be golden on top and bubbling when cooked. Serve with sour cream and avocado slices, as you like.
Per Serving: Calories 447; Fat 28.46g; Sodium 1051mg; Carbs 11.78g; Fibre 3.6g; Sugar 1.51g; Protein 37.04g

Crusted Chicken

Prep Time: 15 minutes | Cook Time: 25 minutes | Serves: 4

30g slivered almonds
2 (150g) boneless, skinless chicken breasts
2 tablespoons full-fat mayonnaise
1 tablespoon Dijon mustard

1. Pulse the almonds with a food processor or chop until finely chopped. Place almonds evenly on a plate and set aside. 2. Completely slice each chicken breast in half lengthwise. 3. Mix the mayonnaise and mustard in a small bowl and then coat chicken with the mixture. 4. Lay each piece of chicken in the chopped almonds to fully coat. Carefully move the pieces into the air fryer basket. 5. Adjust the temperature setting to 175°C and set the timer for 25 minutes. 6. Chicken will be cooked when it has reached an internal temperature of 75°C or more. Serve warm.
Per Serving: Calories 103; Fat 7.1g; Sodium 130mg; Carbs 0.24g; Fibre 0.2g; Sugar 0.04g; Protein 9.06g

Lemon Pepper Chicken Drumsticks

Prep Time: 5 minutes | Cook Time: 25 minutes | Serves: 2

2 teaspoons baking powder
½ teaspoon garlic powder
8 chicken drumsticks
4 tablespoons salted butter,
melted
1 tablespoon lemon pepper seasoning

1. Sprinkle baking powder and garlic powder over drumsticks and rub into chicken skin. Place drumsticks into the air fryer basket. 2. Adjust the temperature setting to 190°C and set the timer for 25 minutes. 3. Use tongs to turn drumsticks halfway through the cooking time. 4. When skin is golden and the internal temperature is at least 75°C, remove from air fryer. 5. In a large bowl, mix butter and lemon pepper seasoning. Add drumsticks to the bowl and toss until coated. Serve warm.
Per Serving (8 drumsticks): Calories 495; Fat 31.68g; Sodium 419mg; Carbs 2.72g; Fibre 0.3g; Sugar 0.16g; Protein 47.34g

Creamy Chicken Corden Bleu Casserole

Prep Time: 15 minutes | Cook Time: 15 minutes | Serves: 4

480g cubed cooked chicken thigh meat
70g cubed cooked ham
50g Swiss cheese, cubed
100g full-fat cream cheese, softened
1 tablespoon heavy cream
2 tablespoons unsalted butter, melted
2 teaspoons Dijon mustard
25g grated parmesan

1. Place chicken and ham into a 15cm round baking pan and toss so meat is evenly mixed. Sprinkle cheese cubes on top of meat. 2. Mix cream cheese, heavy cream, butter, and Dijon mustard in a large bowl and then pour them over the meat and cheese. Top with parmesan. Place pan into the air fryer basket. 3. Adjust the temperature setting to 175°C and set the timer for 15 minutes. 4. The casserole will be browned and bubbling when done. Serve warm.
Per Serving: Calories 357; Fat 25.18g; Sodium 433mg; Carbs 3.49g; Fibre 0.1g; Sugar 2.14g; Protein 27.97g

Cajun Thyme Chicken Tenders

Prep Time: 10 minutes | Cook Time: 17 minutes | Serves: 4

2 teaspoons paprika
1 teaspoon chili powder
½ teaspoon garlic powder
½ teaspoon dried thyme
¼ teaspoon onion powder
⅛ teaspoon ground cayenne
pepper
2 tablespoons coconut oil
445g boneless, skinless chicken mini fillets
60ml full-fat ranch dressing

1. Combine all the spices in a suitable bowl. 2. Drizzle oil over chicken tenders and then generously coat each tender in the spice mixture. Place tenders into the air fryer basket. 3. Adjust the temperature setting to 190°C and set the timer for 17 minutes. 4. Tenders will be 75°C internally when fully cooked. Serve with ranch dressing for dipping.
Per Serving: Calories 209; Fat 10.38g; Sodium 231mg; Carbs 5.24g; Fibre 0.7g; Sugar 1.01g; Protein 23.46g

Fried Chicken

Prep Time: 15 minutes | Cook Time: 25 minutes | Serves: 4

2 (150g) boneless, skinless chicken breasts
2 tablespoons hot sauce
1 tablespoon chili powder
½ teaspoon cumin
¼ teaspoon onion powder
¼ teaspoon ground black pepper
50g ground parmesan

1. Slice both the chicken breast in half lengthwise. Place the chicken into a large bowl and coat with hot sauce. 2. Mix chili powder, cumin, onion powder, and pepper in a small bowl. Sprinkle over chicken. 3. Place the grated parmesan into a large bowl and dip each piece of chicken into the bowl, coating as much as possible. Place chicken into the air fryer basket. 4. Adjust the temperature to 175°C and set the timer for 25 minutes. 5. Halfway through the cooking time, carefully flip the chicken. 6. When done, internal temperature will be at least 75°C and parmesan coating will be dark golden brown. Serve warm.
Per Serving: Calories 114; Fat 5.87g; Sodium 156mg; Carbs 2.11g; Fibre 1g; Sugar 0.66g; Protein 13.03g

Simple Chicken Fajitas

Prep Time: 10 minutes | Cook Time: 15 minutes | Serves: 2

250g boneless, skinless chicken breast, sliced into ½cm strips
2 tablespoons coconut oil, melted
1 tablespoon chili powder
½ teaspoon cumin
½ teaspoon paprika
½ teaspoon garlic powder
¼ medium onion, peeled and sliced
½ medium green pepper, seeded and sliced
½ medium red pepper, seeded and sliced

1. Add chicken and coconut oil into a large bowl and sprinkle with chili powder, cumin, paprika, and garlic powder. Toss chicken until well coated with seasoning. Place chicken into the air fryer basket. 2. Adjust the temperature setting to 175°C and set the timer for 15 minutes. 3. Add onion and peppers into the fryer basket when the timer has 7 minutes remaining. 4. Toss the chicken two or three times during cooking. Vegetables should be tender and chicken fully cooked to at least 75°C internal temperature when finished. Serve warm.
Per Serving: Calories 388; Fat 27.53g; Sodium 421mg; Carbs 5.24g; Fibre 2.2g; Sugar 1.61g; Protein 30.81g

Mayo Chicken

Prep Time: 10 minutes | Cook Time: 25 minutes | Serves: 4

2 (150g) boneless, skinless chicken breasts
½ teaspoon garlic powder
¼ teaspoon dried oregano
½ teaspoon dried parsley
4 tablespoons full-fat mayonnaise, divided
110g shredded mozzarella cheese, divided
50g grated Parmesan cheese, divided
225g low-carb, no-sugar-added pasta sauce

1. Slice both the chicken breasts in half lengthwise and pound out to 2cm thickness. Sprinkle with garlic powder, dried oregano, and dried parsley. 2. Spread 1 tablespoon mayonnaise on top of each piece of chicken, then sprinkle 30g mozzarella on each piece. Sprinkle the parmesan on top of mozzarella. 4. Pour sauce into 15cm round baking pan and place chicken on top. Place pan into the air fryer basket. 5. Adjust the temperature to 160°C and set the timer for 25 minutes. 6. Cheese will be browned and internal temperature of the chicken will be at least 75°C when fully cooked. Serve warm.
Per Serving: Calories 296; Fat 14.15g; Sodium 599mg; Carbs 19.52g; Fibre 0.8g; Sugar 13.2g; Protein 24.1g

Chapter 6 Meat Recipes

Blue Cheese Beef Burgers

Prep Time: 10 minutes | Cook Time: 20 minutes | Serves: 4

Olive oil for spraying
455g lean beef mince
120g blue cheese, crumbled
1 teaspoon Worcestershire sauce
½ teaspoon freshly ground black

pepper
½ teaspoon hot sauce
½ teaspoon minced garlic
¼ teaspoon salt
4 whole-wheat buns

1. Lightly spray the air fryer basket with olive oil. 2. Mix the beef, blue cheese, Worcestershire sauce, pepper, hot sauce, garlic, and salt in a large bowl, then make the mixture into 4 patties. 3. Place the patties in the fryer basket in a single layer, leaving a little room between them for even cooking. 4. Air fry the patties at 180°C for 20 minutes until the meat reaches an internal temperature of at least 70°C, flipping them halfway through cooking. 5. Place each patty on a bun and serve with low-calorie toppings like sliced tomatoes or onions. Enjoy.
Per Serving: Calories 295; Fat 12.39g; Sodium 568mg; Carbs 16.44g; Fibre 2.2g; Sugar 0.47g; Protein 30.7g

Mushroom-Beef Balls

Prep Time: 15 minutes | Cook Time: 15 minutes | Serves: 6

Olive oil
900g lean beef mince
65g finely chopped mushrooms
4 tablespoons chopped parsley
2 eggs, beaten

2 teaspoons salt
1 teaspoon freshly ground black
pepper
100g whole-wheat bread crumbs

1. Lightly spray the air fryer basket with olive oil. 2. Gently mix the beef, mushrooms, parsley, eggs, salt, and pepper in a large bowl, then add the bread crumbs, and mix them until the bread crumbs are no longer dry. Do not overmix. 3. Make the mixture into 24 meatballs. 4. Working in batches, arrange the meatballs in the fryer basket in a single layer, and lightly spray them with olive oil. 5. Air fry the meatballs at 200°C for 10 to 15 minutes until the internal temperature reaches at least 70°C, shaking the basket every 5 minutes for even cooking. 6. Serve and enjoy.
Per Serving: Calories 301; Fat 10.73g; Sodium 1030mg; Carbs 13.88g; Fibre 1.1g; Sugar 1.41g; Protein 37.07g

Steak-Veggie Kebabs

Prep Time: 10 minutes | Cook Time: 15 minutes | Serves: 4

120ml soy sauce
3 tablespoons lemon juice
2 tablespoons Worcestershire
sauce
2 tablespoons Dijon mustard
1 teaspoon minced garlic
¾ teaspoon freshly ground black
pepper
455g sirloin steak, cut into 2.5cm

cubes
1 medium red pepper, cut into big
chunks
1 medium green pepper, cut into
big chunks
1 medium red onion, cut into big
chunks
Olive oil

1. Mix the soy sauce, lemon juice, Worcestershire sauce, Dijon mustard, garlic, and black pepper in a small bowl. 2. Apportion the marinade between two large zip-top plastic bags. 3. Place the steak in one of the bags, seal, and refrigerate for at least 2 hours. Place the vegetables in the other bag, seal, and refrigerate for 1 hour. 4. Soak the skewers in water for at least 30 minutes if using wooden skewers. 5. Lightly spray the air fryer basket with olive oil. Thread the steak and veggies alternately onto the skewers. 6. Working in batches, arrange the skewers in the oiled fryer basket in a single layer. 7. Air fry them at 175°C for 15 minutes until the steak reaches your desired level of doneness, flipping them over and lightly spraying some olive oil halfway through. 8. The internal temperature should read 50°C for rare, 55°C for medium rare, 60°C for medium and 65°C for medium well. 9. When done, serve and enjoy.
Per Serving: Calories 268; Fat 10.28g; Sodium 745mg; Carbs 16.83g; Fibre 2.4g; Sugar 10.36g; Protein 26.43g

Mushroom Steak Bites

Prep Time: 65 minutes | Cook Time: 20 minutes | Serves: 4

455g sirloin steak, cut into 1cm
cubes
200g mushrooms, sliced

1 tablespoon Worcestershire
sauce
1 tablespoon balsamic vinegar

1 tablespoon soy sauce
1 tablespoon olive oil, plus more
for spraying
1 teaspoon Dijon mustard

1 teaspoon minced garlic
Salt
Freshly ground black pepper

1. Toss the steak and mushrooms with Worcestershire sauce, balsamic vinegar, soy sauce, olive oil, Dijon mustard, garlic, salt, and pepper in a large zip-top plastic bag, seal the bag and refrigerate them for at least 1 hour or overnight. 2. Lightly spray the air fryer basket with olive oil. 3. Working in batches, add the steak and mushrooms to the fryer basket in an even layer. 4. Air fry them at 205°C for 20 minutes until the steak reaches your desired level of doneness, shaking the basket halfway through (the internal temperature should read 50°C for rare, 55°C for medium rare, 60°C for medium and 65°C for medium well). 5. Serve warm.
Per Serving: Calories 187; Fat 7.27g; Sodium 249mg; Carbs 4.67g; Fibre 0.7g; Sugar 2.93g; Protein 25.06g

Beef and Broccoli Bowls

Prep Time: 2 hours 15 minutes | Cook Time: 15 minutes | Serves: 4

3 tablespoons dry sherry
60ml soy sauce
4 garlic cloves, minced
1 tablespoon sesame oil
½ teaspoon red pepper flakes
455g flank or skirt steak, trimmed

and cut into strips
Olive oil
225g broccoli florets
60ml beef stock
2 teaspoons corn flour

1. To make the marinade, mix the sherry, soy sauce, garlic, sesame oil, and red pepper flakes in a small bowl. 2. Place the steak strips and 3 tablespoons of the marinade in a large zip-top plastic bag, seal, shake the bag, and then refrigerate them for at least 2 hours. 3. Lightly spray the air fryer basket with olive oil. 4. Add half the steak to the fryer basket along with half the broccoli florets. Lightly spray them with olive oil. 5. Air fry them at 185°C for 15 minutes, shaking the basket to redistribute. 6. Do the same with the remaining steak and broccoli. 7. Transfer the steak and broccoli to a large bowl. 8. While the steak is cooking, add the stock and the remaining marinade to a small saucepan over medium-high heat, and bring to a boil. 9. Combine the corn flour and 1 tablespoon of water to create a slurry in a small ball, then add the slurry to the sauce pan and simmer for a few seconds to 1 minutes until the sauce starts to thicken, stirring occasionally. 10. Pour the sauce over the cooked steak and broccoli, and toss to evenly coat.
Per Serving: Calories 281; Fat 13.41g; Sodium 344mg; Carbs 12.26g; Fibre 2.4g; Sugar 5.91g; Protein 27.67g

BBQ Beef Bowls

Prep Time: 2 hours 10 minutes | Cook Time: 25 minutes | Serves: 4

120ml soy sauce
2 tablespoons brown sugar
2 tablespoons red wine vinegar or
rice vinegar
1 tablespoon olive oil, plus more
for spraying

1 tablespoon sesame oil
455g flank steak, sliced very thin
against the grain
2 teaspoons corn flour
400g cooked brown rice
180g steamed broccoli florets

1. Toss the steak slices with the soy sauce, brown sugar, vinegar, olive oil, and sesame oil in a large bowl, then cover the bowl with plastic wrap, and refrigerate for at least 30 minutes or up to 2 hours. 2. Lightly spray the air fryer basket with olive oil. 3. Remove as much marinade as possible from the steak. Reserve any leftover marinade. 4. Place the steak in the air fryer basket in a single layer. 5. Air fry them at 195°C for 20 minutes, flipping the steak over halfway through. 6. The internal temperature should read 50°C for rare, 55°C for medium rare, 60°C for medium, and 65°C for medium well. 7. Transfer the steak to a large bowl and set aside. 8. Combine the corn flour and 1 tablespoon of water to create a slurry in a small bowl. 9. Bring the remaining marinade to a boil in a small saucepan over medium-high heat; add the slurry to the marinade, lower the heat to medium-low, and simmer them for a few seconds to 1 minutes until the sauce starts to thicken, stirring them occasionally. 10. Pour the sauce over the steak and stir to combine. 11. To assemble the bowls, spoon 100g brown rice and 45g of broccoli into each of four bowls, and top with the steak.
Per Serving: Calories 443; Fat 19.12g; Sodium 550mg; Carbs 36.64g; Fibre 3g; Sugar 10.47g; Protein 29.48g

Tasty Steak Fingers

Prep Time: 15 minutes | Cook Time: 15 minutes | Serves: 4

Olive oil
60g whole-wheat flour
1 teaspoon seasoned salt
½ teaspoon freshly ground black pepper

¼ teaspoon cayenne pepper
2 eggs, beaten
120ml low-fat milk
455g cube steaks, cut into 2.5cm-wide strips

1. Lightly spray the air fryer basket with olive oil. 2. Mix the flour, salt, black pepper, and cayenne in a shallow bowl. 3. Beat the eggs and milk in another bowl. 4. Dredge the steak strips in the flour mixture, then coat them with the egg mixture, and finally dredge them in the flour mixture once more to coat completely. 5. Place the steak strips in the air fryer basket in a single layer, and spray lightly with olive oil. 6. Air fry them at 180°C for 15 minutes until golden brown and crispy, flipping them over and lightly spraying with olive oil halfway through. 7. Serve warm.
Per Serving: Calories 269; Fat 10.03g; Sodium 836mg; Carbs 11.37g; Fibre 1.7g; Sugar 0.25g; Protein 32.44g

Beef-Fried Buttermilk Steak

Prep time: 15 minutes | Cook time: 15 minutes | Serves: 4

4 (150g) beef cube steaks
120ml buttermilk
125g flour
2 teaspoons paprika

1 teaspoon garlic salt
1 egg
100g soft bread crumbs
2 tablespoons olive oil

1. Place the cube steaks on a plate or cutting board and gently pound until they are slightly thinner. Set aside. 2. In a shallow bowl, combine the buttermilk, flour, paprika, garlic salt, and egg until just combined. 3. Add the bread crumbs and olive oil on a plate and coat well. 4. Dip the steaks into the buttermilk batter to coat, and let sit on a plate for 5 minutes. 5. Dredge the steaks in the bread crumbs. Pat the crumbs onto both sides to coat the steaks thoroughly. 6. Air-fry the steaks at 175°C for 12 to 16 minutes or until the meat reaches 70°C on a meat thermometer and the coating is brown and crisp. You can serve this with heated beef gravy.
Per Serving: Calories 467; Fat 18g; Sodium 217mg; Carbs 30.6g; Fibre 1.5g; Sugar 2.2g; Protein 42.6g

Juicy Country Pork Ribs

Prep time: 5 minutes | Cook time: 20 to 25 minutes | Serves: 4

12 country-style pork ribs, trimmed of excess fat
2 tablespoons corn flour
2 tablespoons olive oil
1 teaspoon dry mustard

½ teaspoon thyme
½ teaspoon garlic powder
1 teaspoon dried marjoram
Pinch salt
Freshly ground black pepper

1. Place the ribs on a clean work surface. 2. In a small bowl, combine the corn flour, olive oil, mustard, thyme, garlic powder, marjoram, salt, and pepper, and rub into the ribs. 3. Place the spiced ribs in the air fryer basket and roast at 205°C for 10 minutes. 4. Carefully turn the ribs using tongs and roast for 10 to 15 minutes or until the ribs are crisp and register an internal temperature of at least 65°C.
Per Serving: Calories 905; Fat 40g; Sodium 508mg; Carbs 4g; Fibre 0g; Sugar 0g; Protein 123g

Classic Polish Sausage

Prep time: 10 minutes | Cook time: 10 to 15 minutes | Serves: 4

340g Polish sausage
1 red pepper, cut into 2.5cm strips
80g minced onion
3 tablespoons brown sugar

80g ketchup
2 tablespoons mustard
2 tablespoons apple cider vinegar
120ml chicken stock

1. Cut the sausage into 4cm pieces and put into a 15cm metal bowl. Add the pepper and minced onion. 2. Combine the brown sugar, ketchup, mustard, apple cider vinegar, and chicken broth in a small bowl, and mix well. Pour into the bowl. 3. Roast the sausage at 175°C for 10 to 15 minutes or until the sausage is hot, the vegetables tender, and the sauce bubbling and slightly thickened.
Per Serving: Calories 341; Fat 25g; Sodium 1128mg; Carbs 16.3g; Fibre 1g; Sugar 11.8g; Protein 13g

Beef Chimichangas

Prep Time: 10 minutes | Cook Time: 20 minutes | Serves: 4

Olive oil
455g lean beef mince
1 tablespoon taco seasoning
140g salsa

1 (400g) can fat-free refried beans
4 large whole-wheat tortillas
50g shredded Cheddar cheese

1. Lightly spray the air fryer basket with olive oil. 2. Cook the beef mince in a large frying pan over medium heat for 5 minutes until browned; add the taco seasoning and salsa and stir to combine. Set aside after cooking. 3. Spread ¼. 4. of refried beans onto each tortilla, leaving a 1cm border around the edge. Add ¼ of the beef mixture to each tortilla and sprinkle with 2 tablespoons of Cheddar cheese. 4. Fold the opposite sides of the tortilla in and roll up. 5. Place the chimichangas in the fryer basket with seam side down, lightly spray them with olive oil. 6. Air fry them at 180°C for 5 to 10 minutes until golden brown.
Per Serving: Calories 416; Fat 12.62g; Sodium 1322mg; Carbs 39.07g; Fibre 10.2g; Sugar 4.21g; Protein 36.83g

Roasted Honey Pork Tenderloin

Prep time: 5 minutes | Cook time: 10 minutes | Serves: 4

1 (455g) pork tenderloin, cut into 1cm slices
1 tablespoon olive oil
1 tablespoon lemon juice
1 tablespoon honey

½ teaspoon grated lemon zest
½ teaspoon dried marjoram
Pinch salt
Freshly ground black pepper

1. Add the pork tenderloin slices in a medium bowl. 2. Combine the olive oil, lemon juice, lemon zest, honey, marjoram, salt, and pepper in a small bowl. Mix together. 3. Pour this marinade over the pork slices and massage gently with your hand to work it into the pork. 4. Place the pork tenderloin in the air fryer basket and roast at 205°C for 10 minutes. The pork registers at least 60°C using a meat thermometer.
Per Serving: Calories 235; Fat 12.8g; Sodium 199mg; Carbs 4.7g; Fibre 0g; Sugar 4.4g; Protein 24.2g

Fried Dijon Pork Tenderloin

Prep time: 10 minutes | Cook time: 14 minutes | Serves: 4

455g pork tenderloin, cut into 1-inch slices
Pinch salt
Freshly ground black pepper
2 tablespoons Dijon mustard

1 clove garlic, minced
½ teaspoon dried basil
100g soft bread crumbs
2 tablespoons olive oil

1. Slightly pound the pork slices into about ¾-inch thick. Sprinkle the slices with salt and pepper on both sides. 2. Coat the pork with the Dijon mustard and sprinkle with the garlic and basil. 3. Add the bread crumbs and olive oil on a plate and coat them well. Coat the pork slices with the bread crumb mixture, patting so the crumbs adhere. 4. Place the crumbed pork in the air fryer basket, leaving a little space between each piece. Air-fry at 200°C for 12 to 14 minutes or until the pork reaches at least 60°C on a meat thermometer and the coating is crisp and brown. Serve immediately.
Per Serving: Calories 213; Fat 9.8g; Sodium 335mg; Carbs 5.1g; Fibre 0.6g; Sugar 0.6g; Protein 25g

Sweet and Spicy Chili Pork Ribs

Prep time: 10 minutes | Cook time: 40 minutes | Serves: 4

1 (900g) rack pork spareribs, white membrane removed
50g brown sugar
2 teaspoons salt

2 teaspoons ground black pepper
1 tablespoon chili powder
1 teaspoon garlic powder
½ teaspoon cayenne pepper

1. Preheat the air fryer to 205°C. 2. Place ribs on a work surface and cut the rack into two pieces to fit in the air fryer basket. 3. Whisk together brown sugar, salt, black pepper, chili powder, garlic powder, and cayenne in a medium bowl to make a dry rub. 4. Then rub it over both sides of ribs until well coated. Place a portion of ribs in the air fryer basket, working in batches as necessary. 5. Cook for 20 minutes until internal temperature reaches at least 85°C and no pink remains. Let the spiced ribs rest for 5 minutes before cutting and serving.
Per Serving: Calories 358; Fat 17.5g; Sodium 1295mg; Carbs 16g; Fibre 1g; Sugar 13.5g; Protein 33g

Sriracha Pork Ribs

Prep time: 10 minutes | Cook time: 25 minutes | Serves: 4

1.3kg pork back ribs, white
membrane removed
2 teaspoons salt
1 teaspoon ground black pepper

120ml sriracha
110g honey
1 tablespoon lemon juice

1. Preheat your air fryer to 205°C. 2. Place ribs on a work surface and cut the rack into two pieces to fit in the air fryer basket. 3. Season the pork back ribs with salt and pepper and place in the air fryer basket meat side down. Cook for 15 minutes. 4. Combine the sriracha, honey, and lemon juice in a small bowl to make a sauce. 5. Remove ribs from the air fryer basket and pour sauce over both sides. Return them to the air fryer basket meat side up and cook an additional 10 minutes until they are brown and the internal temperature reaches at least 85°C. Serve warm.
Per Serving: Calories 842; Fat 53.6g; Sodium 2126mg; Carbs 24.8g; Fibre 0g; Sugar 23.4g; Protein 67.4g

Browned Dijon Pork Loin

Prep time: 5 minutes | Cook time: 35 minutes | Serves: 4

455g boneless pork loin
1 tablespoon olive oil
60g Dijon mustard

55g brown sugar
1 teaspoon salt
½ teaspoon ground black pepper

1. Preheat the air fryer to 205°C. Brush pork loin with oil. 2. Mix mustard, brown sugar, salt, and pepper in a small bowl. Brush mixture over both sides of pork loin and let sit for 15 minutes. 3. Place the pork loin in your air fryer basket and cook for 20 minutes until internal temperature reaches 60°C. Let rest 10 minutes before slicing. Serve warm.
Per Serving: Calories 242; Fat 8.5g; Sodium 813mg; Carbs 14.6g; Fibre 1g; Sugar 13.5g; Protein 26g

Barbecue Beef Short Ribs

Prep time: 5 minutes | Cook time: 25 minutes | Serves: 4

1.3kg beef short ribs
2 tablespoons olive oil
3 teaspoons salt

3 teaspoons ground black pepper
120g barbecue sauce

1. Preheat the air fryer to 190°C. 2. Place short ribs in a large bowl. Drizzle them with oil and sprinkle both sides with salt and pepper. 3. Place in the air fryer basket and cook for 20 minutes. Remove from basket and brush with barbecue sauce. 4. Return to the air fryer basket and cook for 5 additional minutes until sauce is dark brown. The internal temperature shall reach at least 70°C. Serve warm.
Per Serving: Calories 673; Fat 37.6g; Sodium 2428mg; Carbs 15.7g; Fibre 0g; Sugar 11.9g; Protein 69g

Enticing Cheeseburgers

Prep time: 5 minutes | Cook time: 10 minutes | Serves: 4

455g beef mince
½ teaspoon salt
¼ teaspoon ground black pepper

4 (25g) slices American cheese
4 hamburger buns

1. Preheat the air fryer to 180°C. 2. Separate beef into four equal portions and form into patties. Sprinkle both sides of patties with salt and pepper. Place the seasoned patties in the air fryer basket and cook for 10 minutes, turning halfway through cooking time, until internal temperature reaches at least 70°C. 3. For each burger, place a slice of cheese on a patty and place on a hamburger bun. Serve warm.
Per Serving: Calories 605; Fat 33.8g; Sodium 939mg; Carbs 35g; Fibre 1g; Sugar 19g; Protein 38g

Pork and Greens Salad

Prep Time: 10 minutes | Cook Time: 15 minutes | Serves: 4

900g pork tenderloin, cut into
2.5cm slices
1 teaspoon olive oil
1 teaspoon dried marjoram
⅛ teaspoon freshly ground black
pepper

180g mixed salad greens
1 red pepper, sliced
1 (200g) package button
mushrooms, sliced
80ml low-sodium low-fat
vinaigrette dressing

1. Coat the pork slices and olive oil, and rub them with the marjoram and pepper. 2. Grill the pork slices in the air fryer at 205°C for 4 to 6 minutes until they reach an internal temperature of at least 60°C. 3. Mix the salad greens, red pepper, and mushrooms in a serving bowl. 4. When the pork is cooked, add the slices to the salad, drizzle with the vinaigrette and toss gently. Enjoy.
Per Serving: Calories 322; Fat 8.83g; Sodium 223mg; Carbs 5.82g; Fibre 3g; Sugar 1.79g; Protein 53.32g

Stuffed Peppers with Cheese

Prep Time: 15 minutes | Cook Time: 20 minutes | Serves: 4

Olive oil
4 large red peppers
455g lean beef mince
160g diced onion
Salt
Freshly ground black pepper
200g cooked brown rice
50g shredded reduced-fat
Cheddar cheese

120ml tomato sauce
2 tablespoons dill pickle relish
2 tablespoons ketchup
1 tablespoon Worcestershire
sauce
1 tablespoon mustard
15g shredded lettuce
75g diced tomatoes

1. Lightly spray the air fryer basket with olive oil. 2. Cut about 1cm off the tops of the peppers, and remove any seeds from the insides. Set aside. 3. Cook the beef mince and onion in a large frying pan over medium-high heat for 5 minutes until browned, then season them with salt and pepper. 4. Mix the beef mixture, rice, Cheddar cheese, tomato sauce, relish, ketchup, Worcestershire sauce, and mustard in a large bowl. 5. Spoon the meat and rice mixture equally into the peppers. 6. Place the stuffed peppers in the air fryer basket. Air fry them at 180°C for 10 to 15 minutes until golden brown on top. 7. Top each stuffed pepper with the shredded lettuce and diced tomatoes, and serve.
Per Serving: Calories 334; Fat 8.84g; Sodium 945mg; Carbs 32.11g; Fibre 4.6g; Sugar 12.38g; Protein 32.15g

Mini Beef Meatloaves

Prep Time: 10 minutes | Cook Time: 20 minutes | Serves: 4

Olive oil
455g lean beef mince
1 egg, beaten
100g whole-wheat bread crumbs
60ml low-fat evaporated milk
60ml plus 2 tablespoons barbeque

sauce, divided
1 teaspoon onion powder
1 teaspoon salt
½ teaspoon freshly ground black
pepper

1. Lightly spray the air fryer basket with olive oil. 2. Combine the beef, egg, bread crumbs, milk, 60ml of barbeque sauce, onion powder, salt, and pepper in a large bowl. 3. Divide the beef mixture into four small meatloaf shapes, spread each meatloaf with ½ tablespoon of the remaining barbeque sauce. 4. Place the meatloaves in the air fryer basket in a single layer. 5. Air fry the meatloaves at 175°C for 15 to 20 minutes until the internal temperature reaches at least 70°C. 6. Serve and enjoy.
Per Serving: Calories 298; Fat 9.83g; Sodium 1041mg; Carbs 22.21g; Fibre 1.7g; Sugar 2.81g; Protein 30.06g

Coconut Pork Satay

Prep Time: 15 minutes | Cook Time: 15 minutes | Serves: 4

1 (455g) pork tenderloin, cut into
4.5cm cubes
40g minced onion
2 garlic cloves, minced
1 jalapeño pepper, minced
2 tablespoons freshly squeezed

lime juice
2 tablespoons coconut milk
2 tablespoons unsalted peanut
butter
2 teaspoons curry powder

1. Combine the pork, onion, garlic, jalapeño, lime juice, coconut milk, peanut butter, and curry powder in a medium bowl. Let stand for 10 minutes at room temperature. 2. Remove the pork from the marinade, and reserve the marinade. 3. Thread the pork onto about 8 bamboo or metal skewers. 4. Grill them at 195°C for 9 to 14 minutes until they reach an internal temperature of at least 60°C, brushing once with the reserved marinade during cooking. 5. Discard any remaining marinade after cooking.
Per Serving: Calories 226; Fat 8.51g; Sodium 71mg; Carbs 4.74g; Fibre 1.2g; Sugar 1.84g; Protein 32.07g

Pork Cabbage Burgers

Prep Time: 20 minutes | Cook Time: 9 minutes | Serves: 4

120g Greek yogurt
2 tablespoons low-sodium mustard, divided
1 tablespoon lemon juice
20g sliced red cabbage
30g grated carrots
455g lean pork mince
½ teaspoon paprika
30g mixed baby lettuce greens
2 small tomatoes, sliced
8 small whole-wheat sandwich buns, cut in half

1. Mix the yogurt, 1 tablespoon mustard, lemon juice, cabbage, and carrots in a small bowl, and then place the bowl in refrigerator. 2. Toss the pork with the remaining mustard, and the paprika in a medium bowl, then form the mixture into 8 small patties. 3. Put the sliders in the air fryer basket. Grill them at 205°C for 7 to 9 minutes until the sliders register 75°C. 4. Assemble the burgers by placing some of the lettuce greens on a bun bottom. Top with a tomato slice, the burgers, and the cabbage mixture. Add the bun top and serve immediately.
Per Serving: Calories 171; Fat 4.85g; Sodium 105mg; Carbs 6.8g; Fibre 1.5g; Sugar 3.99g; Protein 26.09g

Mustard Pork Tenderloin

Prep Time: 10 minutes | Cook Time: 16 minutes | Serves: 4

3 tablespoons low-sodium grainy mustard
2 teaspoons olive oil
¼ teaspoon dry mustard powder
1 (455g) pork tenderloin, silver skin and excess fat trimmed and
discarded
2 slices whole-wheat bread, crumbled
25g ground walnuts
2 tablespoons corn flour

1. Mix the mustard, olive oil, and mustard powder in a small bowl. Spread this mixture over the pork. 2. Mix the bread crumbs, walnuts, and corn flour in a plate. 3. Dip the mustard-coated pork into the crumb mixture to coat. 4. Air-fry the pork at 205°C for 12 to 16 minutes until it registers at least 60°C. 5. Slice to serve after cooking.
Per Serving: Calories 215; Fat 12.75g; Sodium 362mg; Carbs 0.11g; Fibre 0g; Sugar 0g; Protein 23.66g

Pork Tenderloin with Apple Slices

Prep Time: 10 minutes | Cook Time: 20 minutes | Serves: 4

1 (455g) pork tenderloin, cut into 4 pieces
1 tablespoon apple butter
2 teaspoons olive oil
2 Granny Smith apples, sliced
3 celery stalks, sliced
1 onion, sliced
½ teaspoon dried marjoram
80ml apple juice

1. Rub each piece of pork with the apple butter and olive oil. 2. Mix the pork, apples, celery, onion, marjoram, and apple juice in a suitable bowl. 3. Place the bowl into the air fryer and roast the mixture at 205°C for 14 to 19 minutes until the pork reaches at least 60°C and the apples and vegetables are tender. 4. Stir them halfway through cooking. 5. Serve immediately.
Per Serving: Calories 260; Fat 8.37g; Sodium 78mg; Carbs 14.31g; Fibre 2.7g; Sugar 10.24g; Protein 30.3g

Grilled Pork Tenderloin

Prep Time: 15 minutes | Cook Time: 9 to 11 minutes | Serves: 4

1 tablespoon packed brown sugar
2 teaspoons espresso powder
1 teaspoon ground paprika
½ teaspoon dried marjoram
1 tablespoon honey
1 tablespoon freshly squeezed lemon juice
2 teaspoons olive oil
1 (455g) pork tenderloin

1. Mix the brown sugar, espresso powder, paprika, marjoram, honey, lemon juice, and olive oi in a small bowl. 2. Spread the honey mixture over the pork and let stand for 10 minutes at room temperature. 3. Roast the tenderloin in the air fryer at 205°C for 9 to 11 minutes until the pork registers an internal temperature of at least 60°C. 4. Slice the meat after cooking and serve hot.
Per Serving: Calories 174; Fat 4.81g; Sodium 62mg; Carbs 7.89g; Fibre 0.4g; Sugar 6.51g; Protein 24g

Pork Tenderloin with Potatoes

Prep Time: 5 minutes | Cook Time: 25 minutes | Serves: 4

300g potatoes, rinsed and dried
2 teaspoons olive oil
1 (455g) pork tenderloin, cut into 2.5cm cubes
1 onion, chopped
1 red pepper, chopped
2 garlic cloves, minced
½ teaspoon dried oregano
2 tablespoons chicken stock

1. Toss the potatoes and olive oil in a medium bowl, then transfer them to the air fryer basket. 2. Roast the potatoes at 185°C for 15 minutes. 3. Mix the potatoes, pork, onion, red pepper, garlic, and oregano in a suitable bowl, and drizzle with the chicken stock. 4. Put the bowl in the air fryer basket, then roast the mixture for about 10 minutes more until the potatoes are tender and pork reaches an internal temperature of at least 60°C, shaking the basket once during cooking. 5. Serve immediately.
Per Serving: Calories 221; Fat 4.91g; Sodium 69mg; Carbs 17.33g; Fibre 2.4g; Sugar 2.38g; Protein 26.04g

Pork-Fruit Kebabs

Prep Time: 15 minutes | Cook Time: 9 to 12 minutes | Serves: 4

105g apricot jam
2 tablespoons freshly squeezed lemon juice
2 teaspoons olive oil
½ teaspoon dried tarragon
1 (455g) pork tenderloin, cut into 2.5cm cubes
4 plums, pitted and quartered
4 small apricots, pitted and halved

1. Mix the jam, lemon juice, olive oil, and tarragon in a large bowl, then coat the pork cubes with the mixture. Let stand for 10 minutes at room temperature. 2. Alternating the items, thread the pork, plums, and apricots onto 4 metal skewers. 3. Brush them with any remaining jam mixture. Discard any remaining marinade. 4. Grill the kebabs in the air fryer at 195°C for 9 to 12 minutes until the pork cubes reach an internal temperature of 60°C and the fruit is tender. 5. Serve hot.
Per Serving: Calories 267; Fat 4.97g; Sodium 80mg; Carbs 32.15g; Fibre 1.2g; Sugar 25.15g; Protein 24.64g

Steak-Vegetable Kebabs

Prep Time: 15 minutes | Cook Time: 5 to 7 minutes | Serves: 4

2 tablespoons balsamic vinegar
2 teaspoons olive oil
½ teaspoon dried marjoram
⅛ teaspoon freshly ground black pepper
340g round steak, cut into 2.5cm pieces
1 red pepper, sliced
16 button mushrooms
150g cherry tomatoes

1. Stir the balsamic vinegar, olive oil, marjoram, and black pepper in a medium bowl, then coat the steak pieces with the mixture. Let stand for 10 minutes at room temperature. 2. Alternating items, thread the beef, red pepper, mushrooms, and tomatoes onto 8 bamboo or metal skewers that fit in the air fryer. 3. Grill them in the air fryer at 200°C for 5 to 7 minutes until the beef pieces are browned and reach an internal temperature of at least 60°C. 4. Serve immediately.
Per Serving: Calories 182; Fat 8.23g; Sodium 62mg; Carbs 6.26g; Fibre 1.4g; Sugar 4.2g; Protein 20.89g

Simple Grilled Steaks

Prep Time: 10 minutes | Cook Time: 20 minutes | Serves: 4

2 tablespoons low-sodium salsa
1 tablespoon minced chipotle pepper
1 tablespoon apple cider vinegar
1 teaspoon ground cumin
⅛ teaspoon freshly ground black
pepper
⅛ teaspoon red pepper flakes
340g sirloin tip steak, cut into 4 pieces and gently pounded to about 1cm thick

1. Thoroughly mix the salsa, chipotle pepper, cider vinegar, cumin, black pepper, and red pepper flakes in a small bowl. Rub this mixture into both sides of each steak piece. Let stand for 15 minutes at room temperature. 2. Working in batches, grill the steaks in the air fryer at 200°C for 6 to 9 minutes until they reach at least 60°C on a meat thermometer. 3. Remove the steaks to a clean plate and cover with aluminum foil to keep warm. Repeat with the remaining steaks. 4. Slice the steaks thinly against the grain, and serve.
Per Serving: Calories 134; Fat 5.1g; Sodium 55mg; Carbs 3.86g; Fibre 0.3g; Sugar 2.48g; Protein 18.6g

Provolone Spinach and Mushroom Steak Rolls

Prep time: 15 minutes| Cook time: 19 minutes| Serves: 4

½ medium yellow onion, peeled and chopped
50g chopped baby Bella mushrooms
30g chopped fresh spinach

455g flank steak
8 (25g) slices provolone cheese
1 teaspoon salt
½ teaspoon ground black pepper

1. In a medium frying pan, sauté onion over medium heat for 2 minutes until fragrant and beginning to soften. Add mushrooms and spinach and continue cooking 5 more minutes until spinach is wilted and mushrooms are soft. 2. Preheat your air fryer to 205°C. 3. Carefully butterfly steak, leaving the two halves connected. Place slices of cheese on top of steak, then top with cooked vegetables. 4. Place steak so that the grain runs horizontally. Tightly roll up steak and secure it closed with eight evenly placed toothpicks or eight sections of butcher's twine. 5. Slice steak into four rolls. Spritz with cooking spray, then sprinkle with salt and pepper. Place in the air fryer basket and cook for 12 minutes until steak is brown on the edges and internal temperature reaches at least 70°C for well-done. Serve.
Per Serving: Calories 362; Fat 21g; Sodium 1139mg; Carbs 3g; Fibre 0g; Sugar 1g; Protein 39g

Flank Steak Fajita Rolls

Prep time: 10 minutes| Cook time: 12 minutes| Serves: 4

455g flank steak
4 (25g) slices pepper jack cheese
1 medium green pepper
½ medium red pepper

40g finely chopped yellow onion
1 teaspoon salt
½ teaspoon ground black pepper

1. Remove seeds from the peppers and get them finely chopped. 2. Preheat your air fryer to 205°C. 3. Carefully butterfly steak, leaving the two halves connected. Place slices of cheese on top of steak. Scatter peppers and onion over cheese in an even layer. 4. Place steak so that the grain runs horizontally. Tightly roll up steak and secure it with eight evenly spaced toothpicks or eight sections of butcher's twine. 5. Slice steak into four even rolls. Spritz with cooking spray, then sprinkle with salt and black pepper. Place in the air fryer basket and cook for 12 minutes until steak is brown on the edges and internal temperature reaches at least 70°C for well-done. Serve.
Per Serving: Calories 273; Fat 14g; Sodium 811mg; Carbs 3g; Fibre 0g; Sugar 1.6g; Protein 32g

Salsa Empanadas

Prep time: 10 minutes| Cook time: 28 minutes| Serves: 4

455g beef mince
30g taco seasoning
95g salsa

2 (23cm) refrigerated piecrusts
100g shredded Colby-jack cheese

1. Adjust the heat to medium, and brown the beef in a medium frying pan for about 10 minutes until cooked through. Drain fat. Then add the taco seasoning and salsa to the pan. Bring to a boil, then cook for 30 seconds. Reduce heat and simmer for 5 minutes. Remove from heat. Preheat the air fryer to 185°C. 2. Cut three 13cm circles from each piecrust, forming six total. Reroll scraps out to 1cm thickness. Cut out two more 13cm circles to make eight circles total. 3. For each empanada, place ¼ cup of meat mixture onto the lower half of a pastry circle and top with 2 tablespoons of cheese. Dab along the edge of the pastry with a little water and fold the circle in half to fully cover the meat and cheese, pressing the edges together. Gently seal the edges with a fork. Repeat with remaining pastry, meat, and cheese. 4. Spritz empanadas with cooking spray. Then place the empanadas in the air fryer basket and cook for 12 minutes, turning halfway through cooking time, until the crust is golden. Serve warm.
Per Serving: Calories 953; Fat 57g; Sodium 1510mg; Carbs 65g; Fibre 3g; Sugar 2g; Protein 40.6g

Quick Pork Chops

Prep time: 5 minutes| Cook time: 12 minutes| Serves: 4

4 (100g) boneless pork chops
1 teaspoon salt

½ teaspoon ground black pepper
4 tablespoons salted butter,

sliced into 8 (½-tablespoon) pats, divided

1. Preheat your air fryer to 205°C. 2. Sprinkle pork chops with salt and pepper. Top each pork chop with a ½-tablespoon butter pat. 3. Place chops in the air fryer basket and cook for 12 minutes, turning halfway through cooking time, until tops and edges are golden brown, and internal temperature reaches at least 60°C. 4. Use remaining butter pats to top each pork chop while hot, then let cool for 5 minutes before serving warm.
Per Serving: Calories 212; Fat 11.5g; Sodium 699mg; Carbs 0g; Fibre 0g; Sugar 0g; Protein 25.5g

Herbed Crouton-Crusted Pork Chops

Prep time: 10 minutes| Cook time: 14 minutes| Serves: 4

4 (100g) boneless pork chops
1 teaspoon salt
½ teaspoon ground black pepper
80g croutons

½ teaspoon dried thyme
¼ teaspoon dried sage
1 large egg, whisked

1. Preheat your air fryer to 205°C. 2. Sprinkle the boneless pork chops with salt and pepper on both sides. 3. In a food processor, add croutons, thyme, and sage. Pulse five times until croutons are mostly broken down with a few medium-sized pieces remaining. Transfer to a medium bowl. 4. In a separate medium bowl, place egg. Dip each pork chop into egg, then press into crouton mixture to coat both sides. Spritz with cooking spray. 5. Place pork in the air fryer basket and cook for 14 minutes, turning halfway through cooking time, until chops are golden brown and internal temperature reaches at least 60°C. Serve warm.
Per Serving: Calories 224; Fat 6g; Sodium 760mg; Carbs 11.4g; Fibre 0g; Sugar 0g; Protein 29g

Beef-Cheese Meatballs

Prep time: 10 minutes | Cook time: 25 minutes | Serves: 4

225g lean beef mince
225g pork mince
1 large egg, beaten
2 tablespoons no-sugar-added tomato paste
60g ricotta cheese
35g grated Parmesan cheese
3 cloves garlic, peeled and minced

40g peeled and grated yellow onion
½ teaspoon salt
¼ teaspoon freshly ground black pepper
25g almond flour
5g chopped fresh parsley
480ml no-sugar-added marinara sauce

1. Combine beef mince, pork mince, the beaten egg, tomato paste, ricotta cheese, Parmesan cheese, garlic, yellow onion, salt, black pepper, almond flour, and parsley in a large bowl. Form mixture into four meatballs. 2. Heat your air fryer for 3 minutes to at 205°C before cooking. 3. Cut a piece of parchment paper to fit bottom of air fryer basket. Place meatballs on paper. Cook for 20 minutes. 4. In a medium frying pan, heat sauce over medium heat for 3 minutes. Add cooked meatballs and roll them around in sauce for 2 minutes. 5. Transfer meatballs to a large plate and serve warm with sauce over the top.
Per Serving: Calories 444; Fat 27g; Sodium 1470mg; Carbs 12g; Fibre 2.8g; Sugar 5.7g; Protein 37g

Enticing Beef Sliders

Prep time: 5 minutes | Cook time: 18 minutes | Serves: 4

455g lean beef mince
55g peeled and grated yellow onion
½ teaspoon smoked paprika

½ teaspoon salt
¼ teaspoon freshly ground black pepper

1. In a medium bowl, combine all ingredients. Form into eight patties. In the centre of each patty, make a slight indentation. 2. Preheat your air fryer at 175°C for 3 minutes. 3. Place four patties in air fryer basket or on air fryer grill pan lightly greased with olive oil. Cook for 5 minutes. Flip sliders and cook an additional 4 minutes or until desired doneness. 4. Transfer cooked sliders to a large serving plate and repeat cooking with remaining sliders. Serve warm.
Per Serving: Calories 253; Fat 13g; Sodium 361mg; Carbs 0g; Fibre 0g; Sugar 0g; Protein 30g

Barbecue Beef Sliders

Prep time: 5 minutes | Cook time: 18 minutes | Serves: 8

225g beef mince
225g pork mince
1 tablespoon sugar-free barbecue sauce
½ teaspoon salt
¼ teaspoon freshly ground black pepper
4 slices bacon, cooked and crumbled
8 (25g) cubes Cheddar cheese

1. Combine beef mince, pork mince, barbecue sauce, salt, and pepper in a medium bowl. Form into eight equal balls. 2. In the centre of each ball, make a hole with your thumb. Add bacon crumbles and Cheddar cheese cubes to hole. Seal. 3. Heat your air fryer at 175°C for 3 minutes, before cooking. 4. Place four patties in air fryer basket or on the air fryer grill pan lightly greased with olive oil. Cook 5 minutes. Flip sliders and cook an additional 4 minutes or until desired doneness. 5. Transfer cooked sliders to a large plate and repeat cooking with remaining sliders. Serve warm.
Per Serving: Calories 297; Fat 22g; Sodium 478mg; Carbs 1g; Fibre 0g; Sugar 0g; Protein 23g

Mustard Ham

Prep time: 5 minutes| Cook time: 15 minutes| Serves: 8

105g brown sugar
60ml orange juice
2 tablespoons yellow mustard
1 (1.8kg) fully cooked boneless
ham
1 teaspoon salt
½ teaspoon ground black pepper

1. Preheat your air fryer to 190°C. 2. Whisk together brown sugar, orange juice, and mustard in a medium bowl until combined. Brush over ham until well coated. Sprinkle with salt and pepper. 3. Place the seasoned ham in the air fryer basket and cook for 15 minutes until heated through and edges are caramelized. Serve warm.
Per Serving: Calories 428; Fat 19.6g; Sodium 2930mg; Carbs 23.4g; Fibre 3g; Sugar 14g; Protein 38g

Ginger Pork Lettuce Wraps

Prep time: 15 minutes | Cook time: 20 minutes | Serves: 4

1 tablespoon corn flour
1 tablespoon water
1 tablespoon apple cider vinegar
2 tablespoons sugar-free orange marmalade
1 teaspoon smooth orange juice
2 teaspoons sesame oil
⅛ teaspoon cayenne pepper
¼ teaspoon ground ginger
1 (455g) boneless pork loin, cut into 2.5cm cubes
½ teaspoon salt
¼ teaspoon freshly ground white pepper
8 iceberg lettuce leaves

1. In a small bowl, create a slurry by whisking together corn flour and water. Set aside. 2. Combine apple cider vinegar, orange marmalade, orange juice, sesame oil, cayenne pepper, and ginger in a small saucepan over medium heat. Cook for 3 minutes, stirring continuously. Whisk in corn flour slurry and heat another minute. Remove pan from heat and allow to thicken for 3 minutes. 3. Preheat your air fryer at 175°C for 3 minutes. 4. Season pork with salt and white pepper. 5. Add half of pork to air fryer basket lightly greased with olive oil. Cook for 4 minutes. Shake gently. Cook an additional 4 minutes. Using a meat thermometer, ensure internal temperature is at least 60°C. 6. Transfer cooked pork to sauce. Repeat cooking with remaining pork, then add to sauce and toss. Serve warm in lettuce leaves.
Per Serving: Calories 186; Fat 7g; Sodium 348mg; Carbs 3.7g; Fibre 0g; Sugar 1g; Protein 25.6g

Crema Pork and Veggies Bowl

Prep time: 10 minutes | Cook time: 19 minutes | Serves: 4

For Crema
4 tablespoons sour cream
4 tablespoons mayonnaise
1 tablespoon fresh lime juice
½ teaspoon salt
For Vegetables
4 medium radishes, julienned
1 medium shallot, peeled and thinly sliced
3 tablespoons apple cider vinegar
⅛ teaspoon salt
2 medium carrots
435g shredded napa cabbage
10g chopped fresh basil
10g chopped fresh mint
For Pork
1 tablespoon sesame oil
1 tablespoon coconut aminos
2 teaspoons red chili paste
2 teaspoons granular erythritol

1 (2.5cm) knob fresh ginger
1 (455g) pork shoulder
2 tablespoons water

To prepare the ingredients: 1. Peel the carrots and shave them into ribbons. Peel the ginger and mince well. Trim the pork shoulder and thinly slice them into 2.5cm strips.
To make Crema: 1. Whisk together the crema ingredients in a small bowl. Refrigerate covered until ready to use.
To make Vegetables: 1. In a medium bowl, add radishes, shallot, apple cider vinegar, and salt. Refrigerate covered until ready to use.
To make Pork: 1. Whisk together sesame oil, coconut aminos, red chili paste, erythritol, and ginger in a medium bowl. Set aside half of marinade. Add pork strips to the bowl with remaining marinade and toss. Refrigerate covered until ready to use. 2. Heat your air fryer at 175°C for 3 minutes in advance. To ensure minimum smoke from fat drippings, pour water in bottom of air fryer. 3. Add pork to ungreased air fryer basket. Cook for 5 minutes. Toss. Cook them for 6 minutes. Toss once more and cook again for an additional 6 minutes. 4. Transfer the pork to a bowl with remaining marinade and toss. Add carrots to the ungreased air fryer basket and cook 2 minutes.
To assemble: Distribute cabbage, basil, and mint in four medium bowls. Top with pork and vegetables. Drizzle crema over the top and serve.
Per Serving: Calories 341; Fat 17g; Sodium 632mg; Carbs 18g; Fibre 3g; Sugar 7.6g; Protein 28g

Parmesan Pork Meatballs

Prep time: 15 minutes | Cook time: 16 minutes | Serves: 4

455g pork mince
1 large egg
1 tablespoon plain Greek yogurt
40g peeled and grated yellow onion
10g finely chopped fresh parsley
25g grated Parmesan cheese
2 tablespoons almond flour
¼ teaspoon garlic powder
¼ teaspoon salt
¼ teaspoon freshly ground black pepper

1. Heat air fryer at 175°C for 3 minutes in advance. 2. Combine all ingredients in a large bowl. Form into sixteen meatballs. 3. Add eight meatballs to air fryer basket lightly greased with olive oil and cook for 6 minutes. Flip once and cook for an additional 6 minutes. 4. Transfer cooked meatballs to a large serving plate. Repeat cooking with remaining meatballs. Serve warm.
Per Serving: Calories 396; Fat 27.5g; Sodium 363mg; Carbs 2g; Fibre 0g; Sugar 0g; Protein 33g

Buffalo Pork-Celery Meatballs

Prep time: 15 minutes | Cook time: 16 minutes | Serves: 4

455g pork mince
1 large egg
60ml buffalo wing sauce
30g grated celery
10g finely chopped fresh parsley
25g almond flour
¼ teaspoon salt

1. Heat air fryer at 175°C for 3 minutes in advance. 2. Combine all ingredients in a large bowl. Form into sixteen meatballs. 3. Add eight meatballs to air fryer basket lightly greased with olive oil and cook 6 minutes. Flip and cook an additional 2 minutes. 4. Transfer cooked meatballs to a large serving plate. Repeat cooking with remaining meatballs. Serve warm.
Per Serving: Calories 388; Fat 25g; Sodium 437mg; Carbs 7.8g; Fibre 0g; Sugar 6g; Protein 31g

Cheese and Spinach Steak Rolls

Prep Time: 10 minutes | Cook Time: 12 minutes | Serves: 4

1 (445g) flank steak, butterflied
8 (25g, ½ cm-thick) slices provolone cheese
30g fresh spinach leaves
½ teaspoon salt
¼ teaspoon ground black pepper

1. Place steak on a large plate, then place provolone slices to cover it, leaving 2.5cm at the edges. 2. Lay spinach leaves over cheese. 3. Gently roll steak and tie with kitchen twine or secure with toothpicks. 4. Carefully slice the steak into eight pieces. 5. Sprinkle each with salt and pepper. 6. Place rolls into ungreased air fryer basket, cut side up. 7. Adjust the temperature to 205°C and set the timer for 12 minutes. Steak rolls will be browned and cheese will be melted when done and have an internal temperature of at least 65°C for medium steak and 80°C for well-done steak. 8. Serve warm.
Per Serving: Calories 633; Fat 23g; Sodium 1428mg; Carbs 2g; Fibre 0g; Sugar 0g; Protein 98g

Simple Mini Meatloaf

Prep Time: 10 minutes | Cook Time: 25 minutes | Serves: 6

445g lean beef mince
¼ medium yellow onion, peeled and diced
½ medium green pepper, seeded and diced
1 large egg
3 tablespoons blanched finely ground almond flour

1 tablespoon Worcestershire sauce
½ teaspoon garlic powder
1 teaspoon dried parsley
2 tablespoons tomato paste
60ml water
1 tablespoon powdered sweetener

1. Combine beef mince, onion, pepper, egg and almond flour in a large bowl. 2. Pour in the Worcestershire sauce and add the garlic powder and parsley to the bowl, mix until fully combined. 3. Divide the mixture into two and place into two (10cm) loaf baking pans. 4. Mix the tomato paste, water, and sweetener in a small bowl, spoon half the mixture over each loaf, working in batches if necessary, place loaf pans into the air fryer basket. 5. Adjust the temperature setting to 175°C and set the timer for 25 minutes or the until internal temperature is 80°C. 6. Serve warm.
Per Serving: Calories 205; Fat 11.56g; Sodium 80mg; Carbs 2.72g; Fibre 0.7g; Sugar 1.17g; Protein 21.83g

Beef and Chorizo Burger

Prep Time: 10 minutes | Cook Time: 15 minutes | Serves: 4

335g lean beef mince
110g Mexican-style ground chorizo
40g chopped onion
5 slices pickled jalapeños,

chopped
2 teaspoons chili powder
1 teaspoon minced garlic
¼ teaspoon cumin

1. Mix the beef mince, ground chorizo, chopped onion, jalapenos, chili powder, garlic, and cumin in a large bowl. 2. Divide the mixture into four sections and form them into burger patties. 3. Place burger patties into the air fryer basket, working in batches if necessary. 4. Adjust the temperature setting to 190°C and set the timer for 15 minutes. 5. Flip the patties halfway through the cooking time. 6. Serve warm.
Per Serving: Calories 271; Fat 16.29g; Sodium 704mg; Carbs 4.6g; Fibre 1g; Sugar 1.68g; Protein 25.6g

Stuffed Peppers

Prep Time: 15 minutes | Cook Time: 15 minutes | Serves: 4

450g lean beef mince
1 tablespoon chili powder
2 teaspoons cumin
1 teaspoon garlic powder
1 teaspoon salt
¼ teaspoon ground black pepper

250g drained diced tomatoes with green chili
4 medium green peppers
100g shredded Monterey jack cheese, divided

1. Brown the beef mince about 7–10 minutes in a medium frying pan over medium heat. 2. When no pink remains, drain the fat from the frying pan. 3. Return the frying pan to the stovetop and add chili powder, cumin, garlic powder, salt, and black pepper. 4. Add the drained diced tomatoes and chiles to the frying pan. 5. Continue cooking for 3–5 minutes. 6. While it is cooking, cut each pepper in half. Remove the seeds and white membrane. 7. Spoon the cooked mixture evenly into each pepper and top with a 25 g cheese. 8. Place the stuffed peppers into your air fryer basket. 9. Adjust the temperature to 175°C and set the timer for 15 minutes. Peppers will be fork tender and cheese will be browned and bubbling when done. 10. Serve warm.
Per Serving: Calories 410; Fat 23g; Sodium 919mg; Carbs 9.64g; Fibre 2g; Sugar 5g; Protein 40.5g

Bacon and Cheese Burger Casserole

Prep Time: 15 minutes | Cook Time: 20 minutes | Serves: 4

450g lean beef mince
¼ medium white onion, peeled and chopped
1 large egg
4 slices bacon, cooked and

crumbled
2 pickle spears, chopped
100g shredded Cheddar cheese, divided

1. Set a frying pan over medium heat, add the beef mince and then brown for about 7–10 minutes. When no pink remains, drain the fat.

2. Remove from heat and add beef mince to a large mixing bowl. 3. Add onion, 50 g Cheddar and egg to the bowl. 4. Mix them well and add crumbled bacon. 5. Pour the mixture into a 15cm x 15cm round baking dish and top with remaining Cheddar. 6. Place all of them into the air fryer basket, adjust the temperature setting to 190°C and then set the time setting to 20 minutes. The casserole will be golden on top and firm in the middle when fully cooked. 7. Serve immediately with chopped pickles on top.
Per Serving: Calories 303; Fat 17g; Sodium 390mg; Carbs 0.7g; Fibre 0.2g; Sugar 0.2g; Protein 33.8g

Juicy Baked Pork Chops

Prep Time: 5 minutes | Cook Time: 15 minutes | Serves: 2

1 teaspoon chili powder
½ teaspoon garlic powder
½ teaspoon cumin
¼ teaspoon ground black pepper

¼ teaspoon dried oregano
2 (100g) boneless pork chops
2 tablespoons unsalted butter, divided

1. Mix chili powder, garlic powder, cumin, pepper and oregano in a small bowl. 2. Rub the dry rub onto pork chops. 3. Place pork chops into the air fryer basket, adjust the temperature to 205°C and set the timer for 15 minutes. The internal temperature shall reach at least 60°C when fully cooked. 4. Serve warm, each topped with 1 tablespoon butter.
Per Serving: Calories 316; Fat 14.38g; Sodium 136mg; Carbs 2.13g; Fibre 0.7g; Sugar 0.42g; Protein 42.46g

Crispy Stir-fried Beef and Broccoli

Prep Time: 60 minutes | Cook Time: 20 minutes | Serves: 2

225g sirloin steak, thinly sliced
2 tablespoons soy sauce (or liquid aminos)
¼ teaspoon grated ginger
¼ teaspoon finely minced garlic

1 tablespoon coconut oil
180g broccoli florets
¼ teaspoon crushed red pepper
⅛ teaspoon xanthan gum
½ teaspoon sesame seeds

1. Add soy sauce, ginger, garlic, and coconut oil into a large bowl or storage bag to marinate beef. 2. Allow to marinate for 1 hour in refrigerator. 3. Remove beef from marinade, reserving marinade. 4. Place the beef into the air fryer basket, adjust the temperature to 160°C and set the timer for 20 minutes. 5. After 10 minutes, add broccoli and sprinkle red pepper into the air fryer basket and shake. 6. Transfer the marinade to a frying pan over medium heat to boil, then reduce to simmer. 7. Stir in xanthan gum and allow it to thicken. 8. When the air fryer timer beeps, quickly empty air fryer basket into the frying pan and toss. 9. Sprinkle with sesame seeds. Serve immediately.
Per Serving: Calories 333; Fat 22.4g; Sodium 315mg; Carbs 5.4g; Fibre 1.5g; Sugar 3.3g; Protein 26g

Savory Latin American-style Pastries

Prep Time: 15 minutes | Cook Time: 10 minutes | Serves: 4

450g lean beef mince
120ml water
30g diced onion
2 teaspoons chili powder
½ teaspoon garlic powder
¼ teaspoon cumin

170g shredded mozzarella cheese
50g blanched finely ground almond flour
50g full-fat cream cheese
1 large egg

1. Brown the ground beef for about 7–10 minutes in a medium frying pan over medium heat. 2. Drain the fat. Return the frying pan to the stove. Add water and onion to the frying pan. Stir and sprinkle with chili powder, garlic powder, and cumin. 3. Reduce heat and simmer for an additional 3–5 minutes. Remove from heat and set aside. 4. Add mozzarella, almond flour, and cream cheese in a large microwave-safe bowl. Microwave for 1 minute. Stir until smooth. Form the mixture into a ball. 5. Then place it between two sheets of parchment and roll out to ½cm thickness. 6. Cut the dough into four squares. Place ¼ of beef mince onto the bottom half of each square. Fold the dough over and roll the edges up or press with a wet fork to close. 7. Crack the large egg into a small bowl and whisk. Brush the whisked egg over the pastries. 8. Cut a suitable piece of parchment to fit your air fryer basket and place the pastries on the parchment. 9. Place into the air fryer basket, adjust the temperature to 205°C and set the timer for 10 minutes. 10. Flip the pastries halfway through the cooking time. 11. Serve warm.
Per Serving: Calories 460; Fat 25.6g; Sodium 480mg; Carbs 7.9g; Fibre 2.3g; Sugar 2.7g; Protein 49.6g

Classic Pulled Pork

Prep Time: 10 minutes | Cook Time: 2½ hours | Serves: 8

2 tablespoons chili powder	½ teaspoon ground black pepper
1 teaspoon garlic powder	½ teaspoon cumin
½ teaspoon onion powder	1 (1.8kg) pork shoulder

1. Mix chili powder, garlic powder, onion powder, pepper, and cumin in a small bowl. 2. Rub the spice mixture over the pork shoulder, patting it into the skin. 3. Place the pork shoulder into the air fryer basket, adjust the temperature to 175°C and set the timer for 150 minutes. The pork skin will be crispy and meat easily shredded with two forks when done. The internal temperature should be at least 60°C. 4. Serve warm.
Per Serving: Calories 615; Fat 40.5g; Sodium 190mg; Carbs 1.7g; Fibre 0.8g; Sugar 0.3g; Protein 57g

Air Fryer Baby Back Ribs

Prep Time: 5 minutes | Cook Time: 25 minutes | Serves: 4

900g baby back ribs	½ teaspoon garlic powder
2 teaspoons chili powder	¼ teaspoon ground cayenne
1 teaspoon paprika	pepper
½ teaspoon onion powder	120ml sugar-free barbecue sauce

1. Rub ribs with chili powder, paprika, onion powder, and cayenne pepper together. 2. Place into the air fryer basket, adjust the temperature to 205°C and set the timer for 25 minutes. Ribs will be dark and charred with an internal temperature of at least 85°C when done. 3. Brush ribs with barbecue sauce and serve warm.
Per Serving: Calories 511; Fat 36g; Sodium 186mg; Carbs 2.4g; Fibre 0.8g; Sugar 0.3g; Protein 45g

Tasty Seared Ribeye

Prep Time: 5 minutes | Cook Time: 45 minutes | Serves: 2

1 (200g) ribeye steak	softened
½ teaspoon pink Himalayan salt	¼ teaspoon garlic powder
¼ teaspoon ground peppercorn	½ teaspoon dried parsley
1 tablespoon coconut oil	¼ teaspoon dried oregano
1 tablespoon salted butter,	

1. Rub the salt and ground peppercorn over the steak. 2. Place into the air fryer basket, adjust the temperature to 120°C and set the timer for 45 minutes. (Or place it into the air fryer at 205°C for 10–15 minutes for quick cook. Flip halfway through.) 3. After timer beeps, check doneness and add a few minutes until internal temperature is your personal preference. 4. Add coconut oil in a medium frying pan over medium heat. When oil is hot, quickly sear outside and sides of steak until crisp and browned. 5. Remove from heat and allow steak to rest. 6. Whip butter with garlic powder, parsley, and oregano in a small bowl. 7. Slice steak and serve with herbs and butter on top.
Per Serving: Calories 327; Fat 24.8g; Sodium 722mg; Carbs 2.6g; Fibre 0.1g; Sugar 0g; Protein 24.4g

Crusted Buttery Beef Tenderloin

Prep Time: 10 minutes | Cook Time: 25 minutes | Serves: 6

2 tablespoons salted butter, melted	4-peppercorn blend
2 teaspoons minced roasted garlic	1 (900g) beef tenderloin, trimmed of visible fat
3 tablespoons ground	

1. Mix the butter and roasted garlic in a small bowl. Brush it over the beef tenderloin. 2. Place the ground peppercorns onto a plate and roll the tenderloin through them, creating a crust. 3. Place tenderloin into the air fryer basket, adjust the temperature to 205°C and set the timer for 25 minutes. 4.Turn the tenderloin halfway through cooking. 5. Allow tenderloin to rest for 10 minutes before slicing.
Per Serving: Calories 343; Fat 16g; Sodium 107mg; Carbs 0.3g; Fibre 0g; Sugar 0g; Protein 46.2g

Southern-style Breaded Pork Chops

Prep Time: 10 minutes | Cook Time: 15 minutes | Serves: 4

35g grated parmesan	½ teaspoon garlic powder
1 teaspoon chili powder	1 tablespoon coconut oil, melted

4 (100g) pork chops

1. Mix parmesan, chili powder, and garlic powder in a large bowl. 2. Brush coconut oil over each pork chop and then press them into the pork rind mixture, coating both sides. 3. Place each coated pork chop into the air fryer basket, adjust the temperature setting to 205°C and then set the cooking time to 15 minutes. 4. Flip each pork chop halfway through cooking. When the pork chops are fully cooked, they should be golden on the outside and reach an internal temperature of at least 60°C. 5. Serve and enjoy!
Per Serving: Calories 120; Fat 8.5g; Sodium 41mg; Carbs 2.4g; Fibre 0.3g; Sugar 0g; Protein 10g

Lasagna Casserole

Prep Time: 15 minutes | Cook Time: 15 minutes | Serves: 4

170g no-sugar-added pasta sauce	½ teaspoon garlic powder
450g lean beef mince, cooked and drained	1 teaspoon dried parsley
125g full-fat ricotta cheese	½ teaspoon dried oregano
25g grated Parmesan cheese	110g shredded mozzarella cheese

1. Pour 55 g pasta sauce on the bottom of 15cm x 5cm round baking dish. 2. Place ¼ of the beef mince on top of the sauce. 3. Mix ricotta, Parmesan, garlic powder, parsley, and oregano in a small bowl. 4. Place dollops of half the mixture on top of the beef. 5. Sprinkle with ⅓ of the mozzarella. 6. Repeat layers until all beef, ricotta mixture, sauce, and mozzarella are used, ending with mozzarella on top. 7. Cover dish with foil and place into the air fryer basket, adjust the temperature setting to 185°C and then set the timer for 15 minutes. In the last 2 minutes of cooking, remove the foil to brown the cheese. 8. Serve immediately.
Per Serving: Calories 365; Fat 16.5g; Sodium 394mg; Carbs 6g; Fibre 1.6g; Sugar 1.2g; Protein 44.6g

Fajita Flank Steak Rolls

Prep Time: 20 minutes | Cook Time: 15 minutes | Serves: 6

2 tablespoons unsalted butter	1 teaspoon cumin
40g diced yellow onion	½ teaspoon garlic powder
1 medium red pepper	900g flank steak
1 medium green pepper	4 (25g) slices pepper jack cheese
2 teaspoons chili powder	

1. Remove seeds from the peppers and slice them into strips. Melt butter and sauté onion, red pepper and green pepper in a medium frying pan over medium heat. 2. Sprinkle with chili powder, cumin, and garlic powder. Sauté until peppers are tender, for about 5–7 minutes. 3. Lay flank steak flat on a work surface. Spread onion and pepper mixture over entire steak rectangle. Lay slices of cheese on top of onions and peppers, barely overlapping. 4. With the shortest end toward you, begin rolling the steak, tucking the cheese down into the roll as necessary. 5. Secure the roll with twelve toothpicks, six on each side of the steak roll. 6. Place steak roll into the air fryer basket, adjust the temperature to 205°C and set the timer for 15 minutes. Rotate the roll halfway through cooking. 7. Add an additional 1–4 minutes depending on your preferred internal temperature (55°C for medium). 8. When the timer beeps, allow the roll to rest for 15 minutes, then slice into six even pieces. 9. Serve warm.
Per Serving: Calories 267; Fat 12.24g; Sodium 139mg; Carbs 3.02g; Fibre 1g; Sugar 1.48g; Protein 34.32g

Ribeye Steak

Prep Time: 5 minutes | Cook Time: 20 minutes | Serves: 4

4 (200g) ribeye steaks	Salt
1 tablespoon Steak Seasoning	Pepper

1. Season the steaks with the steak seasoning, salt, and pepper. 2. Place 2 steaks in the air fryer. Cook at 180°C for 4 minutes . 3. Open the air fryer and then flip the steaks. Cook for an additional 4 to 5 minutes. 4. Check for doneness to determine how much additional cook time is need. (Check the level of pink with a fork. Or use a meat thermometer) 5. Remove the cooked steaks from the air fryer, then repeat steps 2-4 for the remaining 2 steaks. 6. Cool before serving.
Per Serving: Calories 117; Fat 6.5g; Sodium 206mg; Carbs 3.3g; Fibre 0.5g; Sugar 0.8g; Protein 11.4g

Beef Taco Rolls

Prep Time: 20 minutes | Cook Time: 10 minutes | Serves: 4

225g lean beef mince
80ml water
1 tablespoon chili powder
2 teaspoons cumin
½ teaspoon garlic powder
¼ teaspoon dried oregano
60g canned diced tomatoes and

chiles, drained
2 tablespoons chopped coriander
170g shredded mozzarella cheese
50g blanched finely ground
almond flour
50g full-fat cream cheese
1 large egg

1. Brown the beef mince for about 7–10 minutes in a medium frying pan over medium heat. Drain the meat when it is fully cooked. 2. Add water to the frying pan and stir in chili powder, cumin, garlic powder, oregano, and tomatoes with chiles. Add coriander. 3. Bring them together to a boil, then reduce heat to simmer for 3 minutes. 4. Place mozzarella, almond flour, cream cheese, and the egg in a large microwave-safe bowl. Microwave for 1 minute. Stir the mixture quickly until smooth ball of dough forms. 5. Cut a piece of parchment for your work surface. Press the dough into a large rectangle on the parchment, wetting your hands to prevent the dough from sticking as necessary. Cut the dough into eight rectangles. 6. Place a few spoons of the meat mixture on each rectangle. Fold the short ends of each roll toward the centre and roll the length as you would to make a burrito. 7. Cut a suitable piece of parchment to fit your air fryer basket. Place taco rolls onto the parchment and place into the air fryer basket, adjust the temperature setting to 180°C and set the timer for 10 minutes. Flip halfway through cooking. 8. Cool for 10 minutes before serving.
Per Serving: Calories 374; Fat 23g; Sodium 492mg; Carbs 8g; Fibre 3.5g; Sugar 2.3g; Protein 35g

Italian Parmesan Breaded Pork Chops

Prep Time: 5 minutes | Cook Time: 25 minutes | Serves: 5

5 (90g–125g) pork chops (bone-in
or boneless)
1 teaspoon Italian seasoning
Seasoning salt
Pepper
30g plain flour

2 tablespoons Italian bread
crumbs
3 tablespoons finely grated
Parmesan cheese
Cooking oil

1. Season the pork chops with the Italian seasoning, seasoning salt, and pepper. 2. Sprinkle the flour on both sides of the pork chops, then coat both sides with the bread crumbs and Parmesan cheese. 3. Add the pork chops to the air fryer. Stacking them. Spray the pork chops with cooking oil. Cook at 195°C for 6 minutes. 4. Open the air fryer and then flip the pork chops. Cook for an additional 6 minutes. 5. Cool before serving.
Per Serving: Calories 148; Fat 4.7g; Sodium 200mg; Carbs 15.3g; Fibre 0.9g; Sugar 1.6g; Protein 10.6g

Beef Empanadas with Cheeses

Prep Time: 15 minutes | Cook Time: 25 minutes | Serves: 15

Cooking oil
2 garlic cloves, chopped
50g chopped green pepper
⅓ medium onion, chopped
200g lean beef mince
1 teaspoon burger seasoning
Salt

Pepper
15 empanada wrappers
115g shredded mozzarella cheese
100g shredded Pepper Jack
cheese
1 tablespoon butter

1. Spray a frying pan with cooking oil and turn medium-high heat on. Add garlic, green pepper, and onion. Cook for about 2 minutes until fragrant. 2. Add the beef mince to the frying pan. Season the beef with the hamburger seasoning, salt, and pepper. Use a spatula to break up the beef into small pieces. Cook the beef until browned. Drain any excess fat. 3. Lay the empanada wrappers on a flat surface. 4. Dip a basting brush in water. Glaze each empanada wrapper with a wet brush along the edges to soften the crust and make it easier to roll.) 5. Scoop 2 to 3 tablespoons of beef mixture onto each empanada wrapper. Sprinkle the mozzarella and Pepper Jack cheeses over the beef mixture. 6. Close the empanadas by folding the empanada in half. Press along and seal the edges with the back of a fork. 7. Place 7 or 8 of the empanadas in the air fryer. Spray each with cooking oil. Cook at 205°C for 8 minutes. 8. Open the air fryer and flip the empanadas. Cook for an additional 4 minutes. 9. Remove the cooked empanadas from the air fryer, then repeat the empanada-preparing

steps for the remaining empanadas. 10. For added flavour, melt the butter in the microwave for 20 seconds. Use a cooking brush to spread the melted butter over the top of each. 11. Cool before serving.
Per Serving: Calories 176; Fat 5.3g; Sodium 314mg; Carbs 19.8g; Fibre 0.8g; Sugar 0.5g; Protein 11.5g

Beef and Mushroom Calzones

Prep Time: 10 minutes | Cook Time: 20 minutes | Serves: 6

Cooking oil
60g chopped onion
2 garlic cloves, minced
20g chopped mushrooms
455g lean beef mince
1 tablespoon Italian seasoning
Salt

Pepper
380g pizza sauce
1 teaspoon plain flour
1 (325g) can refrigerated pizza
dough
100g shredded Cheddar cheese

1. Spray a frying pan with cooking oil and turn medium-high heat on. Add the chopped onion, garlic, and mushrooms. Cook them together for 2 to 3 minutes until fragrant. 2. Add the beef mince, Italian seasoning, salt, and pepper and break up the beef into small pieces with a large spoon. Cook the mixture for 2 to 4 minutes until the beef is browned. 3. Add the pizza sauce. Stir to combine. 4. Sprinkle the flour on a flat work surface. Roll out the pizza dough. Cut the dough into 6 equal-sized rectangles. 5. Mound some of the beef mince mixture on each of the rectangles. Sprinkle 1 tablespoon of shredded cheese over the beef mixture. 6. Fold each crust up to close the calzones. Press along and seal the open edges of each calzone with the back of a fork. 7. Place the calzones in the air fryer. Do not stack. Cook in batches. Spray the calzones with cooking oil. Cook at 205°C for 10 minutes. 8. Remove the cooked calzones from the air fryer, then repeat step 7 for the remaining calzones. 9. Cool before serving.
Per Serving: Calories 393; Fat 18.5g; Sodium 750mg; Carbs 26.2g; Fibre 3.3g; Sugar 6g; Protein 29g

Breaded Pork Chops

Prep Time: 5 minutes | Cook Time: 15 minutes | Serves: 5

5 (90g–125g) pork chops (bone-in
or boneless)
Seasoning salt
Pepper

30g plain flour
2 tablespoons panko bread
crumbs
Cooking oil

1. Season the pork chops with the seasoning salt and pepper. 2. Sprinkle the flour on both sides of the pork chops, then coat both sides with panko bread crumbs. 3. Add the pork chops in the air fryer. It's okay to stack them. Spray the pork chops with cooking oil. Cook at 195°C for 6 minutes. 4. Open the air fryer and then flip the pork chops. Cook for an additional 6 minutes. 5. Cool before serving.
Per Serving: Calories 134; Fat 36g; Sodium 105mg; Carbs 2.4g; Fibre 0.8g; Sugar 1.5g; Protein 9.7g

Mouth-watering Pork Chop Salad

Prep Time: 15 minutes | Cook Time: 8 minutes | Serves: 2

1 tablespoon coconut oil
2 (100g) pork chops, chopped
into 2.5cm cubes
2 teaspoons chili powder
1 teaspoon paprika
½ teaspoon garlic powder
¼ teaspoon onion powder
315g chopped romaine

1 medium Roma tomato, diced
50g shredded Monterey jack
cheese
1 medium avocado, peeled,
pitted, and diced
60g full-fat ranch dressing
1 tablespoon chopped coriander

1. Chop the pork into 2.5cm cubes. Drizzle coconut oil over the cubes in a large bowl. Sprinkle them with chili powder, paprika, garlic powder, and onion powder. 2. Place them into your air fryer basket, adjust the temperature setting to 205°C and then set the timer for 8 minutes. The pork cubes will be golden and crispy when fully cooked. 3. Place romaine, tomato, and crispy pork in a large bowl. Top with shredded cheese and avocado. 4. Pour ranch dressing around bowl and toss the salad to evenly coat. 5. Top with coriander. Serve immediately.
Per Serving: Calories 576; Fat 37g; Sodium 354mg; Carbs 10.7g; Fibre 9g; Sugar 4.3g; Protein 34g

Beef Taco Chimichangas

Prep Time: 10 minutes | Cook Time: 20 minutes | Serves: 4

Cooking oil	1 (375g) can diced tomatoes with
55g chopped onion	chiles
2 garlic cloves, minced	4 medium (20cm) flour tortillas
455g lean beef mince	100g Cheddar cheese, shreded (a
2 tablespoons taco seasoning	blend of 50g shredded Cheddar
Salt	and 50g shredded Monterey Jack
Pepper	works great, too)

1. Spray a frying pan with cooking oil and turn medium-high heat on. Add chopped onion and garlic, cook for 2 to 3 minutes until fragrant. 2. Add beef mince, taco seasoning, salt, and pepper. Break up the beef with a spatula. Cook for 2 to 4 minutes until browned. 3. Add the diced tomatoes with chiles. Stir to combine. 4. Mound some of the beef mince mixture on each tortilla. 5. Fold the sides of the tortilla in toward the middle and then roll up from the bottom to form chimichangas. (You can secure the chimichanga with a toothpick. Or you can moisten the upper edge of the tortilla with a small amount of water before sealing. Use a cooking brush or dab with your fingers.) 6. Spray the chimichangas with cooking oil. Place the chimichangas in the air fryer. Do not stack. Cook in batches 205°C for 8 minutes. 7. Remove the cooked chimichangas from the air fryer and top them with the shredded cheese. The heat from the chimichangas will melt the cheese. (Repeat the steps for the remaining chimichangas) 9. Serve.
Per Serving: Calories 494; Fat 16g; Sodium 1552mg; Carbs 49.5g; Fibre 6.5g; Sugar 16.18g; Protein 39.2g

BBQ Meatballs

Prep Time: 10 minutes | Cook Time: 14 minutes | Serves: 4

455g beef mince	4 slices bacon, cooked and
110g Italian sausage meat	chopped
1 large egg	40g chopped white onion
¼ teaspoon onion powder	25g chopped pickled jalapeños
½ teaspoon garlic powder	125g low-carb, sugar-free
1 teaspoon dried parsley	barbecue sauce

1. Mix beef mince, sausage, and egg in a large bowl until fully combined. Mix in all remaining ingredients except barbecue sauce. 2. Form into eight meatballs. Place meatballs into the air fryer basket, adjust the temperature to 205°C and set the timer for 14 minutes. Turn the meatballs halfway through cooking. The beef meatballs should be browned on the outside and have an internal temperature of at least 80°C when done. 3. Remove meatballs from fryer and toss in barbecue sauce. 4. Serve warm.
Per Serving: Calories 419; Fat 25g; Sodium 454mg; Carbs 6.3g; Fibre 0.3g; Sugar 2.5g; Protein 39.9g

Air Fried Sausage, Peppers, and Onions

Prep Time: 5 minutes | Cook Time: 15 minutes | Serves: 5

5 Italian sausages	½ onion, cut into strips
1 green pepper, cut into strips	1 teaspoon dried oregano
without seeds	½ teaspoon garlic powder
1 red pepper, seeded and cut into	5 Italian rolls or buns
strips	

1. Place the sausages in the air fryer. Cook at 180°C for 10 minutes. 2. Season the green and red peppers and the onion with the oregano and garlic powder. 3. Open the air fryer and then flip the sausages. Add the peppers and onion to the basket. Cook them in your air fryer for an additional 3 to 5 minutes, until the vegetables are soft and the sausages are no longer pink on the inside. 4. Serve the sausages (sliced or whole) on buns with the peppers and onion.
Per Serving: Calories 521; Fat 37g; Sodium 1038mg; Carbs 25g; Fibre 1.5g; Sugar 4g; Protein 20.8g

Savory Worcestershire Cheeseburgers

Prep Time: 5 minutes | Cook Time: 15 minutes | Serves: 4

455g lean beef mince	Pepper
1 teaspoon Worcestershire sauce	Cooking oil
1 tablespoon burger seasoning	4 slices cheese
Salt	4 buns

1. Mix the beef mince, Worcestershire, burger seasoning, salt, and pepper in a large bowl. 2. Spray the cooking oil over the air fryer basket. (only a quick spritz, the burgers will produce oil as they cook.) 3. Shape the mixture into 4 patties. Place the burgers in the air fryer. Cook at 180°C for 8 minutes. 4. Open the air fryer and then flip the burgers. Cook for an additional 3 to 4 minutes. 5. Stick a knife or fork in the centre to examine the colour to check the inside of the burgers when they are fully cooked. 6. Add one cheese slice on top of each burger. Cook in your air fryer for an additional minute, or until the cheese has melted. 7. Serve on buns with any additional toppings of your choice.
Per Serving: Calories 648; Fat 37g; Sodium 990mg; Carbs 37g; Fibre 1.2g; Sugar 20g; Protein 39g

Juicy Steak Fajitas

Prep Time: 10 minutes | Cook Time: 10 minutes | Serves: 4

455g beef flank steak, cut into	seasoning
strips	Salt
1 red pepper, cut into strips	Pepper
1 green pepper, cut into strips	2 tablespoons extra-virgin olive
½ red onion, cut into strips	oil
2 tablespoons taco or fajita	8 medium (20cm) flour tortillas

1. Combine beef, red and green peppers, onion, taco seasoning, salt, pepper, and olive oil in a large bowl. Mix them well. 2. Transfer the beef and vegetable mixture to the air fryer. It is okay to stack. Cook at 195°C for 5 minutes. 3. Open the air fryer and shake the basket. Cook for an additional 4 to 5 minutes. 4. Divide the beef and vegetables evenly among the tortillas and serve with any of your desired additional toppings.
Per Serving: Calories 491; Fat 14.3g; Sodium 1098mg; Carbs 55g; Fibre 3.7g; Sugar 6g; Protein 32.8g

Roasted Pork Tenderloin

Prep Time: 5 minutes | Cook Time: 60 minutes | Serves: 6

1 (1.3kg) pork tenderloin	1 teaspoon dried oregano
2 tablespoons extra-virgin olive	1 teaspoon dried thyme
oil	Salt
2 garlic cloves, minced	Pepper
1 teaspoon dried basil	

1. Drizzle the pork tenderloin with the olive oil. 2. Rub the garlic, basil, oregano, thyme, salt and pepper all over the tenderloin. 3. Place the tenderloin in the air fryer. Cook at 180°C for 45 minutes. 4. Use a meat thermometer to test for doneness. 5. Open the air fryer and flip the pork tenderloin. Cook for an additional 15 minutes. 6. Remove the cooked pork from the air fryer and allow it to rest for 10 minutes before cutting.
Per Serving: Calories 348; Fat 10g; Sodium 170mg; Carbs 1g; Fibre 0.3g; Sugar 0.4g; Protein 59.6g

Swedish Meatballs

Prep Time: 10 minutes | Cook Time: 20 minutes | Serves: 10

For the Meatballs

455g lean beef mince	1 egg, beaten
1 (25g) packet Onion Soup Mix	Salt
35g bread crumbs	Pepper

For the Gravy

240ml beef stock	2 tablespoons plain flour
70g heavy cream	

To make the meatballs
1. Combine the beef mince, onion soup mix, bread crumbs, egg, salt, and pepper in a large bowl. Mix thoroughly. 2. Use gloves to assemble the meatballs. Use 2 tablespoons of the meat mixture to create each meatball, rolling the beef mixture around in your hands. Yield about 10 meatballs. 3. Place the beef meatballs in the air fryer. It is okay to stack them. Cook at 185°C for 14 minutes.
To make the gravy
1. Prepare the gravy while the meatballs are cooking. Heat a saucepan over medium-high heat. 2. Add the beef stock and heavy cream. Stir for 1 to 2 minutes. 3. Add the flour and stir. Then simmer the sauce for 3 to 4 minutes, or until thickened. 4. Drizzle the gravy over the meatballs and serve.
Per Serving: Calories 135; Fat 7.5g; Sodium 46mg; Carbs 2.6g; Fibre 0.2g; Sugar 0.6g; Protein 13.4g

Chapter 7 Dessert Recipes

Honey Apple-Peach Crisp

Prep Time: 10 minutes | Cook Time: 10 to 12 minutes | Serves: 4

1 apple, peeled and chopped
2 peaches, peeled, pitted, and chopped
2 tablespoons honey
40g quick-cooking oatmeal
40g whole-wheat pastry flour

3 tablespoons packed brown sugar
2 tablespoons unsalted butter, at room temperature
½ teaspoon ground cinnamon

1. Thoroughly mix the apple, peaches, and honey in a suitable baking pan. 2. Mix the oatmeal, pastry flour, brown sugar, butter, and cinnamon in a medium bowl until crumbly, then sprinkle this mixture over the fruit. 3. Bake them at 195°C for 10 to 12 minutes until the fruit is bubbly and the topping is golden brown. 4. Serve warm.
Per Serving: Calories 209; Fat 5.2g; Sodium 49mg; Carbs 39.94g; Fibre 3.9g; Sugar 27.02g; Protein 3.9g

Strawberry Crumble

Prep Time: 10 minutes | Cook Time: 12 to 17 minutes | Serves: 6

230g sliced fresh strawberries
90g sliced rhubarb
65g sugar
50g quick-cooking oatmeal
65g whole-wheat pastry flour

55g packed brown sugar
½ teaspoon ground cinnamon
3 tablespoons unsalted butter, melted

1. Combine the strawberries, rhubarb, and sugar in a suitable baking pan. 2. Mix the oatmeal, pastry flour, brown sugar, and cinnamon in a medium bowl. 3. Stir the melted butter into the oatmeal mixture until crumbly, then sprinkle this over the fruit. 4. Bake them at 185°C for 12 to 17 minutes until the fruit is bubbling and the topping is golden brown. 5. Serve warm.
Per Serving: Calories 168; Fat 4.99g; Sodium 47mg; Carbs 29.3g; Fibre 2.6g; Sugar 17.55g; Protein 3.31g

Berries Crumble

Prep Time: 10 minutes | Cook Time: 11 to 16 minutes | Serves: 4

75g chopped fresh strawberries
75g fresh blueberries
80g frozen raspberries
1 tablespoon freshly squeezed lemon juice
1 tablespoon honey

80g whole-wheat pastry flour
3 tablespoons packed brown sugar
2 tablespoons unsalted butter, melted

1. Combine the strawberries, blueberries, and raspberries in a suitable baking pan, then drizzle them with the lemon juice and honey. 2. Mix the pastry flour and brown sugar in a small bowl, then stir in the butter and mix until crumbly. 3. Sprinkle this mixture over the fruit. 4. Bake them at 195°C for 11 to 16 minutes until the fruit is tender and bubbly and the topping is golden brown. 5. Serve warm.
Per Serving: Calories 183; Fat 4.6g; Sodium 5mg; Carbs 34.86g; Fibre 3.8g; Sugar 18.3g; Protein 3.38g

Maple Chocolate Chip Cookies

Prep time: 10 minutes | Cook time: 7 minutes | Serves: 6

1 tablespoon refined coconut oil, melted
1 tablespoon maple syrup
1 tablespoon nondairy milk
½ teaspoon vanilla
30g plus 2 tablespoons whole-wheat pastry flour or plain gluten-free flour

2 tablespoons coconut sugar
¼ teaspoon sea salt
¼ teaspoon baking powder
2 tablespoons vegan chocolate chips
Cooking oil spray (sunflower, safflower, or refined coconut)

1. Stir together the oil, maple syrup, milk, and vanilla in a medium bowl. Add the flour, coconut sugar, salt, and baking powder. Stir just until thoroughly combined. Stir in the chocolate chips. 2. Preheat the air fryer basket (with a 15cm round, 5cm-deep baking pan inside) for 2 minutes. Then, spray the pan lightly with oil. Add the batter by teaspoonful to the pan, leaving a little room in between in case they spread out a bit. Bake at 175°C for 7 minutes, or until lightly browned. Be careful not to overcook. 3. Gently transfer to a cooling rack (or plate). Repeat as desired, making all of the cookies at once, or keeping the batter on hand in the fridge to be used later (it will keep refrigerated in an airtight container for about a week). Enjoy warm if possible!

Per Serving: Calories 89; Fat 3g; Sodium 116mg; Carbs 14g; Fibre 0g; Sugar 6g; Protein 1g

Honey Pears with Ricotta

Prep Time: 7 minutes | Cook Time: 18 to 23 minutes | Serves: 4

2 large Bosc pears, halved and seeded
3 tablespoons honey
1 tablespoon unsalted butter

½ teaspoon ground cinnamon
30g walnuts, chopped
60g low-fat ricotta cheese, divided

1. Place the pears in a suitable baking pan with cut-side up. 2. In a small microwave-safe bowl, melt the honey, butter, and cinnamon. Brush this mixture over the cut sides of the pears. 3. Pour 3 tablespoons of water around the pears in the pan, then roast the pears in the air fryer at 175°C for 18 to 23 minutes, or until tender when pierced with a fork and slightly crisp on the edges, basting once with the liquid in the pan. 4. Carefully remove the pears from the pan, and place on a serving plate. 5. Drizzle each with some liquid from the pan, sprinkle the walnuts on top, and serve with a spoonful of ricotta cheese.
Per Serving: Calories 198; Fat 7.07g; Sodium 68mg; Carbs 31.61g; Fibre 3.9g; Sugar 24.32g; Protein 3.66g

Greek Peaches with Blueberries

Prep Time: 10 minutes | Cook Time: 7 to 11 minutes | Serves: 6

3 peaches, peeled, halved, and pitted
2 tablespoons packed brown sugar

240g plain nonfat Greek yogurt
1 teaspoon pure vanilla extract
¼ teaspoon ground cinnamon
150g fresh blueberries

1. Place the peaches in the air fryer basket with cut-side up, and evenly sprinkle them with the brown sugar. 2. Bake the peaches at 195°C for 7 to 11 minutes until they start to brown around the edges and become tender. 3. While baking the peaches, stir the yogurt, vanilla, and cinnamon in a small bowl. 4. When the peaches are done, transfer them to a serving plate. Top with the yogurt mixture and the blueberries. 5. Enjoy.
Per Serving: Calories 67; Fat 0.34g; Sodium 7mg; Carbs 14.25g; Fibre 1.8g; Sugar 12.06g; Protein 2.8g

Walnut-Stuffed Apples

Prep Time: 15 minutes | Cook Time: 12 to 17 minutes | Serves: 4

4 medium apples, rinsed and patted dry
2 tablespoons freshly squeezed lemon juice
35g golden raisins

3 tablespoons chopped walnuts
3 tablespoons dried cranberries
2 tablespoons packed brown sugar
80ml apple cider

1. Peel the apples and remove the core, being careful not to cut through the bottom of the apple. 2. Sprinkle the cut parts of the apples with lemon juice and place in a suitable pan. 3. Mix the raisins, walnuts, cranberries, and brown sugar in a small bowl, then stuff one-fourth of this mixture into each apple. 4. Pour the apple cider around the apples in the pan. 5. Bake the stuffed apples at 175°C for 12 to 17 minutes the apples are tender when pierced with a fork. 6.Serve immediately.
Per Serving: Calories 195; Fat 3.88g; Sodium 4mg; Carbs 42.33g; Fibre 5.2g; Sugar 32.56g; Protein 2.28g

Grilled Fruit Skewers

Prep Time: 10 minutes | Cook Time: 3 to 5 minutes | Serves: 4

2 peaches, peeled, pitted, and thickly sliced
3 plums, halved and pitted
3 nectarines, halved and pitted

1 tablespoon honey
½ teaspoon ground cinnamon
¼ teaspoon ground allspice
Pinch cayenne pepper

1. Thread the fruit, alternating the types, onto 8 bamboo or metal skewers that fit into the air fryer. 2. Stir the honey, cinnamon, allspice, and cayenne in a small bowl, then brush the glaze onto the fruit. 3. Grill the skewers at 205°C for 3 to 5 minutes until lightly browned and caramelized. 4. Cool for 5 minutes and serve.
Per Serving: Calories 95; Fat 0.58g; Sodium 1mg; Carbs 23.68g; Fibre 3g; Sugar 19.4g; Protein 1.61g

Oatmeal-Carrot Cups

Prep Time: 10 minutes | Cook Time: 8 to 10 minutes | Serves: 16

3 tablespoons unsalted butter, at room temperature
55g packed brown sugar
1 tablespoon honey
1 egg white
½ teaspoon vanilla extract

40g finely grated carrot
40g quick-cooking oatmeal
40g whole-wheat pastry flour
½ teaspoon baking soda
30g dried cherries

1. Beat the butter, brown sugar, and honey in a small bowl until well combined, then mix in the egg white, vanilla, and carrot. 2. Stir in the oatmeal, pastry flour, and baking soda. 3. Stir in the dried cherries. 4. Double up 32 mini muffin foil cups to make 16 cups. Fill each with about 4 teaspoons of dough. 5. Working in batches, bake the cookie cups at 175°C for 8 to 10 minutes until light golden brown and just set. 6. Serve warm.
Per Serving: Calories 50; Fat 1.73g; Sodium 58mg; Carbs 7.94g; Fibre 0.5g; Sugar 5.22g; Protein 1.08g

Frosted Chocolate Cake

Prep time: 10 minutes | Cook time: 25 minutes | Serves: 6

For the Cake
90g (whole-wheat pastry, gluten-free plain, or plain)
100g organic sugar
For the Frosting
3 tablespoons vegan margarine
155g icing sugar
120ml nondairy milk
2½ tablespoons neutral flavoured oil (sunflower, safflower, or melted refined coconut)

2 tablespoons cocoa powder
½ teaspoon baking soda
⅛ teaspoon sea salt

½ tablespoon apple cider vinegar
½ teaspoon vanilla
Coconut oil (for greasing)
5 tablespoons cocoa powder
2 teaspoons vanilla
⅛ teaspoon sea salt

To make the cake: 1. Stir together the sugar, flour, cocoa powder, baking soda, and salt in a medium bowl with a wire whisk. When thoroughly combined, add the milk, oil, vinegar, and vanilla. Stir just until well combined. 2. Preheat the air fryer to 175°C for 2 minutes. 3. Grease a 15cm round, 5cm-deep baking pan liberally with some coconut oil to avoid the cake from sticking to the pan. Add the batter to the oiled pan and bake for 25 minutes, or until a knife inserted in the centre comes out clean.
To make the frosting: 1. Cream together the vegan margarine and icing sugar in a medium bowl with an electric beater. 2. Add the cocoa powder, vanilla, and salt and whip with the beaters until thoroughly combined and fluffy. With a rubber spatula, occasionally scrape down the sides as needed. Refrigerate until ready to use.
To assemble: 1. Cool the cake completely, and then run a knife around the edges of the baking pan. Turn it upside-down on a plate so it can be frosted on the sides and top. 2. Allow the cake to cool until no longer hot, usually about 10 minutes. When the frosting is no longer cold, use a butter knife or small spatula to frost the sides and top. Cut into slices and enjoy.
Per Serving: Calories 296; Fat 13g; Sodium 222mg; Carbs 45g; Fibre 3.5g; Sugar 30g; Protein 3.8g

Cinnamon Raisin Oatmeal Cookies

Prep time: 10 minutes | Cook time: 7 minutes | Serves: 18

55g plus ½ tablespoon vegan margarine
2½ tablespoons nondairy milk, plain and unsweetened
100g organic sugar
½ teaspoon vanilla extract
½ teaspoon plus ⅛ teaspoon ground cinnamon
65g plus 2 tablespoons flour

(whole-wheat pastry, gluten-free plain, or plain)
¼ teaspoon sea salt
60g rolled oats
¼ teaspoon baking soda
¼ teaspoon baking powder
2 tablespoons raisins
Cooking oil spray (sunflower, safflower, or refined coconut)

1. Using an electric beater, whip the margarine in a medium bowl until fluffy. 2. Add in the milk, sugar, and vanilla. Stir or whip with beaters until well combined. 3. In a separate bowl, add the cinnamon, flour, salt, oats, baking soda, and baking powder and stir well to combine. Mix the dry mixture to the wet mixture with a wooden spoon until they are well combined. Stir in the raisins. 4. Preheat the air fryer basket (with your 6-inch round, 2-inch deep baking pan

inside) to 175°C for 2 minutes. Then, spray the pan lightly with oil. Add the batter onto the pan with a teaspoon, leaving a little room in between each one as they'll probably spread out a bit. Bake at 175°C for about 7 minutes, or until lightly browned. 5. Gently transfer to a cooling rack (or plate), being careful to leave the cookies intact. Repeat as desired, making all of the cookies at once, or keeping the batter on hand in the fridge to be used later (it will keep refrigerated in an airtight container for a week to 10 days).
Per Serving: Calories 62; Fat 3g; Sodium 53mg; Carbs 8.7g; Fibre 1g; Sugar 3g; Protein 1g

Cinnamon Crisps

Prep time: 2 minutes | Cook time: 5 to 6 minutes | Serves: 4

1 (20cm) tortilla, preferably sprouted whole-grain
Cooking oil spray (sunflower,

safflower, or refined coconut)
2 teaspoons coconut sugar
½ teaspoon cinnamon

1. Cut the tortilla into 8 triangles (like a pizza). Place on a large plate and spray both sides with oil. 2. Sprinkle the tops evenly with the coconut sugar and cinnamon. In short spurts, spray the tops again with the oil. (If you spray too hard for this step, it will make the powdery toppings fly off!) 3. Place directly in the air fryer basket in a single layer (it's okay if they overlap a little, but do your best to give them space). Fry at 175°C for 5 to 6 minutes, or until the triangles are lightly browned, but not too brown—they're bitter if overcooked. Enjoy warm if possible.
Per Serving: Calories 40; Fat 0g; Sodium 83mg; Carbs 7.5g; Fibre 0g; Sugar 1.6g; Protein 1g

Enticing Caramelized Apples

Prep time: 4 minutes | Cook time: 20 minutes | Serves: 2

2 apples, any sweet variety
2 tablespoons water
1½ teaspoons coconut sugar
¼ teaspoon cinnamon

Pinch nutmeg
Dash sea salt
Cooking oil spray (sunflower, safflower, or refined coconut)

1. Cut each apple in half (no need to peel) and then remove the core and seeds, doing your best to keep the apple halves intact—because ideally, you want apple halves, not quarters. 2. Place the apples upright in a 15cm round, 5cm deep baking pan. Add about 2 tablespoons water to the bottom of the dish to keep the apples from drying out (the apples will sit in the water). 3. Sprinkle evenly the tops of the apples with the sugar, cinnamon, and nutmeg. Give each half a very light sprinkle of sea salt. 4. In short spurts, spray the tops with oil (if you spray too hard, it will make the toppings fly off in a tragic whirlwind). Once moistened, spray the tops again with oil. (This will keep them from drying out.) 5. Bake at 200°C for 20 minutes, or until the apples are very soft and nicely browned on top. Enjoy immediately, plain or topped with granola or ice cream.
Per Serving: Calories 112; Fat 1g; Sodium 80mg; Carbs 28g; Fibre 5g; Sugar 21g; Protein 0.6g

Dark Chocolate Cookies

Prep Time: 10 minutes | Cook Time: 8 to 13 minutes | Serves: 30

3 tablespoons unsalted butter
50g dark chocolate, chopped
105g packed brown sugar
2 egg whites
1 teaspoon pure vanilla extract

80g quick-cooking oatmeal
65g whole-wheat pastry flour
½ teaspoon baking soda
30g dried cranberries

1. Mix the butter and dark chocolate in a medium oven-safe bowl. 2. Bake them in the air fryer at 160°C for 1 to 3 minutes until the butter and chocolate melt, then stir until smooth. 3. Beat in the brown sugar, egg whites, and vanilla until smooth. 4. Stir in the oatmeal, pastry flour, and baking soda. 5. Stir in the cranberries, then form the dough into about 30 (2.5cm) balls. 6. Working in batches, bake the dough balls in the air fryer basket at 160°C for 7 to 10 minutes until set. 7. Carefully remove the cookies from the air fryer and cool on a wire rack. 8. Serve and enjoy.
Per Serving: Calories 52; Fat 1.87g; Sodium 39mg; Carbs 7.96g; Fibre 0.6g; Sugar 5.1g; Protein 1.11g

Strawberry Puffs with Cashew Sauce

Prep time: 20 minutes | Cook time: 10 minutes | Serves: 8

For the Filling

455g sliced strawberries, fresh or frozen

320g sugar-free strawberry jam (sweetened only with fruit juice)

1 tablespoon corn flour

Cooking oil spray (sunflower, safflower, or refined coconut)

8 large (33cm x 43cm) sheets of puff pastry, thawed

For the Sauce

130g raw cashew pieces

55g plus 2 tablespoons raw agave nectar

60ml plus 1 tablespoon water

3 tablespoons fresh lemon juice

2 teaspoons (packed) lemon zest

2 tablespoons neutral-flavored oil (sunflower, safflower, or refined coconut)

2 teaspoons vanilla

¼ teaspoon sea salt

To make the filling: 1. In a medium bowl, add the strawberries, jam, and corn flour and stir well to combine. Set aside. 2. Prepare the air fryer basket by spraying it with oil and set aside.

To assemble the puffs: 1. Gently unwrap the puff pastry. Remove 8 sheets and carefully set them aside. Re-wrap the remaining pastry in airtight plastic wrap and place back in the fridge. 2. Remove 1 large sheet of pastry and place on a clean, dry surface. Spray with the oil. 3. Fold it into thirds so that it forms a long, skinny rectangle. As you go, spray each portion of dry pastry, so the exposed pastry continually gets lightly coated with oil. 4. Place about ⅓ cup of the strawberry mixture at the base of the puff pastry rectangle. Fold the bottom of the pastry up and over the mixture. Continue to fold up toward the top, forming it into a triangle as you go. Once fully wrapped, place it in the air fryer basket and spray the top with oil. 5. Repeat with the remaining pastry and strawberry mixture. Note you'll probably only be able to fit 3 puffs in your air fryer at a time, because you don't want them to overlap. 6. Bake at 160°C for 10 minutes, or until beautifully golden-browned.

To make the sauce: 1. Place the cashews, agave, water, lemon juice and zest, oil, vanilla, and salt in a blender. Process until completely smooth and velvety. (Any leftover sauce will keep nicely in the fridge for up to a week.)

Transfer the strawberry puffs to a plate and drizzle with the creamy lemon sauce. If desired, garnish with sliced strawberries. Enjoy while warm.

Per Serving: Calories 391; Fat 22g; Sodium 270mg; Carbs 45.6g; Fibre 4g; Sugar 24g; Protein 6g

Peach Oat Crumble

Prep Time: 10 minutes | Cook Time: 10 minutes | Serves: 6

65g plain flour

20g quick-cooking oats

4 tablespoons cold salted butter, cubed

¼ teaspoon salt

2 teaspoons ground cinnamon, divided

70g brown sugar, divided

1 (365g) can peaches, drained and rinsed

1. Preheat the air fryer to 175°C. 2. Add flour, oats, butter, salt, 1 teaspoon cinnamon, and 3 tablespoons of brown sugar to a food processor. Pulse them fifteen times until large crumbs form. 3. Place peaches in a suitable round baking dish, and sprinkle with the remaining cinnamon and brown sugar. Stir to coat peaches. 4. Completely cover the peaches with the flour mixture, leaving larger crumbs intact as much as possible, and spritz with cooking spray. 5. Place in the air fryer basket, and cook for 10 minutes until the top is golden brown. 6. Serve warm.

Per Serving: Calories 165; Fat 5.52g; Sodium 142mg; Carbs 28.27g; Fibre 1.9g; Sugar 17.6g; Protein 2.05g

Simple Vanilla Cheesecake

Prep Time: 10 minutes | Cook Time: 20 minutes | Serves: 8

6 full digestive biscuits

2 tablespoons salted butter, melted

300g full-fat cream cheese, softened

100g granulated sugar

2 tablespoons sour cream

1 teaspoon vanilla extract

1 large egg

1. Preheat the air fryer to 150°C. 2. Pulse the biscuits in a food processor fifteen times until finely crushed. Transfer crumbs to a medium bowl. 3. Add butter and mix until the texture is sand-like. Press into a suitable round spring-form pan. 4. Combine cream cheese and sugar, stirring in a large bowl until no lumps remain. Mix in sour cream and vanilla until smooth, then gently mix in egg. 5. Pour batter over crust in pan. Place the pan in the air fryer basket and cook for 20 minutes until top is golden brown. 6. Chill cheesecake in refrigerator at least 4 hours to set before serving.

Per Serving: Calories 190; Fat 10.51g; Sodium 231mg; Carbs 18.76g; Fibre 0.4g; Sugar 11.48g; Protein 5g

Apple-Blueberry Pies

Prep Time: 20 minutes | Cook Time: 10 minutes | Serves: 4

1 medium Granny Smith apple, peeled and finely chopped

60g dried blueberries

1 tablespoon freshly squeezed orange juice

1 tablespoon packed brown sugar

2 teaspoons corn flour

4 sheets frozen puff pastry, thawed

8 teaspoons unsalted butter, melted

8 teaspoons sugar

Nonstick cooking spray, for coating the phyllo dough

1. Combine the apple, blueberries, orange juice, brown sugar, and corn flour in a medium bowl. 2. Place 1 sheet of puff pastry on a work surface with the narrow side facing you, lightly brush with 1 teaspoon of butter and sprinkle with 1 teaspoon of sugar. 3. Fold the puff pastry in half from left to right, and place ¼ of the fruit filling at the bottom of the sheet in the centre. 4. Fold the left side of the sheet over the filling, and lightly spray with cooking spray; fold the right side of the sheet over the filling, and then brush with 1 teaspoon of butter and sprinkle with 1 teaspoon of sugar. 5. Fold the bottom right corner of the pastry up to meet the left side of the pastry sheet to form a triangle. Continue folding the triangles over to enclose the filling, as you would fold a flag. 6. Seal the edge with a bit of water, and lightly spray with cooking spray. 7. Do the same the remaining 3 sheets of the pastry, butter, sugar, and cooking spray, making four pies. 8. Place the pies in the air fryer basket, and then bake them at 205°C for 7 to 9 minutes until golden brown and crisp. 9. Remove the pies and let cool on a wire rack before serving.

Per Serving: Calories 225; Fat 6.88g; Sodium 96mg; Carbs 40.32g; Fibre 3.1g; Sugar 24.71g; Protein 2.37g

Raspberry Streusel Cake

Prep time: 15 minutes | Cook time: 45 minutes | Serves: 6

For the Streusel Topping

2 tablespoons organic sugar

2 tablespoons neutral-flavored oil (sunflower, safflower, or refined coconut)

30g plus 2 tablespoons whole-wheat pastry flour (or gluten-free plain flour)

For the Cake

125g whole-wheat pastry flour

100g organic sugar

1 teaspoon baking powder

1 tablespoon lemon zest

¼ teaspoon sea salt

180ml plus 2 tablespoons unsweetened nondairy milk (plain or vanilla)

2 tablespoons neutral-flavored oil (sunflower, safflower, or refined coconut)

1 teaspoon vanilla

125g fresh raspberries

Cooking oil spray (sunflower, safflower, or refined coconut)

For the Icing

60g icing sugar

1 tablespoon fresh lemon juice

½ teaspoon lemon zest

½ teaspoon vanilla

⅛ teaspoon sea salt

To make the streusel: 1. Stir together the sugar, oil, and flour in a small bowl and place in the refrigerator to firm it up and be crumblier later.

To make the cake: 1. In a medium bowl, place the flour, sugar, baking powder, zest, and salt. Stir very well, preferably with a wire whisk. Add the milk, oil, and vanilla. Stir them together to combine with a rubber spatula or spoon. Gently stir in the raspberries. 2. Preheat the air fryer for 3 minutes. Spray or coat the insides of a 15cm round, 5cm deep baking pan with oil and pour the batter into the pan. 3. Remove the streusel from the fridge and crumble it over the top of the cake batter. Carefully place the cake in the air fryer and bake at 155°C for 45 minutes. A toothpick inserted in the centre shall come out clean (the top should be golden-brown).

To make the icing: 1. Stir together the vanilla, icing sugar, lemon juice and zest, and salt in a small bowl. Let the streusel cake cool for about 5 minutes and then slice into 4 pieces and drizzle each with icing. Serve warm if possible. Keep the leftovers in an airtight bowl or resealable bag in your fridge for several days as needed.

Per Serving: Calories 311; Fat 10g; Sodium 170mg; Carbs 52g; Fibre 4g; Sugar 29.6g; Protein 5g

Almond-Shortbread Cookies

Prep Time: 10 minutes | Cook Time: 1 hour 10 minutes | Serves: 8

115g salted butter, softened
50g granulated sugar
1 teaspoon almond extract
1 teaspoon vanilla extract
250g plain flour

1. Mix cream butter, sugar, and extracts in a large bowl, then gradually add flour, mixing until well combined. 2. Roll dough into a 30 x 5cm log and wrap in plastic. Chill the dough in refrigerator for at least 1 hour. 3. Preheat the air fryer to 150°C. 4. Slice dough into ½cm thick cookies. Place in the air fryer basket 5cm apart, working in batches as needed, and cook for 10 minutes until the edges start to brown. 5. Let cool completely before serving.
Per Serving: Calories 196; Fat 8.04g; Sodium 63mg; Carbs 27.07g; Fibre 0.9g; Sugar 3.22g; Protein 3.34g

Delightful Apple Crisp

Prep time: 10 minutes | Cook time: 30 minutes | Serves: 4

For the Topping
2 tablespoons coconut oil
30g plus 2 tablespoons whole-wheat pastry flour (or gluten-free
plain flour)
50g coconut sugar
⅛ teaspoon sea salt
For the Filling
220g finely chopped (or thinly sliced) apples (no need to peel)
3 tablespoons water
½ tablespoon lemon juice
¾ teaspoon cinnamon

To make the topping: 1. In a bowl, combine the oil, flour, sugar, and salt. Mix the ingredients together thoroughly, either with your hands or a spoon. The mixture should be crumbly; if it's not, place it in the fridge until it solidifies a bit.
To make the filling: 1. In a 15cm round, 5cm-deep baking pan, stir the apples with the water, lemon juice, and cinnamon until well combined. 2. Crumble the chilled topping over the apples. Bake them in your air fryer at 160°C for 30 minutes, or until the chopped apples are tender and the crumbles are crunchy and nicely browned.
Serve immediately on its own or topped with nondairy milk, vegan ice cream, or nondairy whipped cream.
Per Serving: Calories 146; Fat 7g; Sodium 79mg; Carbs 21g; Fibre 2g; Sugar 12.7g; Protein 1g

Apple Cinnamon Puffs

Prep time: 20 minutes | Cook time: 10 minutes | Serves: 6

For the Filling
2 medium apples, cored and finely diced (no need to peel)
2 teaspoons cinnamon
2 tablespoons coconut sugar
⅛ teaspoon sea salt
For the Vanilla Caramel Sauce
15cm segment of a vanilla bean
160g plus 1 tablespoon maple syrup
60ml refined coconut oil (or
Cooking oil spray (sunflower, safflower, or refined coconut)
6 large (33cm x 43cm) sheets of puff pastry, thawed (see Ingredient Tip)

vegan margarine), plus 2 tablespoons
50g coconut sugar
½ teaspoon sea salt

To make the filling: 1. Combine the apples, cinnamon, coconut sugar, and salt in a medium bowl and set aside. 2. Spray an air fryer basket with oil and set aside. Gently unwrap the pastry dough. Remove 6 sheets and carefully set them aside. 3. Wrap the remaining pastry in airtight plastic wrap and place back in the fridge.
To assemble the puffs: 1. Remove 1 large sheet of pastry and place on a clean, dry surface. Spray with the oil. Fold it into thirds (the long way, so that you form a long, skinny rectangle). As you go, spray each portion of dry pastry, so the exposed pastry continually gets lightly coated with oil—this will give you a flakier (vs. dry) result. 2. Place ⅓ cup of the apple mixture at the base of the puff pastry rectangle. Fold the bottom of the pastry up and over the mixture. Continue to fold up toward the top, forming it into a triangle as you go. Once you have an apple-filled triangle, place it in the air fryer basket and spray the top with oil. 3. Repeat the steps with the remaining pastry and apple mixture. Note: You'll probably only be able to fit 3 puffs in your air fryer at a time, because you don't want them to overlap. If you don't wish to make a second batch right now, store the pastry wrapped, uncooked puffs in an air-proof container in your fridge and

air-fry them within a day or two. 4. Bake at 160°C for 10 minutes, or until very golden-browned.
To make the sauce: 1. Cut lengthwise all the way down the vanilla bean with a sharp knife and pry it open. Scrape out the insides with a table knife and place in a small pot. 2. Add the maple syrup, oil, coconut sugar, and salt to the pot and set to medium-low heat, stirring very well to combine. After bringing the sauce to a boil, reduce the heat to low and simmer gently for 3 to 5 minutes to slightly thickened the sauce.
Transfer the apple puffs to a plate and top with the caramel sauce. Enjoy while warm.
Per Serving: Calories 304; Fat 13g; Sodium 344mg; Carbs 46g; Fibre 2g; Sugar 31g; Protein 1.6g

Chocolate Cheesecake

Prep Time: 10 minutes | Cook Time: 4 hours 20 minutes | Serves: 8

300g full-fat cream cheese, softened
100g granulated sugar
2 tablespoons sour cream
2 tablespoons cocoa powder
85g semisweet chocolate chips, melted
1 teaspoon vanilla extract
1 large egg

1. Preheat the air fryer to 150°C. Line a suitable round cake pan with parchment paper, and spray with cooking spray. 2. Combine cream cheese and sugar in a large bowl until no lumps remain. 3. Mix in sour cream, cocoa powder, chocolate chips, and vanilla until well combined and smooth. Stir in egg. Pour into prepared pan. 4. Place the pan in the air fryer basket, and cook the food for 20 minutes until the top of cheesecake is firm. 5. Chill cheesecake in refrigerator at least 4 hours to set before serving.
Per Serving: Calories 179; Fat 10.83g; Sodium 166mg; Carbs 17.71g; Fibre 1g; Sugar 14.6g; Protein 4.93g

Cheese Pound Cake

Prep Time: 10 minutes | Cook Time: 25 minutes | Serves: 8

185g plain flour
1 teaspoon baking powder
115g salted butter, melted
100g full-fat cream cheese,
softened
200g granulated sugar
2 teaspoons vanilla extract
3 large eggs

1. Preheat the air fryer to 150°C. Spray a suitable round cake pan with cooking spray. 2. Mix flour and baking powder in a large bowl. 3. In a separate large bowl, mix butter, cream cheese, sugar, and vanilla. 4. Stir wet ingredients into dry ingredients, and add eggs one at a time, making sure each egg is fully incorporated before adding the next. 5. Pour batter into the prepared pan, and then place the pan in the air fryer basket. 6. Cook the cake for 25 minutes until a toothpick inserted into the centre comes out clean. If cake begins to brown too quickly, cover pan with foil and cut two slits in the top of foil to encourage heat circulation. Be sure to tuck foil under the bottom of the pan to ensure the air fryer fan does not blow it off. 7. Allow cake to cool completely before serving.
Per Serving: Calories 261; Fat 11.84g; Sodium 141mg; Carbs 32.08g; Fibre 0.6g; Sugar 13.32g; Protein 5.97g

Double-Layer Chocolate-Nut Brownies

Prep time: 10 minutes | Cook time: 12 minutes | Serves: 9

65g gluten-free plain flour
2 tablespoons unsweetened cocoa
65g granulated sugar
¼ teaspoon baking soda
3 tablespoons unsalted butter, melted
1 large egg
⅛ teaspoon salt
85g semi-sweet chocolate chips
30g chopped pecans
1 tablespoon icing sugar

1. Combine flour, cocoa, sugar, baking soda, and butter in a medium bowl. Stir in egg and salt. Add chocolate chips and chopped pecans, stirring to combine. 2. Preheat air fryer at 175°C for 3 minutes. 3. Press brownie mixture into a 18cm square cake barrel lightly greased with preferred cooking oil. 4. Place cake barrel in the air fryer basket. Cook for 12 minutes. 5. Remove cake barrel from air fryer and let cool for 10 minutes. Slice into nine brownies and garnish with icing sugar.
Per Serving: Calories 131; Fat 7g; Sodium 83mg; Carbs 15g; Fibre 1g; Sugar 5g; Protein 2g

Crusted Lemon Bars

Prep time: 15 minutes | Cook time: 25 minutes | Serves: 6

For the Crust
90g whole-wheat pastry flour
2 tablespoons icing sugar

60ml refined coconut oil, melted

For the Filling
Cooking oil spray
100g organic sugar
1 packed tablespoon lemon zest
1¾ teaspoons corn flour
⅛ teaspoon sea salt

60ml fresh lemon juice
60g unsweetened, plain applesauce
¾ teaspoon baking powder

To make the crust: 1. Stir the icing sugar, flour, and oil together in a small bowl just until well combined. Place the bowl in your fridge.
To make the filling: 1. Add the lemon zest and juice, sugar, salt, applesauce, corn flour, and baking powder in a medium bowl. Stir well.
To assemble the bars: 1. Lightly spray a 15cm round, 5cm-deep baking pan with oil. Then transfer the crust mixture to the bottom of the pan and press gently to form a crust. Place the pan inside your air fryer and bake at 175°C for 5 minutes, or until it becomes slightly firm to the touch. 2. Then spread the lemon filling over the crust. Bake them in your air fryer at 175°C for about 18 to 20 minutes, or until the top is nicely browned. Remove and allow them to cool in the fridge for an hour or more in the fridge. Once firm and cooled, cut them into pieces and serve.
Per Serving: Calories 183; Fat 9.5g; Sodium 53mg; Carbs 25g; Fibre 2g; Sugar 12g; Protein 2g

Caramel Apples

Prep Time: 10 minutes | Cook Time: 16 minutes | Serves: 4

4 medium Pink Lady apples
115g salted butter
8 soft caramel chews

40g rolled oats
50g granulated sugar
1 teaspoon ground cinnamon

1. Preheat the air fryer to 175°C. 2. Carefully core apples by cutting a large, deep square into the centre from the top down. Scoop out seeds and insides, leaving about one-fourth of apple intact at the bottom. 3. Add the butter to a medium microwave-safe bowl, and microwave for 30 seconds; add caramels and microwave 15 seconds more. Stir quickly to finish melting caramels into butter. 4. Add oats, sugar, and cinnamon to caramel mixture, mix them until well combined and crumbly. 5. Scoop mixture into cored apples. Place them in the air fryer basket, and cook for 15 minutes until apples are wrinkled and softened. 6. Serve warm.
Per Serving: Calories 296; Fat 16.47g; Sodium 127mg; Carbs 43.48g; Fibre 6.6g; Sugar 25.22g; Protein 2.69g

Mayonnaise Chocolate Cake

Prep Time: 10 minutes | Cook Time: 25 minutes | Serves: 6

125g plain flour
100g granulated sugar
1 teaspoon baking powder
20g cocoa powder

240g mayonnaise
1 teaspoon vanilla extract
120ml whole milk

1. Preheat the air fryer to 150°C. Spray a suitable round cake pan with cooking spray. 2. Combine flour, sugar, baking powder, and cocoa powder in a large bowl; stir in mayonnaise, vanilla, and milk until thick but pourable. 3. Pour batter into prepared cake pan, and then place the pan in the air fryer basket. 4. Cook the cake for 25 minutes until a toothpick inserted into the centre comes out clean. 5. Serve warm.
Per Serving: Calories 266; Fat 14.02g; Sodium 320mg; Carbs 30.63g; Fibre 2.1g; Sugar 11.31g; Protein 5.79g

Cinnamon Apple-Pecan Jars

Prep time: 15 minutes| Cook time: 24 minutes| Serves: 6

For Apple Filling
3 large diced, peeled, seeded Granny Smith apples
1 tablespoon lemon juice
1 tablespoon gluten-free plain flour

2 tablespoons light brown sugar
½ teaspoon ground cinnamon
1 tablespoon butter, melted
⅛ teaspoon salt
6 (100g) glass jelly jars

For Crumble Topping
2 tablespoons gluten-free plain flour
25g old-fashioned oats
30g chopped pecans
4 teaspoons light brown sugar

¼ teaspoon ground cinnamon
⅛ teaspoon ground nutmeg
2 tablespoons butter, melted
⅛ teaspoon salt

To make Apple Filling: 1. Place diced apples in a medium bowl and toss with lemon juice. Add remaining filling ingredients and toss. 2. Heat your air fryer at 175°C for 3 minutes in advance. 3. Distribute apple mixture among jelly jars. Place three jars in the air fryer basket. Cook for 7 minutes. Repeat with remaining jars.
To make Crumble Topping: 1. While apple mixture is cooking, combine Crumble Topping ingredients in a medium bowl. Spoon Crumble Topping over cooked apples. Bake for an additional 5 minutes in batches of three jars. Let jars cool for 10 minutes before covering. Then refrigerate them until ready to serve, up to 4 days.
Per Serving: Calories 468; Fat 9g; Sodium 186mg; Carbs 101g; Fibre 4g; Sugar 70g; Protein 2g

Awesome Chocolate Cheesecake

Prep time: 10 minutes | Cook time: 24 minutes | Serves: 6

For Crust
80g quick-cooking oats
1 tablespoon peanut butter powder

1 tablespoon granulated sugar
3 tablespoons butter, melted

For Cheesecake
300g cream cheese, room temperature
2 tablespoons sour cream
2 large eggs
20g unsweetened cocoa powder

105g light brown sugar
1 teaspoon vanilla extract
⅛ teaspoon salt
110g peanut butter chips

To make Crust: 1. Pulse oats and peanut butter powder in a food processor until they have a powdered consistency. Pour into a small bowl and add sugar and melted butter. 2. Combine with a fork until butter is well distributed. Press mixture into a 18cm springform pan lightly greased with preferred cooking oil.
To make Cheesecake: 1. Preheat air fryer at 205°C for 3 minutes. 2. Combine cream cheese, sour cream, eggs, cocoa, brown sugar, vanilla, and salt in a large bowl. Spoon over crust. Cover with aluminum foil. 3. Place the springform pan in the air fryer basket and cook for 18 minutes. Remove aluminum foil and cook for an additional 6 minutes. 4. Remove cheesecake from air fryer. Cheesecake will be a little jiggly in centre. Sprinkle with peanut butter chips, cover, and refrigerate for at least 2 hours to allow it to set. Once set, release side pan and serve.
Per Serving: Calories 450; Fat 31g; Sodium 850mg; Carbs 36g; Fibre 2g; Sugar 27g; Protein 10g

Tasty Banana Nut Cake

Prep Time: 15 minutes | Cook Time: 25 minutes | Serves: 6

95g blanched finely ground almond flour
10g powdered sweetener
2 tablespoons ground golden flaxseed
2 teaspoons baking powder
½ teaspoon ground cinnamon

55g unsalted butter, melted
2½ teaspoons banana extract
1 teaspoon vanilla extract
55g full-fat sour cream
2 large eggs
30g chopped walnuts

1. Mix almond flour, sweetener, flaxseed, baking powder, and cinnamon in a large bowl. 2. Stir in butter, banana extract, vanilla extract, and sour cream. 3. Add the 2 eggs to the mixture and gently stir until fully combined. Stir in the walnuts. 4. Pour into 15cm nonstick cake pan and place into the air fryer basket. 5. Adjust the temperature to 150°C and set the timer for 25 minutes. 6. Cake will be golden and a toothpick inserted in centre will come out clean when fully cooked. Allow to fully cool to avoid crumbling.
Per Serving: Calories 276; Fat 23.92g; Sodium 27mg; Carbs 12.87g; Fibre 5.9g; Sugar 1.96g; Protein 9.15g

Crumble-Topped Lemony Pear Jars

Prep time: 15 minutes| Cook time: 24 minutes| Serves: 6

For Pear Filling

4 large diced, peeled, seeded pears	2 tablespoons dark brown sugar
1 tablespoon lemon juice	½ teaspoon ground ginger
1 tablespoon gluten-free plain flour	1 tablespoon butter, melted
	⅛ teaspoon salt
	6 (100g) glass jelly jars

For Crumble Topping

2 tablespoons gluten-free plain flour	4 teaspoons light brown sugar
6 gluten-free gingersnap cookies	⅛ teaspoon ground nutmeg
30g chopped pecans	2 tablespoons butter, melted
	⅛ teaspoon salt

To make Pear Filling: 1. Place pears in a medium bowl and toss with lemon juice. Add remaining filling ingredients and toss. 2. Heat your air fryer at 175°C for 3 minutes in advance. Distribute pear mixture among jelly jars. 3. Place three jars in the air fryer basket. Cook for 7 minutes. Set aside and repeat with remaining jars.
To make Crumble Topping: 1. While jars are cooking, pulse Crumble Topping ingredients together in a food processor until crumbly and a little chunky.
Spoon topping over cooked pear mixture. Place three jars back in the air fryer and bake for an additional 5 minutes. Repeat with remaining jars. Let jars cool for 15 minutes before covering. Refrigerate until ready to serve, up to four days.
Per Serving: Calories 585; Fat 12g; Sodium 232mg; Carbs 124g; Fibre 4g; Sugar 89g; Protein 2g

Pecan Chocolate Chip Bars

Prep time: 10 minutes| Cook time: 20 minutes| Serves: 6

60g gluten-free crispy rice cereal	chips
30g chopped pecans	2 tablespoons semi-sweet chocolate chips
165g light corn syrup	
50g light brown sugar	2 tablespoons butter, melted
85g creamy peanut butter	½ teaspoon vanilla extract
2 tablespoons chocolate toffee	⅛ teaspoon salt

1. Combine all ingredients in a medium bowl. 2. Heat your air fryer at 175°C for 3 minutes in advance. 3. Press bar mixture into a 18cm square cake barrel lightly greased with preferred cooking oil. Cover with aluminum foil. 4. Place the pan in air fryer basket and cook for 15 minutes. Remove foil and cook an additional 5 minutes. 5. Remove the pan from your air fryer and let cool completely, for approximately 15 minutes, to allow to set. Once cooled, flip over on a plate and slice into six bars.
Per Serving: Calories 279; Fat 11g; Sodium 373mg; Carbs 46g; Fibre 1g; Sugar 38g; Protein 2.4g

Chocolate Chip Cookies with Pecans

Prep time: 10 minutes| Cook time: 20 minutes| Serves: 2

65g gluten-free plain flour	2 large eggs
⅛ teaspoon baking soda	40g semi-sweet chocolate chips
55g butter, melted	30g chopped pecans
50g light brown sugar	½ teaspoon vanilla extract
2 tablespoons granulated sugar	⅛ teaspoon salt

1. Preheat your air fryer at 175°C for 3 minutes. 2. Combine all ingredients in a medium bowl. Press half of cookie mixture onto a pizza pan lightly greased with preferred cooking oil. 3. Place the pan in the air fryer basket and cook for 10 minutes. 4. Remove the pan from air fryer and let it cool completely, about 10 minutes, to allow to set. Once cooled, flip over on a plate and repeat with remaining dough. Serve.
Per Serving: Calories 689; Fat 42g; Sodium 502mg; Carbs 70g; Fibre 3g; Sugar 43g; Protein 11.5g

Honey Tortilla Sopapillas

Prep time: 5 minutes | Cook time: 4 minutes | Serves: 8

2 tablespoons granulated sugar	tortillas, quartered
½ teaspoon ground cinnamon	2 tablespoons butter, melted
⅛ teaspoon salt	4 teaspoons honey
8 (15cm) gluten-free flour	1 tablespoon powdered sugar

1. Heat your air fryer at 205°C for 5 minutes in advance. 2. In a small bowl, combine sugar, cinnamon, and salt. Set aside. 3. Brush tortilla quarters with melted butter. Sprinkle sugar mixture over brushed tortillas. 4. Add prepared tortillas to ungreased air fryer basket. Cook for 2 minutes. Toss tortillas, then cook for an additional 2 minutes. 5. Transfer sopapillas to a large plate. Let cool for 5 minutes to allow to harden. 6. Drizzle hardened sopapillas with honey and sprinkle with powdered sugar. Serve.
Per Serving: Calories 190; Fat 5.6g; Sodium 395mg; Carbs 31g; Fibre 1g; Sugar 8.6g; Protein 4g

Vanilla Pancake Cake

Prep Time: 10 minutes | Cook Time: 7 minutes | Serves: 4

50g blanched finely ground almond flour	softened
	1 large egg
5g powdered sweetener	½ teaspoon unflavoured gelatin
½ teaspoon baking powder	½ teaspoon vanilla extract
2 tablespoons unsalted butter,	½ teaspoon ground cinnamon

1. Mix almond flour, sweetener, and baking powder in a large bowl. Add butter, egg, gelatin, vanilla, and cinnamon. Pour into 15cm round baking pan. 2. Place pan into the air fryer basket. 3. Adjust the temperature to 150°C and set the timer for 7 minutes. 4. When the cake is completely cooked, a toothpick will come out clean. Cut cake into four and serve.
Per Serving: Calories 171; Fat 15.22g; Sodium 10mg; Carbs 7.39g; Fibre 3.6g; Sugar 1.13g; Protein 5.78g

Simple Pumpkin Spice Muffins

Prep Time: 10 minutes | Cook Time: 15 minutes | Serves: 6

95g blanched finely ground almond flour	65g pure pumpkin purée
	½ teaspoon ground cinnamon
10g sweetener	¼ teaspoon ground nutmeg
½ teaspoon baking powder	1 teaspoon vanilla extract
55g unsalted butter, softened	2 large eggs

1. Mix almond flour, sweetener, baking powder, butter, pumpkin purée, cinnamon, nutmeg, and vanilla in a large bowl. 2. Gently stir in eggs. 3. Evenly pour the batter into six silicone muffin cups. Place muffin cups into the air fryer basket, working in batches if necessary. 4. Adjust the temperature to 150°C and set the timer for 15 minutes. 5. When completely cooked, a toothpick inserted in centre will come out mostly clean. 6. Serve warm.
Per Serving: Calories 295; Fat 25.61g; Sodium 344mg; Carbs 6.8g; Fibre 2.9g; Sugar 1.31g; Protein 13.11g

Irresistible Raspberry Pavlova with Orange Cream

Prep Time: 15 minutes | Cook Time: 90 minutes | Serves: 2

For Pavlova

2 large egg whites	½ teaspoon pulp-free orange juice
¼ teaspoon cream of tartar	½ teaspoon vanilla extract
10g powdered sweetener	

For Topping

80g heavy whipping cream	2 tablespoons powdered sweetener
1 teaspoon fresh orange juice	
¼ teaspoon orange zest	125g fresh raspberries

1. Cut a piece of parchment paper to the size of a grill pan. Draw a 15cm circle on paper. Flip paper, ink side down, onto grill pan. 2. To make Pavlova: In a medium metal bowl, beat egg whites with a hand held blender on high. Add cream of tartar, then add sweetener, 1 tablespoon at a time, until stiff peaks form. Add orange juice and vanilla and blend. 3. Preheat air fryer at 105°C for 5 minutes. 4. Spoon or pipe egg whites over parchment paper circle, creating higher edges around perimeter, like a pie crust. There should be a divot in the centre. 5. Add grill pan to air fryer and cook 60 minutes. 6. Turn off heat, and let pavlova sit in air fryer an additional 30 minutes. 7. Remove grill pan from air fryer and gently peel off parchment paper from bottom of pavlova. Transfer to a large plate. 8. To make Topping: Whisk together whipping cream, orange juice, orange zest, and sweetener until creamy in a bowl. 9. Fill pavlova with whipped cream and top with raspberries, and enjoy.
Per Serving: Calories 220; Fat 15.47g; Sodium 74mg; Carbs 22.27g; Fibre8.8g; Sugar 4.76g; Protein9.61g

Classic Shortbread Sticks

Prep Time: 10 minutes | Cook Time: 10 minutes | Serves: 4

Oil, for spraying
250g self-rising flour
170g unsalted butter, cubed
40g icing sugar

1. Line the air fryer basket with parchment and sprinkle with oil. 2. Mix together the flour, butter, and icing sugar with your hands until it resembles thick bread crumbs in a bowl. Continue to knead until the mixture forms a dough ball. 3. On a work surface, roll out the dough until it is ½ to 1cm thick. 4. Cut the dough into 8 to 10cm long sticks. 5. Place the sticks in the air fryer basket. 6. Cook the sticks at 360 °F/ 180°C for 10 minutes. If you want the shortbread to be more golden brown, cook for 2 more minutes. Let cool completely on the parchment before serving.
Per Serving: Calories 506; Fat 24.87g; Sodium 761mg; Carbs 63.1g; Fibre 1.7g; Sugar 16.52g; Protein 7.57g

Great Chocolate-Stuffed Wontons

Prep Time: 10 minutes | Cook Time: 10 minutes | Serves: 12

Oil, for spraying
200g cream cheese
95g granulated sugar
20g unsweetened cocoa powder
1 teaspoon almond extract
24 wonton wrappers
15g icing sugar

1. Line the air fryer basket with parchment and sprinkle with oil. 2. Mix together the cream cheese, granulated sugar, cocoa powder, and almond extract until creamy in a bowl. 3. Lay the wonton wrappers on a work surface and place 1 tablespoon of the chocolate filling in the centre of each one. 4. Fill a small bowl with water. Dip your finger in the water and moisten the outer edges of each wrapper. Fold the wonton in half, corner to corner, and pinch the edges together to seal. 5. Place the wontons in the air fryer basket and spray with oil. 6. Cook at 175°C for 5 minutes, shake, spray with oil, and cook for 5 more minutes. 7. Dust with the icing sugar before serving.
Per Serving: Calories 271; Fat 6.65g; Sodium 449mg; Carbs 45.02g; Fibre 1.7g; Sugar 6.81g; Protein 7.96g

Fancy Chocolate Lava Cakes

Prep Time: 7 minutes | Cook Time: 12 minutes | Serves: 4

Oil, for greasing
110g semisweet chocolate chips
8 tablespoons unsalted butter, cubed
60g icing sugar
2 large eggs plus 2 large egg
yolks, at room temperature
1 teaspoon vanilla extract
6 tablespoons plain flour
4 scoops vanilla ice cream, for serving
Chocolate syrup, for serving

1. Preheat the air fryer to 190°C. Grease 4 ramekins and set aside. 2. In a microwave-safe bowl, combine the chocolate chips and butter, and microwave on high for 30 to 45 seconds. 3. Add the icing sugar, eggs, egg yolks, and vanilla and whisk to combine. Fold in the flour. 4. Divide the batter evenly among the ramekins and place them into the air fryer. 5. Cook for 10 to 12 minutes. 6. Let stand for 5 minutes. Invert the ramekins onto individual plates, top with ice cream and a drizzle of chocolate syrup, then serve.
Per Serving: Calories 616; Fat 29.86g; Sodium 127 mg; Carbs 86.94g; Fibre 2.3g; Sugar 57.8g; Protein7.91g

Perfect Overload Dessert Pizza

Prep Time: 8 minutes | Cook Time: 13 minutes | Serves: 4

Oil, for greasing
4 tablespoons unsalted butter, at room temperature
50g granulated sugar
55g packed light brown sugar
½ large egg
½ teaspoon vanilla extract
95g plain flour
¼ teaspoon baking soda
⅛ teaspoon salt
85g semisweet chocolate chips
120g chopped chocolate bars and candies

1. Turn on the air fryer and preheat it to 175°C. Grease a 15 or 18cm round metal cake pan, depending on the size of your air fryer. 2. In a large bowl, beat the butter, granulated sugar, and brown sugar with an electric mixer until creamy. Add the egg and vanilla and beat till combined. 3. Add the flour, baking soda, and salt and beat until smooth. Fold in the chocolate chips. 4. Press the dough into the prepared pan. 5. Cook the dough for 9 to 11 minutes until the edges are lightly browned; top with the chopped candy, and cook for 1 to 2 minutes more until lightly melted. 6. Serve and enjoy.
Per Serving: Calories 379; Fat 19.87g; Sodium 231mg; Carbs 47.76g; Fibre 3.4g; Sugar 13.12g; Protein 6g

Quick and Easy Chocolate Mug Cake

Prep Time: 2 minutes | Cook Time: 13 minutes | Serve: 1

Oil, for spraying
6 tablespoons chocolate cake mix
2 tablespoons unsweetened
applesauce
1 tablespoon water

1. Line the air fryer basket with parchment and sprinkle with oil. 2. Whisk together the cake mix, applesauce, and water until smooth in a mug. 3. Place the mug in the air fryer basket. 4. Cook the cake at 175°C for 12 to 13 minutes. 5. Let the cakes cool for a few minutes before serving.
Per Serving: Calories 137; Fat 7.76g; Sodium 59 mg; Carbs 15.32g; Fibre 0.7g; Sugar 2.86g; Protein 3.28g

Flavourful Chocolate Surprise Cookies

Prep Time: 15 minutes | Cook Time: 8 minutes | Serves: 5

1 tablespoon ground flaxseed
3 tablespoons water
1 teaspoon vanilla extract
1 teaspoon apple cider vinegar
85g natural peanut butter
110g honey
20g cacao powder
¼ teaspoon baking soda

1. Combine the flaxseed, water, vanilla, and apple cider vinegar in a bowl. Let sit for 5 minutes. 2. Add the peanut butter and honey to the bowl, and mix again. Sprinkle in the cacao powder and baking soda and mix until well combined. The mixture should be quite thick. 3. Line the air fryer basket or rack with parchment paper. Scoop the dough into 2-tablespoon balls and place them in the air fryer, leaving some space between each. 4. Bake the dough at 150°C for 8 minutes. 5. Use a fork to flatten each cookie slightly while they're still hot. 6. Let the cookies cool completely before taking them off the parchment paper, as they will still firm and crisp up a bit as they cool.
Per Serving: Calories 167; Fat 7.96g; Sodium 171mg; Carbs 21.08g; Fibre 2.9g; Sugar 11.86g; Protein 6.09g

Butter Lemon Cheesecake

Prep time: 10 minutes | Cook time: 22 minutes | Serves: 6

For Crust
40g cornflakes cereal
2 tablespoons granulated sugar
4 tablespoons butter, melted
For Cheesecake
300g cream cheese, room temperature
2 tablespoons sour cream
2 large eggs
100g granulated sugar
1 tablespoon lemon zest
1 tablespoon fresh lemon juice
1 teaspoon vanilla extract
⅛ teaspoon salt
For Raspberry Sauce
185g fresh raspberries
2 tablespoons lemon juice
100g granulated sugar

To make Crust: 1. Pulse together cornflakes, sugar, and butter in a food processor. Press mixture into a 18cm springform pan lightly greased with preferred cooking oil. 2. Preheat your air fryer at 205°C for 3 minutes.
To make Cheesecake: 1. Combine cream cheese, sour cream, eggs, sugar, lemon zest, lemon juice, vanilla, and salt in a large bowl. Spoon into crust. Cover with aluminum foil. 2. Place the springform pan in the air fryer basket and cook for 16 minutes. Remove aluminum foil and cook for an additional 6 minutes.
To make Raspberry Sauce: 1. While cheesecake is baking, add Raspberry Sauce ingredients to a small saucepan over medium heat and cook together for 5 minutes. 2. Using the back of spoon, smoosh raspberries against side of saucepan while cooking. After berries are smooshed and sauce has thickened, pour through a sieve to filter out seeds. Refrigerate covered until ready to use.
Remove cheesecake from air fryer. Cheesecake will be a little jiggly in centre. Cover and refrigerate for at least 2 hours to allow it to set. Once set, release side pan and serve with Raspberry Sauce poured over slices.
Per Serving: Calories 491; Fat 26g; Sodium 389mg; Carbs 59.6g; Fibre 3g; Sugar 51g; Protein 8g

Delightful Almond Delights

Prep Time: 10 minutes | Cook Time: 18 minutes | Serves: 4

1 ripe banana
1 tablespoon almond extract
½ teaspoon ground cinnamon
2 tablespoons coconut sugar

95g almond flour
¼ teaspoon baking soda
8 raw almonds

1. Mash the banana in a medium bowl; add the almond extract, cinnamon, and coconut sugar and mix until well combined. Add the almond flour and baking soda to the bowl and mix again. 2. Line the air fryer basket or rack with parchment paper. Divide the dough into 8 equal balls and flatten each ball to 1cm thick on the parchment paper. Press 1 almond into the centre of each cookie. 3. Bake the cookies at 150°C for 12 minutes. Then, flip the cookies over and bake for an additional 6 minutes. 4. Let cool slightly before enjoying.
Per Serving: Calories 60; Fat 1.6g; Sodium 83mg; Carbs 11.64g; Fibre 1.3g; Sugar 7.66g; Protein 0.97g

Delicious Candied Walnuts

Prep Time: 5 minutes | Cook Time: 16 minutes | Serves: 6

1 large egg white, beaten
¼ teaspoon vanilla extract
15g brown sugar sweetener

¼ teaspoon ground cinnamon
⅛ teaspoon salt
350g walnut halves

1. Preheat air fryer at 135°C for 3 minutes. Lightly grease the air fryer basket with olive oil. 2. Whisk egg white together with vanilla, brown sugar, cinnamon, and salt in a bowl. Add walnuts and toss until well coated. 3. Place walnuts in air fryer basket, and cook them for 16 minutes, stirring them halfway through. 4. Let cool 10 minutes after cooking, then store in an airtight container at room temperature.
Per Serving: Calories 298; Fat 26.09g; Sodium 62mg; Carbs 13.96g; Fibre 2.7g; Sugar 9.26g; Protein 6.7g

Luscious "Grilled" Watermelon

Prep Time: 10 minutes | Cook Time: 4 minutes | Serves: 4

2 teaspoons olive oil
2 tablespoons fresh orange juice
1 teaspoon orange zest
1 tablespoon granular sweetener

⅛ teaspoon salt
450g 2.5-cm watermelon cubes
1 tablespoon chopped fresh mint

1. Preheat the air fryer at 190°C for 3 minutes. 2. Whisk together olive oil, orange juice, orange zest, sweetener, and salt in a bowl. Toss in watermelon cubes and let marinate 10 minutes. 3. Add watermelon mixture to the air fryer basket, and then cook for 4 minutes, tossing halfway through. 4. Serve warm or at room temperature, garnished with fresh mint.
Per Serving: Calories 73; Fat 2.5g; Sodium 79mg; Carbs 13.32g; Fibre 0.7g; Sugar 10.92g; Protein 1.02g

Sweet Blueberries Jubilee

Prep Time: 10 minutes | Cook Time: 9 minutes | Serves: 4

2 tablespoons butter, melted
5g granular sweetener
2 teaspoons cream of tartar
1 tablespoon fresh orange juice

½ teaspoon orange zest
⅛ teaspoon ground cinnamon
⅛ teaspoon salt
295g fresh blueberries

1. Preheat air fryer at 175°C for 3 minutes. 2. Whisk together butter, sweetener, cream of tartar, orange juice, orange zest, cinnamon, and salt in a bowl. Toss in blueberries. Pour into an ungreased cake barrel. 3. Place cake barrel in air fryer basket, and cook for 9 minutes, stirring every 3 minutes. 4. Enjoy warmed or at room temperature.
Per Serving: Calories 112; Fat 4.59g; Sodium 82mg; Carbs 18.49g; Fibre 1.8g; Sugar 14.91g; Protein 0.889g

Gorgeous Marble Cheesecake

Prep Time: 10 minutes | Cook Time: 20 minutes | Serves: 8

60g digestive biscuit crumbs
3 tablespoons butter, at room temperature
1½ (200g) packages cream cheese, at room temperature

55g sugar
2 eggs, beaten
1 tablespoon plain flour
1 teaspoon vanilla extract
75g chocolate syrup

1. Stir the biscuit crumbs and butter in a bowl. Press the crust into the bottom of a 15-by-5-cm round baking pan and freeze to set while you prepare the filling. 2. Stir together the cream cheese and sugar in a bowl until mixed well. 3. One at a time, beat in the eggs. Add the flour and vanilla and stir to combine. 4. Transfer ⅔ cup of filling to a small bowl and stir in the chocolate syrup until combined. 5. Insert the crisper plate into the air fryer basket, and preheat the air fryer at 160°C for 3 minutes on Bake mode. 6. Pour the vanilla filling into the pan with the crust. Drop the chocolate filling over the vanilla filling by the spoonful. With a clean butter knife stir the fillings in a zigzag pattern to marbleize them. Do not let the knife touch the crust. 7. Once the unit is preheated, place the pan into the air fryer basket. 8. Bake the food at 160°C for 20 minutes. 9. When the cooking is done, the cheesecake should be just set. Cool the dish on a wire rack for 1 hour. Refrigerate the cheesecake until firm before slicing.
Per Serving: Calories 214; Fat 15.62g; Sodium 206mg; Carbs 13.79g; Fibre 0.3g; Sugar 10.44g; Protein 4.84mg

Delicious Pumpkin Mug Cake

Prep Time: 5 minutes | Cook Time: 25 minutes | Serve: 1

1 large egg
1 tablespoon coconut flour
1 tablespoon almond flour
2 tablespoons heavy whipping cream
2 tablespoons granular sweetener

2 teaspoons pumpkin pie spice
¼ teaspoon maple extract
¼ teaspoon baking powder
2 tablespoons chopped walnuts
⅛ teaspoon salt

1. Preheat air fryer at 150°C for 3 minutes. 2. Whisk egg together with remaining ingredients in a bowl. 3. Pour batter into a 10cm ramekin greased with cooking spray. 4. Place ramekin in air fryer basket and cook for 25 minutes. 5. Remove ramekin from air fryer basket and let sit for 5 minutes.
Per Serving: Calories 366; Fat 31.66g; Sodium 829mg; Carbs 9.07g; Fibre 1.9g; Sugar 2.78g; Protein 15.5g

Fresh and Bright Orange Cheesecake

Prep Time: 10 minutes | Cook Time: 19 minutes | Serves: 8

300g cream cheese, at room temperature
2 tablespoons sour cream
2 large eggs
10g granular sweetener

1 tablespoon fresh orange zest
1 tablespoon fresh orange juice
1 teaspoon vanilla extract
⅛ teaspoon salt

1. In a medium bowl, combine cream cheese, sour cream, eggs, sweetener, orange zest, orange juice, vanilla, and salt until smooth. Spoon into an ungreased 23cm spring-form pan. Cover with aluminum foil. 2. Preheat air fryer at 205°C for 3 minutes. 3. Place spring-form pan into air fryer basket and cook 14 minutes. 4. Reduce the cooking temperature to 175°C, remove aluminum foil, and cook an additional 5 minutes. 5. The cheesecake will be a little jiggly in the centre, cover it and refrigerate a minimum of 2 hours to allow it to set. Release sides from pan.
Per Serving: Calories 189; Fat 16.48g; Sodium 469mg; Carbs 3.01g; Fibre 0g; Sugar 1.91g; Protein7.76g

Ultimate Chocolate Bread Pudding

Prep Time: 10 minutes | Cook Time: 10 minutes | Serves: 4

Nonstick baking spray
1 egg
1 egg yolk
180ml chocolate milk
2 tablespoons cocoa powder

3 tablespoons light brown sugar
3 tablespoons peanut butter
1 teaspoon vanilla extract
5 slices firm white bread, cubed

1. Spray a 15-by-5-cm round baking pan with the baking spray. 2. In a medium bowl, whisk the egg, egg yolk, chocolate milk, cocoa powder, brown sugar, peanut butter, and vanilla until thoroughly combined. Stir in the bread cubes and let soak for 10 minutes. Spoon this mixture into the prepared pan. 3. Place the pan into the air fryer basket, and bake the food at 160°C for 12 minutes. 4. Check the pudding after about 10 minutes. It is done when it is firm to the touch. If not, resume cooking. 5. When the cooking is complete, let the pudding cool for 5 minutes. 6. Serve warm.
Per Serving: Calories 277; Fat 7.45g; Sodium 239 mg; Carbs 43.73g; Fibre 4.7g; Sugar 10.83g; Protein 11.02g

Sweet Pineapple Cheese Wontons

Prep Time: 15 minutes | Cook Time: 15 minutes | Serves: 5

1 (200g) package cream cheese
165g finely chopped fresh
pineapple

20 wonton wrappers
Cooking oil spray

1. Add the cream cheese to a small microwave-safe bowl, and heat the cream cheese in the microwave on high power for 20 seconds to soften. 2. Stir the cream cheese and pineapple until mixed well in a bowl. 3. Lay out the wonton wrappers on a work surface. 4. Spoon 1½ teaspoons of the cream cheese mixture onto each wrapper, do not to overfill. 5. Fold each wrapper diagonally across to form a triangle. Bring the 2 bottom corners up toward each other. Do not close the wrapper yet. Bring up the 2 open sides and push out any air. Squeeze the open edges together to seal. 6. Insert the crisper plate into the air fryer basket and the air fryer basket into the unit, and then preheat the air fryer at 200°C for 3 minutes. 7. Once the unit is preheated, spray the crisper plate with cooking oil. 8. Place the wontons into the air fryer basket, and spray the wontons with the cooking oil. Air Fry the wontons at 200°C for 18 minutes. 9. After 10 minutes, remove the air fryer basket, flip each wonton, and spray them with more oil. Reinsert the air fryer basket to resume cooking for 5 to 8 minutes more until the wontons are light golden brown and crisp. 10. If cooking in batches, remove the cooked wontons from the air fryer basket and repeat steps 7, 8, and 9 for the remaining wontons. 11. When the cooking is complete, let the wontons cool for 5 minutes before serving.
Per Serving: Calories 552; Fat 16.59g; Sodium 942mg; Carbs 83.61g; Fibre 2.7g; Sugar 8.88g; Protein 16.16g

Irresistible Honey-Roasted Pears

Prep Time: 7 minutes | Cook Time: 25 minutes | Serves: 4

2 large pears, halved lengthwise
and seeded
3 tablespoons honey
1 tablespoon unsalted butter

½ teaspoon ground cinnamon
30g walnuts, chopped
60g part-skim ricotta cheese,
divided

1. Insert the crisper plate into the air fryer basket, and preheat the air fryer at 175°C for 3 minutes on Air Roast mode. 2. In a 15-by-5-cm round pan, place the pears cut-side up. 3. In a small microwave-safe bowl, melt the honey, butter, and cinnamon. Brush this mixture over the cut sides of the pears. Pour 3 tablespoons of water around the pears in the pan. 4. Once the unit is preheated, place the pan into the air fryer basket. 5. Air Roast the food at 175°C for 23 minutes. After about 18 minutes, check the pears. They should be tender when pierced with a fork and slightly crisp on the edges. If not, resume cooking. 6. When the cooking is complete, baste the pears once with the liquid in the pan. Carefully remove the pears from the pan and place on a serving plate. 7. Drizzle each with some liquid from the pan, sprinkle the walnuts on top, and serve with a spoonful of ricotta cheese.
Per Serving: Calories 194; Fat 6.52g; Sodium 18mg; Carbs 32.35g; Fibre 3.9g; Sugar 24.32g; Protein 3.1g

Unbeatable Gooey Lemon Bars

Prep Time: 15 minutes | Cook Time: 25 minutes | Serves: 6

95g whole-wheat pastry flour
2 tablespoons icing sugar
55g butter, melted
95g granulated sugar
1 tablespoon packed grated lemon
zest
60ml freshly squeezed lemon
juice

⅛ teaspoon sea salt
60g unsweetened plain
applesauce
2 teaspoons cornflour
¾ teaspoon baking powder
Cooking oil spray (sunflower,
safflower, or refined coconut)

1. Stir the flour, icing sugar, and melted butter just until well combined in a bowl. Place in the refrigerator. 2. Stir the granulated sugar, lemon zest and juice, salt, applesauce, cornflour, and baking powder in a bowl. 3. Insert the crisper plate into the air fryer basket, and preheat the air fryer at 175°C for 3 minutes on Bake mode. 4. Spray a 15-by-5-cm round pan lightly with cooking oil. Remove the crust mixture from the refrigerator and gently press it into the bottom of the prepared pan in an even layer. 5. Once the unit is preheated, place the pan into the air fryer basket. 6. Bake the dish at 175°C for

25 minutes. 7. After 5 minutes, check the crust. It should be slightly firm to the touch. Remove the pan and spread the lemon filling over the crust. Reinsert the pan into the air fryer basket and resume baking for 18 to 20 minutes. 8. When baking is complete, let cool for 30 minutes. Refrigerate to cool completely. Cut into pieces.
Per Serving: Calories 173; Fat 8.14g; Sodium 114 mg; Carbs 24.91g; Fibre 1.8; Sugar 12.1g; Protein 2.13g

Traditional Apple-Cinnamon Hand Pies

Prep Time: 15 minutes | Cook Time: 25 minutes | Serves: 8

2 apples, cored and diced
85g honey
1 teaspoon ground cinnamon
1 teaspoon vanilla extract
⅛ teaspoon ground nutmeg

2 teaspoons cornflour
1 teaspoon water
4 refrigerated piecrusts
Cooking oil spray

1. Insert the crisper plate into the air fryer basket, and preheat the air fryer at 205°C for 3 minutes. 2. Stir the apples, honey, cinnamon, vanilla, and nutmeg in a bowl. 3. Whisk the cornflour and water in a small bowl until the cornflour dissolves. 4. Once the unit is preheated, place the metal bowl with the apples into the air fryer basket. 5. Air Fry the apples at 205°C for 5 minutes. 6. After 2 minutes, stir the apples. Resume cooking for 2 minutes. 7. Remove the bowl and stir the cornflour mixture into the apples. Reinsert the metal bowl into the air fryer basket and resume cooking for about 30 seconds until the sauce thickens slightly. 8. When the cooking is complete, refrigerate the apples while you prepare the piecrust. 9. Cut each piecrust into 2 (10cm) circles. You should have 8 circles of crust. 10. Lay the piecrusts on a work surface. Divide the apple filling among the piecrusts, mounding the mixture in the centre of each round. 11. Fold each piecrust over so the top layer of crust is about 2cm short of the bottom layer. (The edges should not meet.) Use the back of a fork to seal the edges. 12. Insert the crisper plate into the air fryer basket, and preheat the air fryer at 205°C for 3 minutes. 13. Once the unit is preheated, spray the crisper plate with cooking oil, line the air fryer basket with parchment paper, and spray it with cooking oil. Working in batches, place the hand pies into the air fryer basket in a layer. 14. Air Fry the pies at 205°C for 10 minutes. 15. When the cooking is complete, let the hand pies cool for 5 minutes before removing from the air fryer basket. 16. Do the same with the remaining pies. 17. Serve and enjoy.
Per Serving: Calories 570; Fat 29.25g; Sodium 469mg; Carbs 74.49g; Fibre 3.4g; Sugar 13.51g; Protein 3.57g

Irresistible Cherry Pie

Prep Time: 15 minutes | Cook Time: 35 minutes | Serves: 6

Plain flour, for dusting
2 refrigerated piecrusts, at room
temperature
1 (310g) can cherry pie filling

1 egg
1 tablespoon water
1 tablespoon sugar

1. Dust a work surface with flour and place the piecrust on it. Roll out the piecrust. Invert a shallow air fryer baking pan, or your own pie pan that fits inside the air fryer basket, on top of the dough. Trim the dough around the pan, making your cut 1cm wider than the pan itself. 2. Repeat with the second piecrust but make the cut the same size as or slightly smaller than the pan. 3. Put the larger crust in the bottom of the baking pan. Don't stretch the dough. Gently press it into the pan. 4. Spoon in enough cherry pie filling to fill the crust. Do not overfill. 5. Using a knife or pizza cutter, cut the second piecrust into 2.5cm wide strips. Weave the strips in a lattice pattern over the top of the cherry pie filling. 6. Insert the crisper plate into the air fryer basket and the air fryer basket into the unit. Preheat the air fryer at 160°C for 3 minutes on Bake mode. 7. Whisk the egg and water in a small bowl. Gently brush the egg wash over the top of the pie. Sprinkle with the sugar and cover the pie with aluminum foil. 8. Once the unit is preheated, place the pie into the air fryer basket. 9. Bake the pie at 160°C for 35 minutes. 10. After 30 minutes, remove the foil and resume cooking for 3 to 5 minutes more. The finished pie should have a flaky golden brown crust and bubbling pie filling. 11. When the cooking is complete, serve warm. Refrigerate leftovers for a few days.
Per Serving: Calories 351; Fat 16.95g; Sodium 410mg; Carbs 44.8g; Fibre 1.3g; Sugar 1.33g; Protein 4.71g

Wonderful Strawberry-Rhubarb Crumble

Prep Time: 10 minutes | Cook Time: 15 minutes | Serves: 6

230g sliced fresh strawberries
90g sliced rhubarb
55g granulated sugar
70g quick-cooking oatmeal
60g whole-wheat pastry flour, or

plain flour
55g packed light brown sugar
½ teaspoon ground cinnamon
3 tablespoons unsalted butter, melted

1. Insert the crisper plate into the air fryer basket, and preheat the air fryer at 190°C for 3 minutes on Bake mode. 2. In a suitable round metal baking pan, combine the strawberries, rhubarb, and granulated sugar. 3. Stir the oatmeal, flour, brown sugar, and cinnamon in a bowl, then stir in the melted butter until crumbly. 4. Sprinkle the crumble mixture over the fruit. 5. Once the unit is preheated, place the pan into the air fryer basket. 6. Bake the food for 17 minutes. 7. After about 12 minutes, check the crumble. If the fruit is bubbling and the topping is golden brown, it is done. If not, resume cooking. 8. When the cooking is complete, serve warm.
Per Serving: Calories 170; Fat 5.19g; Sodium 47mg; Carbs 29.59g; Fibre 2.9g; Sugar 17.28g; Protein3.39g

Wonderful Big Chocolate Cookie

Prep Time: 7 minutes | Cook Time: 9 minutes | Serves: 4

3 tablespoons butter, at room temperature
70g plus 1 tablespoon light brown sugar
1 egg yolk
60g plain flour
2 tablespoons ground white

chocolate
¼ teaspoon baking soda
½ teaspoon vanilla extract
125g semisweet chocolate chips
Nonstick flour-infused baking spray

1. Beat together the butter and brown sugar until fluffy in a bowl. Stir in the egg yolk. 2. Add the flour, white chocolate, baking soda, and vanilla and mix well. Stir in the chocolate chips. 3. Line a 15-by-5-cm round baking pan with parchment paper. Spray the parchment paper with flour-infused baking spray. 4. Insert the crisper plate into the air fryer basket, and preheat the air fryer at 150°C for 3 minutes on Bake mode. 5. Spread the batter into the prepared pan, leaving a 1cm border on all sides. 6. Once the unit is preheated, place the pan into the air fryer basket. 7. Bake the batter for 9 minutes. 8. When the cooking is complete, the cookie should be light brown and just barely set. Remove the pan from the air fryer basket and let cool for 10 minutes. 9. Remove the cookie from the pan, remove the parchment paper, and let cool completely on a wire rack.
Per Serving: Calories 337; Fat 14.67g; Sodium 161mg; Carbs 48.16g; Fibre 0.4g; Sugar 21.87g; Protein 4.05g

Cinnamon Apple Fritters

Prep Time: 10 minutes | Cook Time: 15 minutes | Serves: 6

125g self-raising flour
100g granulated sugar
1½ teaspoons ground cinnamon

60ml whole milk
1 large egg
110g diced Granny Smith apples

1. Preheat the air fryer to 190°C. Line the air fryer basket with parchment paper. 2. Combine flour, sugar, cinnamon, and milk in a large bowl, then stir in egg and gently fold in apples. 3. Scoop dough in ¼-cup portions onto parchment paper. 4. Cook them for 15 minutes until golden brown and a toothpick inserted into the centre comes out clean, turning halfway through cooking time. 5. Let the fritters cool for 5 minutes before serving.
Per Serving: Calories 139; Fat 1.35g; Sodium 265mg; Carbs 28.15g; Fibre 1.4g; Sugar 11.29g; Protein 3.52g

Vanilla Pumpkin Pie

Prep Time: 5 minutes | Cook Time: 2 hours 25 minutes | Serves: 6

1 (375g) can pumpkin pie mix
1 large egg
1 teaspoon vanilla extract

80g sweetened condensed milk
1 (150g) premade piecrust

1. Preheat the air fryer to 160°C. 2. Combine the pumpkin pie mix, egg, vanilla, and sweetened condensed milk in a large bowl. Pour mixture into piecrust. 3. Place them in the air fryer basket, and cook for 25 minutes until pie is brown, firm, and a toothpick inserted into the centre comes out clean. 4. Chill in the refrigerator until set, at least 2 hours, before serving.
Per Serving: Calories 240; Fat 7.76g; Sodium 162mg; Carbs 42.2g; Fibre 5.1g; Sugar 10.01g; Protein 4.98g

Peanut Cookies

Prep Time: 10 minutes | Cook Time: 15 minutes | Serves: 8

115g salted butter, melted
50g granulated sugar
1 teaspoon vanilla extract

125g plain flour
145g peanuts, finely chopped
250g icing sugar

1. Preheat the air fryer to 150°C. 2. Combine the butter, sugar, and vanilla in a large bowl, then gradually add flour and peanuts, and mix until well combined. 3. Form dough into sixteen 2.5cm balls. Place them in the air fryer basket, working in batches as necessary. 4. Cook them for 15 minutes until cookies are golden brown and firm. 5. Let the cool for 5 minutes before rolling in icing sugar. Cool completely before serving.
Per Serving: Calories 423; Fat 20.05g; Sodium 258mg; Carbs 52.89g; Fibre 2.3g; Sugar 30.96g; Protein 11.02g

Low-carb Nutty Chocolate Cheesecake

Prep Time: 10 minutes | Cook Time: 24 minutes | Serves: 6

110g ground pecans (pecan meal)
3 tablespoons butter, melted
3 tablespoons granular sweetener
2 teaspoons instant espresso powder
300g cream cheese, room temperature
2 tablespoons sour cream

2 large eggs
20g unsweetened cocoa
10g powdered sweetener
1 teaspoon vanilla extract
⅛ teaspoon salt
40g mini sugar-free chocolate chips
30g pecan pieces

1. Preheat air fryer at 205°C for 3 minutes. 2. Combine ground pecans, butter, granular sweetener, and espresso powder in a medium bowl. Press mixture into an ungreased 18cm spring-form pan. 3. Place pan in air fryer basket and bake for 5 minutes. Remove from air fryer basket and allow to cool for 15 minutes. 4. In a divide medium bowl, combine cream cheese, sour cream, eggs, unsweetened cocoa, powdered sweetener, vanilla, and salt until smooth. Spoon mixture over crust. Cover with aluminum foil. 5. Place spring-form pan back into air fryer basket and cook 14 minutes. 6. Remove aluminum foil and cook for an additional 5 minutes at 175°C. 7. Remove cheesecake from air fryer basket. Garnish with chocolate chips and pecan pieces. 8. Cover cheesecake and refrigerate at least 2 hours to allow it to set. Once set, release sides of pan.
Per Serving: Calories 431; Fat 41.57g; Sodium 479 mg; Carbs 10.99g; Fibre 4.2g; Sugar 3.08g; Protein 10.38g

Irresistible Carrot Cake Muffins

Prep Time: 10 minutes | Cook Time: 15 minutes | Serves: 6

110g grated carrot
55g chopped pineapple
35g raisins
2 tablespoons pure maple syrup
80ml unsweetened plant-based milk

125g oat flour
1 teaspoon ground cinnamon
½ teaspoon ground ginger
1 teaspoon baking powder
½ teaspoon baking soda
40g chopped walnuts

1. Mix together the carrot, pineapple, raisins, maple syrup, and plant-based milk in a bowl. Then add the oat flour, cinnamon, ginger, baking powder, and baking soda and mix again until just combined. 2. Divide the batter evenly among 6 cupcake molds. Then sprinkle the chopped walnuts evenly over each muffin. Lightly press the walnuts into the batter so they are partially submerged. 3. Bake them at 175°C for 15 minutes. Let the muffins cool completely before enjoying.
Per Serving: Calories 141; Fat 4.79g; Sodium 129mg; Carbs 21.87g; Fibre 2.3g; Sugar 7.84g; Protein 3.92g

Chocolate Pavlova

Prep Time: 15 minutes | Cook Time: 90 minutes | Serves: 2

For Pavlova
2 large egg whites
¼ teaspoon cream of tartar
10g powdered sweetener
1 tablespoon unsweetened cocoa powder

1 teaspoon instant espresso powder
½ teaspoon apple cider vinegar
½ teaspoon vanilla extract

For Topping
60g heavy whipping cream
2 tablespoons powdered sweetener
1 tablespoon sour cream

1 teaspoon instant espresso powder
25g dark chocolate

1. Cut a piece of parchment paper to size of a grill pan. Draw a 15cm circle on paper. Flip paper, ink side down, onto grill pan. 2. To make Pavlova: In a medium metal bowl, beat egg whites with an immersion blender on high. Add cream of tartar, then add sweetener, 1 tablespoon at a time, and blend until stiff peaks form. 3. Fold in cocoa powder and espresso powder. Blend in apple cider vinegar and vanilla. 4. Preheat air fryer at 105°C for 5 minutes. 5. Spoon or pipe egg whites over parchment paper circle, creating higher edges around perimeter, like a pie crust. There should be a divot in the centre. 6. Add grill pan to air fryer and cook for 60 minutes. 7. Turn off heat, and let pavlova stay in air fryer an additional 30 minutes. 8. Remove grill pan from air fryer and gently peel off parchment paper from bottom of pavlova. Transfer to a large plate. 9. To make Topping: Whisk together whipping cream and sweetener in a small bowl. Fold in sour cream and espresso powder. 10. Fill pavlova with whipped cream. Using a vegetable peeler, shave chocolate into curls over pavlova.
Per Serving: Calories 220; Fat 15.47g; Sodium 74mg; Carbs 22.27g; Fibre8.8g; Sugar 4.76g; Protein 9.61g

Tasty Banana Bread Muffins

Prep Time: 10 minutes | Cook Time: 18 minutes | Serves: 6

2 ripe bananas
2 tablespoons ground flaxseed
60ml unsweetened plant-based milk
1 tablespoon apple cider vinegar
1 tablespoon vanilla extract

½ teaspoon ground cinnamon
2 tablespoons pure maple syrup
60g oat flour
½ teaspoon baking soda
3 tablespoons natural peanut butter

1. Use a fork to mash the bananas in a medium bowl, leaving some small chunks intact for texture; add the flaxseed, plant-based milk, apple cider vinegar, vanilla, cinnamon, and maple syrup to the bowl, and mix them until well combined. Then, add the oat flour and baking soda and mix again. 2. Spoon the batter into 6 cupcake molds. Then, place 1½ teaspoons peanut butter on top of each muffin. Swirl it around a little bit so that it sticks. 3. Place the muffins in the air fryer basket, and bake them in the air fryer at 160°C for 18 minutes. Let them cool before enjoying.
Per Serving: Calories 141; Fat 4.02g; Sodium 234mg; Carbs 23.08g; Fibre 2.8g; Sugar 11.3g; Protein 3.24g

Delicious Baked Apples

Prep Time: 6 minutes | Cook Time: 20 minutes | Serves: 4

4 small Granny Smith apples
40g chopped walnuts
55g light brown sugar
2 tablespoons butter, melted

1 teaspoon ground cinnamon
½ teaspoon ground nutmeg
120g water, or apple juice

1. Cut off the top third of the apples. Spoon out the core and some of the flesh and discard. Place the apples in a small air fryer baking pan. 2. Insert the crisper plate into the air fryer basket and the air fryer basket into the unit. Preheat the unit by selecting BAKE, setting the temperature to 175°C, and setting the time to 3 minutes. Select START/STOP to begin. 3. Stir together the walnuts, brown sugar, melted butter, cinnamon, and nutmeg in a bowl. Spoon this mixture into the centres of the hollowed-out apples. 4. Once the unit is preheated, pour the water into the crisper plate. Place the baking pan into the air fryer basket. 5. Select BAKE, set the temperature to 175°C, and set the time to 20 minutes. Select START/STOP to begin. 6. When the cooking is complete, the apples should be bubbly and fork-tender.
Per Serving: Calories 188; Fat 10.76g; Sodium 52mg; Carbs 22.08g; Fibre 4.9g; Sugar 14.28g; Protein 1.91g

Conclusion

This article will dispel all of your questions regarding the healthiness of air frying and the use of air fryers. Overall, it's a fairly nice piece of technology. It may satisfy all of your cravings for mouth-watering, delectable fried cuisine without using any oil. The results are far superior to oil frying, and your kitchen is also kept clean. The air fryer excels in emulating deep frying, even if it performs a commendable job of cooking various types of meat and vegetables.

This article will explain the advantages of using an air fryer for cooking as well as the drawbacks. It will also provide you with a list of mouth-watering dishes that you can prepare in the comfort of your own home. Additionally, it will explain how air fryers operate and their numerous applications for them.

Appendix 1 Measurement Conversion Chart

VOLUME EQUIVALENTS (LIQUID)

US STANDARD	US STANDARD (OUNCES)	METRIC (APPROXIMATE)
2 tablespoons	1 fl.oz	30 mL
¼ cup	2 fl.oz	60 mL
½ cup	4 fl.oz	120 mL
1 cup	8 fl.oz	240 mL
1½ cup	12 fl.oz	355 mL
2 cups or 1 pint	16 fl.oz	475 mL
4 cups or 1 quart	32 fl.oz	1 L
1 gallon	128 fl.oz	4 L

TEMPERATURES EQUIVALENTS

FAHRENHEIT(F)	CELSIUS(C) (APPROXIMATE)
225 °F	107 °C
250 °F	120 °C
275 °F	135 °C
300 °F	150 °C
325 °F	160 °C
350 °F	180 °C
375 °F	190 °C
400 °F	205 °C
425 °F	220 °C
450 °F	235 °C
475 °F	245 °C
500 °F	260 °C

VOLUME EQUIVALENTS (DRY)

US STANDARD	METRIC (APPROXIMATE)
⅛ teaspoon	0.5 mL
¼ teaspoon	1 mL
½ teaspoon	2 mL
¾ teaspoon	4 mL
1 teaspoon	5 mL
1 tablespoon	15 mL
¼ cup	59 mL
½ cup	118 mL
¾ cup	177 mL
1 cup	235 mL
2 cups	475 mL
3 cups	700 mL
4 cups	1 L

WEIGHT EQUIVALENTS

US STANDARD	METRIC (APPROXINATE)
1 ounce	28 g
2 ounces	57 g
5 ounces	142 g
10 ounces	284 g
15 ounces	425 g
16 ounces (1 pound)	455 g
1.5 pounds	680 g
2 pounds	907 g

Appendix 2 Air Fryer Cooking Chart

vegetables	Temp (°F)	Time (min)
Asparagus (1-inch slices)	400	5
Beets (sliced)	350	25
Beets (whole)	400	40
Bell Peppers (sliced)	350	13
Broccoli	400	6
Brussels Sprouts (halved)	380	15
Carrots(½-inch slices)	380	15
Cauliflower (florets)	400	12
Eggplant (1½-inch cubes)	400	15
Fennel (quartered)	370	15
Mushrooms (¼-inch slices)	400	5
Onion (pearl)	400	10
Parsnips (½-inch chunks)	380	5
Peppers (1-inch chunks)	400	15
Potatoes (baked, whole)	400	40
Squash (½-inch chunks)	400	12
Tomatoes (cherry)	400	4
Zucchni (½-inch sticks)	400	12

Meat	Temp (°F)	Time (min)
Bacon	400	5 to 7
Beef Eye Round Roast (4 lbs.)	390	50 to 60
Burger (4 oz.)	370	16 to 20
Chicken Breasts, bone-in (1.25 lbs.)	370	25
Chicken Breasts, boneless (4 oz.)	380	12
Chicken Drumsticks (2.5 lbs.)	370	20
Chicken Thighs, bone-in (2 lbs.)	380	22
Chicken Thighs, boneless (1.5 lbs.)	380	18 to 20
Chicken Legs, bone-in (1.75 lbs.)	380	30
Chicken Wings (2 lbs.)	400	12
Flank Steak (1.5 lbs.)	400	12
Game Hen (halved, 2 lbs.)	390	20
Loin (2 lbs.)	360	55
London Broil (2 lbs.)	400	20 to 28
Meatballs (3-inch)	380	10
Rack of Lamb (1.5-2 lbs.)	380	22
Sausages	380	15
Whole Chicken (6.5 lbs.)	360	75

Fish and Seafood		
Calamari (8 oz.)	400	4
Fish Fillet (1-inch, 8 oz.)	400	10
Salmon Fillet (6 oz.)	380	12
Tuna Steak	400	7 to 10
Scallops	400	5 to 7
Shrimp	400	5

Frozen Foods		
Onion Rings (12 oz.)	400	8
Thin French Fries (20 oz.)	400	14
Thick French Fries (17 oz.)	400	18
Pot Sticks (10 oz.)	400	8
Fish Sticks (10 oz.)	400	10
Fish Fillets (½-inch, 10 oz.)	400	14

Appendix 3 Recipes Index

Printed in Great Britain
by Amazon